MUSIC LITERATURE OUTLINES – SERIES I

Music
in the
Middle Ages
and the
Renaissance

by
Harold Gleason and Warren Becker
Third Edition

Frangipani Press

Division of T.I.S. Enterprises

D1214779

Franigpani Press books are printed in the United States of America by Tichenor Publishing Group, a division of T.I.S. Enterprises.

1986 Printing
Copyright © 1981 by Frangipani Press
All Rights Reserved

ISBN 0-89917-034-X

Library of Congress Catalog Card Number: 79-92456

ISBN 0-89917-034-X

PREFACE TO THE THIRD EDITION

This edition of *Music Literature Outlines*, Series I, *Music in the Middle Ages and the Renaissance*, is a complete revision of the second edition. The *Outlines* are designed as a guide and resource in the study of music from the earliest times through the Renaissance period. The unique outline format of the earlier editions has been maintained and the subject areas and the chronological plan included in the previous outlines have served as the bases for the present edition.

During recent years there has been an increasing interest in the music of the period covered by these outlines. The expanding quantity of significant materials may be noted in the bibliographies of books, articles and music at the end of each *Outline*. The bibliographies have been completely revised and brought up to date; in general they have been limited to those of the English language. Although they are in no way intended to be exhaustive, they nevertheless do give an idea of the scope of the available literature. In order to facilitate study of this period and to use the materials efficiently, references to facsimiles, monumental editions, complete composers' works and specialized anthologies have been given.

The authors present this systematic organization of information in the *Outlines* in the hope that students, teachers and performers may find in it a ready tool for developing a comprehensive understanding of the music of this period. This comprehension should be expanded by performing the music, listening to recordings and performances with scores and consulting the bibliographies.

The authors are indebted to Verne W. Thompson, Catharine Crozier Gleason and Ruth Watanabe, Librarian of the Sibley Music Library, Eastman School of Music, Rochester, New York, for help in the preparation of the earlier editions of the *Outlines*, and to the librarians and staffs of the Central Library, University of California, San Diego and San Diego State University Library for their assistance in making valuable materials available.

March 25, 1981　　　　　　　　　　　　　　　　　　　　　　　　　Harold Gleason
San Diego, California　　　　　　　　　　　　　　　　　　　　　　Warren Becker

CONTENTS

MUSIC IN THE MIDDLE AGES

Monophonic Music

Polyphonic Music

MUSIC IN THE RENAISSANCE

ILLUSTRATIONS

ABBREVIATIONS

A – Periodical article

AC – Antiqua Chorbuch, ed. Mönkmeyer.

ACT – Anthologie de Chants de Troubadours, ed. Maillard.

ActaM (Acta Mus) – Acta Musicologica

AERM – An Anthology of Early Renaissance Music, ed. Greenberg and Maynard.

AIM – Anthology of Instrumental Music, ed. Wasielewski.

AM – Anthology of Music, ed. Fellerer.

AMI – L'Arte Musicale Italia, ed. Torchi.

AMM – Anthology of Medieval Music, ed. Hoppin.

AMO – Archives des Maîtres de l'Orgue, ed. Guilmant & Pirro

AMP – Antiquitates Musicae in Polonia, ed. Feicht.

AnM – Annales Musicologiques

AR – Antiphonale sacrosanctae Romanae ecclesiae

ArM – Archivium musices metropolitanum Mediolenense, ed. Magliavacca.

B – book

BAMS – The American Musicological Society Bulletin

BC – Biblioteca de Catalunya

BMB – Bibliotheca musica Bononiensis

c. – circa (about)

CaMM – Caldwell, John. Medieval Music.

CE – Complete or Collected Edition

CEKM – A Corpus of Early Keyboard Music, ed. Apel.

CM – Collegium Musicum, ed. Schrade.

CMM – Corpus Mensurabilis Musicae, ed. Carapetyan.

CMT – Colorado College Music Press Translations, ed. Seay.

CO – Cantantibus Organis, ed. Kraus.

CP – Capolavori polifonici del secolo XVI, ed. Somma.

ChP – Chansons polyphoniques (Janequin), ed. Merritt and Lesure.

CS – Cantio Sacra, ed. Ewerhart

CSM – Corpus Scriptorum de Musica, ed. Carapetyan.

CW – Das Chorwerk, ed. Blume.

DCS – Dessoff Choir Series, ed. Boepple.

DdT – Denkmäler deutscher Tonkunst, ed. Seiffert.

DPL – Documenta polyphoniae liturgiae Sanctae Ecclesiae Romanae, ed. Feininger.

DM – Documenta Musicologica

DTB – Denkmäler der Tonkunst in Bayern, ed. Sandberger.

DTÖ – Denkmäler der Tonkunst in Österreich, ed. Adler.

EBM – Early Bodleian Music, ed. Stainer.

ed. – edited, editor, edition

EdM – Das Erbe deutscher Musik

EECM – Early English Church Music, ed. Harrison.

EEH – Early English Harmony, ed. Wooldridge.

EFM – Early Fifteenth Century Music, ed. Reaney.

EKMV – Schott's Anthology of Early Keyboard Music. English Virginalists, ed. Dawes.

EL – The English School of Lutenist Song Writers, ed. Fellowes.

ELS – English Lute Songs, ed. Sternfeld.

EM – The English Madrigalists, ed. Fellowes.

EMR – Early Music Reprinted, ed. Edwards.

FCIC – Fourteenth-Century Italian Cacce, ed. Marrocco.

FCVR – Florilege du concert vocal de la renaissance, ed. Expert.

fl. – flourished

FSC – French Secular Compositions of the Fourteenth Century, ed. Apel.

FSM – French Secular Music of the Late Fourteenth Century, ed. Apel.

FVB – Fitzwilliam Virginal Book, ed. Fuller-Maitland.

GD – Grove's Dictionary of Music and Musicians, ed. Blom.

GEx – Examples of Music before 1400, ed. Gleason.

GMB – Geschichte der Musik in Beispielen, ed. Schering.

GR – Graduale sacrosanctae Romanae ecclesiae

HAM – Historical Anthology of Music, ed. Davison and Apel.

HM – Hortus Musicus

HMM – Hoppin, Richard. Medieval Music.

HPM – Harvard Publications of Music

HSMS – Hispaniae Schola Musica Sacra, ed. Pedrell.

ICDMI – I Classici della Musica Italiana, ed. d'Annunzio.

ICMI – I Classici Musicali Italiani, ed. Bravi.

IM – The Italian Madrigal, ed. Einstein.

IMAMI – Istituzione e monumenti dell'arte musicale Italiani

InM – Invitation to Madrigals, ed. Dart.

ISM – Italia sacra musica, ed. Jeppesen.

JAMS – The American Musicological Society Journal

JRBM – Journal of Renaissance and Baroque Musis (MD, v. 1)

LMA – Treize livres de motets parus chez Pierre Attaingnant, ed. Smijers and Merritt.

LO – Liber Organi, ed. Kaller.

LP – Le Pupitre, ed. Lesure.

LU – Liber Usualis

M – Music

MAS – Musical Antiquarian Society

MB – Musica Britannica

MC – Musical Courier

MD – Musica Disciplina

MDa – Musica Divina, ed. Stäblein.

MDaP (ProskeMDa) – Musica Divina, ed. Proske.

MDm – Musikalische Denkmäler

MFCI – Music of Fourteenth Century Italy, ed. Pirrotta.

MH – Musica Hispana

MISC – Miscellanea

ML – Music and Letters

MLi (MLit) – Musica Liturgica, ed. Snow.

MLMI – Monumenta lyrica medii aevi Italica

MM – Masterpieces of Music before 1750, ed. Parrish and Ohl.

MMA – Monuments de la Musique Ancienne

MMB – Monumenta Musicae Belgicae

MME – Monumentos de la Musica Española, ed. Anglés.

MMF – Monuments of Music and Music Literature in Facsimile

MMFR – Les Monuments de la Musique Française au temps de la Renaissance, ed. Expert.

MMMA – Monumenta monodica medii aevi, ed. Stäblein.

MMN – Monumenta Musica Neerlandica

MMRF – Les Maîtres Musiciens de la Renaissance Française, ed. Expert.

MMRL – Music in Medieval and Renaissance Life, ed. Minor.

MOC – Machaut, Oeuvres complètes, ed. Leguy.

MOP – Gleason, Harold. Method of Organ Playing.

MPL – Monumenta Polyphonicae Liturgicae Sanctae Ecclesiae Romanae, ed. Feininger.

MQ – The Musical Quarterly

MR – Music Review

MRM – Monuments of Renaissance Music, ed. Lowinsky.

MS – Musicological Studies

MSD – Musicological Studies and Documents

MSO – Music Scores: Omnibus, ed. Starr and Devine.

MT – The Musical Times

MTNAPro – Music Teachers National Association Proceedings

MTT – Musical Theorists in Translation

NagMA – Musik-Archiv, ed. Nagel.

n. d. – no date

NGD – The New Grove Dictionary of Music and Musicians, ed. Sadie.

NMM – Parrish, Carl. Notation of Medieval Music.

NOH – New Oxford History of Music, ed. Westrup.

n. p. – no publisher

NPM – Apel, Willi. Notation of Polyphonic Music.

OAMB – Old St. Andrews Music Book, ed. Baxter.

OEE – The Old English Edition, ed. Arkwright.

OH – Old Hall Manuscript

OHM – Oxford History of Music

OMM – The Oxford Anthology of Medieval Music, ed. Marrocco and Sandon.

p. – page (pp. – pages)

PäM – Publikationen älterer Musik, ed. Kroyer.

PAM – Publikationen älterer praktischer und theoretischer Musikwerke, ed. Eitner.

PAMS – The American Musicological Society Papers

PCM – Blume, Friedrich. Protestant Church Music.

PM – Paléographie Musicale, ed. Mocquereau.

PMA – The Royal Music Association Proceedings

PMFC – Polyphonic Music of the Fourteenth Century, ed. Schrade.

PMMM – Publication of Medieval Music Manuscripts

PortM – Portugaliae Music

pt. – part

PVSP – Polifonia vocale sacra e profana, ed. Somma.

PWerke – Palestrina, Werke.

RMMA – Reese, Gustave. Music of the Middle Ages.

RMR – Reese, Gustave. Music in the Renaissance.

RRMA – Recent Researches in the Music of the Middle Ages and Early Renaissance, ed. Tischler.

RRMR – Recent Researches in the Music of the Renaissance

SATB – soprano, alto, tenor, bass

SCMA – Smith College Music Archives, ed. Einstein.

sec. – section

ser. – series

SIMg – Sammelbände der Internationalen Musikgesellschaft

SMMA – Summa musicae medii aevi, ed. Gennrich.

SR – Source Readings, ed. Strunk.

SSMS – Study Scores of Musical Style, ed. Lerner.

TCM – Tudor Church Music

TECM – Treasury of English Church Music

TEM – Treasury of Early Music, ed. Parrish.

tr. – translated, translation, translator

transc. – transcribed, transcription, transcriber

T-W – Tallis to Wesley

v. – volume (vols. – volumes)

VOTS – Van Ockeghem tot Sweelinck, ed. Smijers.

WE – The Wellesley Edition, ed. LaRue.

WF – The Worcester Fragments, ed. Dittmer.

WMH – Worcester Medieval Harmony, ed. Hughes.

YMTT – Yale University Music Theory Translation Series, ed. Crocker.

MUSIC IN THE MIDDLE AGES AND RENAISSANCE

OUTLINE I

INTRODUCTION

Ancient Music – Mesopotamia – Egypt
Jewish Music – Greece – Rome

I. **Ancient Music**

    A. The study of ancient non-Western music, particularly in Southwest and Southeast Asia, the Middle and Far East and Africa has occupied scholars for many years.

        1. Present-day knowledge is based mainly on the survival of traditions in old, isolated civilizations, representations, ancient writings and the few instruments which have been preserved.

        2. Music and musical instruments are known to have been a part of the religious and social life for thousands of years before the theoretical writings on music and a system of notation by Greek philosopher/musicians appeared in the early fifth century B. C.

            a. Music was often associated with magic and used in rituals, ceremonies, festivals, war and work.

            b. Primitive instruments were made from natural materials, including wood, skin, bone and reeds.

II. **Mesopotamia**

    A. Civilization was well advanced as early as 4000 B. C. in the land between the Tigris and Euphrates rivers, now known as Iraq.

        1. Mesopotamia was ruled mainly by the successive kingdoms of Sumer, Babylonia and Assyria from about 3500 to 600 B. C. Knowledge of the music is limited principally to representations and the few musical instruments which have been preserved.

    B. The music of the non-Semitic Sumerians (*c*. 3500-2000 B. C.) was liturgical and consisted of chants sung in their temples in honor of the gods. In the words there is some evidence of responsorial and antiphonal singing.

        1. The instruments included reed-pipes, vertical flutes, lyres and harps in a variety of sizes and shapes, kitharas, drums, clappers and the sistrum (a frame with rattling cross-bars).

    C. The Semitic Babylonians (*c*. 2000-1000 B. C.) from the north of Mesopotamia developed a more complete liturgical service with the use of the voice and instruments in an increasingly elaborate way. In addition to the use of Sumerian instruments, the Babylonians favored the more refined flutes, oboe types, lutes and drums.

        1. A Babylonian hymn, dating from about 750 B. C., has signs which are believed to be musical notation, but they have not been successfully transcribed.

    D. The Assyrians (*c*. 1000-600 B. C.) were strongly influenced by foreign music and instruments, particularly Egyptian, and adapted their music to more secular uses. Music became important in festivals and was played at banquets and at the royal palace; performances for the public were also given.

III. Egypt

A.   A high civilization began in Egypt as early as 3000 B. C. and music with foreign influences, possibly from Mesopotamia, began its growth from the ritualistic use of rattles and clappers to drive out evil spirits to elaborate temple services with voices and instruments.

B.   The Old and Middle Kingdoms (*c.* 2780-*c.* 1580 B. C.)
   1.   The history of Egyptian music is told through the remarkable paintings, reliefs and relics found in the tombs of the Pharoahs and elsewhere.
   2.   There were daily services in the temples with chanting by priests and priestesses, often accompanied by instruments which were symbols of divine power.
   3.   Instruments included harps, vertical flutes, sistrums and double clarinet types (two parallel reed-pipes).
      a.   Later in the Middle Kingdom drums, lyres and long-necked lutes are found.
      b.   The popularity of the harp and flute suggests a restrained type of music which was performed mostly by the upper classes.
   4.   Music held considerable importance in the court life of the priest-king Pharoahs, and there are representations showing groups of musicians playing and singing, and accompanying dances.

C.   The New Kingdom (*c.* 1570-*c.* 1090 B. C.)
   1.   Egypt came under the influence of the culture of Mesopotamia about 1500 B. C., and an active musical life began. The older instruments were developed, including the large harp and a type of kithara. New instruments appeared, among them double oboe with two canes set at an angle, one playing a drone bass. Short lutes and gold and silver straight trumpets were found in the tomb of Pharoah Tut-ankh-amen (*c.* 1400 B. C.).
   2.   Secular songs were sung by oriental dancing girls in the harems and women took part in the religious rites. There were choruses of men and women, responsorial and antiphonal singing and other liturgical music.

D.   Little is known of the music in Egypt during the period following the New Kingdom when it was under the domination of foreign rulers. In 332 B. C. Egypt was conquered by Alexander the Great, and there is evidence that the Greeks were influenced by the music and music theory of the Egyptians.

IV. Jewish Music

A.   The knowledge of ancient Jewish music is limited because of the lack of an exact notation, pictures of instruments or musical treatises.

B.   Studies of chants of isolated Jewish tribes in Yemen, Babylonia and Syria show a close correlation and indicate a common source which originated in the late pre-Christian era.
   1.   These melodies are generally diatonic, and some may have survived from as early as the fifth century B. C.

C.   Instruments
   1.   Moses and his people brought to Canaan (Palestine) a knowledge of music and instruments from Egypt during the New Kingdom (*c.* 1570-*c.* 1090 B. C.).
   2.   There are many references to musical instruments in the Bible; Stainer (*B* 34, p. 178) has listed a total of 145, of which only nine are from the New Testament.
      a.   The instruments include the *kinnor* (small lyre), *nevel* (large harp), double oboe, cymbals, small bells, *hasosra* (silver trumpet), sistrum (a frame with jingly crossbars) and the *shofar*, a ram's horn, still used today for signaling during the Services.

D.   Music in the Temple
   1.   The First Temple was built in Jerusalem about 950 B. C. by King Solomon (reigned 973-933 B. C.), the son and successor of King David (reigned 1013-973 B. C.).
      a.   Professional musicians, men from the tribe of Levi, were in charge of the Services.

The principal music was the singing of the Psalms and parts of the Pentateuch by the priests and Levites. The congregation may have sung the responses, Hallelujah and Amen, and there is evidence of antiphonal singing by two choruses.

    b.   The "sweet-toned" *kinnor* and harp were used in the Services as well as the *shofar*, cymbals and trumpets; one hundred-twenty trumpets were blown by the priests at the dedication of Solomon's Temple.

  2. The Second Temple was built about 514 B. C. after the Jews returned to Palestine following the Babylonian Exile (586-538 B. C.).

    a.   Services with music were held, and antiphonal and responsorial chanting became more common with the Levites alternating with the congregation in each half-verse of the Psalms. The trumpet and *shofar* continued to be used for signaling during the Services.

    b.   The Second Temple was destroyed by the Romans in 70 A. D. and the Jews were dispersed throughout the East and West.

      1) The chants used in the singing of the Psalms in the Jewish Temples today are thought to have been preserved by remote civilizations and are very nearly as they were in the pre-Christian era. There is also some evidence of the influence of the chants on Gregorian Psalm tones.

  E. Music
    1. *GEx*, p. 1; *HAM*, No. 6; *M* 2)

V. Greece

  A. The ancient Greeks, through their writings, made contributions in music as well as in law, letters and the other arts. Music is known to have played a part in the religious and secular life in Greece since the time of the epic poems attributed to **Homer** (*c*. 850 B. C.).

    1. **Pythagoras** (*c*. 585-*c*. 479 B. C.) is said to have derived all the tones of the diatonic scale from a perfect fifth. **Plato** (*c*. 427-*c*. 347 B. C.) in his *Republic* (*B* 24, v. 2, pp. 35-37, 241-252, lines 395-403) placed music first in the ideal state and refers to Egypt for his models for the musical education of the youth.

  B. Music was an important part of all Greek life. Epic and lyric poets accompanied their songs on the lyre with their own music. Music was a part of contests (Pythian games, 586 B. C.) and choruses and solo voices took part in the works of the great dramatists (**Aristophanes**, *Frogs*, 405 B. C.). Instrumental music became more important than vocal toward the end of the fifth century B. C., and musicians considered themselves more as performers than composers. Music was used, often improvised, for banquets, ceremonies, various rites and theatrical performances which combined poetry, music and the dance.

  C. Instruments

    1. Aulos: a double-reed instrument consisting of two pipes, one probably used to extend the compass of the other by a few tones. It was associated with the cult of Dionysus and used in contests and during interludes of dramatic performances.

    2. Kithara: an instrument with from three to eleven strings stretched vertically between a sound-chest and a cross-bar. It was associated with the cult of Apollo and had a mild sound in contrast to the shrill aulos.

    3. Lyra: an instrument played with a plectrum which resembled the kithara, but with a sound-chest usually made from a turtle shell.

    4. Hydraulis: a primitive organ with pipes, stops and keys, said to have been invented by the Greek **Ctesibius of Alexandria** (*fl*. 246-221 B. C.). A large tank of water below the wind chest was used to stabilize the air pressure blown by piston pumps.

    5. Castanets, cymbals and tambourines were often used in the ritualistic cults of Cybele and Dionysus.

D.   Music theory
   1.   The many ancient writings on Greek music are often obscure and connected with mysticism, metaphysics, astronomy and number symbolism. The most valuable source for the basic principles of Greek music theory is the treatise of **Aristoxenus of Tarentum** (*fl.* 320 B. C.) who knew the music of the fifth century B. C. as well as that of his own time.
   2.   Scales
      a.   The unit of the tonal organization of the scales was the perfect fourth (tetrachord, four strings) consisting of four notes and three intervals organized in descending order. The two outer notes were "fixed" and the other two notes were "movable" according to three different tetrachords. The interval between f and e in the enharmonic tetrachord was divided into two microtones of about a quarter tone each. Other genera with microtones were also a part of Greek music theory.

   3.   "Greater Perfect System"
      a.   A two-octave scale organized in the fourth century B. C. by adding two pairs of conjunct (connected) diatonic tetrachords above the basic diatonic tetrachord (a–g–f–e) and a conjunct tetrachord below that tetrachord. A disjunct tone (A) was added below to complete two diatonic octaves of the descending scale as follows:

$$a' \underset{t}{-} g' \underset{t}{-} f' \underset{s}{-} e' - d' - c' - b - a \underset{t}{-} g \underset{t}{-} f \underset{s}{-} e - d \overset{t}{-} c \overset{s}{-} B - A$$

      1)   Each tetrachord and each tone was named according to its position on the kithara which was held so that the lowest (shortest) strings were highest in pitch and the highest (longest) strings were lowest in pitch. *Mese* was considered the center of the Greek scale system.
   4.   "Lesser Perfect System"
      a.   A theoretical eleven-note conjunct scale of diatonic tetrachords which made modulation possible as follows:

$$d' - c' - b\flat \overset{t \quad t \quad s}{- a\, (\textit{mese}) - g - f - e} - d - c - B - A$$
$$\underset{t \quad t \quad s}{} \qquad \underset{t \quad t \quad s \quad t}{}$$

   5. Octave species
      a.   Seven segments or species in the form of diatonic octave scales were taken from the "Greater Perfect System." They should not be confused with the medieval church modes.
      b.   Three primary scales were classified according to their intervals and named for Greek tribes. Three secondary scales lay above the primary scales and one below. Each note of the scale is taken as a starting point as follows:

a' − a	Hypodorian
g' − g	Hypophrygian
f' − f	Hypolydian
e' − e	Dorian
d' − d	Phrygian
c' − c	Lydian
b − B	Mixolydian

   1)   The intervals of the above scales are the same as on the white keys of the piano.
   c.   The scales could also be transposed into the vocal range of the original central
        Dorian scale by adding the proper key signature as follows:

Dorian:
$$e' - d' - c' - b - a - g - f - e$$
(intervals: t t t s / t t s)

Phrygian:
$$e' - d' - c\#' - b - a - g - f\# - e$$
(intervals: t t s t / t s t)

Lydian:
$$e' - d\#' - c\#' - b - a - g\# - f\# - e$$
(intervals: t s t t / s t t)

   d.   All the one- and two-octave scales could also be in the chromatic and enharmonic
        genera. The ditone in the latter is one of the most characteristic features of ancient
        Greek music and was preferred by **Aristoxenus** for classical music.
E.   Ethos
   1.   **Aristotle** (384-322 B. C.) (*SR*, pp. 13-24; *B* 2) and other philosophers placed great
        emphasis on the ethical value of music, particularly in reference to the various scales.
        Although writers did not always agree, the Dorian scale was generally considered man-
        ly, strong and ennobling, the Phrygian passionate and headstrong, the Lydian effemi-
        nate and lascivious, the Mixolydian sad and mournful, and the Hypodorian exciting.
   a.   The doctrine of ethos and particularly the writings on music theory were trans-
        mitted to Europe principally through the Latin philosopher and mathematician
        Boethius (*c*. 480-525 A. D.) and in the ninth century by the Arabian writers in
        Spain.
F.   Notation
   1.   There were two types of letter notation used for ancient Greek music, instrumental
        and vocal, but music was rarely written down.
   a.   Instrumental music, evidently used for the kithara, used Phoenician symbols or let-
        ters in different positions for different notes.
   b.   Vocal music made use of Ionic letters placed above the text, but the music was
        learned by rote.
   2.   Instrumental accompaniments for the singers were improvised on the melody with a
        few varied notes or ornaments (heterophony).
G.   Music
   1.   Greek music was rarely written down, and the examples which have been preserved
        are few in number and mostly fragments written on stone or papyrus during the

decline of music after the fourth century B. C., but the dates are often uncertain.

2. The melodies are all monophonic, but singing in octaves and heterophony may have been practiced with voice or instruments. The rhythms appear to be regular in most examples but there is some use of irregular meters (*HAM*, No. 7a).

    a. *Orestes* fragment (*c*. 250 B. C.) (facsimile *M* 4)

        1) One of the earliest examples of Greek music. The fragment on papyrus has a text from *Orestes* by **Euripedes** (*c*. 480-406 B. C.).

    b. Two hymns to Apollo (*c*. 150 B. C.; *c*. 127 B. C.)

        1) These lengthy hymns were discovered on marble slabs at Delphi. The first hymn is an example of irregular meters including 5/8 (*HAM*, No. 7a).

    c. Two hymns to the Muse (*c*. 130 A. D.) are short examples which may be from one composition.

    d. Hymn to Helios (*HAM*, No. 7b) and Hymn to Nemesis.

        1) The two hymns have been ascribed to **Mesomedes of Crete** and may be of an early date A. D.

    e. Epitaph of Seikilos (*GEx*, p. 1; *HAM*, No. 7c; *GMB*, No. 1; *MSO*, v. 1, p. 1)

        1) Found in a tomb at Aidin which is now in Turkey, the epitaph of Seikilos for his wife Euterpe reads: "Throughout your life be happy; do not vex yourself with vain cares. Life is brief and time will demand its ending."

        2) The epitaph probably dates from the second century A. D. and it is doubtful if it is authentic early Greek music.

    f. Five musical fragments on a Berlin papyrus from about 156 A. D.

        1) These fragments contain twelve lines of a Hellenistic paean, three lines of melody for an instrument, four lines on the suicide of Ajax, another three lines of melody for an instrument and half a line of lyrics.

    g. A setting of a Christian hymn from Oxyrynchos, Egypt (*c*. 250 A. D.)

        1) This hymn in praise to the Trinity is the oldest surviving example of Christian music even though it was written with Greek text and Greek notation.

VI. Rome

A. Roman music became a bridge between Egyptian, Hebrew, Greek and early Christian music. It was chiefly an imitation and adaptation of Greek music and no significant developments were made by the Romans. Music was performed by slaves in the homes of the rich, in theatres and at outdoor spectacles. There are many reports of such occasions which made use of instrumental music, large orchestras and choruses.

B. Greek and Egyptian instruments were used and for military purposes the *lituus*, a crooked cavalry trumpet, and the *tuba*, a short military straight trumpet, were used. Another wind instrument was the *cornu*, a circular horn about eleven feet in length, which was used in the Roman armies and at various assemblies and ceremonies. The *hydraulis*, a Greek water organ, became popular at outdoor entertainments.

SELECTED BIBLIOGRAPHY

Books

1. Anderson, Warren D. *Ethos and Education in Greek Music*. Cambridge, MA: Harvard University Press, 1966.

2. Aristotle. *The Works of Aristotle*, ed. W. D. Ross. Oxford: Clarendon Press, 1921.
    Volume VII. *Problemata*, tr. E. S. Forster.
    Volume X. *Politica*, tr. Benjamin Jowett.

3. Bessaraboff, Nicholas. *Ancient European Musical Instruments*. Cambridge, MA: Harvard University Press, 1941.

4. Cumming, Charles Gordon. *Assyrian and Hebrew Hymns of Praise*. New York: Columbia University Press, 1934.

5. Daniélou, Alain. *Introduction to the Study of Musical Scales*. London: The India Society, 1943.

6. Dronke, Peter. *Medieval Latin and the Rise of European Love-Lyrics*, 2 vols. Oxford: Clarendon Press, 1968.

7. Engel, Carl. *The Music of the Most Ancient Nations, Particularly of the Assyrians, Egyptians, and Hebrews*. London: J. Murray, 1864.

8. Farmer, George Henry. *Byzantine Musical Instruments in the Ninth Century*. London: H. Reeves, 1925.

9. ――――――*Historical Facts for the Arabian Musical Influence*. London: William Reeves, 1930; reprint: Hildesheim: Georg Olms Verlag, 1970.

10. ――――――*A History of Arabian Music to the XIIIth Century*. London: Luzac & Co., 1929.

11. ――――――*The Organ of the Ancients from Eastern Sources (Hebrew, Syriac and Arabic)*. London: William Reeves, 1931.

12. ――――――*The Sources of Arabian Music* (from the 2nd to the 17th centuries). Leiden, Netherlands: E. J. Brill, 1965.

13. Galpin, Francis William. *The Music of the Sumerians and Their Immediate Successors, the Babylonians and Assyrians*. Cambridge, England: The University Press, 1937; reprint: Strasbourg: Strasbourg University Press, 1955.

14. Geiringer, Karl. *Musical Instruments; Their History in Western Culture, from the Stone Age to the Present Day*, tr. Bernard Miall. London: G. Allen & Unwin, 1942; reprint: New York: Oxford University Press, 1945. Also appeared as *Instruments in the History of Western Music*, 3rd ed. New York: Oxford University Press, 1978.

15. Gradenwitz, Peter. *The Music of Israel, Its Rise and Growth through 5000 Years*. New York: W. W. Norton, 1949.

16. Haïk-Ventoura, Suzanne. *Le Musique de la Bible Révélée, sa notation millénarie aujourd' hui décryptée*. Paris: Robert Dumas, 1976. Also a phonodisc: Old Testament Cantillations with Instrumental Accompaniment Realized by the Author/Composer. Harmonie Mundi, HMU 989, 1975.

17. Hickman, Hans. "Pharaonic Jingles," in *The Commonwealth of Music in Honor of Curt Sachs*, ed. Gustave Reese and Rose Brandel, pp. 45-70. New York: The Free Press, 1965.

18. Highet, Gilbert A. *The Classical Tradition*. New York: Oxford University Press, 1950.

19. Idelsohn, Abraham Zebi. *Jewish Music in its Historical Development*. New York: H. Holt, 1929; reprint: New York: Schocken, 1967.

20. Lippman, Edward A. *Musical Thought in Ancient Greece*. New York: Columbia University Press, 1964.

21. Monro, David Binning. *The Modes of Ancient Greek Music*. Oxford: Clarendon Press, 1894.

22. Mountford, James Frederick. "Greek Music in the Papyri and Inscriptions," in *New Chapters in the History of Greek Literature*, 2nd series, ed. John Undershell Powell and Eric Arthur Barber. Oxford: Clarendon Press, 1929.

23. Oates, Whitney Jennings, and Eugene O'Neill, Jr. *The Complete Greek Drama*. New York: Random House, 1938.

24. Plato. *The Dialogues of Plato*, tr. Benjamin Jowett. New York: Liveright, 1954. Volume II: *Republic*.

25. Rosowsky, Solomon. *The Cantillation of the Bible: The Five Books of Moses*. New York: The Reconstructionist Press, 1957.

26. Rothmüller, Aron Marko. *The Music of the Jews*. Cranbury, NJ: A. S. Barnes, 1967.

27. Sachs, Curt. *Altägyptische musikinstrumente*. Leipzig: J. C. Hinrichs, 1920.

28. ———*Die Musikinstrumente des alten Ägyptens*. Berlin: K. Curtius, 1921.

29. ———*Real-Lexikon der Musikinstrumente*. Berlin: Max Hesse, 1913; Hildesheim: Georg Olms Verlagsbuchhandlung, 1962.

30. Salvador-Daniel, Francesco. *The Music and Musical Instruments of the Arabs*. New York: C. S. Scribner's Sons, 1915; reprint: Portland, ME: Longwood Press, 1976.

31. Schlesinger, Kathleen. *The Greek Aulos*. London: Metheun & Co., 1939; reprint: Groningen: Bouma, 1970.

32. Sendrey, Alfred. *Music in Ancient Israel*. New York: Philosophical Library, 1969.

33. ———*Music in the Social and Religious Life of Antiquity*. Cranbury, NJ: Associated University Presses, 1974.

34. ʼStainer, John. *The Music of the Bible*. London: Novello, 1914; reprint: New York: Da Capo Press, 1970.

35. Strunk, Oliver. *Essays on Music in the Byzantine World*. New York: W. W. Norton, 1977.

36. Tillyard, Henry J. W. *Byzantine Music and Hymnography*. London: Faith Press, 1923; reprint: New York: AMS Press, 1976.

37. ———"The Rediscovery of Byzantine Music," in *Essays Presented to Egon Wellesz*, ed. Jack Westrup, pp. 3-6. Oxford: Clarendon Press, 1966.

38. Wellesz, Egon. *A History of Byzantine Music and Hymnography*, 2nd ed. Oxford: Clarendon Press, 1961.

39. Werner, Eric. "Greek Ideas on Music in Judeo-Arabic Literature," in *The Commonwealth of Music in Honor of Curt Sachs*, ed. Gustave Reese and Rose Brandel, pp. 71-96. New York: The Free Press, 1965.

40. ———*The Sacred Bridge. The Interdependence of Liturgy and Music in Synagogue and Church during the First Millenium*. London: Dennis Dobson, 1959; New York: Columbia University Press, 1959.

41. Williams, Charles Francis Abdy. *The Aristoxenian Theory of Musical Rhythm*. Cambridge, England: University Press, 1911.

42. Williams, Peter; *New History of the Organ: From the Greeks to the Present Day*. London: Faber, 1980.

43. Wilson, Nigel Guy, and Dimitrije I. Stefanovic. *Manuscripts of Byzantine Chant in Oxford*. Oxford: Bodleian Library, 1963.

44. Winnington-Ingram, Reginald P. *Mode in Ancient Greek Music*. Cambridge, England: University Press, 1936.

Articles

1. Adkins, Cecil. "The Technique of the Monochord." *Acta Mus* 39 (1967), pp. 34-43.

2. Antcliffe, Herbert. "Music in the Life of the Ancient Greeks." *MQ* 16 (1930), pp. 263-275.

3. Apel, Willi. "Early History of the Organ." *Speculum* 23 (1948), pp. 191-216.

4. Avenary, Hanoch. "Formal Structure of Psalms and Canticles in Early Jewish and Christian Chant." *MD* 7 (1953), pp. 1-13.

5.   Barbour, J. Murray. "The Principles of Greek Notation." *JAMS* 13 (1960), pp. 215-242.
6.   Barry, Philipps. "Greek Music." *MQ* 5 (1919), pp. 578-613.
7.   Cohen, Francis L. "Ancient Musical Traditions of the Synagogue." *PMA* 19, (1892-1893), pp. 135-158.
8.   Cohon, Baruch Joseph. "The Structure of the Synagogue Prayer-Chant." *JAMS* 3 (1950), pp. 17-32.
9.   Edmiston, Jean. "Boethius and Pythagorean Music." *MR* 35 (1974), pp. 179-184.
10. Farmer, Henry George. "Mediaeval Jewish Writers on Music." *MR* 3 (1942), pp. 183-189.
11. Friedlander, A. M. "Discovery of an Ancient Hebrew Manuscript Containing Neumes." *MT* 62 (1921), pp. 170-172.
12. Gombosi, Otto. "Key, Mode, Species." *JAMS* 4 (1951), pp. 20-26.
13. ———————"The Melody of Pindar's Golden Lyre." *MQ* 26 (1940), pp. 381-392.
14. ———————"New Light on Ancient Greek Music." *International Congress of Musicology Papers* (1939), p. 168.
15. Handschin, Jacques. "The *'Timaeus'* Scale." *MD* 4 (1950), pp. 3-42.
16. Harap, Louis. "Some Hellenic Ideas on Music and Character." *MQ* 24 (1938), pp. 153-168.
17. Henderson, M. I. "The Growth of Ancient Greek Music." *MR* 4 (1943), pp. 4-13.
18. ———————"The Growth of the Greek *'Apmoniai'*." *The Classical Quarterly* 36 (1942), pp. 94-103.
19. Herzog, George. "Speech Melody and Primitive Music." *MQ* 20 (1934), pp. 452-466.
20. Lippman, Edward A. "The Sources and Development of the Ethical View of Music in Ancient Greece." *MQ* 49 (1963), pp. 188-209.
21. MacLean, Charles. "The Principle of the Hydraulic Organ." *SIMg* 6 (1905), p. 183.
22. Mountford, James Frederick. "Greek Music and its Relation to Modern Times." *Journal of Hellenic Studies* 40 (1920), pp. 13-42.
23. ———————"The Musical Scales of Plato's *Republic*." *The Classical Quarterly* 17 (1923), pp. 125-136.
24. Nettl, Paul. "Some Early Jewish Musicians." *MQ* 17 (1931), pp. 40-46.
25. Page, Christopher. "Biblical Instruments in Medieval Manuscripts." *Early Music* 5 (1977), pp. 299-309.
26. Perrett, Wilfrid. "The Heritage of Greece in Music." *PMA* 58 (1932), pp. 85-103.
27. Pulver, Jeffrey. "The Music of Ancient Egypt." *PMA* 48 (1921-1922), pp. 29-55.
28. Reaney, Gilbert. "The Greek Background of Medieval Musical Thought." *Monthly Musical Record* 87 (1957), pp. 124-130.
29. Rosowsky, Solomon. "The Music of the Pentateuch." *PMA* 60 (1933-1934), pp. 39-66.
30. Sabaneev, Leonid. "The Jewish National School in Music." *MQ* 15 (1929), pp. 448-468.
31. Sachs, Curt. "The Mystery of the Babylonian Notation." *MQ* 27 (1941), 62-69.
32. Schlesinger, Kathleen. "The Greek Foundations of the Theory of Music." *Mus Standard* 27 (1925), pp. 23, 44, 62, 96, 109, 143, 162, 197; 28 (1926), pp. 31, 34.
33. ———————"The Harmonia, Creator of the Modal System of Ancient Greek Music." *MR* 5 (1944), pp. 7-39, 119-141.
34. Schrade, Leo. "Music in the Philosophy of Boethius." *MQ* 33 (1947), pp. 188-200.
35. Sendrey, Alfred. "Bibliography of Jewish Music." *MQ* 37 (1951), pp. 432-435.
36. Shirlaw, Matthew. "Claudius Ptolemy as Musical Theorist." *MR* 16 (1955), pp. 181-190.
37. ———————"The Music and Tone Systems of Ancient Greece." *MR* 4 (1943), pp. 14-27.
38. ———————"The Music and Tone-System of Ancient Greece." *ML* 32 (1951), p. 131.
39. Warman, John W. "The Hydraulic Organ of the Ancients." *PMA* 30 (1903-1904), pp. 37-56.
40. Winnington-Ingram, Reginald P. "Ancient Greek Music." *ML* 10 (1929), pp. 326-345.

Music

1. Gombosi, Otto. *Tonarten und Stimmungen der antiken Musik*. Kopenhagen: E. Munksgaard, 1939.
2. Idelsohn, Abraham Zebi. *Hebräisch-Orientalischer Melodienschatz*, 10 vols. Leipzig: Breitkopf & Härtel, 1914-1932. (A Thesaurus of Hebrew-Oriental Melodies)
3. Reinach, T. *La Musique grecque*. Paris: Payot, 1926.
4. Sachs, Curt. *Die Musik der Antike*. Wildpark-Potsdam: Akademische Verlagsgesellschaft Athenaion m. b. h., 1928.
5. ——————*Musik des Altertums*. Breslau: F. Hirt, 1924.
6. Werner, Eric. *Hebrew Music* (*AM*, v. 20). Cologne: Arno Volk Verlag, 1961.

1.   Greek musicians with harp, kithara and lyre

OUTLINE II

GREGORIAN CHANT

The Roman Catholic Liturgy — Notation — Music of the Chant
The Eight Church Modes — Psalmody
Chants of the Ordinary — Chants of the Proper
Hymns — Tropes — Sequences — Harmonization of Gregorian Chant
Liturgical Drama

I. **The Roman Catholic Liturgy**

A. The liturgies, which borrowed elements (Psalms, *Sanctus*, Benediction) from the Jewish Synagogue Services, developed in the Christian Church from the earliest times. The Last Supper, called the Eucharist, was first described in the second century A. D. and further developments were described in writings of the fourth century. Since then changes have been made at infrequent intervals. The liturgy and music developed together and are inseparable. The older name, "*Eucharistia*," was replaced by the term "*Missa*" from the closing benediction, *Ite, missa est.*

B. The two principal types of Services are 1) the Mass, celebration of the Holy Eucharist, and 2) the Divine Office, also known as Daily or Canonical Hours. Both Services are used throughout the Church Year: 1) Advent, 2) Christmas, 3) Epiphany, 4) Septuagesima (the ninth Sunday before Easter), 5) Sexagesima, 6) Quinquagesima, 7) Quadragesima (the first Sunday in Lent), 8) Easter, 9) Ascension and 10) Pentecost.

   1. The principal liturgical books containing music appear in various editions. Those being used in this *Outline* are commonly known as the *Graduale Romanum (GR)* for the Masses, the *Antiphonale Romanum (AR)* for the Offices and the *Liber usualis (LU)*, a practical compilation of the liturgy for use in both Masses and Offices.

C. Classes of days of the liturgical year

   1. The Services for the liturgical days, including both Masses and Offices, are divided into two categories: 1) *Temporale* (feasts of the Lord) and 2) *Sanctorale* (feasts of the Saints).

      a. The *Temporale* includes the *Proprium de Tempore* (Proper of the Time) (*LU*, pp. 317-1110) for the Masses (*GR*, pp. 1-365) and Offices (*AR*, pp. 185-483). The Offices for Sundays and weekdays (*feria*) are included in the *Ordinarium Divini Officii* (*AR*, pp. 1-183; *LU*, pp. 112-316).

      b. The *Sanctorale* includes Masses (*GR*, pp. 366-606) and Offices (*AR*, pp. 485-776) for individual Saints (*Proprium Sanctorum* [Proper of the Saints]) (*LU*, pp. 1303-1762), as well as for groups of Saints, such as Apostles or Martyrs (*Commune Sanctorum* [Common of the Saints]) (*LU*, pp. 1111-1272; *GR*, pp. [1-76]; *AR*, pp. [1-68]).

D. The Mass

   1. Liturgical books for the Mass

      a. *Missale*: The Missal contains only the texts for all the Masses.

      b. *Graduale Romanum (GR)*: The Gradual contains the chants and their music for the Masses according to the following. (Note the pagination of both the *Graduale* and the *Antiphonale*. After a long section using regular numbers there is a section with page numbers in brackets, then sections with one and two asterisks following the page number.)

1) *Proprium de Tempore* (Proper of the Time), *GR*, pp. 1-365.
2) *Proprium Sanctorum* (Proper of the Saints), *GR*, pp. 366-606.
3) *Commune Sanctorum* (Common of the Saints), *GR*, pp. [1-76].
4) *Aliae Missae Votivae* (Some Votive Masses), *GR*, pp. [77-132].
5) *Ordinarium Missae* (Ordinary of the Mass), *GR*, pp. 1*-94*.
6) *Missa pro defunctis* (Requiem Mass), *GR*, pp. 95*-108*.
7) *Toni Communes Missae* (Common Tones of the Mass), *GR*, pp. 109*-128*.
8) *Missae Aliquibus in Locis* (Some Masses for Certain Localities), *GR*, pp. 1**-76**.

   c. *Liber usualis (LU)*: This is a compilation from the four liturgical books: Missal, Breviary, Gradual and Antiphonal. Several important Services have been omitted (*HMM*, pp. 527-529).

2. Types of Masses
   a. *Missa solemnis*: the Solemn or High Mass is sung by the choir with a deacon chanting the Gospel and a subdeacon the Epistle.
   b. *Missa cantata*: the sung Mass is without deacon and subdeacon.
   c. *Missa lecta*: the Low Mass is read, not sung.
   d. *Missa pro defunctis* (*GR*, p. 95*; *LU*, p. 1807): the Requiem (Burial) Mass has the Credo and Gloria omitted. The Alleluia is replaced by a Tract followed with the sequence, *Dies irae*. A special form of Agnus Dei is used.
   e. Votive Mass (*GR*, p. [77-127]; *LU*, p. 1273): the Mass for private devotions can be celebrated upon request any day.
   f. *Missa pro Sponso et Sponsa* (*GR*, p. [123]; *LU*, p. 1288): the Nuptial Mass.
   g. Mass of the Presanctified: the Mass for Good Friday for which the Host is consecrated the day before.

3. Structure of the Solemn Mass
   a. In the following chart the first two columns show the sung parts of the Mass, and the third column shows the parts which are sung to simple plainsong in liturgical recitative.

THE MASS

Ordinarium Missae (Ordinary of the Mass)	Proprium Missae (Proper of the Mass)	
	1) Introit	
2) Kyrie eleison		
3) Gloria in excelsis Deo		
		4) Collect (Proper)
		5) Epistle (Proper)
	6) Gradual	
	7) Alleluia or Tract	
	8) Sequence at Easter, Whitsuntide, Corpus Christi, Seven Dolours; also at Requiem Mass	
		9) Gospel (Proper)
10) Credo		
	11) Offertory	
		12) Preface (Proper)
13) Sanctus – Benedictus		
		14) Canon (Ordinary) (Elevation of the Host) Lord's Prayer
15) Agnus Dei		
	16) Communion	
		17) Post-Communion Prayers (Proper)
		18) Ite, missa est or Benedicamus Domino (Ordinary)

b. The liturgy of the appointed Mass is the same whether sung or said. It is divided into two parts: 1) the Proper in which the texts are variable, thus appropriate to the particular day, and 2) the Ordinary in which the texts are invariable.

c. The Mass may be said or sung at any hour from dawn until noon. Solemn Mass is celebrated usually between Terce and Sext. On Christmas Eve, however, it is sung at midnight.

E. The Divine Offices (Canonical Hours)

  1. Liturgical books

    a. *Breviarium*: the Breviary contains only the texts for all the Offices.

    b. *Antiphonale Romanum (AR)*: the Antiphonal or Antiphonary contains the chants and their music for the Offices according to the following:

      1) *Ordinarium Divini Officii* (Ordinary of the Divine Offices), *GR*, pp. 1-183.

      2) *Proprium de Tempore* (Proper of the Time), *AR*, pp. 185-483.

      3) *Proprium Sanctorum* (Proper of the Saints), *AR*, pp. 485-776.

      4) *Commune Sanctorum* (Common of the Saints), *AR*, pp. [1]-[108].

      5) *Officia Propria pro Aliquibus Locis* (Offices Appropriate to Certain Localities), *AR*, pp. [109]-[221].

      6) *Toni Communes* (Common Tones), *AR*, pp. 1*-53*.

    c. *Liber usualis* (*HMM*, pp. 527-529).

  2. Canonical Hours

    a. The appointed times for the eight daily Hours are as follows. All the Hours must be celebrated each day, but a few sometimes may be celebrated at one time.

      1) Matins, at midnight, is divided into three Nocturns on Sundays and greater festivals.

      2) Laudes: 3:00 A. M.;   3) Prime: 6:00 A. M.

      4) Terce: 9:00 A. M.;   5) Sext: 12:00 M.;   6) None: 3:00 P. M.

      7) Vespers: 6:00 P. M. This is the only Office in which composed music is used, except *Tenebrae*, which is sung at Matins and Lauds on the last three holy days of Holy Week.

      8) Compline: 9:00 P. M. This includes the four Antiphons B. V. M. (Blessed Virgin Mary), one for each season of the year.

  3. Structure of the Offices

    a. The Office Services consist of Psalms and Canticles (non-Psalm Scriptures) with Antiphons (short texts sung before and after the Psalm or Canticle), Lessons (Scripture readings) and Chapters (single scriptural sentences) with Responsories, and Hymns. In addition, there are Collects (prayers of the day) and Versicles (sentences sung by the Priest with choir response).

    b. At Lauds the lesser Canticles (from the Old Testament) are used. The major Canticles (from the New Testament) are assigned each to a particular Office; Lauds: Canticle of Zacharias, *Benedictus Dominus*; Vespers: Canticle of the Virgin Mary, *Magnificat*; and Compline: Canticle of Simeon, *Nunc dimittis* (*LU*, p. 91* "Canticles").

    c. The melodies used for the chants of the Offices are generally simple. However, more elaborate melodies are used for the important Services of Matins, Vespers and Compline.

F. Texts of the chants

  1. Latin has been the official language of the Roman Church since the early fourth century.

    a. Pronunciation of Church Latin may be found in *LU*, pp. xxxv-xxxix.

  2. The majority of the texts in the Mass and the Offices are taken from the Psalms (prose poems).

    a. Scriptural texts other than the Psalms are used in the Canticles, some Introits and Graduals.

b.   The texts of the Ordinary of the Mass are nonscriptural prose.
3.   Metrical poetic texts are used in Hymns and Sequences.
4.   The four Antiphons of the Blessed Virgin Mary (B. V. M.) are independent chants with free poetic texts. Each of the four Marian Antiphons is sung for one quarter of the year to conclude the Office of Compline, and on occasion are used at Lauds and Vespers.
  a.   *Alma Redemptoris Mater* (*AR*, p. 54; *LU*, p. 273; *AMM*, p. 1)
  b.   *Ave Regina coelorum* (*AR*, p. 55; *LU*, p. 274)
  c.   *Regina coeli laetare* (*AR*, p. 56; *LU*, p. 275)
  d.   *Salve Regina* (*AR*, p. 56; *LU*, p. 276)

II.   Notation (*PM* v. 1, p. 121)

A.   Origin and history of neumes
1.   Latin neumes were derived from the Greek and Latin grammatical accents which indicated the inflections of the voice. The acute (´), indicating a rise of the voice, became the *virga*, and the grave (`), indicating a lowering of the voice, became the *punctum*. The neumatic signs served as a guide in recalling the memorized melodies.
2.   Early neumatic, or cheironomic, notation (*PM*, v. 1, pp. 96-122) indicated the movements of a conductor's hand in interpreting the rise and fall of the melody. These neumes indicated the number and groups of notes, higher and lower pitches, but not the exact intervals between pitches.
3.   Fragments of manuscripts with neumes come from the 8th century, but the earliest complete manuscripts with neumes (*PM*, Ser. II, v. 2) date from the 9th century. Late in the 10th century neumes began to be arranged above and below an imaginary horizontal line to give an idea of pitch. Gradually the two-, three- and four-line staffs developed. A unique manuscript of the 11th century (*PM*, v. 8) makes use of both letters and neumes for a more exact reading. By the 12th century neumes began to take on shapes somewhat resembling the square notation (*PM* vols. 9, 13) used today in the liturgical books of the Roman rite.
B.   Simple neumes (*LU*, pp. xj, xix)

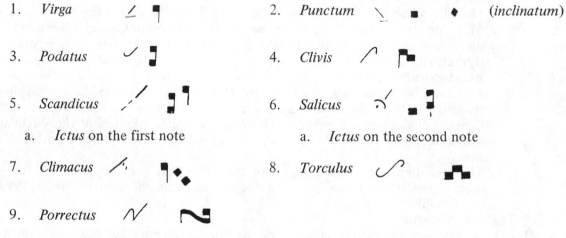

1.   *Virga*   2.   *Punctum*   (*inclinatum*)

3.   *Podatus*   4.   *Clivis*

5.   *Scandicus*   6.   *Salicus*

   a.   *Ictus* on the first note   a.   *Ictus* on the second note

7.   *Climacus*   8.   *Torculus*

9.   *Porrectus*

C.   Compound nuemes are combinations of four or more notes (*LU*, p. xxj). "Special" neumes, such as the *bistropha* (■ ■), *tristropha* (■ ■ ■), *pressus* ( ) and *quilisma* ( ) also suggest special techniques of performance.

D. Liquescent neumes
   1. A liquescent (semivocal) neume ends with a smaller note than the preceding note and is designed to create a smooth transition from one syllable to another. It is used when a word has two successive consonants (*al-leluia*) or when two vowels form a diphthong (*la-uda*).

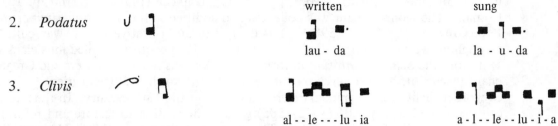

   2. *Podatus*

written

sung

lau - da

la - u - da

   3. *Clivis*

al - - le - - - lu - ia

a - l - - le - - lu - i - a

E. Modern plainsong notation
   Note: Books with plainsong notation (square and diamond-shape notes) should be used when possible.
   1. A four-line staff is used with C and F clefs and quarter, half, full or double barlines to indicate divisions of the chant.
   2. The *custos* (direct) is a small note at the end of a staff to indicate the first note on the next staff. The asterisk (*) indicates a change from a solo voice to the choir. To repeat a phrase two or three times, ij or iij is used.
F. Rhythmic signs
   1. The *ictus* (*LU*, p. xxvij) usually indicates the beginning of groups of two or three notes and never is used as an accent.
   2. The horizontal *episema* (*LU*, p. xxvij) indicates a slight lengthening of a note.
   3. Romanian signs, found in 9th (*PM*, Ser. II, v. 2) and early 10th century manuscripts (*PM*, v. 1), are letters which suggest certain subtle nuances, such as "*t*" for *tenere* (hold back, slower), "*c*" *celeriter* (accelerate), and "*x*" *expectare* (ritard).
   4. All the notes of plainsong are basically of the same duration but are slightly influenced by the text and rhythm.
G. Interpretation of rhythm (*LU*, p. xxx)
   1. The two main schools of thought regarding the rhythm of Gregorian chant are known as 1) "mensuralists" and 2) "equalists."
      a. The mensuralists believe there is more than one time value to the notes of the chants, but disagree as to which notes are short or which are long. The *Editio Medicaea*, 1614, based on the mensural concept, interprets the neumes as measured notation.
      b. The equalists are divided into two branches: 1) "accentualists" and 2) Solesmes School.
         1) The accentualists believe in a uniform value of notes with musical accent based on textual accent.
         2) The Solesmes School believes in basically uniform values, but not in musical accent based on textual accent.
            a) In the Solesmes School of rhythmic interpretation, the basic time values, units or pulses, defined by the *punctum* or the *virga*, are organized into binary groups of one arsis (rising) and one thesis (falling), and ternary groups of one arsis and two theses or two arses and one thesis. These are marked by the *ictus* and in turn make up rhythmic divisions of incises, phrases and periods.

III. Music of the Chant

A. Origin and development
   1. Roman chant (plainsong, plainchant, Gregorian chant), the chant used in the liturgy of

the Roman Catholic Church, developed during the early centuries of Christianity and was strongly influenced by Jewish tradition.   Chants of the eastern branches of the Christian Church in Syria, Armenia and Byzantium are closely related to those of the Western Church and must have derived from a common source.   The chief branches of chant in the Western Church were Ambrosian (Milan)   (*HAM*, Nos. 9, 10;   *OMM*, p. 17), Mozarabic (Spain) (*OMM*, pp. 16, 17), Gallican (France) (*OMM*, p. 15) and Roman.   The Roman chant was collected and codified in the *Antiphonarium cento* by **Pope Gregory** the Great (590-604) and, as the authoritative chant, was cultivated throughout western Europe.   From the 7th to the 12th centuries skilled musicians were sent from the *Schola Cantorum* in Rome to the various religious centers and Gregorian chant reached its highest development during the 9th to the 12th centuries.

2.   Gregorian chant began a gradual deterioration about the 13th century.   In the late 16th century **Pope Gregory XIII** (1572-1585) gave authorization to restore and reform the music of the chants (*SR*, p. 358).   The first printed edition, *Editio Medicea*, 1614, edited by **Felice Anerio** and **Francesco Suriano** [Soriano], and the later *Editio Ratisbonensis*, 1871-1881, edited by Franz X. Haberl, are both spurious editions.

3.   The Benedictine monks of Solesmes, through extensive studies of early manuscripts in the late 19th century, began the work of restoring Gregorian chant as it was at the high point of its development.   In 1889 they published the first volume of facsimiles and commentaries on the chants in the *Paléographie musicale*, a monumental series of 21 volumes to date.   The Solesmes edition of restored Roman chant, *Editio Vaticana*, was officially adopted by the Roman Catholic Church in 1904.

B.   Classes of chants
1.   Strophic
   a.   Hymns and Psalms: each stanza is sung to the same melody.
   b.   Sequences, Kyries, Agnus Dei: mostly strophic, but with some free phrases.
2.   Through-composed
   a.   Glorias, Credos, Sanctus, Offertories, Communions: there is new music throughout, without repetition.
3.   Psalmodic
   a.   Responsorial and antiphonal psalmody (Introits, Alleluias, Graduals): repetition of various sections or rondo-like form is common.

C.   Origin of the chant melodies
1.   The chant melody may be made up of preexisting melodic motives or formulas, a process known as "centonization."   There may be some repetition of material (*LU*, pp. 44, 507) or melodic sequence (*LU*, p. 696).
2.   The chant melody may be based on a traditional melody, or it may be freely composed.

D.   Melodic styles
1.   Syllabic
   a.   There is frequent use of one note to a syllable.   These chants include Recitation Tones, Psalm Tones, Credos, Hymns and Sequences, chants sung by the clergy and the congregation.
2.   Neumatic
   a.   There is frequent use of several notes to a syllable.   These chants are developed for the choir and include Introits, Communions, Kyries, Sanctus, Agnus Dei.
3.   Melismatic
   a.   These chants are very florid with many notes to one syllable. They were originally sung by soloists and include Graduals (*Haec dies, LU*, p. 778; *HAM*, No. 12), Alleluias (*Angelus Domini, LU*, p. 786; *HAM*, No. 13), Tracts, Offertories (*Jubilate Deo, GR*, p. 58) and some Kyries (*Kyrie fons bonitatis, GR*, p. 8*; *LU*, p. 19).

E.   Melodies
1.   Melodic progression in plainchant is primarily by seconds, and skips of a third are

common.   Fourths are less frequent, and wider skips of fifths, sixths and octaves are rare except as "dead" intervals between phrases.

    a.   Characteristic skips include the opening dramatic skip of a fifth, two successive thirds outline a triad and the upward progression of a fourth made up of a second and a third.

  2.   The melodic contour is delineated by a rise, often rapidly, to a high point and then a gradual descent.

    a.   At times the melody may begin on the fifth or fourth note of the mode and descend. It may also revolve about the final (*In illa, LU*, p. 323; *AR*, p. 188).

  3.   The approach to the final at the cadence is usually from above by a second or a third.

    a.   Ascending to the final by half step is almost always avoided. However, ascending to the final by whole step is used.

  4.   Transposition

    a.   Transposition a fifth higher is used to avoid an E-flat (*Passer, LU*, p. 556; *GR*, p. 115; *LU*, pp. 344-347). Transposition is often found in Graduals in modes I and II.

      1) Melodies may end on the fifth of the mode (*confinalis*) when transposed a fifth higher.

  5.   Range

    a.   The majority of chants have a range within an octave. However, some chants (Sequences and Graduals) make use of a 10- or 11-note range of the authentic and plagal modes combined (*LU*, p. 335; *Universi, LU*, p. 320; *GR*, p. 2).

    b.   Many chants (Office Antiphons and Alleluias) move in the restricted range of a fifth or sixth (*LU*, p. 361).

  6.   Modulation

    a.   Sections of a chant may sometimes occur in another mode. The Offertory, *Tui sunt* (*LU*, p. 410; *GR*, p. 35) is in the Hypophrygian mode with the word *"ejus"* using the "dominant" and cadence of the Hypodorian mode.

F.   Tonic accent

  1.   A higher note of a chant when accompanied by a strong syllable of the text produces what is known as a tonic accent.

    a.   Tonic accent is not reflected in chants based on the monotone principle, such as Psalm and Recitation tones; nor does it function in later chants (Hymns, Sequences and Tropes) when the rules of Latin prosody were little regarded.

    b.   In the case of melismatic or florid melodies, tonic accent seems to maintain when the motion from one group to another is considered.

    c.   Accented syllables may be set either syllabically or melismatically. The final syllable, which is generally unaccented, is often set melismatically.

    d.   The tonic accent and the ictus rarely coincide.

IV. The Eight Church (Medieval) Modes

A.   The modes came into use in the ninth and tenth centuries in order of the Greek *tonoi* (scales). Although they are known by the Greek names, it is doubtful they were derived from the Greek octave-species. Some variations from the eight modes indicate that a large portion of the plainchants existed long before the modes were established (*c*. 800).

B.   Names of the modes

  1.   Medieval theorists of the eighth to the thirteenth centuries called these scales *maneraie*, and used the Greek ordinal numbers.

    a.   *Protus authenticus, Protus plagius* (modes 1 and 2)

    b.   *Deuterus authenticus, Deuterus plagius* (modes 3 and 4)

    c.   *Tritus authenticus, Tritus plagius* (modes 5 and 6)

    d.   *Tetrardus authenticus, Tetrardus plagius* (modes 7 and 8)

C.   Mode characteristics
1.   The "final" of the mode is the tone on which it rests.
2.   The "reciting-tone" (*tenor*) in the authentic modes is a fifth above the final, except in the Phrygian mode. In the plagal modes the reciting-tone is a third below those of the authentic modes, except in the Mixolydian mode. About the eleventh century, c replaced b as the reciting-tone in the Phrygian and Hypomixolydian modes in order to avoid the tritone.
3.   In modern liturgical books the mode number is usually indicated at the beginning of the plainchant.
D.   Modes (*OMM*, p. 18)

			Range	Reciting-tone	Final
1.	Dorian	Authentic	d-d'	a	d
2.	Hypodorian	Plagal	A-a	f	d
3.	Phrygian	Authentic	e-e'	c'	e
4.	Hypophrygian	Plagal	B-b	a	e
5.	Lydian	Authentic	f-f'	c'	f
6.	Hypolydian	Plagal	c-c'	a	f
7.	Mixolydian	Authentic	g-g'	d'	g
8.	Hypomixolydian	Plagal	d-d'	c'	g

V.   Psalmody

A.   Psalmody is the oldest part of Christian church music (Ephesians 5:19; Colossians 3:16). The 150 Psalms (prose poems) form a major part of the texts for the Offices. In the Mass, single Psalms are used in Introits, Graduals, Alleluias, Tracts, Antiphons, Responses, Communions and Offertories.
1.   The Latin Bible (*Vulgate*) used in the Roman Church has the Psalms numbered differently from those in the English King James Version. When citing references these variances should be taken into consideration.
a.   Vulgate Psalm 9 is   King James Psalms 9 and 10
b.   Vulgate Psalm 113 is   King James Psalms 114 and 115
c.   Vulgate Psalms 114 and 115 are   King James Psalm 116
d.   Vulgate Psalms 146 and 147 are   King James Psalm 147.
2.   Each Psalm verse is divided into two lines, the second containing a thought which is the complement or antithesis of the first.
B.   Methods of Psalm singing (developed 400-800 A. D.)
1.   Direct psalmody
a.   The Psalm, or part of it, is sung without any additional text.
2.   Responsorial psalmody
a.   Responsorial psalmody is derived from the Jewish service. Originally the cantor (soloist) sang the Psalm verse and the congregation (later the choir) responded after each verse with an Amen, Alleluia or other short response (*HAM*, No. 11; *OMM*, pp. 19, 21; *AMM*, p. 2; *MM*, pp. 3, 6).
1)   Psalm 135 (*LU*, p. 295) has the same response at the end of each verse.
2)   *Subvenite* (*GR*, p. 106*; *LU*, p. 1765) shows an early form: Respond (soloist, choir) - Verse I (soloist) - Respond (choir) - Verse II (soloist) - Respond (choir).
b.   Responsorial chants today are very much reduced in the number of verses and responses.
1)   *Responsorium prolixa* (melismatic) (*LU*, pp. 375, 761, 766, 767; *HAM*, No. 14)
2)   *Responsorium brevia* (syllabic) (*LU*, pp. 229, 1380; *AMM*, No. 3)
3)   The Alleluia and Gradual are examples from the Mass (see Section VIII below).

3. Antiphonal Psalmody
   a. Originally antiphonal psalmody consisted of singing the Psalm verses alternately by two half-choirs. It was introduced by **St. Ambrose** from Syria. Later a short phrase (Antiphon), added before and between the verses, was sung by the full choir.
      1) *Lumen* (*LU*, p. 1357) has the form: Antiphon - Verse - A - V_2 - A - V_3 - A - V_4 - A - V_5 - A.
   b. The antiphonal chants used today, like the responsorial chants, have been very much reduced in the number of verses and responses.
C. Psalm tones (*LU*, p. 112)
   1. A Psalm tone is a melody in the character of an inflected monotone used for the singing of a complete Psalm during an Office. On great feasts (doubles) the Psalm is preceded and followed by an Antiphon. However, on lesser feasts (semi-doubles) the officiant intones the first Antiphon only to the asterisk and then the Psalm and Antiphon follow as usual.
   2. There is a Psalm tone for each mode and, of necessity, the Antiphon must be in the same mode as the Psalm. Another tone, rarely used, is the *Tonus peregrinus* (wandering tenor) which belongs to the Dorian mode. On the second half of the Psalm the tenor is g instead of a (*LU*, pp. 117, 160; *AR*, p. 24*; *Angeli Domini, LU*, p. 1660; *OMM*, p. 20).
   3. Parts of the Psalm tones
      a. Part I (first half of the Psalm)
         1) Intonation
            a) The Intonation leads from the Antiphon to the tenor (reciting-tone) and is sung only with the first verse of the Psalm.
         2) Tenor (reciting-tone)
            a) The tenor is on the fifth of the mode. In long verses it may be interrupted by an inflection (*flexa*) in order to take a breath.
         3) Mediant cadences
            a) The mediant cadence ends the first half of the verse and is followed by a pause (*caesura*). All the modes have only one mediant cadence except mode VI.
      b. Part II (second half of the Psalm)
         1) Tenor (reciting-tone)
            a) Like the first half of the Psalm, the tenor is on the fifth of the mode.
         2) Termination (final cadence)
            a) Optional terminations (*differentiae*), except in modes II, V, and VI, are given in order to lead back to the Antiphon smoothly. The letters *"e u o u a e"* represent the vowels of *seculorum Amen* at the end of the *Gloria Patri* (*LU*, p. 14), which is always the last verse of the Psalm. The Antiphon ends on the final of the mode.
   4. Recitation tones
      a. The recitation tones, distinguished from Psalm tones, are used for reading texts, such as Lessons, Epistles, Gospels, Collects and Prayers.
      b. Although short rising or falling cadences are used, the recitation tones have no musical significance or value apart from the text. They only serve for presenting the texts clearly and audibly.

VI. Chants of the Ordinary of the Mass

A. All the musical parts of the Ordinary were originally sung by the congregation. They were taken into the liturgy after 500 A. D. in the following order: Sanctus, Kyrie, Gloria, Agnus Dei and Credo.
B. *Kyrie eleison* (Greek text)
   1. The Kyrie developed from a recitative-like chant to a neumatic chant, and rarely is

melismatic. The Kyries today are named after the tropes originally associated with them, *e. g. Kyrie "lux et origo" eleison* (Lord, "light and origin of the world," have mercy); *"Omnipotens genitor, Deus omnium creator," eleison* ("Omnipotent Father, Lord creator of all," have mercy) (*HAM*, No. 15b).

   2.   There are three main forms:

      a.   Kyrie A - A - A, Christe B - B - B, Kyrie A - A - A' (*LU*, p. 28)

      b.   Kyrie A - A - A, Christe B - B - B, Kyrie C - C - C' (*LU*, p. 19)

      c.   Kyrie A - B - A, Christe C - D - C, Kyrie E - F - E' (*LU*, p. 22)

         1)   The final phrase of each Kyrie is generally more elaborate.

C.   *Gloria in excelsis Deo* (Greater Doxology)

   1.   The oldest Gloria melody (Mass XV) is like a simple psalm-tone. Later Glorias are free compositions in syllabic-neumatic style. The Priest always sings the first phrase and the choir begins at *"Et in terra pax."*

      a.   The musical settings of the Gloria are indexed under *"Et in terra pax."*

      b.   Of the 18 Glorias in the *Graduale*, 13 of them are in a plagal mode.

D.   *Credo in unum Deum*

   1.   The Credo (a through-composed, syllabic chant) was established in the Roman Mass *c.* 1000 A. D. (Credo I, *LU*, p. 64). The Priest always sings the first phrase and the choir begins at *"Patrem omnipotentem."* The musical settings of the Credo are indexed under *"Patrem."*

      a.   The Credos are grouped separately from the other chants of the Ordinary (Credos I-VI, *LU*, pp. 64-78). Credos II, V, VI are variants of Credo I.

E.   *Sanctus*

   1.   The chants of the Sanctus (normally through-composed) are neumatic, and the word "Sanctus" is generally in melismatic style. The cantor sings through the first *"Sanctus"* and the choir continues through the first *"Hosanna."* The Elevation of the Host follows and the choir then sings *"Benedictus."*

F.   *Agnus Dei*

   1.   This chant is neumatic but sometimes partly syllabic. There are two common three-part forms: A - B - A or A - A - A.

VII. Chants of the Proper of the Mass

A.   Introit

   1.   The Introit was introduced into the Mass by **Pope Celestine** in the early fifth century. It is a neumatic chant sung at the opening of the Mass to accompany the entrance of the Priest to the altar.

      a.   Originally the entire Psalm was sung antiphonally with an antiphon between each verse. Today it consists of an Antiphon - Psalm verse - Gloria Patri (except at Requiems and during Lent) - Antiphon (*Puer natus est, LU*, p. 408; *GR*, p. 33).

   2.   All eight tones are used for the Psalm verses in the Introits.

B.   Gradual, originally called *Responsorium*, then *Responsorium graduale*, and ultimately *Graduale*

   1.   The Gradual is a melismatic chant which is sung from the steps (*gradus*) of the altar (*clamaverunt, LU*, p. 1170; *GR*, p. [30]).

      a.   Originally the entire Psalm was sung responsorially with the cantor singing each verse and the congregation or choir singing the response. Today the Gradual consists of Response - Verse - Response (optional).

      b.   Centonization occurs frequently in the Graduals and produces a strongly unified chant (*Benedicite Dominum, LU*, p. 1654; *GR*, pp. 432, 580).

   2.   The Gradual is omitted on Sundays after Easter until the first Sunday after Pentecost.

C.   Alleluia [Latin spelling for the Hebrew *Hallelu Jah* (Praise ye Jehovah)]

   1.   The Alleluia is a melismatic chant sung responsorially on all Sundays except during

Lent, and consists of Response (Alleluia) - Verse - Response (Alleluia). The cantor sings the Alleluia, the choir repeats it and continues with the *jubilus* on the vowel "a". The Verse to the asterisk is then sung by the cantor after which the choir continues. The melody of the *jubilus* is usually repeated after the Verse except when a Sequence follows (*AMM*, No. 23).

D.   Tract

   1.   The Tract is a melismatic chant used in place of the Alleluia during Lent, Ember days and the Requiem Mass. It consists of several Psalm verses sung in direct psalmody, *i. e.* straight through without an Antiphon. Modes II and VIII are the only ones used in the Tracts. The same melodies are used for many texts, and the melody of the first verse is varied when set to other verses (*Qui confidunt in Domino, LU*, p. 561; *GR*, p. 128; *OMM*, p. 22).

   2.   Centonization is more common in the Tracts than anywhere else.

E.   Offertory

   1.   The Offertory is a melismatic chant which is sung while people present their gifts. In the early manuscripts the Offertory consisted of three or four verses with a response after each verse. However, the present form consists only of an Antiphon.

F.   Communion

   1.   The Communion is a relatively short and simple neumatic chant sung after the Priest returns the Sacrament to the tabernacle. Originally the Communion was a Psalm verse with an Antiphon before and after. The present form consists of an Antiphon only.

Note: Chants of the Proper and Ordinary for Easter Day, with directions for performance, may be found in *GEx*, pp. 3-6; *OMM*, pp. 22-45; *AMM*, pp. 7-29.

VIII.   Hymns

A.   Latin hymnody is divided according to the purpose for which the hymn is intended.

   1.   Liturgical hymns

      a.   Latin hymns are rarely found in the liturgy of the Mass, but in the Offices they are frequently used.

         1)   **St. Ambrose** and **Prudentius** wrote hymns for specific hours of the day, but it was **St. Benedict** (6th century) who finally established the hymn as a regular part of the Office service.

         2)   Of the vast number of hymns written during medieval times, only about 120 are in use today.

      b.   Latin hymns were also intended to be sung at private devotions.

B.   Characteristics of the hymns

   1.   Texts of the hymns of the first four centuries were taken from the Psalms and Old and New Testament Canticles. Later the term "hymn" signified newly-written poems.

      a.   **St. Ambrose** established the basic principles of hymn writing.

         1)   A hymn is divided into strophes (stanzas), and each strophe has the same number of lines (generally four), the same metrical pattern and, when present, the same rhyme.

   2.   Little is known about the music of the hymns until it began to be written down in the ninth and tenth centuries.

      a.   The melody, set syllabically, is repeated for each strophe and makes use of all the church modes.

      b.   Melodic sequence is common and musical rhyme is of various patterns.

      c.   Various repeat forms are used, *e. g.* A - B - C - A (*Deus tuorum Militum, AR*, p. 241; *LU*, p. 419), A - B - A - B (*Lucis Creator optime, AR*, p. 39; *LU*, p. 256), and A - A - B - C (*Jam sol recedit, AR*, p. 433; *LU*, p. 312).

   3.   Interchange of text and music was fairly common in the hymns.

      a.   The same melody was used for *Jesu Redemptor omnium* (*AR*, p. 228; *LU*, p. 365),

Deus tuorum Militum (*AR*, p. 240; *LU*, p. 419), *Exsultet orbis gaudiis* (*AR*, p. 244; *LU*, p. 425) and *Salvete flores Martyrum* (*AR*, p. 248; *LU*, p. 431).

  b. The text *Te lucis* has twelve different melodies listed in the *Antiphonale*, each for a different occasion: Ascension, Advent, Easter, *etc.*

C. Early hymn writers

  1. **St. Ambrose** (340-397)

  a. **Ambrose** defined a hymn as "a song in praise of God." Only four of his hymns are definitely known.

  1) *Aeterne rerum conditor* (Eternal Maker of all things) (*AR*, p. 5; *AM* v. 18, p. 79; *AMM*, No. 4), *Deus Creator omnium* (God, Creator of all), *Jam surgit hora tertia* (Now came the third hour) and *Veni Redemptor gentium* (Come, Redeemer of the people)

  2) *Splendor paternae gloriae* (From the Father's glory shining) (*AR*, p. 61) is also ascribed to **Ambrose**. The music form is A - A - B - A for each stanza.

  2. **Aurelius Prudentius** (348-*c*. 413)

  a. **Prudentius** was a Spanish-Latin poet who wrote many hymns for private devotions.

  b. Three of his hymns are set to the same music; the form is A - A' - B - A.

  1) *Ales diei nuntius* (The winged herald of the day) (*AR*, p. 92), *Nox, et tenebrae, et nubila* (Night, and darkness, and clouds) (*AR*, p. 109) and *Lux ecce surgit aurea* (Behold the golden dawn arise) (*AR*, p. 127) for Lauds on Thursday.

  c. *Salvete flores Martyrum* (*AR*, p. 248; *LU*, p. 431) is a hymn to the Holy Innocents. Its form is A - B - C - A.

  3. **Venantius H. C. Fortunatus** (530-609)

  a. *Vexilla Regis prodeunt* (The royal banner is unfurled) (*AR*, pp. 340, 588; *LU*, p. 575)

  1) This hymn on the Crucifixion, in honor of the Holy Cross, entered the liturgy as the Vesper hymn in Passiontide. Its form is A - B - C - D.

  b. *Pange lingua gloriosi lauream certaminis* (Sing, my tongue, the glorious battle) (*AR*, p. [167]; *LU*, p. 742; *OMM*, p. 15; *AM*, v. 18, p. 81) is sometimes ascribed to **Claudianus Mamertus**.

  1) On a Crucifixion theme, this processional hymn is part of the Good Friday service. It was incorporated into the Roman rite from Gallican chant. Its form is A - B - C - D - C - D.

  4. **Pope Gregory** the Great (*c*. 548-604)

  a. *Lucis Creator optime* (Blest Creator of the light) (*AR*, p. 39; *LU*, p. 256)

  1) The form for each stanza is A - B - A - B.

D. Miscellaneous hymns

  1. *Veni Creator Spiritus* (Come Thou Creator God) (*AR*, p. 420; *LU*, p. 885)

  a. The text is ascribed to Rhabanus Maurus [Hraban Maur] (780-856) and contains a couplet from a Christmas hymn of **St. Ambrose**, *Veni Redemptor Gentium*.

  2. *Lustra sex qui iam peregit* (Thirty years among us dwelling) (*AR*, p. 344)

  a. This may be by **Ambrose** or **Fortunatus**. The form is A - B - C - D - C - D.

  3. *Jam sol recedit igneus* (Now the fiery sun is setting) (*AR*, pp. 180, 433; *LU*, p. 312)

  a. This hymn is a revision of *O Lux beata Trinitas*. The poetic rhyme is A - B - B - A and the musical rhyme is A - A - B - A.

IX. Tropes

A. Tropes are texts usually added between two words of the authorized liturgical texts. These texts which varied from a few words to entire poems often explained or amplified the liturgical text, or were related to a particular feast, day or season.

  1. Two centers primarily associated with troping were the monasteries of St. Gall in Switzerland where **Tuotilo** [Tutilo] (d. 915) was a master of troping and St. Martial

at Limoges.

B.   Tropes were sometimes set syllabically to preexisting melismas in the original chant (Kyries), or at times additional texts and music extended the chant (Glorias, Sanctus, Agnus Dei).

1.   Texts added to the final melisma of the Alleluia developed into the Sequence.

C.   The chants most frequently troped were the Kyrie (*AM*, v. 18, p. 84; *MSO*, v. 1, p. 11), Gloria, Sanctus (*AM*, v. 18, p. 83) and *Benedicamus Domino* (*AMM*, pp. 32, 33; *HAM*, No. 15b; *OMM*, p. 29).

D.   Tropes were banished by the Council of Trent (1545-1563), but the Kyries are known today by the texts of the tropes associated with them, *e. g.* Kyrie *Cunctipotens Genitor* (Omnipotent Father) (*GR*, p. 15*; *LU*, p. 25).

X.   Sequences

A.   The Sequence was perfected by **Notker Balbulus** (Notker the stutterer) (*c.* 840-912); his collection of A. D. 884 has many fine examples (*GMB*, No. 4). Originally the Sequence was a long melisma after the final vowel (*jubilus*) of the Alleluia. Later a free poetic text (*prosa*) was syllabically set to the melisma. Some 4500 Sequences had been written but all except four were banned at the Council of Trent. A fifth Sequence, *Stabat Mater*, was added in 1727. When Sequences are sung the final Alleluia after the Verse is omitted.

B.   Texts

1.   The Sequence texts are long poems of two-line stanzas, often beginning and ending with a single line, *e. g.* X - AA - BB - CC - DD - *etc.* - Y. They developed in three phases.

a.   During the first phase the lines of each stanza have the same number and accentuation of syllables but the stanzas vary greatly in length, maybe 8 to 20 syllables.

b.   In the second phase the stanzas become more regular in length with occasional rhyme, *e. g. Victimae paschali*.

c.   In the final phase (*c.* 1175) the stanzas are regular in rhythm and do away with the single opening and closing lines (*HAM*, No. 16c).

1)   **Adam** (d. 1192) of the Abbey of St. Victor in Paris, the principal Sequence composer of his time, composed some 50 Sequences.

C.   Music

1.   The music, set syllabically, is the same for each two lines. The relationship between the music of the Sequence and that of the Alleluia *jubilus* is vague. In fact, the Sequence melody often continues freely after the Alleluia and shows little resemblance to the Alleluia (*HAM*, No. 16a). Wide range, sequential treatment and repetition of motives and phrases are common characteristics.

2.   *Dies irae*, **Thomas of Celano** (d. 1250) (*LU*, p. 1810; *GR*, p. 97*; *AM*, v. 18, p. 97; *MSO*, v. 1, p. 9)

a.   Used in the Requiem Mass, this Sequence has the form: AA - BB - CC - AA - BB - CC - AA - BB - CDEF.

3.   *Lauda Sion*, **St. Thomas Aquinas** (d. 1274) (*LU*, p. 945; *GR*, p. 295)

a.   For the Mass of Corpus Christi, this Sequence contains a poem of 12 stanzas and a form: AA - BB - CC - DD - EE - FF - GG - HH - II - JJ - KK - LL.

4.   *Veni Sancte Spiritus*, attributed to **Innocent III** (1198-1216) (*LU*, p. 880; *GR*, p. 273; *GMB*, No. 5)

a.   For Whit Sunday, its form is AA - BB - CC - DD - EE. The rhyme scheme of the six phrases in each two line stanza is AAB - CCB.

5.   *Victimae paschali*, **Wipo of Burgundy** (d. 1048) (*LU*, p. 780; *GR*, p. 222; *HAM*, No. 16b; *MM*, p. 8; *GMB*, No. 6; *AM*, v. 18, p. 92; *GEx*, p. 4; *AMM*, p. 15)

a.   This is for the Easter Mass and the form is irregular: X - AA - BC - BC - Y. It is the only one of the remaining five Sequences that contains the single lines to open and close.

6.   *Stabat Mater*, **Jacopone da Todi** (d. 1306) (*LU*, p. 634; *GR*, p. 445; *AM*, v. 18, p. 99)

   a.   This Sequence is for the Feast of the Seven Dolours and its form is AA - BB - CC - DD - EE - FF - GG - HH - II - JJ, 10 stanzas. The rhyme scheme of the six phrases in each two-line stanza is AAB - CCB.

XI.   Harmonization of Gregorian Chant

  A.   **Joseph Yasser** (*A* 44) advanced the theory that if Gregorian chant, which is unison music, is to be harmonized, it should be done in a manner consistent with the harmonic practice of the period near that of the final development of the chant (13th century).

    1.   The modes are considered pentatonic, therefore in the Dorian mode E and B are *pien* (deviating) tones.

    2.   The fourth, the smallest consonant interval, is the basic chord equivalent to the major or minor triad in the tertian system.

    3.   Examples of two- and three-part harmonizations are below.

Kyrie (*Clemens Rector*)

The pentatonic species used.   The fundamental dyads in the species.

Ex. 1

Ex. 2

XII.   Liturgical Drama

A.   Presentation of Bible stories
1.   Liturgical drama developed during the 10th and 11th centuries as an outgrowth of troping and a means of embellishing the liturgy. Bible stories were presented with music and limited acting. Early examples in dialogue form (question and answer) on the stories of Christmas and Easter were probably sung antiphonally or responsorially. Later developments include the addition of costumes, use of other themes, even other than Scripture, and the removal of the drama from the chancel to the churchyard or on to the village green (*TEM*, p. 20).
   a.   The music was in the style of plainchant, written syllabically but with short melismas near the end of the phrases to heighten interest (*Play of Daniel, MSO*, v. 1, p. 11; *SSMS*, pp. 16, 17). Instruments of various kinds were probably used.

B.   Music
1.   *Hodie cantandus* (Today we must sing) (*c.* 900) attributed to **Tuotilo** (*GMB*, No. 3)
   a.   This is a trope-like introduction to the Introit for Christmas sung antiphonally by two choirs.
2.   *Quem quaeritis* (Whom do you seek?) (*B* 7; *GMB*, No. 8)
   a.   This 10th-century trope introduction to the Easter Introit was probably sung antiphonally and tells the story of the three Marys who visited the opened tomb of Christ.
3.   *The Play of Herod* (*OMM*, pp. 47-60)
   a.   The 12th-century drama of the Christmas story was performed at the Office of Matins, a position which allowed the drama to expand more than when sung in the Mass.
4.   Fleury Play Book (13th century)
   a.   The Fleury Play Book from the monastery of St. Benoit-sur-Loire includes ten liturgical dramas. The miracles of St. Nicholas make up the first four, then come two plays each on Christmas and Easter, and the last two are based on New Testament stories, "The Conversion of Paul" and "The Raising of Lazarus."
   b.   *The Slaughter of the Innocents*
      1)   "Lament of Rachel" (*AMM*, No. 28)
   c.   Four Latin plays of St. Nicholas (*M* 1)
5.   *Orientis partibus* (Out from lands of Orient) (*HAM*, No. 17a)
   a.   Commonly known as "The Song of the Ass," this is a secular conductus used in a liturgical play in which Virgin Mary rides a donkey into the cathedral.

C.   The Passion
1.   The story of the suffering (Passion) of Christ on the Cross (*Passio Domini nostri Jesu Christi*) is taken from one of the four Gospels: St. Matthew (Palm Sunday), St. Mark (Holy Thursday), St. Luke (Holy Wednesday) and St. John (Good Friday).
2.   The Passion story was first read without music. Dramatic tendencies led to the reading of the Gospel narrative of the Passion before the Gospel proper and then dramatic action was gradually added for particular episodes, such as the rending of the temple veil. One of the influences in Passion plays was the extra-liturgical lament which expressed the emotions of the people present at the Crucifixion, especially of Mary. It began as a dialogue and later was presented with several voices.
3.   Plainsong Passion (*LU*, pp. 106-109)
   a.   In the 4th century a deacon recited the Mass and the words of Christ were sung to a Gospel tone.
   b.   By the 8th century the text was solemnly declaimed on a fixed tone and the words of Christ were sung to a Gospel tone with inflections and cadences.
   c.   In the 12th century a more dramatic character was given to the presentation. The

parts of Christ (*Vox Christi*), Narrator (*Evangelista, Chronista*) and the crowd (*Turba Judaeorum*) were sung in an inflected monotone by the Priests. Different registers and tempos were used for the three parts.

SELECTED BIBLIOGRAPHY

Books

1. Apel, Willi. *Gregorian Chant*. London: Burns & Oates, 1958.
2. Arnold, J. H. *Plainsong Accompaniment*. London: Oxford University Press, 1927.
3. Benedictine of Stanbrook. *The Grammar of Plainsong*. Liverpool: Rushworth & Dreaper, 1934.
4. Brandel, Rose. "Some Unifying Devices in the Religious Music Drama of the Middle Ages," in *Aspects of Medieval and Renaissance Music: A Birthday Offering to Gustave Reese*, ed. Jan LaRue, pp. 40-55. New York: W. W. Norton, 1966.
5. Bryden, John R. and David G. Hughes. *An Index of Gregorian Chant*, 2 vols. Cambridge, MA: Harvard University Press, 1969.
6. Carpenter, Nan Cooke. *Music in the Medieval and Renaissance Universities*. Norman: University of Oklahoma Press, 1958.
7. Chambers, Edmund Kerchover. *The Medieval Stage*. London: Oxford University Press, 1903; reprint: 1963.
8. Chase, Gilbert. *The Music of Spain*. New York: W. W. Norton, 1941; 2nd rev. ed., New York: Dover Publications, 1959.
9. Collins, Jr., Fletcher. *The Production of Medieval Church Music-Drama*. Charlottesville: The University Press of Virginia, 1972.
10. Crocker, Richard L. *The Early Medieval Sequence*. Berkeley: University of California Press, 1977.
11. Deiss, Lucien. *Spirit and Song of the New Liturgy*, rev. ed. Cincinnati: World Library Publications, 1976.
12. Donovan, Richard B. *The Liturgical Drama in Medieval Spain*. Toronto: Pontifical Institute of Mediaeval Studies, 1958.
13. Douglas, Charles Winfred. *Church Music in History and Practice*. New York: C. Scribner's Sons, 1937; rev. ed., London: Faber & Faber, 1962.
14. Draeger, Hans-Heinz. "The Order of the Arts in the Catholic Service," in *Paul A. Pisk, Essays in His Honor*, ed. John Glowacki, pp. 1-9. Austin: University of Texas Press, 1966.
15. Ellinwood, Leonard Webster. *Musica Hermanni Contracti*. Rochester, NY: Eastman School of Music, 1936.
16. Evans, Paul. *The Early Trope Repertory of Saint Martial de Limoges*. Princeton: Princeton University Press, 1970. (Transcriptions of the Proper Tropes of Paris 1121, pp. 129-169).
17. Farmer, Henry George. *Historical Facts for the Arabian Musical Influence*. London: William Reeves, 1930; Hildesheim: Georg Olms Verlag, 1970.
18. Fellerer, Karl G. *The History of Catholic Church Music*, tr. Francis A. Brunner. Baltimore: Helicon Press, 1961.
19. Fortescue, Adrian. *The Ceremonies of the Roman Rite Described*. London: Burns, Oates and Washbourne, 1932.
20. Hammerich, A. *Medieval Musical Relics of Denmark*, tr. Margaret Williams Hamerik. Leipzig: Breitkopf & Härtel, 1912.
21. Hoppin, Richard H. "Tonal Organization in Music Before the Renaissance," in *Paul A. Pisk, Essays in His Honor*, ed. John Glowacki, pp. 25-37. Austin: University of Texas Press, 1966.
22. Hughes, Andrew. *Medieval Music*. Toronto: University of Toronto Press, 1974.

23. Johner, Father Dominicus. *A New School of Gregorian Chant*. New York: F. Pustet, 1906; 3rd ed., Ratisbon and New York: F. Pustet, 1925.

24. Julian, John. *A Dictionary of Hymnology*. London: J. Murray, 1908; rev. ed., 1925; reprinted in 2 vols., 1957.

25. Lapierre, Eugene. *Gregorian Chant Accompaniment*. Toledo: Gregorian Institute of America, 1949.

26. Murray, Dom Gregory. *Gregorian Chant According to the Manuscripts*, with musical supplement. London: L. J. Cary, 1963.

27. Peacock, Peter. "The Problem of the Old Roman Chant," in *Essays Presented to Egon Wellesz*, ed. Jack Westrup, pp. 43-47. Oxford: Clarendon Press, 1966.

28. Peeters, Flor. *A Practical Method of Plain Chant Accompaniment*. Malines, Belgium: H. Dessain, 1950.

29. Pierik, Marie. *Dramatic and Symbolic Elements in Gregorian Chant*. New York: Desclée & Co., 1963.

30. Potiron, Henri. *Treatise on the Accompaniment of Gregorian Chant*, tr. Ruth C. Gabain. Tournai, Belgium: Desclée & Co., 1933.

31. Randel, Don Michael. *An Index to the Chant of the Mozarabic Rite*. Princeton: Princeton University Press, 1973.

32. Rayburn, John. *Gregorian Chant. A History of the Controversy Concerning its Rhythm*. New York: n. p., 1964.

33. Robertson, Alec. *The Interpretation of Plain Chant*. London: Oxford University Press, 1937; reprint: Westport, CT: Greenwood Press, 1970.

34. Smits van Waesberghe, Joseph. *Gregorian Chant and its Place in the Catholic Liturgy*, tr. W. A. G. Doyle-Davidson. Stockholm: Continental Book Co., 1947.

35. Strawley, James Herbert. *The Early History of the Liturgy*, 2nd ed. Cambridge, England: University Press, 1949.

36. Suñol, Dom Gregorio Maria. *Introducció à la paléographie musicale grégorienne*. Montserrat: Abadia de Montserrat, 1925; Paris: Société de Saint Jean l'Evangéliste, Desclée et cie., 1935.

37. ———————*Text Book of Gregorian Chant According to the Solesmes Method*. Tournai, Belgium: Société de Saint Jean l'Evangéliste, Desclée et cie., 1930.

38. Terry, Richard Runciman. *The Music of the Roman Rite*. Boston: E. C. Schirmer, 1931.

39. Treitler, Leo. "On the Source of the Alleluia Melisma: A Western Tendency in Western Chant," in *Studies in Music History: Essays for Oliver Strunk*, ed. Harold Powers, pp. 59-72. Princeton: Princeton University Press, 1968.

40. Vollaerts, Jan W. A. *Rhythmic Proportions in Early Medieval Ecclesiastical Chant*, 2nd ed. Leiden, Netherlands: E. J. Brill, 1960.

41. Wagner, Peter J. *Introduction to the Gregorian Melodies*, 2nd ed., tr. Agnes Orme and E. G. P. Wyatt. London: Plainsong and Medieval Society, 1901.

42. Weakland, Rembert G. "The Performance of Ambrosian Chant in the 12th Century," in *Aspects of Medieval and Renaissance Music: A Birthday Offering to Gustave Reese*, ed. Jan LaRue, pp. 856-882. New York: W. W. Norton, 1966.

43. Wellesz, Egon. *Eastern Elements in Western Chant. Studies in the Early History of Ecclesiastical Music*. Copenhagen: Munksgaard, 1947.

44. Werner, Eric. "The Genesis of the Liturgical Sanctus," in *Essays Presented to Egon Wellesz*, ed. Jack Westrup, pp. 19-32. Oxford: Clarendon Press, 1966.

45. ———————*The Origin of the Eight Modes of Music*. Cincinnati: Hebrew Union College, 1948.

46. Yasser, Joseph. *Medieval Quartal Harmony*. New York: American Library of Musicology, 1938.

47. Young, Karl. *The Drama of the Medieval Church*, 2 vols. Oxford: Clarendon Press, 1933; reprint: 1951.

Articles

1. Apel, Willi. "The Central Problem of Gregorian Chant." *JAMS* 9 (1956), pp. 118-127.
2. Bjork, David A. "The Kyrie Trope." *JAMS* 33 (1980), pp. 1-41.
3. Bonvin, Ludwig. "Liturgical Music from the Rhythmical Standpoint up to the Twelfth Century." *MTNAPro* 10 (1915), pp. 215-225.
4. ————"The 'Measure' in Gregorian Music." *MQ* 15 (1929), pp. 16-28.
5. Bowles, Edmund A. "Musical Instruments in the Medieval Corpus Christi Procession." *JAMS* 17 (1964), pp. 251-260.
6. ————"The Role of Musical Instruments in Medieval Sacred Drama." *MQ* 45 (1959), pp. 67-84.
7. Brockett, Clyde Waring. "Unpublished Antiphons and Antiphon Series Found in the Gradual of St. Yrieix." *MD* 26 (1972), pp. 5-35.
8. Bukofzer, Manfred. "Speculative Thinking in Mediaeval Music." *Speculum* 17 (1942), pp. 165-180.
9. Cochrane, Marian Bennett. "The Alleluia in Gregorian Chant." *JAMS* 7 (1954), pp. 213-220.
10. Crocker, Richard L. "Hermann's Major Sixth." *JAMS* 25 (1972), pp. 19-37.
11. ————"The Repertory of Proses at Saint Martial de Limoges in the 10th Century." *JAMS* 11 (1958), pp. 149-164.
12. ————"Some Ninth-Century Sequences." *JAMS* 20 (1967), pp. 367-402.
13. ————"The Troping Hypothesis." *MQ* 52 (1966), pp. 183-203.
14. Cutter, Paul F. "The Old Roman Chant Tradition: Oral or Written? " *JAMS* 20 (1967), pp. 167-181.
15. ————"The Question of the 'Old-Roman' Chant: a Reappraisal." *Acta Mus* 39 (1967), pp. 2-20.
16. Dutka, Joanna. "The Twelfth-Century Sequence: Text and Music." *Medieval Studies* 29 (1967), pp. 344-350.
17. Emerson, John A. "The Recovery of the Wolffheim Antiphonal." *AnM* 6 (1958-1963), pp. 69-97.
18. Frere, Walter Howard. "Key-Relationship in Early Medieval Music." *PMA* 37 (1911), pp. 129-149.
19. Grutchfield, E. J. "Hucbald." *MT* 71 (1930), pp. 507-510, 704-710.
20. Holman, Hans-Jörgen. "Melismatic Tropes in the Responsories for Matins." *JAMS* 16 (1963), pp. 36-45.
21. Homan, Frederic W. "Final and Internal Cadential Patterns in Gregorian Chant." *JAMS* 17 (1964), pp. 66-77.
22. McGee, Timothy J. "The Liturgical Placements of the *Quem quaeritis* Dialogue." *JAMS* 29 (1976), pp. 1-29.
23. McKinnon, James. "Musical Instruments in Medieval Psalm Commentaries and Psalters." *JAMS* 21 (1968), pp. 3-20.
24. More, Mother Thomas. "The Performance of Plainsong in the Later Middle Ages and the Sixteenth Century." *PMA* 92 (1965-1966), pp. 129-134.
25. Murray, George. "The Authentic Rhythm of Gregorian Chant." *Caecilia* 86 (1959), pp. 57-71.
26. Perl, Carl Johann. "Augustine and Music." *MQ* 41 (1955), pp. 496-510.
27. Robertson, Alec. "The Fathers of the Church and Music." *MR* 1 (1940), pp. 279-284.
28. Schlesinger, Kathleen. "The Utrecht Psalter." *Musical Antiquary* 2 (1910), pp. 18-33.
29. Schuler, Richard J. "The Roman Chant." *Caecilia* 86 (1959), pp. 129-137.
30. Smoldon, William L. "The Easter Sepulchre Music-Drama." *ML* 27 (1946), pp. 1-17.
31. ————"Medieval Church Drama and the Use of Musical Instruments." *MT* 103 (1962), pp. 836-840.
32. ————"Medieval Lyrical Melody and the Latin Church Dramas." *MQ* 51 (1965), pp. 507-517.

33. Smoldon, William L. "The Music of the Medieval Church Drama." *MQ* 48 (1962), pp. 476-497.
34. Steiner, Ruth. "Some Questions about the Gregorian Offertories and Their Verses." *JAMS* 19 (1966), pp. 162-181.
35. Stevens, George. "The Gregorian Chant, the Greatest Unison Music." *MQ* 30 (1944), pp. 205-225.
36. Stevens, John. "Music in Medieval Drama." *PMA* 86 (1957), pp. 81-95.
37. Strunk, Oliver. "The Notation of the Chartres Fragment." *AnM* 3 (1955), pp. 7-37.
38. van der Werf, Hendrik. "Concerning the Mensurability of Medieval Music." *Current Musicology* 10 (1970), pp. 69-73.
39. Van Dijk, S. J. P. "Medieval Terminology and Methods of Psalm Singing." *MD* 6 (1952), pp. 7-26.
40. Weakland, Rembert. "Beginnings of Troping." *MQ* 44 (1958), pp. 477-488.
41. ————"The Rhythmic Modes and Medieval Latin Drama." *JAMS* 14 (1961), pp. 131-146.
42. Wellesz, Egon. "The Interpolation of Plainchant." *ML* 44 (1963), pp. 343-349.
43. ————"Recent Studies in Western Chant." *MQ* 41 (1955), pp. 177-190.
44. Yasser, Joseph. "Mediaeval Quartal Harmony." *MQ* 23 (1937), pp. 170-197, 333-366; 24 (1938), pp. 351-358.

Music

1. Albrecht, Otto Edwin. *Four Latin Plays of St. Nicholas from the 12th Century Fleury Play-Book*. Philadelphia: University of Pennsylvania Press, 1935.
2. *Antiphonale sacrosanctae Romanae ecclesiae*. Rome: Vatican Press, 1912.
3. Brockett, Clyde Waring. *Antiphons, Responsories, and Other Chants of the Mozarabic Rite*. Brooklyn: Institute of Mediaeval Music, 1968.
4. Coussemaker, Edmond de. *Drames Liturgiques de Moyen Age*. Rennes: H. Vatar, 1860; reprint: New York: Broude Brothers, 1964.
5. *The Fleury Play of Herod*, ed. Terence Bailey. Toronto: Pontifical Institute of Mediaeval Studies, n. d.
6. Frere, Walter Howard. *The Winchester Troper*. London: Harrison and Sons, 1894.
7. *Graduale sacrosanctae Romanae ecclesiae*. Rome: Vatican Press, 1907; Solemes edition, Tournai and Paris: Desclée et cie, 1924.
8. *Graduale Sarisburiense* (reproduction of a thirteenth-century manuscript), ed. Walter Howard Frere. London: Barnard Quaritch, 1894; reprint: Farnborough, England: Gregg Press, 1966.
9. Jeanroy, Alfred. *Le Jeu de Sainte Agnès, drame provençal du XIVe siècle*. Paris: E. Champion, 1931.
10. *The Liber Usualis*, ed. Benedictines of Solesmes. Tournai: Desclée et cie, 1961. (with rubrics in English)
11. *Medieval Church Music-Dramas. A Repertory of Complete Plays*, ed. and transc. Fletcher Collins, Jr., Charlottesville: University of Virginia, 1978.
12. Messenger, Ruth Ellis. *Latin Hymns of the Middle Ages*. New York: Hymn Society of America, 1948.
13. *The New Roman Missal*, in Latin and English by Rev. F. X. Lasance. New York: Benziger Brothers, 1937.
14. Planchart, Alejandro E. *The Repertory of Tropes at Winchester*, 2 vols. Princeton: Princeton University Press, 1977.
15. *The Play of Daniel; A Thirteenth-Century Musical Drama*, ed. Noah Greenberg. New York: Oxford University Press, 1959.
16. *The Play of Herod: A Twelfth-Century Musical Drama*, ed. Noah Greenberg and William L. Smoldon. New York: Oxford University Press, 1965.

17. *The Play of Herod; A Medieval Nativity Play*, ed. William L. Smoldon. New York: Oxford University Press, 1960.

18. Plummer, John. *Liturgical Manuscripts for the Mass and the Divine Offices*. New York: Pierpont Morgan Library, 1964.

19. Randel, Don Michael. *The Responsorial Psalm Tones for the Mozarabic Office*. Princeton: Princeton University Press, 1969.

20. Tack, Franz. *Gregorian Chant*, tr. Everett Helm (*AM*, v. 18). Cologne: Arno Volk Verlag, 1960.

21. *Vesperale Romanum*. Paris: Desclée et cie, 1924.

2. Orlando di Lasso (seated at the harpsichord) and
other famous 16th-century composers

OUTLINE III

SECULAR MONOPHONIC MUSIC

Secular Latin Songs – Jongleurs – Troubadours – Trouvères

I. **Secular Latin Songs**

    A. 7th-10th centuries
      1. Early secular Latin songs with Visigothic neumes (as yet undeciphered) dealt with a variety of subjects, such as the virtues of royalty, marriages and coronations, epitaphs and laments (*planctus*). Occasional settings (9th century) from Horace, Virgil and others show the interest in classical poets.
          a. *"Planctus"* is the title given to several of the religious Sequences. Many of these melodies are made by reiterating a simple motive in varied forms.
    B. Goliards (10th-13th centuries)
      1. The Goliards were men who roamed Europe and had discontinued association with religious orders. Their activities and songs were generally related to the pleasures of the tavern.
      2. Cambridge Songs (11th century)
          a. This collection of more than 40 songs is one of the oldest collections of Latin songs. The texts reveal a wide range of religious and secular subjects. Most of the melodies have been lost.
          b. *O Roma nobilis* (O noble Rome) (*GEx*, p. 7; *NOH*, v. 2, facing p. 221, facsimile)
             1) This song in praise of Rome appears with its melody notated in the letters of the Guidonian hand in a manuscript at Monte Cassino. In a Vatican manuscript it is associated with the song *O admirabile Veneris idolum* (O lovely image of Venus) (*HMM*, p. 261) which was notated with staffless neumes. *O admirabile Veneris* also appears with staffless neumes in the Cambridge manuscript.
      3. *Carmina Burana* (Songs of Benediktbeuern)
          a. This famous 13th-century manuscript, entitled *Carmina Burana* in an 1847 edition, contains over 200 poems on religious and secular subjects. Included are six religious plays, moral-satiric songs, love songs, parodies of religious songs, and gambling and drinking songs. Forty-eight of the songs are in the Bavarian dialect. Some of these songs appear also in French and English sources.
          b. Several poems have melodies notated in staffless neumes. These have been deciphered by comparing them to other sources having readable notation.
          c. *Olim sudor Herculis* (Once the sweat of Hercules) (*AMM*, No. 39)
             1) Some resemblance to the Sequence is noted in the four two-line stanzas, each stanza with its own music. A refrain is added, although it is not indicated where it should be used.
          d. *Sic mea fata* (Singing thus I ease my sorrow) (*AMM*, No. 40)
             1) The music form of this song of love and youth is A - A - B - C - D. Note the repetitions of melodic phrases in the A part and the ends of parts C and D.
    C. Monophonic conductus (12th-13th centuries)
      1. Conductus generally signifies a strophic song used in the liturgy as a transition piece while the officiant moves from one function to another in the Service. It preserved its solemn characteristics also as a ceremonial entry or procession in secular music and liturgical plays.
      2. Usually the strophes had the same music (not Gregorian plainsong), but in some there

was new music for each strophe. The music became more elaborate with the addition of long melismas.

   3.   *Beata viscera* (The blessed offspring of the Virgin Mary) (*GEx*, p. 7; *HAM*, No. 17c)
      a.   This conductus is in A - A - B - C form with melismas in the refrain.
   4.   *Sol oritur* (The sun rises in the sky) (*HAM*, No. 17d)
      a.   A conductus with very elaborate melismas.
   5.   *Christo psallat* (The church sings psalms to Christ) (*HAM*, p. 17b)
      a.   This conductus is in the form of a *Rondellus*, AA - AB - AB.
   6.   *Mors vite propitia* (Death, the propitiation of our life) (*OMM*, p. 62)
      a.   This typical rhymed, metrical, strophic Latin song from about 1200 is known as a conductus.

II.   **Jongleurs** (9th-12th centuries)

   A.   The jongleurs, known in England as gleemen and in Germany as *Gaukler*, were men and women vagabond minstrels who entertained at church festivities and at a wide variety of functions for the nobility. Their activities centered in northern France and included dancing, singing, juggling, playing instruments and story-telling. The repertoire of the jongleurs included troubadour and trouvère songs and epic poems in the vernacular known as *chansons de geste*.
   B.   *Chanson de geste*
      1.   Subjects for these epic poems included the lives of saints and the deeds of heroes. *The Song of Roland* is the best known.
      2.   The *chanson de geste* is divided into stanzas (*laisses*) of unequal length. Each *laisse*, made up of several rhymed lines and a closing unrhymed line, is concerned with one central thought or event.
      3.   Each line of the *laisse* is set syllabically with the same melody except for the closing line which had new music. This closing line of the *laisse* may have been repeated by instruments.
      4.   The music has not survived except in a few cases.
         a.   **Adam de la Halle's** play, *Le Jeu de Robin et Marion*, contains an actual *chanson de geste* melody (*Audigier, CE*, p. 409; *GEx*, p. 19; *RMMA*, p. 204).
         b.   *C'est d'Aucassin et de Nicolete* from *Chanson de Roland* (*c.* 1100) (*NOH*, v. 2, p. 223)
         c.   **Johannes de Grocheo** in his *Theoria* describes a *chante-fable* in the style of a *chanson de geste* (*NOH*, v. 2, p. 224).
   C.   Instrumental music
      1.   The earliest known *estampie* was used by the troubadour **Raimbaut de Vaqueiras** (*fl.* 1180-1207) to set the text *"Kalenda maya"* (refer to IV. C. 6. a. 2) below). It was played by two French jongleurs on their *"vieles."*

III.   **Troubadours** (1100-1300)

   A.   The Troubadours were poet-musicians, both knights and commoners, whose vernacular art flourished in aristocratic circles in Old Provençal, the part of France south of the Loire river. More than 2500 poems by some 450 authors have been preserved. About 300 melodies are extant.
      1.   **Guilhem IX** [Guillaume, William], Count of Poitiers and Duke of Aquitaine (1071-1127) (*SMMA*, v. 3, pp. 25, 277)
         a.   **Guilhem**, the first known troubadour, has only eleven surviving poems and one fragment of a melody.
      2.   **Cercamon** (*fl.* 1130-1150)
         a.   **Cercamon**, the teacher of **Marcabru**, wrote seven poems. His patron was William X

of Aquitaine for whom he wrote a *planh* at the time of his death in 1137.

3.   **Marcabru** (*fl.* 1129-1150) (*AMM*, No. 43; *AM*, v. 2, p. 12; *ACT*, p. 26; *SMMA*, v. 3, pp. 26-28, 278-279)

  a.   **Marcabru** wrote 41 poems, four with music. Like **Cercamon**, **Marcabru** enjoyed the patronage of William X of Aquitaine. He wandered over northern France and also Spain where he spent considerable time and fought against the Moors.

  b.   He influenced later troubadours in manipulating words and introducing difficult rhyme schemes and involved meters.

  c.   *Pax in nomine Domini* (Peace in the name of the Lord), 1138 (*HAM*, No. 18a; *ACT*, p. 28; *SMMA*, v. 3, p. 28)

    1)   This is **Marcabru's** famous crusading song written to incite the Christians to war against the Saracens in Spain. The word *"lavador"* (washing place, signifying the washing away of sin) is used to close the sixth line of each of the 9-line stanzas.

4.   **Guiraut de Borne[i]lh** (1175-1220) (*HAM*, No. 18c; *RMMA*, p. 215; *AM*, v. 2, p. 14; *ACT*, p. 20; *SMMA*, v. 3, pp. 63-65)

5.   **Jaufré Rudel** (*fl.* 1130-1147) (*AMM*, No. 41; *AM*, v. 2, p. 12; *SMMA*, v. 3, pp. 29-31)

  a.   As Prince of Blaye, **Rudel** must have gone on the second crusade in 1147.

  b.   Six of his poems are extant; four are with music.

  c.   *Lanquan li jorn son lonc en may* (When in May the days are long) (*ACT*, p. 24; *M* 15, pp. 63, 249; *SMMA*, v. 3, p. 29)

    1)   The word *"lonh"* (far away) appears at the end of lines 2 and 4 in each stanza. This song closes with a *tornada*, a short stanza corresponding to the last half of a full stanza.

6.   **Peire d'Alvernhe**, a contemporary of **Bernart de Ventadorn**, has 20 poems extant, one with music.

  a.   *Dejosta . ls breus jorns e . ls loncs sers* (Near the time of brief days and long nights) (*SMMA*, v. 3, p. 46; *M* 15, pp. 75, 253)

7.   **Bernart de Ventadorn** (d. *c.* 1180) (*AMM*, No. 42; *AM*, v. 2, p. 13; *ACT*, pp. 8, 10; *SMMA*, v. 3, pp. 31-44, 280)

  a.   **Bernart**, one of the greatest troubadours, the son of a baker, was honored by the Viscount of Ventadorn for his poetry and song. Later he enjoyed the patronage of the Duchess of Normandy (Eleanor of Aquitaine). When she married King Henry of England, **Bernart** spent some time in England (1154) and later entered the order of Dalon, a Cistercian monastery.

  b.   Forty-one of his poems survive, 8 with melodies.

  c.   *Can vei la lauzeta mover* (When I see the lark joyously move) (*OMM*, p. 62; *M* 15, pp. 91, 260)

B.   Texts

1.   The texts of the troubadour songs were based on any subject. However, the theme of courtly love was most common. While Latin remained the language of the Church and the educated, *langue d'oc*, the Old Provençal dialects in which *"oui"* (yes) is *"oc,"* was used by the troubadours. The medieval and modern language of southern France is now called *"occitan."*

  a.   The strophic form with a variety of rhyme schemes was common. Types of poems were not associated with specific poetic or musical forms.

  b.   *Vers* was the term often used by the troubadours to indicate any poem to be sung. Various types were common.

    1)   *Canso*, a love song (*AMM*, Nos. 42, 43; *OMM*, pp. 62, 65, 66; *MSO*, v. 1, p. 12)

    2)   *Sirventes*, a song of service addressed to the nobility, may be based on political, moral or literary subjects, often satirical.

      a)   The *eneug*, from the French *"ennui"* (nuissance, vexation), gave an account of an annoyance or irritation.

      b)   The *planh*, a mourning song similar to the Latin *planctus*, expressed intense grief, particularly over the death of a hero (*OMM*, p. 64).

3) The *tenso*, a dispute or debate, makes use of dialogue, often between two troubadours.

    a) The *partimen* or *joc partit (jeu-parti)* is a dialogue debate usually about love.

4) The *pastorela* [*Pastourelle*] is on the subject of the repulsed knight and the shepherdess (*AMM*, No. 42; *OMM*, p. 67).

5) The *chanson de toile* is a spinning song about the fate of a distraught woman lover (*AMM*, No. 44).

6) The *alba* is a morning song in which a friend warns lovers of approaching dawn (*GEx*, p. 12; *MMRL*, pp. 10-15).

C. Music

1. The melodies are monophonic, without independent accompaniments. Melodies may be through-composed or phrases may be repeated in a variety of repeat patterns, not necessarily following the rhyme scheme of the text.

    a. Instruments, *vieles* and harps particularly, no doubt accompanied the voice more or less in unison. Opening and closing phrases may have been used for preludes, postludes and interludes between stanzas.

2. The normal range of the melodies was an octave. Cadences, melodic direction and intervals differ little from plainchant. The Dorian and Mixolydian modes were common. *Musica falsa*, suggesting more of the modern major or minor modes, was used.

3. The settings are generally syllabic with some use of two- to five-note ornamental figures.

4. Notation is on a staff in uniform square notes with some ligatures.

5. No note values are indicated and the rhythm probably follows the natural accentuations of the text and the fancy of the performer.

    a. Dance songs probably used rhythms based on the rhythmic modes (see IV.B. below).

6. The musical forms are ingenious and diverse, and no common formal structure may be found.

    a. To designate a repeat form as *"canso"* and the continuous through-composed form as *"vers"* is purely arbitrary.

IV. Trouvères

A. The Trouvères were aristocratic poet-musicians from northern France. By the last half of the 13th century many of them were university educated, members of the clergy, as well as of the bourgeoisie, who established guilds in various cities. Some 20 *chansonnieres* from Paris, Rome, London and Milan preserve approximately 1700 melodies and 4000 poems. The songs of the trouvères, written in *langue d'oïl*, generally manifested the same characteristics as those of the troubadours, but the poetry is more sophisticated.

1. **Blondel de Nesle** (1150-1200), contemporary of **Bernart de Ventadorn** (*MMMA*, v. 11, pp. 3-122; *AM*, v. 2, p. 23)

    a. *A l'entrant d'esté* (At the beginning of the summer) (*GEx*, p. 14; *CaMM*, p. 104; *MMMA*, v. 11, p. 26; *M6*, No. 17)

        1) The melodic structure of this five-stanza song as AB - AB - CC - B.

2. **King Richard the Lionhearted** (1157-1199), son of Eleanor of Aquitaine, patroness of **Bernart de Ventadorn.**

    a. *Ja nuns hons pris* (Indeed, a captive cannot tell his story) (*GEx*, p. 8; *HAM*, No. 19a; *M6*, No. 152)

3. **Perrin d'Agincourt** (*fl.* 1250)

    a. *Quant voi en la fin d'estey* (When I see, at the end of the summer, the leaves fall) (*GEx*, p. 11; *HAM*, no. 19b; *AM*, v. 2, p. 35; *M6*, No. 291)

    b. *Il covient qu'en la chandoile* (A candle must be threefold in substance) (*OMM*, p. 72; *M6*, No. 162)

4. **Thibaut IV**, King of Navarre (1201-1253) (*MMMA*, v. 12, pp. 3-311; *AM*, v. 2, p. 33)
  a. Great-grandson of Eleanor of Aquitaine and former Count of Champagne, **Thibaut** was one of the most prolific and outstanding trouvères.
  b. *Dex est ausi comme li pellicans* (God is like the pelicans) (*MMMA*, v. 12, p. 18; *OMM*, p. 73; *M6*, No. 91)
  c. *Dame, merci* (Lady, have mercy) (*MMMA*, v. 12, p. 43; *OMM*, p. 75; *M6*, No. 90)
    1) The form of this *jeu-parti* is AAB with an *envoi*.
  d. *De touz max* (*MMMA*, v. 12, p. 23; *M 6*, No. 86; *NMM*, Plate XIII, facsimile)
5. **Adam de la Halle** (*c*. 1230-1288) (*CE*; *MMMA*, v. 12, pp. 483-680; *CMM*, 44)
  a. *Le Jeu de Robin et Marion* (*CE*, p. 347; *GEx*, p. 16)
    1) This is a comic play with monophonic music presented at the French court in Naples in 1285. The melodies are probably folksongs and there are instruments indicated in the text.

B. Rhythm
1. In the trouvère songs no defined rhythm is indicated. To avoid strained and unnatural emphasis, it is necessary to sing these folklike melodies with rhythmic freedom following the normal accentuation of the text.
2. Various theories regarding the use of modal rhythms in the interpretation of trouvère music are problematical and must be applied with discretion. The troubadours and trouvères continued to use unmeasured notation long after measured notation was available and commonly used in polyphonic music.
3. The rhythmic modes make up a system of modal notation in which two values, the *longa* and *brevis*, repeat rhythmic patterns in ternary meter. The *ordo* (plural is *ordines*) indicated the number of times a modal pattern was repeated before being interrupted with a rest.

4. Rhythmic modes
  a. Trochaic
  b. Iambic
  c. Dactylic
  d. Anapaestic
  e. Spondaic
  f. Tribrachic

C. Music and Text
1. Melodies were simple, monophonic and essentially syllabic. With a preference for repetition and the refrain, the structural forms became organized and in greater variety than those of the troubadours.
2. At times ornamentation was used for expressive purposes. Many of the texts took on a spontaneity and lighthearted quality which was reflected in the music.
3. Important musical forms developed and may be classified into two main types: 1) narrative and 2) refrain.
4. Narrative songs
  a. *Chanson de geste* (see II. B. above)
  b. *Lai* or *descort* ("disorder")
    1) The *lai* is a narrative poem (Roman) written in rhymed couplets, but apparently not sung originally. When a melody is supplied some similarity to the liturgical Sequence may be noted. However, the irregularities of the *lai* overbalance the similarities.
      a) In addition to the repetition for a couplet, the music may repeat three or four times, or appear as a single phrase (*MSO*, v. 1, p. 12).
    2) The line length (3 to 8 syllables), the number of lines to a stanza (4 up to 56) and the number of stanzas all may vary considerably.
    3) In the 14th century the *lai* became more standardized, usually with 12 stanzas, the first and the last being the same and accompanied with the same music.

4) *Au renouvel du tene* (At the renewing of the season)   (*MMMA*, v. 12, p. 411; *OMM*, p. 71)

    a)   A 13th century *pastourelle* in the form of a *lai*: AA - BB - CC - BB.

5.   Refrain songs

  a. *Rotrouenge*

    1)   The relatively few examples of the *rotrouenge* may be identified by textual reference. However, repetition of the music and a refrain seem to be characteristic. As a musical form, no uniform pattern exists.

    2)   The closing line of a stanza may be used as a refrain for each of three to seven stanzas. Some internal repetition may also be present.

    3)   **Gillebert de Berneville**, *De moi dolereus* (*AMM*, p. 93; *AM*, v. 2, p. 55)

       a)   A song with four stanzas of five lines each with the melodic form of AA - BB - C. The last line of each stanza is a refrain.

    4)   *Cuidoient li losengier* (*OMM*, p. 73)

       a)   Five nine-line stanzas set to a melody in the form AB - AB - CC - DEF. The last two lines form a refrain.

  b. *Rondeau (carole, ronde, rondet, rondel, rondelet)*

    1)   The *rondeau*, *ballade* and *virelai* each consist of two sections of music: 1) that which is sung by a soloist or leader of the dance and 2) that sung by the chorus or dancers as a refrain. In the form analyses the chorus part is indicated by capital letters and the solo part by lower case letters. Ultimately the chorus part was sung by a soloist and the songs were no longer danced.

    2)   One stanza consists of two musical phrases (AB) repeated in various ways by a soloist and chorus. Further developments of the *rondeau* continued in the polyphonic songs of the 14th and 15th centuries.

    3)   **Guillaume d'Amiens** (13th century)

       a)   *Prendès i garde* (*GEx*, p. 9; *AM*, v. 2, p. 38) *AB aA ab AB*

       b)   *De ma dame vient* (*HMM*, p. 297) *AB aA ab AB*

       c)   *Vos n'aler* (*HAM*, No. 19e) *AB aA ab AB*

    4)   **Adam de la Halle** (*c.* 1230-1288) *Le Jeu de Robin et Marion*

       a)   *Robins m'aime* (*CE*, p. 347; *AM*, v. 2, p. 38; *RMMA*, p. 223; *GEx*, p. 16) *AB a ab AB*

    5)   Anonymous, *C'est la jus* (*GEx*, p. 9) *aA ab AB*

    6)   Anonymous, *En ma dame* (In my lady) (*HAM* No. 19d) *AB aA ab AB*

  c. *Ballade*

    1)   The *ballade* is a refrain form which usually has a poem of three stanzas with 7 to 10 lines each. The last one or two lines are the same in each stanza and form a refrain.

    2)   The *ballade*, even though similar to the *canzo* and the *bar*, should not be identified with these non-refrain forms.

    3)   **Adam de la Halle** (*c.* 1230-1288)

       a)   *Diex [Dieus] soit* (*CE*, p. 232; *GEx*, p. 10; *AM*, v. 2, p. 41) *AB cd cd ef AB*

    4)   **Jehannot de l'Escurel** (d. 1303)

       a)   *Amours, cent mille* (*GEx*, p. 10) *ab ab cd E*

    5)   **Perrin d'Agincourt** (13th century)

       a)   *Quant voi en la fin* (*GEx*, p. 11; *M6*, No. 291) *ab ab cd ef gh GH*

    6)   Anonymous, *Enmi! brunette jolie* (*GEx*, p. 11) *AB cd cd ef AB*

  d. *Virelai*

    1)   The *virelai*, related to the *rondeau*, is another dance song with soloist and chorus. Usually consisting of three stanzas, its form is *AbbaA bbaA bbaA*.

    2)   **Guillaume d'Amiens** (13th century)

       a)   *C'est la fins* (This is the end) (*GEx*, p. 10; *HAM*, No. 19f; *AM*, v. 2, p. 38)

    3)   Anonymous, *Or la truix* (I find it hard to woo her) (*MM*, p. 12; *MSO*, v. 1, p. 12)

6.   Monophonic instrumental music
   a.   *Estampie*
      1)   The *estampie*, a principal type of monophonic instrumental dance, resembles the Sequence and the *lai* in having repeated sections (AA BB CC DD). There may be four to seven repeated sections (*puncta*) with each section having an open or closed ending.
         a)   In some examples the first and second endings are the same for all stanzas. Portions of a melody may be repeated in any *puncta*.
      2)   *Kalenda maya* (The month of May) (*GEx*, p. 13; *HAM*, No. 18d; *GMB*, No. 11; *AM*, v. 2, p. 16)
         a)   The earliest *estampie* was also sung to a text by the troubadour **Raimbault de Vaqueiras** (d. 1207).
      3)   *Dansse Real* (*AMM*, No. 57; *AM*, v. 27, p. 17; *NMM*, Plate XLII)
         a)   In this dance the second phrase, with its first and second endings, is the same for each of the three *puncta*.
      4)   *La quinte estampie real* (*OMM*, p. 82)
         a)   Each of the four *puncta* closes with the same pair of endings.
      5)   *Danse Royale* (*HAM*, No. 40b)
   b.   *Ductia*
      1)   The *ductia*, according to **Johannes de Grocheo** (13th century), is a shortened form of the *estampie*.
      2)   *Danse Royale* (*HAM*, No. 40a; *GEx*, p. 57)

SELECTED BIBLIOGRAPHY

Books

1.   Aston, Stanley Collins. *Peirol, Troubadour of Auvergne*. Cambridge, England: The University Press, 1953.
2.   Aubry, Pierre. *Trouvères and Troubadours: A Popular Treatise*, tr. Claude Aveling. New York: G. Schirmer, 1914; reprint: New York: Cooper Square Publishing Co., 1969.
3.   Briffault, Robert S. *The Troubadours*. Bloomington: Indiana University Press, 1965.
4.   Beck, Jean Baptiste. *Le Melodie dei Trovadori*, tr. Gaetano Cesari. Milano: Editore Ulrico Hoepli, 1939. (Italian)
5.   ------*Le Melodien der Troubadours*. Strassburg: Karl J. Trübner, 1908. (same as above in German)
6.   Burkhalter, A. Louis [pseudonym: Romain Goldron]. *Byzantine and Medieval Music*. New York: H. S. Stuttman Co., 1968.
7.   ------*Minstrels and Masters*. New York: H. S. Stuttman Co., 1968.
8.   *Carmina Burana*, ed. Bernhard Bischoff. Brooklyn: Institute of Mediaeval Musicology, 1967.
9.   Chaytor, Henry John. *The Troubadours*. Cambridge, England: The University Press, 1912; New York: G. P. Putnam's Sons, 1912.
10. Cohen, Gustave. *Le Jeu de Robin et Marion*. Paris: Delagrave, 1935.
11. Coussemaker, Charles Edmond Henri. *Histoire de l'harmonie au moyen âge*; Paris: V. Didron, 1852.
12. Gérold, Théodore. *La musique au moyen âge*. Paris: H. Champion, 1932.
13. Karp, Theodore. "Modal Variants in Medieval Secular Monophony," in *The Commonwealth of Music in Honor of Curt Sach*, ed. Gustave Reese and Rose Brandel. New York: The Free Press, 1965.
14. Maillard, Jean. *Roi-Trouvère du XIIIème Siècle Charles d'Anjou*. Rome: American Institute of Musicology, 1967. (*MSD*, v. 18)

15. Wicher, George F., tr. *The Goliard Poets; Medieval Latin Songs and Satires*, bilingual ed. New York: New Directions, 1965.

Articles

1. Apel, Willi. "Rondeaux, Virelais, and Ballades in French 13th-Century Song." *JAMS* 7 (1954), pp. 121-130.
2. Gastoué, Amédée. "Three Centuries of French Medieval Music." *MQ* 3 (1917), pp. 173-188.
3. Hibberd, Lloyd. *"Estampies* and *Stantipes." Speculum* 19 (1944), pp. 222-249.
4. Karp, Theodore C. "Borrowed Material in Trouvère Music." *Acta Mus* 34 (1962), pp. 87-101.
5. Kirby, Percival R. "A Thirteenth Century Ballad Opera [*Le Jeu de Robin et de Marion,*]" *ML* 11 (1930), pp. 163-171.
6. Maillard, Jean. "Charles d'Anjou, Roi-Trouvère di XIIIème Siècle." *MD* 21 (1967), pp. 7-64.
7. Perrin, Robert H. "Descant and Troubadour Melodies; A Problem in Terms." *JAMS* 16 (1963), pp. 313-324.
8. ––––––"Some Notes on Troubadour Melodic Types," *JAMS* 9 (1956), pp. 12-18.
9. Pope, Isabel. "Mediaeval Latin Background of the Thirteenth-Century Galician Lyric." *Speculum* 9 (1934), pp. 3-25.
10. Reaney, Gilbert. "Concerning the Origins of the Medieval Lai." *ML* 39 (1958), pp. 343-346.
11. Smythe, Barbara. "Troubadour Songs." *ML* 2 (1921), pp. 263-273.
12. van der Werf, Hendrik. "The Trouvère Chansons as Creations of a Notationless Musical Culture." *Current Musicology* 1 (1965), pp. 61-68.
13. Wolf, Johannes. "Die Musiklehre des Johannes de Grocheo." *SIMg* 1 (1899), p. 69.
14. Wright, L. M. "Misconceptions Concerning Troubadours, Trouvères and Minstrels." *ML* 48 (1967), pp. 35-39.

Music

1. Adam de la Halle. *Oeuvres Complètes de Trouvère Adam de la Halle*, ed. Edmond de Coussemaker. Paris: A. Durand and Pédone-Lauriel, 1872; reprints: New York: Broude Brothers, 1964; Ridgewood, NJ: Gregg Press, 1965; Geneva: Slatkine Reprints, 1970.
2. *Das altfranzösische Rondeau und Virelai im 12. und 13. Jahrhundert*. Frankfurt: Langen, 1963. (*SMMA*, v. 10)
3. Appel, C. *Die Singweisen Bernarts von Ventadorn*. Halle: M. Niemeyer, 1934.
4. Aubry, Pierre. *Estampies et danses royales*. Paris: Fischbacher, 1907.
5. ––––––*Les plus anciens monuments de la musique française*. Paris: H. Welter, 1905.
6. Beck, Jean Baptiste and Louise Beck. *Les Chansonniers des Troubadours et des Trouvères, Numéro 2. Le Manuscript du Roi*. 2 vols. Philadelphia: University Press, 1938; reprint: New York: Broude Brothers, 1970. (facsimile and commentary)
7. Beck, Jean. *Les Chansonnieres des Troubadours et des Trouvères. Le Chansonnier Cangé*, 2 vols. Philadelphia: University of Pennsylvania Press, 1927; reprint: New York: Broude Brothers, 1964. (facsimile and transcription)
8. *Le Chansonnier de l'Arsenal* (*Trouvères du XIIe - XIIIe Siècle),* tr. Pierre Aubry. Paris: Paul Geuthner, 1909-1912. (facsimile and transcription)
9. Gennrich, Friedrich. *Rondeaux, Virelais, und Balladen,* 2 vols. Volume I, Dresden: Gesellschaft für Romanische Literatur, 1921; Volume II, Göttingen, 1927.
10. Hill, Raymond Thompson, and Thomas Goddard Bergin. *Anthology of the Provençal Troubadours*, 2 vols., 2nd ed. New Haven: Yale University Press, 1973.

11.   Jeanroy, Alfred, Louis Branden and Pierre Aubry, eds. *Lais et descorts français du XIIIe siècle*, 3 vols. Paris: H. Welter, 1901.
12.   Jeanroy, Alfred. *Le Chansonnier d'Arras*. Paris: Société des anciens textes français, 1875-1925.
13.   Maillard, Jean. *Anthologie de Chants de Troubadours*. Nice, France: Georges Delrieu & Cie, 1967. (*ACT*)
14.   *Der musikalische Nachlass der Troubadours*, 3 vols. Darmstadt, 1958, 1960, 1965. (*SMMA*, vols. 3, 4, 15)
15.   *Songs of the Troubadours*, ed. and tr. Anthony Bonner. New York: Schocken Books, 1972.
16.   *Troubadours Medieval Music to Sing and Play*, ed. Brian Sargent. Cambridge, England: University Press, 1974.
17.   *Troubadour-Melodien*, ed. Adolf Lang. Kassel: Bärenreiter, 1956. (*MMMA*, v. 5)
18.   *Troubadours, Trouvères, Minnesang and Meistergesang*, ed. Friedrich Gennrich; tr. Rodney G. Dennis. Köln: Arno Volk Verlag, 1960. (*AM*, v. 2)
19.   *Trouvères-Melodien*, 2 vols., ed. Hendrik van der Werf. Kassel: Bärenreiter, v. 1, 1977; v. 2, 1979. (*MMMA*, vols. 11, 12)
20.   van der Werf, Hendrik. *The Chansons of the Troubadours and Trouvères*. Utrecht: A. Oosthoek's Uitgeversmaatschappij NV, 1972.

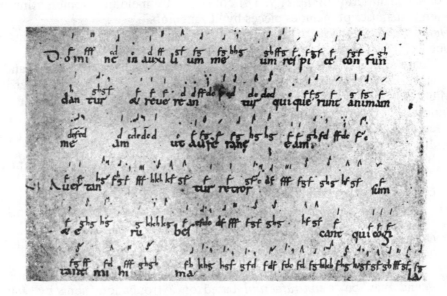

3.   Manuscript with neumes and alphabetical
notation (11th century)

OUTLINE IV

SECULAR MONOPHONIC MUSIC

Minnesinger — Laude — Geisslerlieder — Cantigas — English Songs

I. **Minnesinger**

A. The *Minnesinger* were aristocratic poet-musicians, who like their French counterparts, the troubadours and trouvères, were preoccupied with courtly love. Their techniques and forms, as well as some melodies, were borrowed from the French. The period of the *Minnesinger* extends from about 1160 to the early 14th century. Two main types of songs exist: 1) the *Minnelied* having to do with courtly love and 2) the *Spruchdichtung*, a more serious song similar to the troubadour *sirventes*.

B. Collections of poems and music
   1. Jena manuscript (*SMMA*, v. 11) contains 91 melodies, some of which are from the early 13th century.
   2. Colmar manuscript (*SMMA*, v. 18) contains 109 melodies, some dating from *c*. 1250.
   3. Vienna manuscript includes pieces by "Frauenlob."
   4. *Manessische Handschrift* from the 13th and 14th centuries contains pictures and poems.
      a. These were collected by the knight Ruediger Manesse (d. 1304) and his son, and since 1888 this collection has been in the library of Heidelberg University.
   5. Münster fragment contains portions of five melodies by **Walther von der Vogelweide**.

C. Composers
   1. **Spervogel** (12th century) (*SMMA*, v. 11, p. 31; *HAM*, No. 20a; *GEx*, p. 21)
   2. **Walther von der Vogelweide** (*c*. 1170-1228)
      a. Born in Tyrol, **Walther** for a time was a patron of the court of Vienna and in 1220 settled in Würzburg (*SMMA*, v. 18, pp. 182, 183, 184).
      b. *Under der linden* (Under the linden) (*OMM*, p. 79)
         1) This is an example of a *contrafactum* in that the original German lyrics were set to an anonymous trouvère chanson *En Mai au douz ten nouvel*.
      c. *Nû al'erst lebe ich mir werde* (Now at last my life seems worthwhile) (*HAM*, No. 20b; *GMB*, No. 12, 1)
         1) This Palestine song, probably written in 1228, makes use of the common *bar* form and may be a *contrafactum* based on a troubadour song by **Jaufré Rudel**, although it is more probably an original tune.
   3. **Neidhart von Reuenthal** (*c*. 1190-*c*. 1240) (*SMMA*, v. 18, p. 83)
      a. **Neidhart**, a knight, was born in the same region as **Walther** and, like **Walther**, performed at various courts in Bavaria and Austria.
      b. Poems by **Neidhart** may be classified as "summer" songs and "winter" songs. A large number of his melodies remain.
      Note: In the following references to *DTÖ*, vols. 71 and 18, the first page number will indicate a facsimile and the second page number the transcription.
         1) The summer songs are generally short and simple.
            a) *Ine gesach die heide* (I never saw the heath) (*AMM*, No. 48; *AM*, v. 2, p. 53; *DTÖ*, v. 71, pp. 7, 23; *SMMA*, v. 9, p. 4; *M 9*, v. 2, p. 81)
            b) *Der may* (May has lifted up many hearts) (*HAM*, No. 20c; *DTÖ*, v. 71, pp. 8, 33)

2)   The winter songs have longer lines and stanzas, and their melodies make frequent use of the *bar* form.

   a)   *Winder wie ist nu dein kraft* (Winter, how is your strength?) (*HAM*, No. 20d; *DTÖ*, v. 71, pp. 4, 32; *M 9*, v. 2, p. 38), in *bar* form.

   b)   *Owê dirre sumerzît* (Alas, the dear summertime) (*OMM*, p. 80; *SMMA*, v. 1, p. 12; *DTÖ*, v. 71, pp. 17, 38; *M 9*, v. 2, p. 262), in *bar* form.

   c)   *Owê, lieber sumer* (Alas, dear summer) (*AMM*, No. 39; *DTÖ*, v. 71, pp. 17, 38; *SMMA*, v. 1, p. 13; *M 9*, v. 2, p. 258), a poem of five stanzas with ten lines each in the common *bar* form.

   d)   *Willekommen Mayenschein* (Welcome art thou, May's bright sun) (*MM*, p. 15; *DTÖ*, v. 71, pp. 4, 31; *M 9*, v. 2, p. 31)

4.   **Wolfram von Eschenbach** (*fl. c.* 1200-1220) (*SMMA*, v. 18, pp. 181, 185)

5.   **Meister Alexander** (*SMMA*, v. 11; *AM*, v. 2, p. 56)

6.   **Tannhäuser** (*c.* 1200-1266) (*SMMA*, v. 11, pp. 20-24; v. 18, p. 194)

  a.   **Tannhäuser's** songs reveal information about his life. He participated in the crusade of 1228 and in the Cyprian war in 1231. The German Emperor Frederick II was his patron.

  b.   *Ez ist huite eyn wunnychlicher tac* (Today is a joyful day) (*OMM*, p. 80) in *bar* form.

7.   **Meyster Rumelant** (*AM*, v. 2, p. 59; *SMMA*, v. 18, p. 191; v. 11, pp. 53-67)

  a.   *Daz Gedeones wollenvlius* (On Gideon's woolen fleece) (*RMMA*, p. 235; *SMMA*, v. 11, p. 56)

   1)   **Rumelant** used the extended *bar* form (A A B A) to set this 11-line poem.

8.   **Heinrich von Meissen**   (1260-1318), known as *"Frauenlob"* (praise of ladies) (*AM*, v. 2, p. 60; *SMMA*, v. 18, pp. 1, 20, 30, 88-108)

  a.   **Frauenlob** travelled extensively in Germany and finally settled in Mainz (1312) under the patronage of Archbishop Peter von Aspelt. His songs are less distinguished than those of the trouvère **Adam de la Halle**.

  b.   *Myn vroud ist gar szugangyn* (My joy has completely vanished) (*OMM*, p. 81; *GMB*, No. 21; *NMM*, Plate XVII)

   1)   This song in *bar* form concludes with the last line of the stollen.

9.   **Prinze Wizlaw von Rügen** (*c.* 1268-1325), a contemporary of **Frauenlob** (*SMMA*, v. 11, pp. 76-89)

  a.   *Wê, ich han gedacht* (Ah! I thought this whole night) (*GEx*, p. 20; *AM*, v. 2, p. 61; *SMMA*, v. 11, p. 83)

  b.   *Ich warne dich* (I warn you) (*OMM*, p. 82; *SMMA*, v. 11, p. 82)

   1)   Several melismas make this song quite florid, and some internal repetition in the *abgesang* of the *bar* form is apparent.

10.   **Count Hugo von Montfort** (1357-1423)

  a.   Count **Hugo** admits that he employed a minstrel, **Burk Mangolt**, to compose his melodies. He makes some use of instrumental interludes.

11.   **Oswald von Walkenstein** (1377-1445) (*DTÖ*, v. 18; *AM*, v. 2, p. 64 [*DTÖ*, v. 18, pp. 25, 164])

  a.   The most gifted of the late *minnelied* composers, **Oswald** travelled to the near east, north Africa, Spain, Italy and Russia. In *DTÖ*, v. 18 there are 127 songs by **Oswald**.

D.   Texts

1.   The texts are generally narrative and often religious in character.

2.   The *Tagelied* (day-song) and *Wächterlied* (guardian-song) were similar to the troubadour *alba*. Sometimes it was a warning song or a morning prayer.

3.   The *Leich (lai)*, adopted from the troubadours in the 14th century, commonly used poems in praise of the Virgin or addressed to a lady.

4.   The *Lied* was similar to the troubadour *canzo*.

5.   *Spruch*, meaning proverb, was often a fable or related social or political details.

E.   Melodies
   1.   Melodies generally do not have the texts set under the music. Single unmeasured note values predominate and an occasional ligature appears. Phrase endings are not indicated. Transcription into duple meter is common.
   2.   The melodies tend to be angular, with skips along chord lines. Modality, especially Dorian and Phrygian, is freely used and a pentatonic character is often apparent.
F.   Forms
   1.   *Bar*
      a.   The *bar* form, derived from the *canso* and *ballade* of the troubadours and trouvères, is a three-line stanza made up of two *Stollen* with the same melody and a concluding *Abgesang* with different music (A A B). There are many variations to this basic form.
         1)   The *Stollen* phrase may be added at the end (A A B A), and the endings of each phrase may all be the same.
         2)   The "rounded" *bar* form concludes with a portion of the *Stollen*.
   2.   *Leich (lai)*
      a.   The *Leich* is the German counterpart of the trouvère *lai* but maintains a more regular double versicle repetition than the *lai*.
      b.   *Ey ich sach in dem trone* (*MSO*, v. 1, p. 12; *NOH*, v. 2, p. 258)

II.   Lauda

A.   The *laude* (plural of *lauda*) were Italian non-liturgical hymns of praise and devotion. They originated at the time of St. Francis of Assisi (1182-1226) and their development was continued through the 13th and 14th centuries by groups of penitents (flagellants).
   1.   Many congregations, called *Companie de Laudesi* or *Laudisti*, were organized for the singing of religious songs. Their musical and dramatic presentation anticipated the 16th century oratorio.
B.   *Lauda* collections
   1.   The Cortona manuscript of the 13th century contains 46 pieces with relatively simple melodies.
   2.   Two Florentine manuscripts from the 14th century contain about 100 pieces of which the melodies seem to be more elaborate than those of the Cortona manuscript.
C.   Music
   1.   The *laude* in the 13th century, which show troubadour influences, were made up of several stanzas set monophonically. The music was modal but it also tended toward major and minor tonalities. The melodies were written in plainsong notation and their rhythm is thought to be binary.
   2.   The refrain form of the French *virelai* and the Italian *ballata* with various modifications was common.
      a.   The *lauda* is generally divided into three parts: 1) a *ripresa* (a refrain indicated by capital letters), 2) a middle section made up of two *piedi* and a *volta* and 3) a repetition of the *ripresa* (*AB cc ab AB*).
         1)   The two *piedi* may have the same or different music, or the music of the *ripresa* may be repeated.
            a)   When the two *piedi* have the same music the complete middle section is similar to the German *bar* form: *piedi (A A), volta (B)*.
         2)   The forms may include: *AB cc ab AB* (*HAM*, No. 21c), *AB cd ab AB* and *AB ab ab AB*.
         3)   At times the *volta* may borrow its second phrase from the *ripresa*: *AB cd c'b AB* (*Gloria in cielo*, *HAM*, No. 21a; *GEx*, p. 22).
   3.   *Laude novella sia cantata* (Let a new song of praise be sung) (*AMM*, No. 50; *GEx*, p. 22; *M 5*, v. 1, p. 261) The musical structure of this anonymous *lauda* is *AB cd eb AB*.
   4.   *Lo'ntellecto divino* (Divine understanding of heavenly light) (*OMM*, p. 76; *M 5*, v. 2,

p. 361) The musical form is *AB cc' ab*.

5. *Venite a laudare* (Come to praise) (*RMMA*, p. 238) This *lauda*, in the form of *AB cd ab AB*, is from the Cortona manuscript.

6. *Santo Lorenzo* (Saint Laurence) (*HAM*, No. 21c) form: *AB cc' ab AB*.

III. Geisslerlieder

A. The German *Geisslieder* were religious "folksongs" sung by penitent flagellants (*Geissler*) to accompany their processions and ceremonial rites, particularly during the year of the Black Plague, 1349. In some ways the *Geisslerlied* anticipates the Lutheran chorale.

B. Collections

1. *"Chronikon"* of **Hugo Spechtshart von Reutlingen** (*c.* 1285-1360) gives a description of the rites of the *Geissler* and their songs.

C. Music and texts

1. Generally the four-line stanzas are made up of rhyming couplets.

2. The texts are adapted to only a few tunes often with the basic melodic pattern of *AA BB*.

3. *Nu ist diu* (Now is the pilgrimage) (*GEx*, p. 23)

4. *Maria, muoter* (Mary, mother) (*RMMA*, p. 239; *GMB*, No. 25; *M* 11, p. 30) form: *AA BB*.

5. *Maria, unser frowe* (Mary, our lady) (*HMM*, p. 318)

   a. The first line of each of the 57 rhymed couplets ends with the words *Kyrie eleison* and the second line of each concludes with *Alleluia! Globet sis du, Maria*.

IV. Cantigas

A. The *cantigas* are thirteenth century Spanish monophonic songs most of which pay homage to the Virgin Mary. Frequent interaction among the courts of the Spanish and French rulers suggests that the troubadours had some influence on the development of Spanish music.

B. Collections

1. *Siete Canciones de Amor*, seven love songs (six with music) by **Martin Codax** in the Galician-Portuguese language. These early thirteenth century folk songs and dance tunes are relatively simple.

2. *Cantigas de Santa Maria* (*c.* 1270), assembled by Alfonso X the Wise, King of Castile and León (1252-1284), is a collection of more than 400 songs in four volumes, mostly extolling the Virgin Mary.

   a. Each song describes a miracle, and every tenth song is more general in praise.

      1) *Prologo* (*MSO* v. 1, p. 13); *Gran Dereit'* (Grand delight) (*TEM*, p. 36); *Maria villosos* (Mary, who guides us) (*NOH*, v. 2, p. 262)

   b. The songs are numbered, identified and distinguished by miniatures of more than 70 musicians playing on various instruments (*GD*, v. 3, opposite p. 848; v. 4, opp. pp. 496, 500; v. 5, frontispiece; *B* 4, opp. p. 33).

C. Music and Texts

1. Most of the poems open with a refrain which is repeated after each stanza.

2. The *cantigas* are generally syllabic with occasional use of short ornamentations. The melodies, most often stepwise, are dance-like in character and have well-defined cadences (*TEM*, p. 33).

3. Mensural notation is used throughout.

4. The common form of the *cantiga* is that of the *villancico*; the form was later established in the French *virelai*, the Italian *ballata* and the German *Geisslerlied*. At times the form may vary.

5. *Santa Maria amar* (We should love Holy Maria) (*AMM*, No. 51; *BC* v. 15, p. 13; v. 19, p. 36 *verso*)

6. *Nas mentes senpre tẽer* (We should always carry in our minds) (*OMM*, p. 77; *BC*, v. 15, p. 37; v. 19, p. 53 *verso*)

7. *Maldito seja quen non loará* (Cursed be he who will not praise) (*OMM*, p. 78; *BC*, v. 15, p. 321; v. 19, p. 260)

8. *Rosa das rosas* (Rose of all roses) (*RMMA*, p. 247; *BC*, v. 15, p. 18; v. 19, p. 39 *verso*)

9. Villancicos: *A Madre* (The mother) (*HAM* No. 22a; *BC*, v. 15, p. 8; v. 19, p. 31 *verso*); *Mais nos faz sancta Maria* (Oft indeed does Holy Mary) (*HAM* No. 22b; *BC*, v. 15, p. 7; v. 19, p. 30 *verso*); *A que serven* (She who all celestial beings serve) (*HAM*, No. 22c; *BC*, v. 15, p. 124; v. 19, p. 120)

10. *Alegria! Alegria!* (*GEx*, p. 22; *BC*, v. 15, p. 455; *B* 4, p. 28)

   a. The Easter *cantiga* on the Resurrection of Christ has the musical structure of the *virelai: AB cc ab AB.*

V. English Songs

A. From the time of the Norman Conquest (1066) of England, few, if any, English songs show direct influence of the French trouvères. Among the comparatively few surviving early songs, from the late twelfth century there are three religious songs in unmeasured notation attributed to St. Godric, a Saxon monk (d. 1170).

   1. *Crist and Sainte Marie* (*RMMA·*, p. 241)

      a. This song is interpolated between two renditions by angels of *Kyrie eleison.*

      b. *Sainte Marie virgine* (*HAM*, No. 23a)

B. Religious and moralizing songs of the thirteenth century

   1. *Worldes blis ne last* (*HAM*, No. 23b; *NOH*, v. 2, p. 251; *NMM*, Plate XIX, facsimile; *MSO*, v. 1, p. 14; *Early Bodleian Music*, v. 1, Plate IV; v. 2, p. 196)

   2. *Man mei longe him lives wene* (*RMMA*, p. 243)

C. Secular songs of the 13th and early 14th centuries

   1. *Mirie it is while sumer ilast* (*c.* 1225) (*EBM*, v. 1, Plate III, v. 2, p. 5)

   2. *Byrd one brere* (Bird on a briar) (*AMM*, No. 52; *SSMS*, p. 29)

D. Manuscript Arundel 248 (13th century) (*EEH*, v. 1, Plates 32-36)

   1. Included in this manuscript are Latin, French and English songs, some monophonic and others of two and three voices.

   2. *Is milde Lomb* (*GEx*, p. 23; *EEH*, v. 1, Plate 34)

E. Manuscript Harley 978 (13th century) (*EEH*, v. 1, Plates 12-22)

   1. *Samson dux fortissime* (*EEH*, v. 1, Plates 12-17)

      a. This Latin lament (*plantus*) contains solo parts for Samson and Delilah and other monophonic portions to be sung by a chorus as in a Greek drama.

F. Manuscript Douce 139 (13th century)

   1. Included is a rhythmical dance; the first part is monophonic but ends by expanding into three polyphonic parts (*HAM*, No. 40c; *EBM*, v. 1, Plate VII).

SELECTED BIBLIOGRAPHY

Books

1. Anglés, Higinio. "The Musical Notation and Rhythm of the Italian Laude," in *Essays in Musicology: A Birthday Offering for Willi Apel*, ed. Hans Tischler, pp. 51-60. Bloomington Indiana University School of Music, 1968.
2. Burkhalter, A. Louis [pseudonym: Romain Goldron]. *Minstrels and Masters*. New York: H. S. Stuttman Co., 1968.
3. *Die Colmarer Liederhandschrift*, ed. Friedrich Gennrich. Frankfurt: Langen, 1967. (facsimile; *SMMA*, v. 18)
4. Chase, Gilbert. *The Music of Spain*, 2nd ed. New York: Dover Publications, 1959.
5. Eberth, F. *Die Liedweisen der Kolmarer Handschrift*. Göttingen, 1933.
6. Hagen, Friedrich Heinrich van der. *Minnesänger*, 5 vols. Leipzig: J. A. Barth, 1838-1861.
7. *Die Jenaer Liederhandschrift*, ed. Friedrich Gennrich. Frankfurt: Langen, 1963. (facsimile; *SMMA*, v. 11)
8. *Die Kontrafaktur im Liedschaffen des Mittelalters*, ed. Friedrich Gennrich. Frankfurt: Langen, 1965. (*SMMA*, v. 12)
9. Linker, Robert White. *Music of the Minnesinger and Early Meistersinger* (A Bibliography). Chapel Hill: University of North Carolina Press, 1961.
10. *Die Manessische Lieder-Handschrift*, eds; Rudolf Sillib, Friedrich Panzer, Arthur Haseloff. Heidelberger Liederhandschrift, Grosse, 1929. (facsimile)
11. Maurer, Friedrich. *Frühester deutscher Minnesang*. Berlin: Walter de Gruyter, 1969.
12. Moser, Hans Joachim. *Geschichte der deutschen Musik*, 3 vols. Stuttgart and Berlin: J. G. Cotta, 1928-1930.
13. Müller, K. K. *Die Jenaer Liederhandschrift*. Jena: F. Strobel, 1896. (facsimile)
14. Padelford, F. M. *Old English Musical Terms*. Bonn: P. Hanstein, 1899.
15. Ribera y Tarragó, Julian. *Music in Ancient Arabia and Spain*. London: Oxford University Press, 1926.
16. Riano, Juan F. *Critical and Bibliographical Notes on Early Spanish Music*. London: Bernard Quaritch, 1887.
17. Saintsbury, G. *A History of English Prosody*, 3 vols. New York: Macmillan Co., 1923.
18. Saran, Franz Ludwig. *Die Jenaer Liederhandschrift*, 2 vols. Leipzig: C. L. Hirschfeld, 1901.
19. Sayce, Olive. *Poets of the Minnesang*. Oxford: Clarendon Press, 1967.
20. Trend, John Brande. *The Music of Spanish History to 1600*. London: Oxford University Press, 1926; reprint: New York: Krause Reprint Corp., 1965.

Articles

1. Anglés, Higini. "Hispanic Musical Culture from the 6th to the 14th Century." *MQ* 26 (1940), pp. 494-528.
2. Molitor, Raphael Fidelis. "Die Lieder des Münsterer Fragments." *SIMg* 12 (1911), p. 475.
3. Saltmarsh, John. "Two Medieval Love-Songs Set to Music." *Antiquaries Journal* 15 (1935).
4. Steiner, Ruth. "Some Monophonic Latin Songs Composed Around 1200." *MQ* 52 (1966), pp. 59-70.
5. Trend, John Brande. "The First English Songs." *ML* 9 (1928), pp. 111-128.

Music

1. *Le Còdex Musical de las Huelgas (Música a veus dels segles XIII-XIV)*, 3 vols. Barcelona: Institut d'estudis Catalans, 1931. (v. 1: explanation; v. 2, facsimile; v. 3, transcription)

2. *Early Bodleian Music*, 3 vols.; vols. 1, 2, ed. John Stainer, v. 3, ed. Edward Williams Byron Nicholson. London: Novello, 1901, 1901, 1913.

3. *Gesänge von Frauenlob, Reinmar von Zweter und Alexander, nebst einem anonymen Bruchstück nach der Handschrift 2701 der Wiener Hofbibliothek*, ed. Heinrich Rietsch. (*DTÖ*, v. 41)

4. Gülke, Peter. *Mönche/Bürger Minnesänger*. Vienna: Verlag Hermann Böhlaus, 1975.

5. Liuzzi, Fernando. *La Lauda e i primordi della melodia italiana*, 2 vols. Roma: La Libreria dello stato, 1935. (facsimiles, transcriptions, commentary)

6. *La música de las Cantigas de Santa María del Rey Alfonso el Sabio*, ed. Higinio Anglés. Barcelona: Institut d'estudio Catalans, 1964. (*Biblioteca de Catalunya [Publicaciones de la Sección de Música]*, v. 15 (1943), v. 18 (1958), v. 19 (1964).

7. *Neidhart-Lieder*, ed. Friedrich Gennrich. Frankfurt: Langen, 1962. (*SMMA*, v. 9)

8. Neidhart von Reuenthal. *Lieder*, ed. Wolfgang Schmieder. (*DTÖ*, v. 71)

9. *Neidharts Sangweisen*, 2 vols., ed. Ernst Rohloff. Berlin: Akademie-Verlag, 1962.

10. Oswald von Wolkenstein. *Geistliche und weltliche Lieder*. (*DTÖ*, v. 18)

11. Runge, Paul. *Die Lieder und Melodien der Geissler des Jahres 1349*, ed. Hugo von Reutlingen. Leipzig: 1900.

12. *The Songs of the Minnesingers*, eds. Barbara A. G. Seagrave and Wesley Thomas. Urbana: University of Illinois Press, 1966.

13. Taylor, Ronald J. *The Art of the Minnesinger: Songs of the Thirteenth Century Transcribed and Edited with Textual and Musical Commentaries*, 2 vols. Cardiff: University of Wales Press, 1968.

14. Thomas, Wesley, and Barbara Seagrave. *The Songs of the Minnesinger, Prince Wizlaw of Rügen*. Chapel Hill: University of North Carolina Press, 1967.

15. Wooldridge, Harry Ellis, and Dom Anselm Hughes. *Early English Harmony*, 2 vols. v. 1, London: Bernard Quaritch, 1897; v. 2, London: Plainsong and Mediaeval Society, 1913.

a. Fiddles

b. Bagpipes

c. Double flutes

4.   Miniatures from the *Cantigas de Santa Maria* (13th century)

OUTLINE V

ORGANUM

Early Part Singing – Strict Organum – Free Organum

Compositions in Organum Style

I. **Early Part Singing**

    A. Singing in parallel motion, playing instruments with drone basses and developing melodic imitation are characteristics of polyphonic music in the Eastern World that foreshadowed the part music of the West. In order to perpetuate music it was necessary for the West to develop a system of notation.

    B. **St. Augustine** (354-430) in his *De musica* and the Roman **Boethius** (*c.* 480-*c.* 524) in *De institutione musica* are among early writers who refer to what may have been part music.

    C. Speculation on the origins of part music has produced various theories, some seemingly more valid than others (*RMMA*, p. 250).

    D. **Hucbald** (840-930), a Flemish monk

        1. *De harmonica institutione* (Concerning Harmonic Instruction) (*B* 9, v. 1, p. 103)

            a. **Hucbald**, in his instruction on harmony, defined the fundamental harmonic consonances and taught a system of pitch notation and expression, but no music examples survive.

                1) "Consonance is the calculated and harmonious mixture of two notes, which . . . are combined in one musical unity" (*B* 9, v. 1, p. 107; *NOH*, v. 2, p. 277; *RMMA*, p. 253).

    E. **Regino** of Prüm (d. 915)

        1. *De harmonica institutione* (*B* 9, v. 1, p. 230)

            a. In this book, as in **Hucbald's**, *organum* is mentioned, and consonance and dissonance are explained.

II. **Strict (Parallel) Organum** (9th-10th centuries)

    A. Organum (to organize) is the name given to polyphonic music from 800 to *c.* 1250. It consists of a plainsong tenor with one or more contrapuntal parts added to it.

    B. Strict simple organum (diaphony)

        1. Added below the plainsong tenor (*vox principalis*) is the parallel melody (*vox organalis* or *duplum*) in consonant fifths (*diapente*) or fourths (*diatessaron*). In this note-against-note strict counterpoint the effect of being in two modes simultaneously is apparent. A slow tempo was recommended for the performance of organum.

            a. In the late 13th century in England a type of organum in parallel thirds was called *gymel*.

    C. Strict composite organum

        1. Composite organum results when the *vox principalis* is doubled an octave below and the *vox organalis* is doubled an octave above.

    D. *Musica Enchiriadis* (Manual of Music) and *Scholia Enchiriadis* (Notes on the Manual)

        1. The *Musica Enchiriadis* manuscript contains the earliest known examples of polyphony (*c.* 850) and gives rules for writing organum. Authorship, although frequently ascribed to **Hucbald**, is debatable.

2. Strict parallel organum generally appears only in the middle of the phrase, especially with organum at the fourth. Since the phrase begins and ends on a unison, oblique and some contrary motion appear. The resulting seconds and thirds are considered as passing tones and free organum is anticipated.

    a. The scale delineated in the "Manuals" was an arbitrary arrangement of disjunct medieval Dorian tetrachords ranging from G to c-sharp".

        1) It is easy to see that the scale was made to favor simple organum at the fifth since tritones and augmented octaves were occasionally created.

        2) The rule for avoiding the tritone was that the *vox organalis* should not go below c of the lower tetrachord or g of the second tetrachord.

3. The notation of the "Manual" is called Daseian derived from *prosodia daseia*, the ancient Greek aspirate sign (⊢).

    a. Each tetrachord consists of a set of four signs. The first, second and fourth signs are similar to the letter F, but the third, which indicates a half step above the previous sign, is different in each tetrachord. To indicate the position of the tetrachord in the scale, there is a different position for each set of signs: the signs backwards for the first tetrachord, straight for the second, inverted for the third and inverted backwards for the fourth or highest tetrachord.

    b. There are three indications of the notes to be sung (*NPM*, p. 205).

        1) Each syllable of the text is written on an invisible line of a staff corresponding to the desired pitch of the syllable.

        2) At the beginning of the staff the tetrachord signs may be placed between the lines to indicate the pitches.

        3) The letters *t* (tone) and *s* (semitone) may be used to indicate the intervals between adjacent lines of the staff.

4. *Rex coeli Domine* (King of heaven, Lord) (*B* 9, v. 1, p. 167; *HAM*, No. 25b2; *GEx*, p. 24; *MM*, p. 17; *MSO*, v. 1, p. 14; *NMM*, Plate XXa, facsimile)

Simple Organum at the fourth   *Musica Enchiriadis*

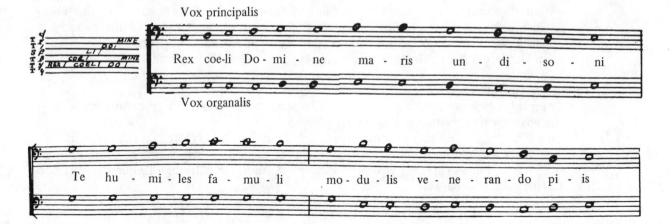

Vox principalis

Rex coe-li Do - mi - ne   ma - ris   un - di - so - ni

Vox organalis

Te hu - mi - les fa - mu - li   mo - du - lis ve - ne - ran - do pi - is

5.   *Sit gloria Domini* (May the glory of the Lord)   (*M* 9, v. 1, p. 185; *HAM*, No. 25b1;
     GEx, p. 24)

Strict Composite Organum at the Fifth   *Musica Enchiriadis*

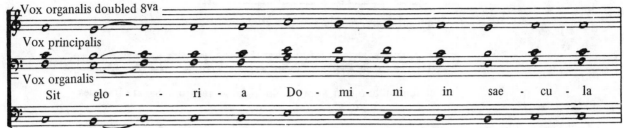

III.   **Free Organum** (11th-early 12th centuries)

   A.   **Guido d'Arezzo** (*c*. 995-1050)

     1.   *Micrologus* (short account)   (*c*. 1040)   (*B* 9, v. 2, p. 1; *CSM*, v. 4)

       a.   In this "Little Discourse" strict organum is recognized but parallel fifths are consid-
ered harsh. Parallel fourths are considered softer and more pleasing. Primarily
Guido discusses free or modified parallel organum which he prefers.

       b.   The permitted intervals, in addition to the unison, include the perfect fourth, major
and minor thirds and the major second. The perfect fifth and the minor second
(semitone) are excluded.

       c.   The *vox principalis* is still above the *vox organalis*.

       d.   Parallel, oblique and contrary motion is used for pleasing combinations of sounds
as well as to avoid the tritone. Increased emphasis is placed on contrary motion
with a greater awareness of its possibilities.

       e.   One note in the *vox organalis* is permitted against several in the *vox principalis*. The
vox principalis occasionally is permitted to cross below the *vox organalis* while the
latter remains stationary.

       f.   The *occursus* (cadence) becomes more important.

        1)   The unison at the cadence is approached from a whole tone or a major third. The
minor third at a cadence is not permitted. The *vox organalis* may conclude before
the *vox principalis* (*GEx*, p. 27; *HMM*, p. 195), or the reverse may occur (*GEx*,
pp. 26, 27).

       g.   The scale was formed of conjunct and disjunct medieval Dorian tetrachords from A
to g'.

     2.   Solmization

       a.   The modern system of using syllables to designate notes of the scale was invented by
Guido as an aid to memorizing, and remained essentially unaltered until the increased use of chromatics about the end of the 16th century. Each succeeding
phrase of the Latin hymn to St. John the Baptist, *Ut queant laxis* (*LU*, p. 1504),

began a note higher. **Guido** took the first syllable of each line of the text as a name for each of the notes in the hexachord c to a (*ut, re mi, fa, sol, la*).

Ut quant laxis **re**-sona-re fibris **Mi**- ra gesto-

rum famu-li tu-o-rum, **Sol**-ve pollu-ti labi-i re-a-tum, Sancte Jo-annes.

b. The hexachord consists of a semitone bounded on either side by two tones (*t t s t t*).

c. The solmization system is based on three equal hexachords, each built on a different scale tone: G (*gamma*), c, f. The entire range from G to e" is made up of seven hexachords. The hexachords including B (those built on G) are called *hexachordum durum* (hard), using B-flat (built on F) are called *hexachordum molle* (soft) and those without B or B-flat (built on C) are called *hexachordum naturale* (natural).

d. In order to identify a note or in some cases a particular octave, the letter name of the note with the appropriate syllables in the following chart denotes terms for common use, such as *C fa ut (Cefaut), A la mi re (Alamire), etc.*

e"							la	E	la
d"						la	sol	D	la sol
c"						sol	fa	C	sol fa
b'							mi	B	mi
b-flat'							fa	B	fa
a'					la	mi	re	A	la mi re
g'					sol	re	ut	G	sol re ut
f'					fa	ut	Durum	F	fa ut
e'				la	mi	Molle	(hard)	E	la mi
d'			la	sol	re	(soft)		D	la sol re
c'			sol	fa	ut			C	sol fa ut
b				mi	Naturale			B	mi
b-flat			fa		(natural)			B	fa
a		la	mi	re				A	la mi re
g		sol	re	ut				G	sol re ut
f		fa	ut	Durum				F	fa ut
e	la	mi	Molle	(hard)				E	la mi
d	sol	re	(soft)					D	sol re
c	fa	ut						C	fa ut
B	mi	Naturale						B	mi
A	re	(natural)						A	re
G	ut							G	ut
	Durum								
	(hard)								

e. When a melody exceeds the range of one hexachord it is necessary to pass from one hexachord into another, a practice known as mutation. Mutation is generally accomplished at *re* of a new hexachord when ascending and at *la* when descending. *Mi-fa* always represents a semitone and is never broken in passing from one hexachord to another.

1) The term solmization is derived from the two syllables of the Guidonian system (*sol-mi*), but in reality the syllable *mi* is understood to belong to the F hexachord. Therefore the principle of mutation is inherent in the word "sol-mi-zation."

    f.   Hexachords contain only one semitone (*mi-fa*), whereas the octave system of church modes contains two semitones.

B.   Theoretical treatises after **Guido**

  1. **Hermannus Contractus** (Herman the cripple) (1013-1054)

    a. *De musica* (*B* 9, v. 2, p. 124)

      1) **Hermannus** made no mention of organum. He did, however, present a new system of notation. Letters representing various melodic intervals are placed above the text to indicate successive intervals in a melody. There is no indication of rhythm.

e	*(equaliter)*	= unison
s	*(semitonium)*	= half step
t	*(tonus)*	= whole step
ts	*(tonus cum semitonus)*	= minor third
tt	*(ditonus)*	= major third
d	*(diatesseron)*	= perfect fourth
△	*(diapente)*	= perfect fifth
△ *s*	*(diapente cum semitonus)*	= minor sixth
△ *t*	*(diapente cum tonus)*	= major sixth

      2) To indicate the direction of the interval, a dot placed under a letter indicates descending motion and letters without a dot indicate ascending motion. The starting point is given by letter name (*NMM*, Plate XII).

      3) A major disadvantage of this system is that if a mistake is made all succeeding notes are also wrong.

  2. **John Cotton** (John of Afflighem)

    a. *De musica* (*c.* 1100)   (*B* 9, v. 2, p. 230; *CSM*, v. 1)

      1) Free organum is described but only one short example is given (*HMM*, p. 197).

      2) All the consonant intervals (unison, octave, fifth and fourth) are used in any order to create variety. Seconds and thirds are used as before.

      3) Similar motion is allowed but contrary motion is preferred. The crossing of parts is also desirable. Two or three notes of the organal voice are permitted against one note of the principal voice, the plainsong.

      4) New rules for the *occursus* allow endings on either octaves or unisons. John suggests that unison cadences alternate with octave cadences; preference is given to the unison cadence.

  3. Anonymous French author, *Ad Organum faciendum* (On composing organa) (*c.* 1100)

    a. Free organum is described and several examples are given.

      1) The *vox principalis* is now below the *vox organalis*. Cadences close on fourths and fifths as well as on unisons and octaves.

      2) B-flat is introduced to avoid the tritone rather than holding the organal voice on the same tone.

      3) Included are several examples of the same *principalis* having different melodies in the organal voice.

    b. *Cunctipotens genitor Deus* (All powerful Father, Lord) (*GEx*, p. 30; *HAM*, No. 26a; *GMB*, No. 9)

      1) This example of note-against-note organum is based on the Kyrie-trope (*LU*, p. 25).

    c. *Alleluia Justus ut palma* (Alleluia, the righteous shall flourish like a palm-tree) (*OMM*, p. 86)

      1) Only the sections normally sung by a soloist have been set with an organal part in note-against-note style (*LU*, p. 1207).

2) The motion is basically contrary (50%) and similar or parallel (40%). The remaining motion is oblique with one example of a repeated interval.
3) The principal intervals used are fifths (30%), fourths (29%), unisons (16%) and octaves (15%). The remaining 10% is made up equally of thirds and sixths.
4) Motion and intervallic analyses of this piece of free organum rather clearly shows the creative advancement of polyphonic art by the early 12th century.

IV. Compositions in Organum Style

A. England
1. *Winchester Troper* (early 11th century)
   a. The 11th-century copy is a revision of an earlier version dated *c.* 980 and contains a supplement of 166 two-part *organa* for use in Masses and Offices (*EBM*, v. 3, Plates 17-25).
   b. It is notated in neumes, note-against-note, without a staff or clefs, but recent research has made it decipherable. Parallel motion is common and contrary motion is used more than at the cadences (*HMM*, p. 199).
   c. The *vox principalis* below the *vox organalis* is an early example of this important development.
   d. *Alleluia Te martyrum* (Alleluia, the noble army of martyrs) (*OMM*, p. 85)
2. *Ut tuo propitiatus* (By thy intervention) (late 11th century) (*GEx*, p. 29; *HAM*, No. 26b; *EEH*, v. 1, Plate 1, facsimile)
   a. Notated in letters without staff lines, this example is in note-against-note style and is melismatic rather than syllabic. The two voices, often moving in contrary motion, cross parts and make use of all intervals within the octave, fourths and fifths being most frequent.
3. *Nobilis humilis* (Noble, humble Magnus) (12th century) (*GEx*, p. 47; *HAM*, No. 25c; *ML* 20 (1939), p. 353, facsimile)
   a. A two-part hymn in praise of St. Magnus (d. 1115), patron saint of the Orkney Islands, this piece makes regular use of parallel thirds with unisons mostly at the cadences. By the 15th century the name *gymel* was given to this style of writing.

B. France
1. The Chartres manuscript (11th century) includes a group of five "Alleluias" sung responsorially. The polyphonic section (*organum*) set the verses of the text (to be performed by soloists) and the plainsong (monophonic), not written out in the Chartres manuscript, was sung by a chorus.
   a. In these two-part *organa* the *vox principalis* is in the lower part.
   b. *Alleluia Angelus Domini* (Alleluia the angel of the Lord) (*HAM*, No. 26c; *GEx*, p. 28; *LU*, p. 786)
      1) In the "Alleluias," as in this one in particular, there is an increased use of contrary motion. The consonant intervals (fourths, fifths, octaves) are still predominate, but there is an increase in the number of thirds, many in parallel groups of two or three.
2. The St. Martial Abbey manuscripts (early 12th century) at Limoges show that two main types of *organum* were used at St. Martial: 1) the older note-against-note style, called *discant* and 2) the sustained-tone or melismatic style.
   a. *Discant* style
      1) *Mira lege* (By a wonderful law) (*c.* 1100) (*GEx*, p. 31)
         a) In this piece of *discant organum* the *vox principalis* is a metrical song rather than the usual plainsong. Note-against-note style predominates. However, there are several examples of two notes against one and some crossing of parts. Contrary motion is very common with some parallel, similar and oblique motion mixed in. The interval of a fifth is most common; the third appears much more frequently than the fourth.

Mira lege, miro modo

Translation: By a wonderful law, in a miraculous manner, God makes man. More marvelously He remakes him; see, a marvelous order.

b.   Melismatic or sustained-tone style
   1)   The *vox organalis* (upper part, or *duplum*) becomes more elaborate and rhythmi-
      cally free, and the notes of the *vox principalis* (tenor, or *cantus firmus*) become
      increasingly longer.
      a)   *"Tenor,"* from the Latin *tenere* (to hold), becomes the name of one of the
         polyphonic parts, usually the lowest.
   2)   In a composition the sustained-tone or melismatic style may be used throughout,
      or it may be combined with the note-against-note style.
   3)   *Benedicamus Domino* (Let us bless the Lord) (*GEx*, p. 30; *MM*, p. 20; *MSO*, v. 1,
      p. 14)
      a)   The tenor, a plainsong melody (*LU*, p. 124), is drawn out to accommodate ex-
         tended melismas in the upper voice. Only the beginning of the composition is
         given in the examples.
   4)   *Laude jocunda* (With joyful praise) (*AMM*, No. 29)

C.   Transitional organum
   1.   While the older St. Martial manuscripts show a preference for melismatic organum, later manuscripts include compositions which are a mixture of both discant and melismatic styles.
      a.   Chants in syllabic style usually were set in melismatic organum, and melismatic chants were generally set in discant style.
   2.   *Rex omnia tenens* (The King holding sway over all things) (*OMM*, p. 87)
      a.   In this composition the two styles, melismatic and discant, are combined.
   3.   *De monte lapis* (A stone is broken) (*OMM*, p. 88)
      a.   Note the free melismatic style at some cadences, particularly the last, in distinction to the note-against-note discant style used throughout the main body of the piece.
   4.   *Viderunt Hemanuel* (All the ends of the earth have seen Emmanuel) (*GEx*, p. 32; *HAM*, No. 27a; *CaMM*, p. 125; *NPM*, p. 211, facsimile)
      a.   Melismatic organum is mixed with note-against-note style. The tenor or *cantus firmus* is a trope on the Christmas Gradual *"Viderunt omnes"* (*LU*, p. 409). Soloists sing the opening phrase *"Viderunt"* and the following trope in organum, and the chorus sings the plainsong beginning with *"omnes."*
   5.   *Verbum bonum et suave* (Good and pleasant word) (*GEX*, p. 35; *GMB*, No. 10; *AM*, v. 9, p. 18)
      a.   This polyphonic sequence, mostly in note-against-note style, has three strophes of music and six stanzas of text. The tenor melody resembles the Sequence *Lauda Sion* (*LU*, p. 945).
D.   Spain
   1.   *Codex Calixtinus* (*c.* 1140) of Santiago de Compostela
      a.   It is possible that the Benedictines of Cluny (France) assembled this collection from various sources and presented it to the Cathedral of Santiago. The concluding appendix to the codex contains 20 polyphonic pieces and one more appears in the main body of the codex.
      b.   *Nostra phalans plaudit leta* (Let our company praise joyfully) (*AMM*, No. 32; *NMM*, Plate XXIII, facsimile)
         1)   The last line of the text for each of the four stanzas is the same and serves as a refrain.
      c.   *Kyrie Rex immense, Pater pie* (Great King, dear father) (*OMM*, p. 90)
         1)   The troped Kyrie, based on the Kyrie similar to *Pater cuncta* (*LU*, p. 48), is basically in discant organum with some use of melismatic organum.
      d.   *Huic Jacobo* (This James was consoled by the Lord) (*AMM*, No. 31)
      e.   *Congaudeant Catholici* (Let Catholics rejoice together), attributed to Magister **Albertus** of Paris (*RMMA*, p. 268; *NOH*, v. 2, p. 305; *NMM*, pp. 68, 70, 71; Plate XXIII, facsimile)
         1)   This appears to be the first known example of three-part polyphony, excluding composite organum. The lower two voices, one in red and one in black, are written on one staff and are in note-against-note style. The third and upper voice is written on a separate staff in melismatic style.
      f.   *Benedicamus Domino* (Let us bless the Lord) (*HAM*, No. 28b)
         1)   The plainsong *Benedicamus Domino* (*LU*, p. 124) was frequently used as a tenor and appears here as the lower voice in a two-part example of melismatic organum.
      g.   *Cunctipotens genitor* (All-powerful father) (*HAM*, No. 27b; *AM*, v. 9, p. 15)
         1)   The tenor for this melismatic organum is from a Kyrie trope (*LU*, p. 25; *NPM*, p. 213).

SELECTED BIBLIOGRAPHY

Books and Music

1. Bannister, Henry Mariott. *Monumenti Vaticani di paleografia musicale latina.* Leipzig: O. Harrassowitz, 1913.

2. Briggs, Henry B. *The Musical Notation of the Middle Ages.* London: J. Masters & Co., 1890. (facsimiles)

3. Chappell, William. *Old English Popular Music*, v. 1. London: Chappell & Co., 1893.

4. Coussemaker, Charles Edmond Henri. *L'art harmonique aux XIIe et XIIIe siècle*s. Paris: A. Durand, 1865.

5. ————————*Histoire de l'harmonie au moyen-âge.* Paris: V. Didron, 1852.

6. Ellinwood, Leonard. *Musica Hermanni Contracti.* Rochester, NY: Eastman School of Music, 1936.

7. Evans, Paul. *The Early Trope Repertory of St. Martial de Limoges.* Princeton: Princeton University Press, 1970.

8. Frere, Walter Howard. *The Winchester Troper.* London: Harrison and Sons, 1874.

9. Gerbert, Martin. *Scriptores Ecclesiastici De Musica Sacra Potissimum*, 3 vols. Hildesheim: Georg Olm Verlagsbuchhandlung, 1963. (reprint of 1784 edition)
    Volume I: Hucbald, *De musica,* pp. 103-152; *Musica enchiriadis*, pp. 152-212.
    Volume II: Guido, *Micrologus,* pp. 1-24; John Cotton, *Musica,* pp. 230-265; Hermanus Contractus, *Opuscula Musica,* pp. 124-153.

10. Guido d'Arezzo. *Micrologus,* ed. Joseph Smits van Waesberghe. Rome: American Institute of Musicology, 1955. (*CSM*, v. 4)

11. ————————*Micrologus*, in Martin Gerbert, *Scriptores Ecclesiastici De Musica Sacra Potissimum*, v. 2, pp. 1-24. Hildesheim: Georg Olm Verlagsbuchhandlung, 1963.

12. ————————*Micrologus*, in *Hucbald, Guido, and John on Music: Three Medieval Treatises*, tr. Warren Babb, pp. 49-86. New Haven: Yale University Press, 1978.

13. Hermanus Contractus. *Opuscula Musica*, in Martin Gerbert, *Scriptores Ecclesiastici De Musica Sacra Potissimum*, v. 2, pp. 124-153. Hildesheim: Georg Olm Verlagsbuchhandlung, 1963.

14. Hughes, Dom Anselm. *Anglo-French Sequelae.* London: The Plainsong and Medieval Music Society, 1934.

15. Hucbald. *De musica,* in Martin Gerbert, *Scriptores Ecclesiastici De Musica Sacra Potissimum,* v. 1, pp. 103-152. Hildesheim: Georg Olm Verlagsbuchhandlung, 1963.

16. ————————*Musica enchiriadis*, in Martin Gerbert, *Scriptores Ecclesiastici De Musica Sacra Potissimum*, v. 1, pp. 152-212. Hildesheim: Georg Olm Verlagsbuchhandlung, 1963.

17. *Hucbald, Guido, and John on Music: Three Medieval Treatises*, tr. Warren Babb. New Haven: Yale University Press, 1978. (Hucbald, *De harmonica institutione*, p. 3; Guido, *Micrologus*, p. 49; John, *De musica*, p. 87)

18. Husman, Heinrich. *Medieval Polyphony*, tr. Robert Kolben. Köln: Arno Volk Verlag, 1962. (*AM*, v. 9)

19. John Cotton [Johannis Affligemensis]. *De Musica*, in *Hucbald, Guido, and John on Music: Three Medieval Treatises*, tr. Warren Babb, p. 87. New Haven: Yale University Press, 1978.

20. ————————*De Musica cum Tonario*, ed. Joseph Smits van Waesberghe. Rome: American Institute of Musicology, 1950. (*CSM*, v. 1)

21. ————————*Musica*, in Martin Gerbert, *Scriptores Ecclesiastici De Musica Sacra Potissimum*, v. 2, pp. 230-265. Hildesheim: Georg Olm Verlagsbuchhandlung, 1963.

22. *Liber Sancti Jacobi, Codex Calixtinus.* Santiago de Compostela: The Monastery, 1944.

23. *Musica Enchiriadis* (Music Handbook), tr. Léonie Rosenstiel. Colorado Springs: The Colorado College Music Press, 1976. (*CMT*, No. 7)

24. Planchart, Alejandro Enrique. *The Repertory of Tropes at Winchester*. Princeton: Princeton University Press, 1977.
25. Ringer, Alexander. "Eastern Elements in Medieval Polyphony," in *Studies in Medieval Culture*, pp. 2, 75-83. Kalamazoo: The Medieval Institute, Western Michigan University, 1966.
26. Waite, William G. *The Rhythm of Twelfth-Century Polyphony*. New Haven: Yale University, 1954.

Articles

1. Apel, Willi. "From St. Martial to Notre Dame." *JAMS* 2 (1949), pp. 145-158.
2. Bukofzer, Manfred. "Popular Polyphony in the Middle Ages." *MQ* 26 (1940), pp. 31-49.
3. Crocker, Richard L. "The Repertory of Proses at Saint Martial de Limoges in the 10th Century." *JAMS* 11 (1958), pp. 149-164.
4. Dyer, Joseph. "A Thirteenth-Century Choirmaster: The *Scientia Artis Musicae* of Elias Salomon." *MQ* 66 (1980), pp. 83-111.
5. Ferand, Ernst T. "The 'Howling in Seconds' of the Lombards." *MQ* 25 (1939), pp. 313-324.
6. Flindell, Edwin Frederick. "Joh[ann]is Cottonis." *MD* 20 (1966), pp. 7-30; 23 (1969), pp. 7-11.
7. Fox Strangways, Arthur H. "A Tenth Century Manual [Hucbald]." *ML* 13 (1932), pp. 183-193.
8. Grutchfield, E. J. "Hucbald: a Millenary Commemoration." *MT* 71 (1930), pp. 507-510. 704-710.
9. Handschin, Jacques. "Two Winchester Tropers." *Journal of Theological Studies*, old series 37 (1936), pp. 34-49, 156-172.
10. Hughes, Dom Anselm. "The Origins of Harmony." *MQ* 24 (1938), pp. 176-185.
11. Karp, Theodore. "St. Martial and Santiago de Compostela: An Analytical Speculation." *ActaM* 39 (1967), pp. 144-160.
12. Marshall, Judith M. "Hidden Polyphony in a Manuscript from St. Martial de Limoges." *JAMS* 15 (1962), pp. 131-144.
13. Pulver, Jeffrey. "The English Theorists." *MT* 74 (1933), pp. 892-895; 75 (1934), pp. 26, 220, 408, 708, 804, 900.
14. Roesner, Edward. "The Performance of Parisian Organum." *Early Music* 7 (1977), pp. 174-189.
15. Sachs, Curt. "A Strange Medieval Scale." *JAMS* 2 (1949), pp. 169-170.
16. Salzer, Felix. "Tonality in Early Medieval Polyphony: Towards a History of Tonality." *The Music Forum* 1, pp. 35-98.
17. Sanders, Ernest H. "Consonance and Rhythm in the Organum of the 12th and 13th Centuries." *JAMS* 33 (1980), pp. 264-286.
18. ———"Peripheral Polyphony of the 13th Century." *JAMS* 17 (1964), pp. 261-287.
19. Sandon, Nicholas. "Fragments of Medieval Polyphony at Canterbury Cathedral." *MD* 30 (1976), pp. 37-53.
20. Schrade, Leo. "Music in the Philosophy of Boethius." *MQ* 33 (1947), pp. 188-200.
21. Seay, Albert. "An Anonymous Treatise from St. Martial." *AnM* 5 (1957), pp. 7-42.
22. Smits van Waesberghe, Joseph. "Guido of Arezzo and Musical Improvisation." *MD* 5 (1951), pp. 55-63.
23. ———"John of Affligem or John Cotton? " *MD* 6 (1952), pp. 139-153.
24. ———"The Musical Notation of Guido d'Arezzo." *MD* 5 (1951), pp. 15-53.
25. Spiess, Lincoln Bunce. "The Diatonic 'Chromaticism' of the Enchiriadis Treatise." *JAMS* 12 (1959), pp. 1-6.
26. ———"Discant, Descant, Diaphony, and Organum, a Problem of Definitions." *JAMS* 8 (1955), pp. 144-147.

27.   Spiess, Lincoln Bunce. "An Introduction to the Pre-St. Martial Practical Sources of Early Polyphony." *Speculum* 22 (1947), pp. 16, 17.
28.   Strunk, Oliver. "The Notation of the Chartres Fragments." *AnM* 3 (1955), pp. 7-37.
29.   Treitler, Leo. "The Polyphony of St. Martial." *JAMS* 17 (1964), pp. 29-42.

5.   From the Squarcialupi Codex (14th century), a miniature of Francesco Landini and part of his madrigal *Musica son*

6.   Examples of organum from Guido's *Micrologus*

7.   *Mira lege* from an 11th-century manuscript

8.   Strict organum from *Musica enchiriadus* (9th century)

OUTLINE VI

THE EARLY GOTHIC PERIOD (1150-1325)

Classes of Polyphony — Notre Dame School
Conductus — Motet — Hocket — Cantilena
Polyphony in the British Isles to 1350 — Instruments

I. **Classes of Polyphony**

A. Organum, Clausula, Conductus, Motet, Cantilena
  1. Harmonic basis of pre-tertian harmony
    a. 1050-1200
      1) Consonances in two-part writing were the unison, fourth, fifth and octave. Thirds and sixths were treated as dissonances, and second and sevenths were used as passing tones and appoggiaturas.
    b. 1200-1350
      1) Three-part writing used open triads: 1-5-8 with a perfect or diminished fifth as the principal consonant. Triads, 1-3-5, were used in weak positions. The fourth became less common as a consonant interval above the lowest voice, but it continued as an acceptable interval between the upper voices. Harsh consecutives of seconds and sevenths were allowed as passing tones and appoggiaturas (**Johannes de Garlandia**, *c*. 1250, *B* 6, v. 1, p. 97). **Franco of Cologne** in 1250 said there should be a "consonance at the beginning of every perfection" (*B* 6, v. 1, p. 132; *RMMA*, p. 295; see *Outline*, p. 55, *B* 9, v. 3, p. 13).
  2. The term *"organum"* (plural is *organa*) was originally used for all polyphonic music. However, during the period of the Notre Dame School, the term was confined to compositions based on plainsong, and more specifically to Graduals, Alleluias, responsories and *organa* on *"Benedicamus Domino."* The *conductus* and *motet* became independent styles. *Organa* and *conducti* were written in score and motets were written in separate parts on one or two pages of manuscripts.
  3. Thirteenth-century music (*organa, clausulae,* motets) was written in modal notation making use of the rhythmic modes. The change from the free rhythm of the St. Martial School to the strict modal rhythm of the Notre Dame School was one of the most important developments in all music.

II. **Notre Dame School** of Paris (1160-1225) (beginning of the *Ars antiqua*)

A. *Anonymous IV* (*B* 1, v. 1, pp. 327-364), written in the latter part of the 13th century (*c*. 1275), mentions works and composers of the period including **Leonin** and **Perotin**. An English student at the University of Paris probably compiled all this information. Some music examples are indicated by letters rather than being notated on a staff.
B. Manuscripts containing music of the Notre Dame School
  1. *MS Wolfenbüttel 677* (*W₁; St. Andrews MS; Helmstedt 628; M* 13, 20; *NPM*, p. 259)
    a. Now in the Ducal Library of Wolfenbüttel, Germany, this manuscript belonged to St. Andrews Priory in Scotland early in the 14th century and contains the earliest examples of Notre Dame polyphony (*NMM*, Plates XXV; XXVI a, b; XXVII a; XXVIII; XXX; XXXI).
  2. *MS Wolfenbüttel 1206* (*W₂; Helmstedt 1099*), also in the Ducal Library, was written in France in the mid-13th century (*NPM*, pp. 233, 275, 281; *M* 21).

3. *Florence MS, Pluteo* ("bookshelf") *29,1 (F)*, in the Biblioteca Mediceo-Laurenziana, Florence, was written near the end of the 13th century in France and includes about 485 *clausulae*. By the mid-15th century it was in the Medici Library (*PMMM*, vols. 10, 11; *NPM*, pp. 229, 247, 255, 257; *NMM*, Plates XXIV, XXVIIb).

4. *Madrid Biblioteca Nacional 20486 (Hh 167), Toledo Codex* (*NMM*, Plate XXIX)

5. There are several other examples of Notre Dame polyphony held in other libraries of Europe.

C. **Leonin** (*c.* 1150-1185)

1. **Leonin**, according to *Anonymous IV*, was known as the greatest composer of organa (*optimus Organista*) (*B* 1 [*MTT*, v. 1], p. 342, tr. p. 36).

2. *Magnus liber organi de Gradali et Antiphonario pro servitio divinio multiplicando* (Great Book of Organa for the Mass and Office) (between 1160 and 1180)

   a. The "Great Book," found in its most complete form in *Pluteo 29,1*, contains 35 responsories for the Offices and 60 organa for the Mass. In addition there is a cycle of two-part organa (*organa dupla*) for the entire church year beginning with Christmas Day. The original manuscript has not been preserved.

   b. Plainsong melodies from Graduals, Alleluias, Responsoria and *Benedicamus Domino* have been used for the tenors (*MSO*, v. 1, p. 14).

3. Organa of **Leonin** combines sections of two different styles: 1) melismatic style in free rhythm and 2) discant or measured style where both parts are in rhythmic modes.

   a. The sustained-tone tenor with the upper part in melismatic style is called *organum purum*. The upper part is said to be in modal rhythm, even though irregular (*non rectus*) (*HAM*, No. 29; *M* 20, p. 120).

   b. Measured sections are sometimes called *clausulae*.

   c. The soloist sections of the chants, *i. e.* the *incipit* or intonation and most of the verse are generally set in two-part organum. The upper part is textless. The remainder of the intonation and the closing portion of the verse are sung in plainsong. A small group of soloists sang the polyphony and the full choir sang the plainsong.

   d. *Hec* [*sic*] *dies* (This is the day) (*HAM*, No. 29; *LU*, p. 778; *GR*, p. 221; *M* 20, p. 120; *AM*, v. 9, p. 19)

Hec dies *	quam facit . . . in ea.	℣ Confitemini . . . saeculum	Misericordia ejus.
Organum: [soloists]	Plainsong: [choir]	Organum: [soloists]	Plainsong: [choir]

   e. *Alleluia: Non vos relinquam* (I shall not abandon you) (*OMM*, pp. 90-92; *LU*, p. 856)

   f. *Alleluia: Nativitas* (The birth of the glorious virgin) (*AMM*, No. 33; *M* 20, p. 195)

   g. The melodic style includes stepwise motion, repeated notes and some thirds, but rarely wider intervals. There is use of sequence, filled in fifths and passages running through an octave. Broken triads are not used.

D. **Perotin** (*c.* 1160-1220)

1. **Perotin** was called the *"optimus discantor"* (greatest composer of discant). He substituted new *clausulae* in discant style for discant and free rhythm (*organum purum*) sections in the organa of **Leonin's** *Magnus liber* (*HAM*, Nos. 28d, 28e; *RMMA*, p. 300).

2. The number of parts in the organa was increased from two to three and, in only three known examples, to four parts.

3. *Clausulae*

   a. Over 500 examples of *clausulae* are known. The clausula is a polyphonic composition in which the tenor is taken from a melisma of a plainsong instead of from the solo sections of an entire plainsong as in organa. The tenors use only one or two words, and at times only a syllable, from the text, but both parts are vocalized. The two parts are in modal rhythms. Many clausulae were later used as independent compositions.

    b.   The tenor melody is usually in *ordines*, reiterated rhythmic patterns forming a type of rhythmic ground bass. The melody is sometimes repeated and may begin on another value of the rhythmic pattern or coincide with it.

    c.   The addition of a text to a wordless upper part began the development of the motet (*HAM*, Nos. 28f, 28g, 28h2, 28i).

        1)   *Ex semine* (*AMM*, No. 38; *RRMA*, vols. 4-5, Part II, p. 52)

   4.   *Organa tripla*

    a.   *Alleluia Posui adjutorium* (*M*18, v. 2, p. 31; *RRMA*, vols. 2-3, Part I, p. 27)

    b.   *Alleluia Nativitas* (*M*18, v. 2, p. 16; *RRMA*, vols. 2-3, Part I, p. 13; *NMM*, Plate XXV).

    c.   *Hec dies* (*HAM*, No. 31; *LU*, p. 778; *GR*, p. 221; *AR*, p. 373)

        1)   In the style of Perotin.

   5.   *Organa quadrupla*

    a.   *Viderunt omnes* (*c.* 1200) (*GEx*, p. 36; *M* 20; *NMM*, Plate XXVIb)

    b.   *Sederunt principes* (*AMM*, No. 35)

    c.   *Mors* (*M* 20; *AM*, v. 9, p. 24; *NMM*, Plate XXVIa)

   6.   In the example of the quadrupla *Viderunt*, only the first word of the text is given. The text in the duplum is a later addition. In the complete work the text of the tenor and plainsong sections are from the Gradual for Christmas Day (*LU*, p. 409; *GR*, p. 33). The text *"Viderunt omnes"* is set in four parts and vocalized by soloists; the following text *"fines terrae . . . terra"* is sung in plainsong by the choir and then *"Notum fecit . . . revelavit"* in four parts sung by soloists is followed with *"justitiam suam"* in plainsong sung by the choir.

   7.   Technical devices found in the first part of the quadupla *Viderunt* include short phrases, the three upper parts in trochaic modal rhythm, the tenor in sustained-tone style and *Stimmtausch*. Other devices include melodic repetition, sequence, imitation, augmentation and triadic motives. Measures in the following refer to *GEx*, p. 36, not counting the first measure marked 12/4. The abbreviation for the quadruplum part is *Q*, triplum is *Tr*, duplum is *D* and tenor is *T*.

    a.   *Stimmtausch*, "interchange of melodies," results in canonic imitation at the unison: *Tr* and *D*, meas. 3-4-5-6. With equal voices it is not invertible counterpoint.

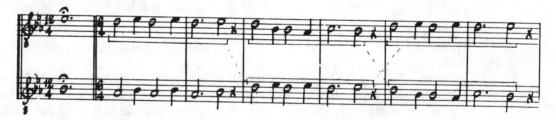

    b.   Repetition is repeating in the same part at the same pitch: *Q*, meas. 1-2, 3-4; meas. 9-10, 11-12. Repetition with open (*D*, meas. 22-25) and closed (*D*, meas. 26-29) endings.

    c.   Sequence is repetition in the same part but at a different pitch: *D*, meas; 1-2, 3-4; *Tr*, meas. 15-16-17-18.

    d.   Imitation is repetition in a different part at a different pitch: *Tr*, meas. 15 – *D*, meas. 16; *Tr*, meas. 17 – *D*, meas. 18; *Tr*, meas. 18 – *D*, meas. 19 (also hocket).

    e.   Canonic or exact imitation at the unison: *Tr*, meas. 7-8 – *Q*, meas. 9-10.

    f.   Melody as a broken triad: *D*, meas. 45. The melody may be varied in repetition: *Tr*, meas. 39-40 – 41-42.

g.   Filling in fifths: *D*, meas. 9-12.
h.   Parallel, oblique and contrary motion is used.
   1)   Parallel fifths: *Q* and *D*, meas. 34, 35; parallel thirds: *Q* and *Tr*, meas. 39-40.
i.   Augmentation of the *Tr*, meas. 54, in the *D*, meas. 55-58.
j.   Cadences
   1)   Contrary motion is emphasized and the outer voices usually progress stepwise to the final intervals which in two-part organa might be the unison, fifth or octave. In three-part writing various combinations of these intervals are used at the cadence.

III.   Conductus

A.   Conductus is a Latin metrical poem set to music for one to three, or rarely four, voices. It developed from rhymed tropes which were used to accompany the entrance of the Priest. They were used for festivals and processions and became one of the chief types of early 13th-century polyphony. Later in the century the conductus gave way to the motet.
B.   Characteristics of 13th-century conducti
   1.   The conductus is not based on a tenor borrowed from a liturgical chant. Each voice is composed separately and the third voice (triplum) is consonant with either the duplum or tenor, or both.
   2.   All parts move in a uniform modal rhythm in note-against-note style, often called "conductus style." Therefore the tenor is not in the usual sustained-note style of the early organa.
   3.   The text of the conductus is generally set syllabically. Often the closing cadence, or even the interior phrase cadences, may be embellished and thus called *"cauda."*
      a.   *Pange melos lacrimosum* (O tearful elegy) (*OMM*, p. 111)
      b.   *Praemii dilatio* (The postponement of a reward) (*OMM*, p. 112) with phrase *caudae*.
   4.   One metrical Latin text, either sacred or secular, is shared by all the voices; the conductus is notated in score.
   5.   The clef and tessitura do not indicate the pitch. The conductus is sung either by men or women, in any case, in equal voices. In general this applies to all music written before the introduction of the bass voice about 1450.
   6.   *Procurans odium* (Averting ill will) (*AMM*, No. 36; *PMMM*, vols. 10-11, fol. 226)
      a.   In this three-voice conductus note the *Stimmtausch* between the tenor and triplum in measures 1 and 2, and between the duplum and triplum in measures 3 and 4. Measures 1-4 are repeated in measures 5-8; measures 9-12 are repeated in measures 17-20.
C.   Other music examples: *OMM*, p. 114; *AMM*, No. 37; *GEx*, pp. 41, 43, 44, 49; *HAM*, Nos. 38, 39; *RMMA*, p. 309; *MM*, p. 31; *GMB*, No. 16; *MSO*, v. 1, p. 22; *AM*, v. 9, pp. 34-37.

IV.   Motet

A.   **Johannes de Grocheo** in *c*. 1300 described the motet as a "song composed of several parts, with several texts, in which two voices at a time are consonant with each other. This type of song, however, is not suitable for the common people, because they neither sense its subtleties nor are they delighted when listening to it. But it is fitting for the educated and for those who seek the refinements of the arts" (*CMT*, v. 1, p. 25).
B.   Early period of the motet (before 1250)
   1.   The motet originated about 1200 with the addition of a complete text to the upper part of a clausula. The text, from the French *"mot"* (word), added to the duplum was called the *motetus*, which name was given to the entire composition. Therefore a

motet is a polyphonic setting of a tenor taken from a whole plainsong (*GEx*, p. 33; *HAM*, Nos. 28f, 28g; *GMB*, Nos. 18, 19).

    a.   A double motet is a three-part motet with two added texts, and a triple motet is a four-part motet with three added texts.

  2.   The conductus motet is one in which the two upper parts have the same rhythm and text while the tenor is in a slower rhythm and has a different text (*HAM*, No. 32c).

C.   Classical period of the motet (*c.* 1250-1275)

  1.   The classical motet, usually in three parts, occasionally in four, has a different Latin, or French, text for each of the upper parts and a tenor *incipit*. The text of the *motetus* is often related to that of the tenor. With the beginning use of French texts the motet became a secular as well as a religious class of composition (*GEx*, p. 60; *MM*, p. 27; *RRMA*, vols. 4-5, Part II, p. 110).

    a.   *Pucelete–Je languis–Domino* (Fair maid–I languish–The Lord) (*HAM*, No. 28h,2; *RRMA*, vols. 4-5, Part II, p. 165; *MSO*, v. 1, p. 19)

  2.   The tenor is borrowed from a preexistent melody, usually a melismatic passage from a plainsong (Gradual, Alleluia, Responsorium). It is identified with the word or syllable with which it occurs in the plainsong. *In saeculum*, taken from the third line of the verse in the Gradual for Easter Sunday (*LU*, p. 779; *GR*, p. 221; *GEx*, p. 4; *OMM*, p. 32), became a very popular motet tenor (*GEx*, pp. 58, 62, 70; *HAM*, Nos. 32d, 32e). The tenor may be vocalized or played on instruments.

  3.   Individual modal rhythms are used in each part. The first, second and sixth rhythmic modes are often used in the upper parts, and the third and fifth modes are used in the tenor.

  4.   *Ordines*, reiterated rhythmic patterns, are used in the tenor.

    a.   *Ordo* indicates the number of times a pattern is repeated without interruption. However, modifications are allowed. Melodic repetition, known as *color* could coincide with the rhythmic pattern or overlap it.

D.   The motet after 1275

  1.   The triplum with greater rhythmic independence became the predominant part. French secular texts became common in both upper parts (*HAM*, No. 32d; *GEx*, p. 62; *RRMA*, vols. 4-5, Part II, p. 85), and a Latin text in one voice combined with a French text in another voice is also used (*HAM*, No. 32b; *RRMA*, vols. 4-5, Part II, p. 25). Motets are extant with German and English texts also.

  2.   Tenors were borrowed from a variety of sources of melodies: tropes (*Alleluya, GEx*, p. 67; *RRMA*, vols. 6-7, Part III, p. 223; *HAM*, No. 33a; *Kyrie fons bonitatis, RRMA*, vols. 6-7, Part III, p. 81), instrumental dances (*Chose Tassin, RRMA*, vols. 6-7, Part III, p. 95), Trouvère melodies (*Portare, GEx*, p. 65; RRMA, vols. 6-7, Part III, p. 88; *CaMM*, p. 150) and a Paris street cry (*Frèse nouvele, GEx*, p. 63; *RRMA*, vols. 6-7, Part III, p. 189; *HAM*, No. 33b).

  3.   Various types of repetition and imitation continued in the motets and rhythmic relationships among the parts became more free. Motivic repetition in the tenor was common. In one example of a tenor an ostinato was developed with 31 repetitions of a three-note figure (*RRMA*, vols. 6-7, Part III, p. 203). The tenor does not always move in strict *ordines*. Devices used in organa, such as *Stimmtausch* (meas. 1-6, *Tr* and *D*, in *GEx*, p. 67; *RRMA*, vols. 6-7, Part III, p. 223; *HAM*, No. 32a) and canon (meas. 9-15, *D* and *Tr*, in *GEx*, p. 60; meas. 5-7 in *MM*, p. 29; *RRMA*, vols. 4-5, Part II, p. 110) appear also in the motet.

E.   **Pierre de la Croix** (Petrus de Cruce) (late 13th century)

  1.   Pierre made innovations in notation and rhythm by introducing as many as nine *semibreves* to be sung to one *breve* (*HAM*, No. 35; *RRMA*, vols. 6-7, Part III, p. 209).

    a.   *Aucun–Lonc tans–Annuntiantes* (Some invent their songs–For a long time–Announcing) (*HAM*, No. 34; *RRMA*, vols. 6-7, Part III, p. 65)

F. Chief sources of 13th-century motets, in addition to the Notre Dame manuscripts listed above under II. B.
   1. *Codex Montpellier, H 196* (*RRMA*, vols. 2-3; *AM*, v. 47, pp, 23, 28; *NMM*, Plates XXXVIII-XLI; *NPM*, pp. 291, 293, 316, 317, 321)
      a. This codex, assembled early in the 14th century, is the largest extant collection of 13th-century polyphony from **Perotin** to **Pierre de la Croix**. In all it contains 345 compositions, including 16 repetitions and 6 motet texts without music. In mensural notation, the types of compositions include 76 two-part motets, 214 three-part motets, 19 four-part motets, 4 incomplete motets, 2 three-part hockets, 2 three-part conducti and 6 organa.
      b. Other composers identified in addition to **Perotin** and **Pierre** are **Adam de la Halle**, **Gilon Ferrant** and "a Spaniard."
   2. *Codex Bamberg Ed. IV.6* (*CMM*, 75; *NPM*, p. 305; *AM*, v. 47, p. 27; *TEM*, p. 49)
      a. The Bamberg manuscript dates from the late 13th century. However, it contains some earlier Notre Dame music (*NMM*, Plate XXXV). Included are 100 motets, a conductus and 7 textless (instrumental) motets (*NMM*, Plate XXXVI). In the contents there is one four-voice motet with two tenors.
   3. *El Còdex musical de Las Huelgas* (*CMM*, 79; *NMM*, Plate, XXXVII; *NPM*, p. 309; *AM*, v. 47, p. 27)
      a. Copied during the late 13th and early 14th centuries, this Spanish codex consists of 186 compositions, both monodic and polyphonic. As the above codices, this one also is representative of the whole repertoire of the *ars antiqua*. It includes French, Spanish and English texts; 49 organa, 31 one- and two-voice sequences, 16 conducti and 55 motets. Fifteen monophonic songs are also included.
      b. Various types of motets have been copied from other sources. However, there are 21 motets known to this codex only. The codex is written in mensural notation and new parts are often added; rhythmic and other alterations are made. Frequent repetitions of tenor melodies suggest the later *basso ostinato*.
   4. *An Old St. Andrews Music Book* (*Wolfenbüttel 677*) (*M 13*)
      a. This is a transcription (1931) by James H. Baxter of **Leonin's** *Magnus liber*, the earliest examples of Notre Dame polyphony. Of the 46 two-part organa that make up this book, 13 are for Offices and 33 for Masses (*TEM*, p. 44).
   5. *Oeuvres complètes du trouvère Adam de la Halle* (*M 1*)
      a. Among **Adam's** complete works there are 4 three-voice polytextual motets and one for two voices (*M1*, pp. 239-272). All of the texts are French with Latin tenors.

V. Hocket (*hoquet, hoquetus, hoketus*)

  A. Used as a device and a form
   1. Hocket is a unique compositional device in which the single notes of a melody alternate between two voices so that a melody note appears in one voice against a rest in the other. Each note may be repeated alternately and, in some cases, groups of notes may alternate. Hocket is also the name given to the musical form in which the alternating effect is developed, generally in the duplum and triplum of three-voice motets.
   2. Hocket is defined by **Walter Odington** (*c.* 1300) as a "truncation over the tenor, made in such a way that one voice is always silent while the other sings" (*CSM*, v. 14, p. 144; *MSD*, v. 31, p. 34; *B 6*, v. 1, p. 248). **Johannes de Grocheo** says that hocket "suits the taste of farmers and young people because of its mobility and speed" (*B 16*).
   3. The earliest examples appear in the early 13th century. In six of the instrumental pieces at the end of the Bamberg manuscript hocket plays a major role (*HAM*, No. 32e; *CMM*, 75, No. 108; *NMM*, Plate XXXVI).
   4. *Ja n'amerai autre—In seculum* (I shall have no other) (*GEx*, p. 70; *RRMA*, vols. 2-3, Part I, pp. 2, 4; *TEM*, p. 59)

Ja n'amerai autre – In seculum

Example of Hocket (Montpellier, MS H 196)   XIII Century

5.   Hocket (*RRMA*, vols. 4-5, Part II, p. 69; vols. 6-7, Part III, p. 203)

VI.   Cantilena

A.   The polyphonic *cantilenae* were secular vocal pieces which correspond to the monodic cantilenas and include dance songs with refrains, such as rondeaux, virelais and ballades. In the cantilenas there is only one text for all voices, or instruments might have played two of the parts.

B.   **Adam de la Halle** (*c.* 1230-1288)

   1.   **Adam** was born in Arras, France, and died in Naples. In addition to his monophonic songs, motets and the play "Robin and Marion," there remain 16 polyphonic cantilenas for which **Adam** wrote the texts also.

   2.   *Fines amouretes* (My delicate love), a virelai: A bba A (*GEx*, p. 74; *CE*, p. 211)

   3.   *A Dieu commant amouretes* (To God I commend my love), a rondeau – ABaAabAB (*GEx*, p. 76; *CE*, p. 215)

   4.   *Tant con je vivrae* (As long as I live), a rondeau (*HAM*, No. 36b; *CE*, p. 230)

   5.   *Diex soit en cheste maison* (May God dwell in this house), a rondo – ABABA (*HAM*, No. 36c; *CE*, p. 232)

   6.   *Hé Diex! quant verrai* (O God! when shall I see her) , a rondeau (*OMM*, p. 117; *CE*, p. 225)

VII.   Polyphony in the British Isles to 1350

A.   Free organum (see *Outline* V)

B.   *An Old St. Andrews Music Book*, commonly known as Wolfenbüttel 677 (see II. B. 1. above) contains mostly examples of French compositions also found in several Notre Dame collections. However, the last of eleven fascicles is devoted mainly to two-part compositions of British origin in a slightly different style.

   1.   In some compositions, in contrast to the Notre Dame style, the responsorial compositions are completely set polyphonically rather than having the plainsong sung monophonically.

   2.   At times a third voice enters near the end of these otherwise two-part pieces.

   3.   The English organa are less melismatic and make use of more melodic repetition than those of the Notre Dame school.

C.   *Gymel (gimel, cantus gemellus)*, meaning twin song

   1.   Gymel is a style of two-part composition which makes use of thirds, sixths and tenths, often in parallel motion.

    a.   *Nobilis humilis* (*GEx*, p. 47; *HAM*, No. 25c; *A*3, p. 353, facsimile)
      1) Parallel organum (*c*. 1270)
    b.   *Foweles in the Frith* (Birds in the thicket) (*GEx*, p. 47; *EBM*, v. 1, Plate 6; *EEH*, v. 1, Plate 7; *NOH*, v. 3, p. 343)
    c.   *Jesu Cristes milde moder* (Jesus Christ's gentle mother) (*c*. 1270) (*GEx*, p. 48; *EEH*, v. 1, Plate 35; *NOH*, v. 2, p. 324)
      1) A two-part polyphonic sequence of double versicles.
    d.   *Edi beo thu* (Blessed be thou) (*OMM*, p. 118; *NOH*, v. 2, p. 342)

D.   Worcester Fragments (*MSD*, v. 2; *PMMM*, v. 5)
  1.   These fragments of music of the 13th century have been collected from various types of manuscripts in which the music has been written on covers and flyleafs. They contain important polyphonic settings of tropes for the Mass, motets, conducti, organa and rondelli.

E.   Rondellus
  1.   **Walter Odington** (*c*. 1300) in his *De speculatione Musicae* (*CSM* 14; *B*24, pp. 182-250) discusses intervals, harmony, notation, rhythms and musical instruments. Among other definitions, he includes "rondellus," a piece in which two or three melodies are sung at the same time, each voice singing each melody through in turn (*GEx*, p. 46; *MSD*, v. 31, p. 29; *B* 6, v. 1, pp. 182-250).
  2.   *Fulget coelestis* (*WMH*, p. 141; p. 143, facsimile; *WF*, No. 31; *PMFC*, v. 14, p. 81; *TECM*, v. 1, p. 46)
  3.   *De supernis sedibus* (*WMH*, p. 127, facsimile; *WF*, No. 5; *PMFC*, v. 14, p. 53)

F.   Conductus
  1.   *Hac in annui Janua* (At the beginning of the year) (*NPM*, pp. 259-260; *GEx*, p. 29; *HAM*, No. 39; *OAMB*, fol. 78r)
    a.   This three-voice conductus is a secular song in which the text describes the pleasure of students on returning to school after the Christmas holidays, and their resolve to improve their behavior. Note the extended *cauda* on the closing syllable.
  2.   *Beata viscera* (Blessed offspring) (*WF*, No. 91; *PMMM*, v. 5, p. 42, facsimile; *WMH*, p. 108; *TECM*, v. 1, p. 41.
    a.   The 13th century conductus uses six-three chords, English discant style (see below).

G.   Motet
  1.   *Puellare gremium* (A maiden's womb spreads joy) (early 14th century) (*WF*, No. 76; *WMH*, p. 100; *NOH*, v. 2, p. 384; *B* 8, p. 25)
    a.   The early 14th century three-part motet makes use of thirds, complete triads and some crossing of parts.
    b.   The textless tenor is made up of two repeated phrases which alternate in a type of *ostinato*: aa bb aa bb aa bb.
  2.   *Alleluia psallat* (Sing Alleluia) (*WMH*, p. 83; *HAM*, No. 57a; *WF*, No. 46, pp. 64, 65; *TECM*, v. 1, p. 43
    a.   The upper motet voices (meas. 2-6) make use of *Stimmtausch*, a device frequently found in early English motets.
  3.   *Excelsus in numine - Benedictus Dominus* (Raised up by your power - Blessed by the Lord) (*OMM*, p. 105)
    a.   In this 13th century motet, *Stimmtausch* is used in regular four-measure phrases, except for short phrases at the beginning, end and in the middle.
  4.   London Manuscript 27630 (*EdM*, v. 52, facsimile; v. 53, transcription)
    a.   This volume contains examples of organum and the two-voice motet in the earlier style of the twelfth century.

H.   Rota (round)
  1.   *Sumer is icumen in* (13th century) (*GEx*, p. 45; *GMB*, No. 17; *HAM*, No. 42; *HMM*, p. 508, facsimile; *MSO*, v. 1, p. 17)
    a.   "Sumer" is a four-voice canon sung over a two-voice tenor (*pes*) in *Stimmtausch*.

I.   English discant and *fauxbourdon*
   1.   In contrast to authentic discant of the St. Martial School, English discant is a term used to identify compositions in chordal style, frequently made up of six-three chords. However, perfect as well as imperfect intervals are common.
      a.   If a preexistent melody is present, it most frequently appears in the middle voice.
   2.   English writers mention that English discant was originally a type of improvisation by means of a "sight" system (*RMMA*, p. 401).
   3.   *In te Domine speravi* (In Thee, Lord, have I trusted) (*RMMA*, p. 399)

SELECTED BIBLIOGRAPHY

Books

1.   *Anonymous IV*, tr. Luther Dittmer.   Brooklyn: Institute of Mediaeval Music, 1959. (*MTT*, v. 1)
2.   *Anonymous IV*, in Charles Edmond Henri Coussemaker, *Scriptorum de Musica Medii Aevi, Nova series*, v. 1, pp. 327-365.
3.   Bergsagel, John D. "An English Liquescent Neume," in *Essays Presented to Egon Wellesz*, ed. Jack Westrup, pp. 94-102. Oxford: Clarendon Press, 1966.
4.   Bowles, Edmund A. "The Symbolism of the Organ in the Middle Ages: A Study in the History of Ideas," in *Aspects of Medieval and Renaissance Music: A Birthday Offering to Gustave Reese*, ed. Jan LaRue, pp. 27-39. New York: W. W. Norton, 1966.
5.   Bukofzer, Manfred. *Sumer is icumen in. A Revision*. Berkeley: University of California Press, 1944.
6.   Coussemaker, Charles Edmond Henri. *Scriptorum de Musica Medii Aevi, Nova Series*, 4 vols. Paris: A. Durand, 1864, 1867, 1869, 1876; reprint: Hildesheim: Georg Olm Verlagsbuchhandlung, 1963.
7.   Dittmer, Luther A. *The Worcester Fragments. A Catalogue Raisonné and Transcription*. Rome: American Institute of Musicology, 1957. (*MSD*, v. 2)
8.   ———————*Auszug aus The Worcester Music-Fragments*. Brooklyn: The Institute of Mediaeval Music, 1957. (*Musicological Studies*, v. 1)
9.   Farmer, Henry George. *Music in Mediaeval Scotland*. London: William Reeves, 1930.
10.   Flood, William Henry Grattan.   *A History of Irish Music*, 4th ed. Dublin: Browne and Nolan, Ltd., 1927.
11.   Galpin, Francis William. *Old English Instruments of Music*. Chicago: A. C. McClurg, 1911; 3rd rev. ed., London: Metheun & Co., 1932.
12.   Harrison, Frank Llewellyn. *Music in Medieval Britain*. London: Routledge and K. Paul, 1963.
13.   ———————"Tradition and Innovation in Instrumental Usage 1100-1450," in *Aspects of Medieval and Renaissance Music: A Birthday Offering to Gustave Reese*, ed. Jan LaRue, pp. 319-335. New York: W. W. Norton, 1966.
14.   Haskins, Charles Homer. *The Rise of Universities*. New York: H. Holt, 1923; reprint: New York: P. Smith, 1940.
15.   Hurry, Jamieson Boyd. *Sumer is icumen in*, 2nd ed. London: Novello, 1914.
16.   Johannes de Grocheo. *Concerning Music (De musica)*, tr. Albert Seay. Colorado Springs: Colorado College Music Press, 1967. (*CMT*, No. 1)
17.   Johannis de Garlandia. *Concerning Measured Music (De Mensurabili Musica)*, tr. Stanley H. Birnbaum. Colorado Springs: Colorado College Music Press, 1978. (*CMT*, No. 9)
18.   ———————*De Musica Mensurabili*, in Charles Edmond Henri Coussemaker, *Scriptorum de Musica Medii Aevi, Nova series*, v. 1, pp. 97-116. Hildesheim: Georg Olm Verlagsbuchhandlung, 1963.
19.   Kenney, Silvia W. "The Theory of Discant," in *Walter Frye and the "Contenance Angloise,"* Chapter 5. New Haven: Yale University Press, 1965.

20. Ludwig, Friedrich. *Repertorium Organorum Recentioris et Motetorum Vetustissimi Stili*. Halle: M. Niemeyer, 1910; reprint: ed. Luther Dittmer. Brooklyn: Institute of Mediaeval Music, v. 1, Part 1, 1964; v. 1, Part 2 and v. 2, 1978.

21. Mathiassen, Finn. *The Style of the Early Motet (c. 1200-1250)*. Copenhagen: Dan Fog Musikforlag, 1966. (concerning the Montpellier Manuscript)

22. Montagu, Jeremy. *The World of Medieval and Renaissance Musical Instruments*. Woodstock, NY: The Overlook Press, 1976.

23. *The Music of the St. Victor Manuscript, Paris lat. 15139. Polyphony of the 13th Century*, ed. Ethel Thurston. Toronto: Pontifical Institute of Mediaeval Studies, 1959.

24. Odington, Walter. *De Speculatione Musicae*, Part VI, tr. Jay A. Huff. Rome: American Institute of Musicology, 1973. (*MSD*, v. 31)

25. ———————*De Speculatione Musicae*, ed. Frederick F. Hammond. Rome: American Institute of Musicology, 1970. (*CSM*, v. 14)

26. Tischler, Hans. "Perotinus Revisited," in *Aspects of Medieval and Renaissance Music: A Birthday Offering to Gustave Reese*, ed. Jan LaRue, pp. 803-817. New York. W. W. Norton, 1966.

Articles

1. Anderson, Gordon A. "Clausuale or Transcribed Motets in the Florence Manuscript? " *ActaM* 42 (1970), pp. 109-128.

2. ———————"Notre Dame and Related Conductus—A Catalogue Raissonĕ." *Miscellanea Musicologica—Adelaide Studies in Musicology* 6 (1972), p. 1-81.

3. ———————"Notre Dame Latin Double Motets c. 1215-1250." *MD* 25 (1971), pp. 35-92.

4. ———————"The Rhythm of *cum littera* Sections of Polyphonic Conductus in Mensural Sources." *JAMS* 26 (1973), pp. 288-304.

5. ———————"Thirteenth-Century Conductus: *Obiter Dicta*." *MQ* 58 (1972), pp. 349-364.

6. Anglés, Higini. "Hispanic Music Culture from the 6th to the 14th Century." *MQ* 26 (1940), pp. 494-528.

7. Apel, Willi. "From St. Martial to Notre Dame." *JAMS* 2 (1949), pp. 145-158.

8. Baltzer, Rebecca. "Thirteenth-Century Illuminated Miniatures and the Date of the Florence Manuscript." *JAMS* 25 (1972), pp. 1-18.

9. Bent, Margaret. "New and Little Known Fragments of English Medieval Polyphony." *JAMS* 21 (1968), pp. 137-156.

10. Beveridge, John. "Two Scottish Thirteenth-Century Songs." *ML* 20 (1939), pp. 352-364.

11. Blum, Fred. "Another Look at the Montpellier Organum Treatise." *MD* 13 (1959), pp. 15-24.

12. Boos, Elizabeth L. "Alleluia cum psallite." *MD* 25 (1971), pp. 93-98.

13. Branner, Robert. "Manuscript-Makers in Mid-Thirteenth Century Paris." *Art Bulletin* 48 (1966), pp. 65-67.

14. Bukofzer, Manfred. "The First Motet with English Words." *ML* 17 (1936), pp. 225-233.

15. ———————"The Gymel. The Earliest Form of English Polyphony." *ML* 16 (1935), pp. 77-84.

16. ———————"Interrelations between Conductus and Clausula." *AnM* 1 (1953), pp. 65-103.

17. ———————"Popular Polyphony in the Middle Ages." *MQ* 26 (1940), pp. 31-49.

18. Daglish, William E. "The Hocket in Medieval Polyphony." *MQ* 55 (1969), pp. 344-363.

19. ———————"The Use of Variation in Early Polyphony." *MD* 26 (1972), pp. 37-51.

20. Dittmer, Luther A. "Binary Rhythm, Musical Theory and the Worcester Fragments." *MD* 7 (1953), pp. 39-57.

21. ———————"The Dating and Notation of the Worcester Fragments." *MD* 11 (1957), pp. 5-11.

22. ———————"An English *Discantuum Volumen*." *MD* 8 (1954), pp. 19-58.

23. ———————"The Ligatures of the Montpellier Manuscript." *MD* 9 (1955), pp. 35-56.

24. Ellinwood, Leonard. "The Conductus." *MQ* 27 (1941), pp. 165-204.

25.   Ficker, Rudolf von. "Polyphonic Music in the Gothic Period." *MQ* 15 (1929), pp. 483-505.

26.   Flindell, E. Fred. "Syllabic Notation and Change of Mode." *ActaM* 39 (1967), pp. 21-34.

27.   Flood, W. H. Grattan. "The Eschequier Virginal; an English Invention." *ML* 6 (1925), pp. 151-153.

28.   Gastoué, Amédée. "Three Centuries of French Medieval Music." *MQ* 3 (1917), pp. 173-188.

29.   Günther, Ursula. "The 14th-Century Motet and Its Development." *MD* 12 (1958), pp. 27-58.

30.   Handschin, Jacques. "A Monument of English Medieval Polyphony." *MT* 73 (1932), pp. 510-513; 74 (1933), pp. 697-704.

31.   ————"The Summer Canon and Its Background." *MD* 3 (1949), pp. 55-94.

32.   Harbinson, Denis. "Consonance and Dissonance in the Old Corpus of the Montpellier Motet Manuscript." *MD* 22 (1968), pp. 5-13.

33.   ————"The Hocket Motets in the Old Corpus of the Montpellier Motet Manuscript." *MD* 25 (1971), pp. 99-112.

34.   ————"Imitation in the Early Motet." *ML* 45 (1964), pp. 359-368.

35.   Harrison, Frank Llewelyn. "Benedicamus, Conductus, Carol: A Newly Discovered Source." *ActaM* 37 (1965), pp. 35-48.

36.   Hibberd, Lloyd. "Instrumental Style in Early Melody." *MQ* 32 (1946), pp. 107-130.

37.   ————"*Musica Ficta* and Instrumental Music *c.* 1250-*c.* 1350." *MQ* 28 (1942), pp. 216-226.

38.   Hughes, Andrew, and Margaret Bent. "The Old Hall Manuscript: A Reappraisal and an Inventory." *MD* 21 (1967), pp. 97-147.

39.   Hughes, Dom Anselm. "Old English Harmony." *ML* 6 (1925), pp. 154-160.

40.   ————"The Origins of Harmony with Special Reference to an Old St. Andrews MS." *MQ* 24 (1938), pp. 176-185.

41.   Husman, Heinrich. "The Enlargement of the 'Magnus liber organi' and the Paris Churches St. Germain l'Auxerrois and Ste. Geneviève-du-Mont." *JAMS* 16 (1963), pp. 176-203.

42.   ————"The Origin and Destination of the *Magnus liber organi*." *MQ* 49 (1963), pp. 311-330.

43.   Jeffery, Peter. "Notre Dame Polyphony in the Library of Pope Boniface VIII." *JAMS* 32 (1979), pp. 118-124.

44.   Knapp, Janet. "Musical Declamation and Poetic Rhythm in an Early Layer of Notre Dame Conductus." *JAMS* 32 (1979), pp. 383-407.

45.   Machabey, Armand. "A Propos des Quadruples Perotiniens." *MD* 12 (1958), pp. 3-25.

46.   Montgomery, Franz. "The Musical Instruments in 'The Canterbury Tales'." *MQ* 17 (1931), pp. 439-448.

47.   Nathan, Hans. "The Function of Text in French 13th Century Motets." *MQ* 28 (1942), pp. 445-462.

48.   Pirrotta, Nino. "On the Problem of 'Sumer is icumen in'." *MD* 2 (1948), pp. 205-216.

49.   Reaney, Gilbert. "The Musician in Medieval England." *The Monthly Musical Record* 89 (1959), pp. 3-8.

50.   ————"Some Little-Known Sources of Medieval Polyphony in England." *MD* 15 (1961), pp. 15-26.

51.   Ripin, Edwin M. "The Early Clavichord." *MQ* 53 (1967), pp. 518-538.

52.   Sanders, Ernest H. "Peripheral Polyphony of the 13th Century." *JAMS* 17 (1964), pp. 261-287.

53.   Schofield, Bertram. "The Provenance and Date of *Sumer is icumen in*." *MR* 9 (1948), pp. 81-86.

54.   Schrade, Leo. "Political Compositions in French Music of the 12th and 13th Centuries." *AnM* 1 (1953), pp. 9-63.

55.   Smith, Norman E. "Interrelationships between the Alleluias of the *Magnus liber organi*." *JAMS* 25 (1972), pp. 175-202.

56. Smith, Norman E. "Tenor Repetition in the Nore-Dame Organa." *JAMS* 19 (1966), pp. 329-351.

57. Stevens, Denis. "Alleluia Psallat." *MT* 106 (1965), pp. 27-28.

58. Tischler, Hans. "Another English Motet of the 13th Century." *JAMS* 20 (1967), pp. 274-279.

59. —————"A Propos the Notation of the Parisian Organa." *JAMS* 14 (1961), pp. 1-8.

60. —————"Classicism and Romanticism in Thirteenth-Century Music." *Revue belge de musicologie* 16 (1962), pp. 3-12.

61. —————"The Dates of Perotin." *JAMS* 16 (1963), pp. 240-241.

62. —————"The Early Cantors of Notre Dame." *JAMS* 19 (1966), pp. 85-87.

63. —————"English Traits in the Early 13th-Century Motet." *MQ* 30 (1944), pp. 458-476.

64. —————"The Evolution of Forms in the Earliest Motets." *ActaM* 31 (1959), pp. 86-90.

65. —————"The Evolution of the Harmonic Style in the Notre-Dame Motet." *ActaM* 28 (1956), pp. 87-95.

66. —————"How were Notre Dame Clausulae Performed? " *ML* 50 (1969), pp. 273-277.

67. —————"Intellectual Trends in Thirteenth-Century Paris as Reflected in the Texts of Motets." *MR* 29 (1968), pp. 1-11.

68. Treitler, Leo. "The Polyphony of St. Martial." *JAMS* 17 (1964), pp. 29-42.

69. —————"Regarding Meter and Rhythm in the *Ars Antiqua*." *MQ* 65 (1979), pp. 524-558.

69. Waite, William G. "The Abbreviation of the Magnus liber." *JAMS* 14 (1961), pp. 147-158.

70. —————"Johannis de Garlandia, Poet and Musician." *Speculum* 35 (1960), pp. 179-195.

Music

1. Adam de la Halle. (*CE*) *Oeuvres Complètes du Trouvère Adam de la Halle*, ed. Charles Edmond Henri Coussemaker. Paris: A. Durand and Pédone-Lauriel, 1872. (reprint: New York: Broude Brothers, 1964; Ridgewood, NJ: Gregg Press, 1965; Geneva: Slatkine Reprints, 1970)

2. *A Central Source of Notre-Dame Polyphony*, ed. Luther Dittmer. Brooklyn: Institute of Mediaeval Music, 1959. (*PMMM*, v. 3)

3. *Cent Motets du XIIIe siècle* (Bamberg Ed. IV. 6), 3 vols., ed. Pierre Aubry. Paris: A. Rouart, Lorelle & Co., 1908.

4. *El códex musical de Las Huelgas*, 3 parts, ed. Higini Anglés. Barcelona: Biblioteca de Catalunya, 1931. (Publicacions del department de música, v. 6)

5. *Early Bodleian Music*, 3 vols., eds. John Stainer (vols. 1, 2). London: Novello, 1901; Edward W. B. Nicholson (v. 3). London: Novello, 1913. (reprint: Farnborough, England: Gregg Press, 1967)

6. *Firenze, Biblioteca Medico-Laurenziana, Pluteo 29, 1*, ed. Luther Dittmer. Brooklyn: Institute of Mediaeval Music, n. d. (*PMMM*, vols. 10, 11)

7. Gennrich, Friedrich. *Rondeaux, Virelais, und Balladen*, 2 vols. Volume I, Dresden: Gesellschaft für Romanische Literatur, 1921. Volume 2, Göttingen, 1927.

8. Hughes, Dom Anselm. *Worcester Mediaeval Harmony of the Thirteenth and Fourteenth Centuries*. Nashdom Abbey, Burnham, Bucks: The Plainsong and Mediaeval Music Society, 1928; reprint: Hildesheim: Georg Olms Verlag, 1971.

9. Knapp, Janet. *Thirty-five Conductus for Two and Three Voices*. New Haven: Yale University Press, 1965.

10. *London Ms 27630*. (*EdM*, vols. 52, 53) (14th- and 15th-century organa and two-voice motets in the style of the early 12th century)

11. *A Medieval Motet Book: A Collection of 13th Century Motets*, ed. Hans Tischler. New York: Associated Music Publishers, 1973.

12. *The Monpellier Codex*, ed. Hans Tischler. Madison: A-R Editions, 1978. (*RRMA*, vols. 2, 3)

13. *An Old St. Andrews Music Book*, ed. James Houston Baxter. London: Oxford University Press, 1931. (facsimile of MS Wolfenbüttel 677, Codex Helmstadt 628)

14. *Oxford, Latin Liturgical D-20; London, Add. Ms. 25031; Chicago, Ms 654 App.* ed. Luther Dittmer. Brooklyn: Institute of Mediaeval Music, 1960. (*PMMM*, v. 6)

15. *Paris, B. N. Ms nouv. acq. fr. 13521; Ms Lat. 11411*, ed. Luther Dittmer. Brooklyn: Institute of Mediaeval Music, 1959. (*PMMM*, v. 4)

16. *Polyphonic Music of the Fourteenth Century*, ed. Kurt von Fischer, 14 vols. Monaco: Éditions de L'Oiseau-Lyre, 1959.

17. Reaney, Gilbert, ed. *Manuscripts of Polyphonic Music* (11th to early 14th centuries). München-Duisberg: Henle, 1969.

18. Rokseth, Yvonne. *Polyphonies du XIIIe siècle* (Montpellier MS H-196), 4 vols. Paris: Éditions de L'Oiseau-Lyre, 1935-1939.

19. Thurston, Ethel. *The Works of Perotin*. New York: Kalmus, 1970.

20. Waite, William G., transc. Leonin, *Magnus liber organi de gradali et antiphonarie*, Wolfenbüttel 677, Olim Helmstadt 628, in *The Rhythm of Twelfth-Century Polyphony, its Theory and Practice*, pp. 1-254. New Haven: Yale University Press, 1954.

21. *Wolfenbüttel Ms 1099 Helmstadiensis (1206)*, ed. Luther Dittmer. Brooklyn: Institute of Mediaeval Music, 1960. (*PMMM*, v. 2)

22. Wooldridge, Harry Ellis, and Dom Anselm Hughes. *Early English Harmony*, 2 vols. Vol. 1, London: Bernard Quaritch, 1897. Vol. 2, London: Plainsong and Mediaeval Society, 1913.

23. *Worcester Add. 68; Westminster Abbey 33327; Madrid, Bibl. Nac. 192*, ed. Luther Dittmer. Brooklyn: Institute of Mediaeval Music, 1959. (*PMMM*, v. 5)

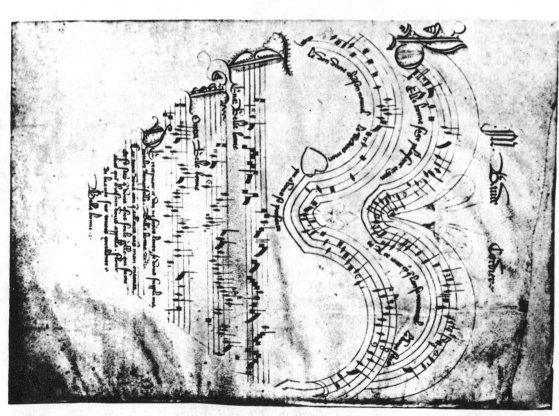

9. Belle bonne by Baude Cordier from the Chantilly manuscript 1047 (c. 1400)

OUTLINE VII

FRENCH MUSIC OF THE FOURTEENTH CENTURY

Le Roman de Fauvel – Isorhythm – French Notation
Early Fourteenth Century Manuscripts – Guillaume de Machaut
Late Fourteenth Century Secular Music

I. **Le Roman de Fauvel** (Paris, Bibl. Nat. fr. 146), Part I, 1310; Part II, 1314

    A.   This 3280-line poem was written by Gervais de Bus, a clerk (1313-1338) in the French court.

    B.   The allegory is a satirical attack on the social corruption and abuses against the church by religious orders, symbolized by Fauvel, an ass or horse. The name *"Fauvel,"* explained to represent a dingy, brownish-yellow color (*fauve*), is an acrostic of six words representing his character: *Flaterie, Avarice, Vilanie, Variété, Envie, Lascheté.*

    C.   By 1316 musical interpolations had been inserted in the story by Chaillou de Pesstain, probably also of the French court.

        1.   The music comes from various sources representing a broad range of styles and generally using Latin texts.

            a.   34 motets: 10 two-voice, 23 three-voice, one four-voice

            b.   25 monophonic conducti and sequences

            c.   52 Alleluias, antiphons, responses, hymns, versets

            d.   Four *lais*, four *rondeaux*, nine *ballades*, including two with the *virelai* form

            e.   15 refrains

            f.   12 *sottes chansons* (foolish songs)

        2.   Some pieces, unchanged, were chosen to fit the particular situation in the poem; others were adapted with new texts or special references; new texts were set to old music, and still others were completely new compositions, words and music.

        3.   There is some use of isorhythms.

II. **Isorhythm** (same rhythm)

    A.   Isorhythm is derived from 13th century modal rhythms (rhythmic modes). It usually occurs in the tenor but **Philippe de Vitry** and succeeding composers apply it also to the upper voices.

        1.   The simple *ordo* lengthens into an isorhythmic structure consisting of one or more repetitions of a phrase made up of a rhythmic pattern called *talea* (plural *taleae*).

        2.   The repetition of the melody is called *color* (plural is *colores*).

        3.   The repetitions of *talea* (rhythm) and *color* (melody) may coincide or occur at different times; *e. g.* two rhythmic repetitions (*taleae*) may occur within the same time as three melodic repetitions (*colores*): 2 T = 3 C.

    B.   **Philippe de Vitry** (October 31, 1292-June 9, 1361)

        1.   Composer, theorist, poet and Priest, **Vitry** was appointed Canon of the Church in 1323. In 1351 he became Bishop of Meaux where he remained until his death. He made two diplomatic journeys to the papal court at Avignon and was a friend of the Italian poet Francesco Petrarch.

        2.   *Ars Nova*, *c.* 1325 (*CSM*, 8)

            a.   This treatise on the "New Art," which gave the period its name, deals primarily with a new notational and rhythmical organization.

3. Several motets by **Vitry** were cited by him in his *Ars Nova*. They show the use of iso-rhythm in the tenor and at times in the upper voices.
   a. *Garrit Gallus - In nova fert - Neuma* (*AMM*, No. 59; *PMFC*, v. 1, p. 68; *NPM*, p. 331, facsimile; *DTÖ*, v. 76, p. 2)
      1) The isorhythmic tenor consists of 2 *colores* = 6 *taleae*.
   b. *Douce playsence - Garison selon nature - Neuma quinti toni* (*CaMM*, p. 167; *PMFC*, v. 1, p. 72)
4. *Vos qui admiramini - Gratissima virginis - Gaude gloriosa* (*OMM*, p. 120; *PMFC*, v. 1, p. 76)
   a. In this four-voice motet the typical isorhythmic tenor is from the antiphon *Ave Regina caelorum*.
   b. The isorhythms proceed in the following plan: meas. 1-91: 1 *color* = 6 *taleae* of 15 bars each; meas. 92-154: 1 *color* = 7 *taleae* of 9 bars each.
   c. The use of hocket is apparent in meas. 100-103, 118-121, 136-139, and the triplum takes on isorhythmic characteristics (meas. 94-108, 111-126, 129-144) (*RMMA*, p. 338).
5. Hocket, used for expressive purposes, may be found in many motets.
   a. *Hugo princeps - Cum structura* (*DTÖ*, v. 76, p. 4; *PMFC*, v. 1, p. 82)
C. Pope John XXII in 1322, during the exile of the popes in Avignon (1305-1378), issued a famous decree denouncing secularism and elaborate polyphony in the "new" style in music for the church. Restrained temporarily, composers seemed little affected by the decree (*OHM*, v. 1, pp. 294-296).

III. French Notation

A. During the *Ars Nova* **Vitry** reorganized notation. Duple and triple notation became equally important and smaller time values were introduced: *semiminima* (♪), *fusa* (♫), *semifusa* (♬).

1. The time values changed: the *longa* (⌐) now became equal to our whole note, the *brevis* (⊟) to our half note, the *semibrevis* (◆) to our quarter note and the *minima* (♩) to our eighth note. The *semibrevis* was performed at an average tempo, probably about ♩ = 60. New subtleties in rhythm were also introduced.

B. Relationships between note values
   1. Mood (*modus*), subdivision of the *longa*, was rarely used and was usually imperfect.
      a. O_3 (perfect) ⌐ = 3 ■
      b. O_2 (imperfect) ⌐ = 2 ■
   2. Time (*tempus*), subdivision of the *brevis*, is indicated by a circle or semi-circle.
      a. O (perfect) ■ = 3 ◆
      b. C (imperfect) ■ = 2 ◆
   3. Prolation (*prolatio*), subdivision of the *semibrevis*, is indicated by a dot (dots) or ab-sence of dots.
      a. ⊙ or ⊙ (major) ◆ = 3 ♩   Sometimes indicated by three dots.

    b.   O or C (minor)   ◆ = 2 ↓   Sometimes indicated by two dots.
    4.   Modern transcriptions
        a.   Ꝋ = 9/8; O = 3/4; ₵ = 6/8; C = 2/4.
    5.   In the tenor of two motets of *Le Roman de Fauvel* there is occasional use of red notes
          which indicates imperfect mode.

IV. Fourteenth Century Manuscripts

   A.   **Jehannot de Lescurel** (*CMM*, 30, facsimile and transcription)
       1.   The songs of **Lescurel** are included in the manuscript containing *Le Roman de Fauvel*.
             The collection comprises 15 ballades, 11 rondeaux and 5 virelais, all monophonic
             except the opening three-voice rondeau refrain.
       2.   **Lescurel's** name is used as an acrostic in No. 29, *Dis tans plus qu'il ne faudroit flours*
             (*CMM*, 30, p. 18).
   B.   Ivrea Codex (*c.* 1360) (*PMFC*, v. 5; *CMM*, 29)
       1.   The codex, originating at the papal court in Avignon, is an anthology of motets (21
             Latin, 14 French, one Latin and French) and 25 movements from the Ordinary of the
             Mass (9 Glorias and Credos each). Included also are 15 French secular songs, 6 ron-
             deaux, 5 virelais and 4 chaces.
       2.   Although no composer is identified, motets by **Vitry** and **Machaut** are included.
       3.   The four chaces, except for *Sumer is icumen in*, are the earliest examples of the canon
             as a complete composition.
           a.   *Se je chant* (If I sing) (*AMM*, No. 60)
   C.   Apt Codex (*c.* 1400) (*M 2*; *CMM*, 29; *MMA*, v. 10)
       1.   The Apt manuscript contains about 50 Mass movements and hymns used in the Papal
             Chapel at Avignon. Compositions appear in the three common styles: 1) motet, 2)
             discant (song) and 3) simultaneous (conductus). They range from two to four voices.
             Several composers are identified (**de Fronciaco, Guymont, Tapissier** and others).
   D.   Mass movements: Toulouse, Tournai, Barcelona and Sorbonne Masses (*CMM*, 29)
       1.   The performance of a polyphonic setting of the Ordinary gradually became an ac-
             cepted practice. Four Masses common to the Avignon repertory are known by their
             present locations.
       2.   The Tournai and Toulouse Masses are both for three voices; the first generally in con-
             ductus style and the latter in polyphonic song style (*PMFC*, v. 1).
       3.   The five-movement Barcelona Mass, without plainsong, contains a variety of styles and
             was probably written in the later 14th century.
       4.   In the Sorbonne Mass sections of the Kyrie and Sanctus are used in the Agnus Dei, a
             unifying feature which anticipates the cyclic Mass. The Credo is omitted.

V. Guillaume de Machaut

   A.   Life
       1.   Composer, Priest and prolific poet, **Guillaume de Machaut** enjoyed the patronage of
             nobility throughout most of his life. In 1323 he entered the employ of John, Count
             of Luxembourg and King of Bohemia and was installed as a Canon at Reims Cathedral
             in January, 1337. Remaining there the rest of his life, **Machaut** nevertheless continued
             a life of freedom associating with nobility. After the death of King John, **Machaut**
             served Charles V, King of France, and his brother John, Duke of Berry.
           a.   **Machaut's** poetry reveals he was afflicted with blindness in one eye and endured
                 hardships in the Black Plague (1348-1349) and the Hundred Years' War (1337-
                 1453).
       2.   The Italian Francesco Petrarch (1304-1374) and the English Geoffrey Chaucer (1340-
             1400) were his contemporaries.

B.   Music
  1.   A catalog of **Machaut's** works reveals a wide range of musical and poetical accomplishments. Included is a Mass, motets and several secular forms.
    a.   At least two poems had musical compositions interpolated in them (*Remède de Fortune, c.* 1345 and *Le Livre du Voi Dit, c.* 1365).
C.   Characteristics
  1.   **Machaut's** secular music, except for the motets, in general follows the rules given in the *Ars nova*, in regard to both rhythm and harmony.
    a.   Binary rhythm and the minim are used and both are new to French music. The themes and the same rhythmic motives, usually stated at the beginning, are often used throughout the composition.
    b.   "Accompanied melody" is the characteristic of the new style. The *cantus firmus* treatment is given up. Two, three, four and in some cases five parts are used.
    c.   The free contrapuntal texture is rarely built up from the tenor and the polyphony often contrasts with chordal sections. The polyphony moves independently from consonance to consonance (fourths, fifths, octaves). Thirds appear frequently.
    d.   There is a bold use of syncopation and dissonance.
  2.   The motets make use of the old (*Ars antiqua*) style with extensive use of isorhythms.
  3.   The rondeau, virelai and ballade forms of the Trouvères continued on in polyphonic texture but, with the possible exception of the virelai, they were no longer danced.
D.   Forms
  1.   Lai (*CE*, v. 4, pp. 24-81; *PMFC*, v. 2, pp. 1-102; *MOC*, v. 4)
    a.   The influence of the double versicle of the Sequence is apparent. At times triple and quadruple versicles are used.
    b.   Characteristics include phrases repeated in transposed version, repetition of rhythmic motives suggesting isorhythms and contrast of pitch level suggesting the possibility of two performers.
      1)   The range of a stanza may be a ninth, but the total range of a lai may be almost two octaves.
    c.   The same melody is used for the first and last stanzas.
    d.   Four lais are polyphonic, either to be sung in canon or with other melodic combinations.
    e.   *J'aim la flour* (I love that worthy flower) (*CE*, v. 4, p. 25; *MOC*, v. 4, p. 3; *PMFC*, v. 2, p. 2; *OMM*, p. 155)
  2.   Rondeaux (*CE*, v. 1, pp. 52-69; *MOC*, v. 2; *PMFC*, v. 3, pp. 142-166)
    a.   Twenty-one in all: 7 in two parts, 11 in three parts, 2 in four parts and one in five parts.
    b.   The form of the eight-line rondeaux as expressed in music and rhyme scheme is AB aA ab AB (one stanza). Capital letters indicate the refrain sung by a chorus and lower case letters indicate a soloist.
      1)   Expansion of the form developed by adding an extra line to the first section of the refrain and necessarily then adding lines at the repeats of the first section.
    c.   Only one part is set with a text.
    d.   *Tant doulcement* (So sweetly I feel) (*CE*, v. 1, p. 58; *MOC*, v. 2, p. 10; *PMFC*, v. 3, p. 150; *OMM*, p. 159)
    e.   *Se vous n'estes* (If you are not) (*CE*, v. 1, p. 56; *MOC*, v. 2, p. 8; *PMFC*, v. 3, p. 146; *HMM*, p. 427, facsimile)
    f.   *Ma fin est mon commencement et mon commencement ma fin* (My end is my beginning and my beginning my end) (*CE*, v. 1, p. 63; *MOC*, v. 2, p. 22; *PMFC*, v. 3, p. 156; *GEx*, p. 81; *MSO*, v. 1, p. 26)
  3.   Virelai (called by **Machaut** *chanson baladée*) (*CE*, v. 1, pp. 70-92; *MOC*, v. 1; *PMFC*, v. 3, pp. 167-192)
    a.   Twenty-five monodic and eight with instrumental tenor, including one with instru-

mental contratenor also.

b. Form with three stanzas: A bba A bba A bba A.

c. *Dame, mon cuer* (Lady, favorite of my heart) (*CE*, v. 1, p. 88; *MOC*, v. 1, p. 18; *PMFC*, v. 3, p. 188; *GEx*, p. 80)

d. *Plus dure* (Harder than a diamond) (*CE*, v. 1, p. 86; *MOC*, v. 1, p. 16; *PMFC*, v. 3, p. 187; *HAM*, No. 46b)

e. *De bonté, de valour* (With goodness, courage) (*CE*, v. 1, p. 74; *MOC*, v. 1, p. 5; *PMFC*, v. 3, p. 172; *AMM*, No. 64)

f. *Se je souspir* (If I sigh) (*CE*, v. 1, p. 89; *MOC*, v. 1, p. 19; *PMFC*, v. 3, p. 189; *GMB*, No. 26b; *MSO*, v. 1, p. 25)

4. *Ballade notée* (ballade with music) (*CE*, v. 1, pp. 1-51; *MOC*, v. 3; *PMFC*, v. 3, pp. 68-140)

a. Forty-two examples: one is monodic and the remaining are in two, three or four parts.

b. Some have texts in all parts and some have instrumental parts.

   1) Sequence, canon, hocket and some imitation is used.

c. The typical form is ab ab cd E (F) or a a b C where a = ab and b = cd. There are usually three stanzas each ending with the refrain.

   1) The refrain often rhymes musically with a recurring section of the stanza.

d. One double ballade (with two texts): *Quant Theseus* (*CE*, v. 1, p. 40; *PMFC*, v. 3, p. 124)

e. Two triple ballades (with three texts)

   1) *De triste cuer - Quant vrais amans - Certes, je di* (*CE*, v. 1, p. 32; *PMFC*, v. 3, p. 114)

   2) *Sanz cuer m'en vois - Amis, dolens - Dame, par vous* (I leave without my heart - Sorrowing friend - Lady, I feel myself consoled) (*CE*, v. 1, p. 16; *PMFC*, v. 3, p. 88; *OMM*, p. 157)

     a) This is **Machaut's** only canonic ballade.

f. *Mes esperis* (My hope) (*CE*, v. 1, p. 47; *PMFC*, v. 3, p. 134; *GEx*, p. 85)

g. *Je puis trop bien* (I can well compare) (*CE*, v. 1, p. 31; *PMFC*, v. 3, p. 112; *HAM*, No. 45; *GMB*, No. 26a)

h. *Dous [Doulz] amis* (Gentle friend) (*CE*, v. 1, p. 5; *PMFC*, v. 3, p. 77; *AMM*, p. 140; *NPM*, p. 357, facsimile)

5. Motets (*CE*, v. 3, pp. 2-87; *MOC*, v. 5)

a. Twenty-three motets: 19 in three parts and 4 in four parts.

b. The texts may be religious, moralizing or political and show a preference for the French language.

   1) Fifteen have complete French texts, two have a combination of French and Latin, and only six have complete Latin texts.

c. Isorhythms are found in all but three tenors. In the upper parts there is some use of isorhythms (*CE*, v. 3, p. 13; *PMFC*, v. 2, p. 119; *GEx*, p. 88), and hocket, syncopation (*CE*, v. 3, p. 30; *PMFC*, v. 2, p. 134; *AMM*, No. 61) and rhythmic sequence may be introduced. In the closing section of half of the motets diminution is used in melodic repetition of the tenors. The repetition of the melody and the rhythm does not always agree. Therefore the melody will have a new rhythm on its repetition (*CE*, v. 3, p. 24; *PMFC*, v. 2, p. 127; *HAM*, No. 44).

d. In some motets the isorhythmic tenor is preceded by an instrumental introduction.

e. The mensural notation of imperfect time with major prolation (6/8) predominates in the upper voices and perfect mood is most common in the tenor (15 motets).

f. *Trop plus est bele* (*CE*, v. 3, p. 71; *PMFC*, v. 3, p. 11; *GMB*, No. 27) is a puzzle canon; the tenor is to be sung: a b a a a b a b.

g. *Felix virgo* (*CE*, v. 3, p. 82; *PMFC*, v. 3, p. 26; *NPM*, p. 360, facsimile) employs a rhythmic *Stimmtausch* in the tenor and contratenor.

    h.   *Aucune gent m'ont demandé* (*CE*, v. 3, p. 18; *PMFC*, v. 2, p. 123) makes use of the rhythmic *Stimmtausch* in the tenor and contratenor. However, the rhythmic design is in retrograde resulting in a rhythmic palindrome.

6.   Hocket (*CE*, v. 4, p. 21; *PMFC*, v. 3, p. 65)
    a.   Based on the melisma of the word "David" in the *Alleluia: Nativitas*, the David hocket in three voices resembles the instrumental motets of the Bamberg Codex.

7.   *Messe de Nostre Dame* (*CE*, v. 4, p. 2; *MOC*, v. 6; *PMFC*, v. 3, p. 37; *CMM*, 2, v. 1)
    a.   This Mass is the earliest complete polyphonic setting of the Ordinary of the Mass by one composer. During the 12th and 13th centuries the Proper was composed as *organa*. The *Nostre Dame Mass* was performed at the coronation of Charles V in 1364, although it was probably written earlier. It is bound together by a descending five-note scale motive.
    b.   The five movements, and in addition the *Ite, missa est* (not usually a part of later polyphonic Masses), were all set in four voices.
    c.   Two distinct styles are contrasted: 1) isorhythmic motet style (Kyrie, Sanctus, Agnus Dei, Ite, missa est) and 2) note-against-note conductus style.
    d.   A contrast in modality is marked by the first three movements (Kyrie, Gloria, Credo) in Dorian mode and the last three movements (Sanctus, Agnus Dei, Ite, missa est) in Lydian or Hypolydian modes ending on F.
    e.   Kyrie (*CE*, v. 4, p. 2; *PMFC*, v. 3, p. 37; *AM*, v. 30, p. 33; *MSO*, v. 1, p. 22)
      1)   The plainsong tenor is from Mass IV, *Cunctipotens Genitor Deus* (*LU*, p. 25).
      2)   The form is the characteristic: aaa bbb ccc.
    f.   Gloria (*CE*, v. 4, p. 41; *PMFC*, v. 4, p. 5)
      1)   Conductus style
    g.   Credo (*CE*, v. 4, p. 8; *PMFC*, v. 3, p. 46)
      1)   Conductus style. The plainsong melody is paraphrased in the motetus part. An example of symbolism occurs when the melody becomes broader in the *Et incarnatus est*; dissonance occurs on the word *"Crucifixus."*
    h.   Sanctus (*CE*, v. 4, p. 14; *PMFC*, v. 3, p. 55)
      1)   This is based on the plainsong melody from Mass XVII (*LU*, p. 61).
    i.   Agnus Dei (*CE*, v. 4, p. 17; *PMFC*, v. 3, p. 60; *GEx*, p. 97; *MM*, p. 43)
      1)   This is based on the plainsong melody also from Mass XVII (*LU*, p. 61). The first part is in isorhythmic motet style.
    j.   Ite, missa est (*CE*, v. 4, p. 20; *PMFC*, v. 3, p. 64)

VI. Late Fourteenth Century Secular Music

A.   The principal forms during the transitional period between **Machaut** and **Dufay** (1350-1400) include the rondeau, virelai and ballade. Three overlapping styles may define this period.

1.   *c.* 1350-1370: The music shows the influence of **Machaut** in the use of short phrases (*FSM*, No. 62, p. 103*; *FSC*, v. 3, p. 35), one rhythmic element or motive (*FSM*, No. 74, p. 126*; *FSC*, v. 3, p. 87), short phrases (*FSM*, No. 62, p. 103*; No. 63, p. 104*; *FSC*, v. 3, p. 35) and four parts (*FSM*, No. 35, p. 54*; *FSC*, v. 1, p. 189). The beginning of greater complexity (*FSM*, No. 32, p. 47*; No. 34, p. 52*; *FSC*, v. 1, pp. 94, 181), extended syncopation (*FSM*, No. 53, p. 86*; *FSC*, v. 2, p. 7) and lengthy imitation (*FSM*, No. 54, p. 88*; *FSC*, v. 2, p. 83) may be noted.
    a.   **Solage**, a representative composer, anticipates the later style (*FSM*, Nos. 31-40, pp. 45*-64*; *FSC*, v. 1, pp. 179-200).

2.   *c.* 1370-1390: The music becomes extraordinarily complex rhythmically; long syncopated passages (*FSM*, No. 57, p. 94*; *FSC*, v. 1, p. 41; *FSM*, No. 59, p. 98*; *FSC*, v. 1, p. 48; *FSM*, No. 66, p. 108*; *FSC*, v. 1, p. 25); cross rhythms (*FSM*, No. 24, p. 33*; *FSC*, v. 1, p. 7). Examples of the augmented sixth (*FSM*, No. 46, p. 75*; *FSC*,

v. 1, p. 218), augmented fifth (*FSM*, No. 58, p. 96*; *FSC*, v. 1, p. 88), Neopolitan type (*FSM*, No. 33, p. 50*; *FSC*, v. 1, p. 179) chords. The third, and sometimes the sixth, are treated as consonant. The cadences II–I and III–I are frequent. Fauxbourdon (*FSM*, No. 7, p. 13*; No. 74, p. 126*; *FSC*, v. 1, p. 111; v. 3, p. 87).

    a.   Representative composers include **Anthonello de Caserta**   (*FSM*, Nos. 23-30, pp. 31*-44*; *FSC*, v. 1, pp. 3-16; *PMFC*, v. 10), **Trebor** (*FSM*, Nos. 41-46, pp. 65*-76*; *FSC*, v. 1, pp. 209-220) and **Jacob Senleches** (*FSM*, Nos. 47-51, pp. 77*-84*; *FSC*, v. 1, pp. 167-178).

   3.   *c*. 1390-1400: The music returns to a more lyrical, less complex style leading to the Burgundian School (*FSM*, No. 18, p. 26*; *FSC*, v. 1, p. 128; *FSM*, No. 20, p. 28*; *FSC*, v. 1, p. 122; *FSM*, No. 80, p. 132*; *FSC*, v. 3, p. 32). Use of imitation (*FSM*, No. 4, p. 7*; *FSC*, v. 1, p. 102); hocket (*FSM*, No. 71, p. 120*; *FSC*, v. 3, p. 38).

    a.   **Matheus de Perusio** (*FSC*, v. 1, pp. 96-133; *FSM*, Nos. 1-22, pp. 1*-30*), an Italian writing in the French style, is a representative composer. He also wrote in the complex style of the preceding period.

 B.   **Jacob Senleches** (a corruption of Sentluck [St. Luke]) [Jacopin Selesses] (late 14th century)

   1.   *En atendant* (While waiting) (*HAM*, No. 47; *FSM*, No. 49, p. 81*; *FSC*, v. 1, p. 167; *NPM*, p. 423, facsimile). This extremely rhythmical complex ballade is in the "mannered" style, that of the second period above.

 C.   **Baude Cordier** (*c*. 1400)

   1.   *Amans, ames* (Lovers Love) (*HAM*, No. 48a; *EFM*, v. 1, p. 7) is a rondeau with complex rhythms.

   2.   *Belle bonne* (Fair, good lady) (*HAM*, No. 48b; *EFM*, v. 1, p. 9; *NPM*, p. 427, facsimile in the shape of a heart)

    a.   The rondeau is progressive in the use of imitation, leading to the Burgundian School.

SELECTED BIBLIOGRAPHY

Books

1.   Hagopian, Viola L. *Italian Ars Nova Music; A Bibliographic Guide to Modern Editions and Related Literature.* Berkeley: University of California Press, 1964.

2.   Hoppin, Richard H. "Tonal Organization in Music before the Renaissance," in *Paul A. Pisk. Essays in His Honor*, ed. John Glowacki, pp. 25-37. Austin: University of Texas, 1966.

3.   Levarie, Siegmund. *Guillaume de Machaut*, ed. John J. Becker. New York: Sheed and Ward, 1954; reprint: New York: Da Capo Press, 1954.

4.   Machabey, Armand. *Guilaume de Machault: La vie et l'oeuvre*, 2 vols. Paris: Richard-Masse, 1955.

5.   *Machaut's World: Science and Art in the Fourteenth Century*, eds. Madeleine Pelner Cosman and Bruce Chandler. New York: New York Academy of Sciences, 1978.

6.   Mendel, Arthur. "Some Ambiguities of the Mensural System," in *Studies in Music History: Essays for Oliver Strunk*, ed. Harold Powers, pp. 137-160. Princeton: Princeton University Press, 1968.

7.   Reaney, Gilbert. *Guillaume De Machaut*. London: Oxford University Press, 1971.

8.   ————— "Notes on the Harmonic Technique of Guillaume de Machaut," in *Essays in Musicology: A Birthday Offering for Willi Apel*, ed. Hans Tischler, pp. 63-68. Bloomington: Indiana University School of Music, 1968.

9.   Salop, Arnold. "The Secular Polyphony of Guillaume Machaut," in *Studies in the History of Musical Style,* ed. Arnold Salop, pp. 39-80. Detroit: Wayne State University Press, 1971.

10.   Vitry, Philippe de. *Ars Nova*, eds. Gilbert Reaney, Jean Maillard, André Gilles. Rome: American Institute of Musicology, 1964. (*CSM*, v. 8)

11.   ————*Ars Nova*, in *Scriptorum de Musica Medii Aevi, Nova series*, ed. Edmond de Coussemaker, v. 3, pp. 13-22. Hildesheim: Georg Olm Verlagsbuchhandlung, 1963.

12.   ————*Ars Nova*, tr. Leon Plantinga. *Journal of Music Theory* 5 (1961), pp. 204-223.

Articles

1.   Apel, Willi. "Rondeaux, Virelais, and Ballades in French 13th-Century Song." *JAMS* 7 (1954), pp. 121-130.

2.   Cape, Safford. "The Machaut Mass and Its Performance." *Score* 25 (1959), pp. 38-57; 26 (1960), pp. 20-29.

3.   Fallows, David. "Guillaume de Machaut and the Lai." *Early Music* 5 (1977), pp. 477-483.

4.   Ficker, Rudolf von. "Polyphonic Music of the Gothic Period." *MQ* 15 (1929), pp. 483-505.

5.   Gilles, André, and Gilbert Reaney. "A New Source for the *Ars Nova* of Philippe de Vitry." *MD* 12 (1958), pp. 59-66.

6.   Gombosi, Otto. "Machaut's *Messe Notre Dame*." *MQ* 36 (1950), pp. 204-224.

7.   Günther, Ursula. "The 14th-Century Motet and its Development." *MD* 12 (1958), pp. 27-58.

8.   Harbinson, Denis. "Isorhythmic Technique in the Early Motet." *ML* 47 (1966), pp. 100-109.

9.   Harden, Jean. " 'Musica Ficta' in Machaut." *Early Music* 5 (1977), pp. 473-477.

10,   Harrison, Frank Llewelyn. "Ars Nova in England; A New Source." *MD* 21 (1967), pp. 67-85.

11.   Hasselman, Margaret, and Thomas Walker. "More Hidden Polyphony in a Machaut Manuscript." *MD* 24 (1970), pp. 7-16.

12.   Hoppin, Richard H. "Notational Licenses of Guillaume de Machaut." *MD* 14 (1960), pp. 13-27.

13.   ————"An Unrecognized Polyphonic Lai of Machaut." *MD* 12 (1958), pp. 93-104.

14.   Jackson, Roland. "Musical Interrelations between 14th Century Mass Movements (A Preliminary Study)." *ActaM* 29 (1957), pp. 54-64.

15.   Keitel, Elizabeth A. "The Musical Manuscripts of Guillaume de Machaut." *Early Music* 5 (1977), pp. 469-472.

16.   Page, Christopher. "Machaut's 'Pupil' Deschamps on the Performance of Music: Voices or Instruments in the 14th-Century Chanson?" *Early Music* 5 (1977), pp. 484-491.

17.   Perle, George. "Integrative Devices in the Music of Machaut." *MQ* 34 (1948), pp. 169-176.

18.   Plantinga, Leon. "Philippe de Vitry's *Ars Nova*: a Translation." *J Mus Theory* 5 (1961), pp. 204-223.

19.   Gilbert, Reaney, André Gillis, Jean Maillard. "The 'Ars Nova' of Philippe de Vitry." *MD* 10 (1956), pp. 35-53; 11 (1957), pp. 12-30.

20.   Reaney, Gilbert. "A Chronology of the Ballades, Rondeaux and Virelais set to Music by Guillaume de Machaut." *MD* 6 (1952), pp. 33-38.

21.   ————"Concerning the Origins of the Rondeau, Virelai and Ballade Forms." *MD* 6 (1952), pp. 155-166.

22.   ————"Fourteenth Century Harmony and the Ballades, Rondeaux and Virelais of Guillaume de Machaut." *MD* 7 (1953), pp. 129-146.

23.   ————"Guillaume de Machaut, Lyric Poet." *ML* 39 (1958), pp. 343-346.

24.   ————"Machaut's Influence on Late Medieval Music." *The Monthly Musical Record* 88 (1958), pp. 50-58, 96-101.

25.   ————"New Sources of Ars Nova Music." *MD* 19 (1965), pp. 53-67.

26.   ————"The Poetic Form of Machaut's Musical Works." *MD* 13 (1959), pp. 25-41.

27.   Reaney, Gilbert. "A Postscript to Philippe de Vitry's *Ars Nova*." *MD* 14 (1960), pp. 29-33.
28.   ———"The 'Roman de Fauvel' and Its Music." *The Monthly Musical Record* 89 (1959), pp. 99-103.
29.   ———"Towards a Chronology of Machaut's Musical Work." *MD* 21 (1967), pp. 87-96.
30.   Sachs, Curt. "Some Remarks about Old Notation." *MQ* 34 (1948), pp. 365-370.
31.   Sanders, Ernest H. "The Early Motets of Philippe de Vitry." *JAMS* 28 (1975), pp. 24-45.
32.   Schrade, Leo. "A Fourteenth-Century Parody Mass." *ActaM* 27 (1955), pp. 13-39.
33.   ———"The Mass of Toulouse." *Revue belge de musicologie* 8 (1954), pp. 84-96.
34.   ———"Philippe de Vitry: Some New Discoveries." *MQ* 42 (1956), pp. 330-354.
35.   Smith, F. Joseph. "Ars Nova—a Re-definition? " *MD* 18 (1964), pp. 19-35; 19 (1965), pp. 83-97.
36.   Smits van Waesberghe, Joseph. "Some Music Treatises and Their Interrelations. A School of Liége (c. 1050-1200)? " *MD* 3 (1949), pp. 95-118.
37.   Werner, Eric. "The Mathematical Foundation of Philippe de Vitri's *Ars Nova*." *JAMS* 9 (1956), pp. 128-132.
38.   Williams, Sarah Jane. "Vocal Scoring in the Chansons of Machaut." *JAMS* 21 (1968), pp. 251-257.

Music

1.   *Die Altfranzösische Rotrouenge*, ed. Friedrich Gennrich. Halle: Max Niemeyer, 1925.
2.   *Apt, Bibliothèque Capitulaire, Ms. 16 bis*. New York: Broude Brothers. (*MMF*, Ser. 3, v. 3)
3.   *Cent motets du XIIIe siècle*, 3 vols., ed. Pierre Aubry. Paris: A. Rouart, Lerolle & Co., 1908.
4.   *Early Fifteenth-Century Music*, 6 vols., ed. Gilbert Reaney. Rome: American Institute of Musicology. (*CMM*, 11)
5.   *Fourteenth Century Mass Music in France*, ed. Hanna Stäblein-Harder. Rome: American Institute of Musicology. (*CMM*, Ser. 29; *MSD*, v. 7)
6.   *A 14th Century Repertory from the Codex Reina*, ed. Nigel E. Wilkins. Rome: American Institute of Musicology, 1966.
7.   *French Secular Compositions of the Fourteenth Century*, 3 vols., ed. Willi Apel. Rome: American Institute of Musicology, 1970. (*CMM*, 53, vols. 1-3)
8.   *French Secular Music in the Late Fourteenth Century*. Cambridge, MA: Mediaeval Academy of America, 1950.
9.   Jehannot de L'Escurel. *Balades, Rondeaux et Diz entez sus Refroiz de Rondeaux*, ed. Friedrich Gennrich. Langen bei Frankfurt: Gennrich, 1964. (*SMMA*, v. 13)
10.   Jehan du Lescurel. *The Works of Jehan de Lescurel*, ed. Nigel E. Wilkins. Rome: American Institute of Musicology, 1966. (*CMM*, 30)
11.   *La Louanges des dames*, ed. Nigel E. Wilkins. New York: Barnes & Noble, 1973.
12.   Guillaume de Machaut
    a.   (*CE*) *Musikalische Werke*, 4 vols., ed. Friedrich Ludwig. Leipzig: Breitkopf & Härtel, 1926-1928.
    b.   (*MOC*) *Guillaume de Machaut Oeuvres Complètes*, 7 vols., transc. Sylvette Leguy. Paris: Le Droict Chemin de Musique, 1977.
    c.   *The Works of Guillaume de Machaut*, ed. Leo Schrade. (*PMFC*, vols. 2, 3)
    d.   *La Messe de Nostre-Dame*, ed. Friedrich Gennrich. Frankfurt: Langen, 1957. (*SMMA*, v. 1, facsimile)
    e.   *La Messe de Nostre-Dame*, ed. Guillaume de Van. Rome: American Institute of Musicology, 1949. (*CMM*, Ser. 2)

13.   *Le Manuscrit de Bayeux (Texte et Musique d'un recueil de Chansons de XVe Siècle)*, ed. Théodore Gérold. New York: Columbia University Press, 1921.

14.   *Le Manuscrit de musique polyphonique de Trésor d'Apt*, ed. Amédée Gastoué. Paris: La Société Française de Musicologie, 1936. (*MMA*, v. 10)

15.   Masses of Tournai, of Toulouse and of Barcelona, ed. Leo Schrade, in *Polyphonic Music of the Fourteenth Century*, v. 1. Monaco: Éditions de L'Oiseau-Lyre, 1959.

16.   *A Medieval Motet Book: A Collection of 13th-Century Motets*, ed. Hans Tischler. New York: Associated Music Publishers, 1973.

17.   *Mélanges de Musicologie Critique*, 4 vols., ed. Pierre Aubry. Paris: H. Welter, 1900-1905.
     I.   *Le Musicologie Médiévale*
     II.   *Les Proses d'Adam de Saint-Victor* (text and music)
     III.   *Lais et Descorts Français du XIIIe Siècle*
     IV.   *Les Plus Anciens Monuments de la Musique Française*

18.   *Music in Medieval and Renaissance Life: Anthology of Vocal and Instrumental Music, 1200-1614*, ed. Andrew C. Minor. Columbia: University of Missouri Press, 1964.

19.   *One Hundred Ballades, Rondeaux and Virelais from the Late Middle Ages*, ed. Nigel E. Wilkins. London: Cambridge University Press, 1969.

20.   *Les plus anciens monuments de la musique française*, ed. Pierre Aubry. Paris: H. Welter, 1905.

21.   *Polyphonic Music of the Fourteenth Century*, 14 vols., ed. Kurt von Fischer. Monaco: Éditions de L'Oiseau-Lyre, 1959.

22.   *Le Roman de Fauvel*, ed. Pierre Aubry. Paris: H. Welter, 1907. (facsimile)

23.   *Le Roman de Fauvel*, ed. Leo Schrade, in *Polyphonic Music of the Fourteenth Century*, v. 1. Monaco: Éditions de L'Oiseau-Lyre, 1959.

24.   Vitry, Philippe de. *Motets*, ed. Leo Schrade, in *Polyphonic Music of the Fourteenth Century*, v. 1. Monaco: Éditions de L'Oiseau-Lyre, 1959.

25.   Vitry, Philippe de. Some works in *Trienter Codices VI*, ed. Rudolf von Ficker. (*DTÖ*, v. 76)

10.   Dufay and Binchois from
Martin le Franc's poem
Le Champion des dames (1441-1442)

OUTLINE VIII

ITALIAN MUSIC OF THE FOURTEENTH CENTURY

Polyphony of the Trecento (1325-1425)
Composers – Music and Social Life – Secular Forms
Technical Features of Trecento Music – Instrumental Music

I. **Polyphony of the Trecento (1325-1425)**

A. The influence of Troubadour melodies caused a continued interest in monophonic songs and a development of Italian secular polyphony. The earliest surviving Italian treatise on polyphonic music is by **Marchetus de Padua**, *Pomerium artis musicae mensuratae* (Orchard-Garden of the Art of Measured Music) (*c.* 1325), which deals with Italian notation and rhythm. The general style is more florid than the contemporary French and anticipates the Renaissance style. There are no known composers of Italian polyphony before 1300. Sacred polyphony found little interest for the *trecento* composer, although most composers wrote some.

B. The secular forms evolved from the conductus in that one text was common to all parts. The French motet style with several texts and a *cantus firmus* tenor was abandoned. Duple time was common.

C. The principal melody is in the upper part (*superius*); it is frequently ornamented and varied rhythmically. The tenor part is the simplest, although there are more skips when it is without a text. The contratenor (between the *superius* and the tenor) serves as a harmonic complement to the other parts.

D. The principal forms of secular polyphonic music include the madrigal, caccia and ballata.

E. *Trecento* music
  1. *Rossi Codex* (Vatican, Codex 215) (*MFCI*, v. 2, pp. 15-45; *MLMI*, Ser. III, v. 2)
    a. Thirty-seven pieces are included in this codex; no composers are identified. However, later manuscripts do confirm two composers: **Giovanni da Firenze** and **Piero**, each with two pieces.
    b. The secular polyphonic songs make use of three forms: madrigal (29), ballata (5) and cacce (2). One Italian rondeau is included.
  2. *Squarcialupi Codex* (*B* 15)
    a. The codex is named for its first owner, **Antonio Squarcialupi** (1417-1480), a famous Florentine organist. This, the largest collection of *trecento* music, contains 352 compositions, mostly two- and three-part pieces. It includes 145 compositions by Francesco Landini and works of twelve other composers.

F. Notation
  1. Italian notation, a parallel development with the French, appears to have a common background with the early French.
  2. The use of the "point of division" gives 2, 3, 4, 5, 6 or 7 semibreves the value of one breve. The breve may also be divided into three equal parts and subdivided into 6, 9 or 12, or divided into 4, 6 or 8 parts.

II. **Composers**

A. The period of the *trecento* composers, which in fact extends into the first two decades of the fifteenth century, may be divided into three generations.
  1. The first group of composers include **Maestro Piero** (*MFCI*, v. 2, pp. 1-15; *PMFC*, v.

6, pp. 2-21), **Giovanni da Firenze [Johannes de Florentia, Giovanni da Cascia]** (*PMFC*, v. 6, pp. 22-79; *TEM*, p. 79), **Vincenzo d'Arimini** (*PMFC*, v. 7, pp. 1-26; *FCIC*, p. 57; *MFCI*, v. 4, pp. 43-52) and **Jacopo da Bologna [Jacobus de Boninia]** (*PMFC*, v. 6, pp. 80-169; *MFCI*, v. 4, pp. 1-43), the teacher of **Landini**. These were all connected with ruling families in the northern Italian cities of Padua, Verona and Milan.

    a.   Characteristics of their style include singing the texts simultaneously in both voices. Occasional points of imitation occur but return to the simultaneous style during the phrase or line. The madrigal was the predominate form used.

    b.   **Jacopo Bologna**

       1)   Of his 34 pieces, 24 are two-voice madrigals and five are three-voice madrigals including one tritextual madrigal. In addition there are three *cacce* and only two sacred pieces.

  2.   The composers of the second generation located principally in Florence: **Gherardello da Firenze** (*PMFC*, v. 7, pp. 75-119; *MFCI*, v. 1, pp. 53-80), **Lorenzo (Masini) da Firenze** (*PMFC*, v. 7, pp. 120-173; *MFCI*, v. 3, pp. 1-21), **Donata da Firenze (da Cascia)** (*PMFC*, v. 7, pp. 30-74; *MFCI*, v. 3, pp. 23-42) and the great **Francesco Landini**.

    a.   Concerning their style often called "manneristic," melismas became excessively long and the voices achieved a greater independence. Frequent points of imitation prevent the simultaneous rendering of the text. Syncopation, conflicting rhythms and unusual rhythmic combinations show considerable complexity.

    b.   **Gherardello da Firenze** (d. *c.* 1363) wrote 10 two-part madrigals, five monophonic ballatas and one caccia.

    c.   **Lorenzo da Firenze** (*fl.* 1350-1370), a Priest, wrote the same number of compositions as **Gherardello**.

    d.   **Francesco Landini** (1325-September 2, 1397)

       1)   Blinded by smallpox in childhood, Landini turned to music and became a skillful performer on many instruments, including the organ. His compositions include 11 madrigals (two are in three voices) and 141 ballatas (91 in two voices).

          a)   The three-voice ballatas appear with the text in one, two or all three voices, with the remaining voices played on instruments.

  3.   The third generation of Italian *ars nova* composers flourished during the last of the fourteenth and early fifteenth centuries. They include **Niccolo de Perugia** (*PMFC*, v. 8, pp. 101-200), **Bartolino da Padova** (*PMFC*, v. 9. pp. 1-93), **Andrea da Firenze** (*PMFC*, v. 10, pp. 1-50), **Paolo Tenorista da Firenze** (*PMFC*, v. 9, pp. 102-191), **Matteo da Perugia** (*PMFC*, v. 10, pp. 95-100) and **Johannes Ciconia**, a Belgian who spent considerable time in Italy. By far the majority of these composers' works were devoted to the ballata; the madrigal is of less importance.

    a.   Characteristics of their style show restraint; the melismas are not so long nor virtuosic. There is some use of "text painting" to suggest bird calls, dramatic effects and unusual emphasis of the text.

III.   Music and Social Life

  A.   There developed a wide interest in art, letters and music, especially in Florence.

    1.   Giovanni Boccaccio (1313-1375) refers to music in his *Decameron*.

      a.   After the telling of ten stories each evening by members of a party brought together in Florence to avoid the plague of 1348, instruments were brought out and songs were sung.

  B.   Art music was represented by polyphonic compositions.

    1.   **Landini** in a madrigal text (*PMFC*, v. 4, p. 213; *B* 8b, p. 26; *B* 15, p. 197) wrote, "I am Music, who weeping regret to see intelligent people forsaking my sweet and perfect sounds for street-songs."

C. Popular music
1. Street songs developed into the *frottola, strambatta* and *villanella* of the late fifteenth century; these in turn furnished the basis for sixteenth century madrigals.

IV. Secular Forms

A. Madrigal (from *matricale*—in mother tongue)
1. The madrigal was the most popular form with the early group of *trecento* composers: **Jacopo da Bologna, Giovanni da Cascia. Landini** wrote only 12 examples of the madrigal: nine in two parts, three in three parts.
2. Form
   a. The texts consist of two or three stanzas (*terzetti*) of three lines each and a *ritornello* of two lines (not a repeating refrain). The texts are serious, expressive and varied, from moralizing to amorous, and at times satirical. The rhyme scheme of the stanza is usually a b b.
   b. All the stanzas are sung through to the same music (a) and the concluding *ritornello* is sung to new music (b) in a contrasting rhythm.
      1. Eight-line madrigal: a a b; eleven-line madrigal: a a a b.
3. Characteristic features
   a. The text is sung by both voices in two-part polyphony. Considerable alternations of melismas and almost syllabic style occur. The parts remain independent; rarely do they cross. The French motet style is rare.
   b. Octaves, fifths and unisons in parallel motion are common. The cadence generally progresses from a third to a unison.
   c. Some use of imitation appears (*GEx*, p. 99), as well as two- and three-part canon (*GEx*, p. 108); occasional use of triads; repetition of the tenor melody occurs in the style of a ground bass (*GEx*, p. 113).
4. **Giovanni da Firenze:** *Nel mezzo a sei paon* (In the midst of six peacocks) (*HAM*, No. 50; *PMFC*, v. 6, p. 48; *MFCI*, v. 1, p. 24; *B* 15, p. 9)
5. **Jacopo Bologna**
   a. *Non al suo amante* (Not her lover) (*HAM*, No. 49; *PMFC*, v. 6, p. 114; *MFCI*, v. 4, p. 15; *B* 15, p. 23)
   b. *Fenice fu'* (I was a phoenix) (*GEx*, p. 99; *PMFC*, v. 6, p. 90; *MFCI*, v. 4, p. 6; *B* 15, p. 35; *B* 10, p. 40; *SSMS*, p. 50)
   c. *Aquila altera* (Lofty eagles), tritextual (*OMM*, p. 171; *PMFC*, v. 6, p. 80; *AM*, v. 9, p. 50; *MFCI*, v. 4, p. 1; *B* 15, p. 19; *B* 10, p. 31)
6. **Lorenzo da Firenze**
   a. *Dà, dà, a chi avareggia* (Give, give to him who hoards) (*MFCI*, v. 3, p. 3; *PMFC*, v. 7, p. 29; *AMM*, No. 65; *B* 15, p. 87)
   b. *Povero çappator* (A poor tiller), isorhythmic madrigal (*OMM*, p. 178; *PMFC*, v. 7, p. 160; *MFCI*, v. 3, p. 12; *B* 15, p. 95)
7. **Francesco Landini**
   a. *Una conlonba candid'e gentile* (*GEx*, p. 106; *PMFC*, v. 4, p. 208; *B* 15, p. 215; *B* 8b, p. 19)
   b. *Fa metter bando* (Let it be proclaimed) (*OMM*, p. 176; *PMFC*, v. 4, p. 192; *B* 15, p. 200; *B* 8b, p. 3)
   c. *De! dinmi tu che*, canonic madrigal (*GEx*, p. 108; *PMFC*, v. 4, p. 216; *FCIC*, p. 37; *B* 15, p. 206; *B* 8b, p. 22)
   d. *Si dolce* (So sweetly) (*HAM*, No. 54; *GEx*, p. 113; *PMFC*, v. 4, p. 210; *B* 15, p. 201; *B* 8b, p. 31)
8. Anonymous: *E con chaval* (Count Hugo riding along the road) (*OMM*, p. 170; *PMFC*, v. 8, p. 28)

B.   Caccia   (*B* 4)
1.   The caccia possibly developed from the older French *chace*, a two-part canon, or the canonic madrigal.
2.   The most common subject of the texts is hunting, but included also are the subjects of love, fire, sailing, fishing scenes, rural scenes and market scenes with street cries.
3.   Form
   a.   The caccia is divided into two sections.
     1)   The first section is a strict canon in unison between the two upper parts at a distance of eight or more measures. Triple canon also appears.
     2)   The second and shorter section is a *ritornello*, usually in canon between the two upper parts or with points of less strict imitation.
     3)   In some cases the *ritornello* may be deleted and the parts may not appear in canon.
4.   Characteristic features
   a.   These include the free instrumental tenor part in longer notes; strong rhythms; use of hocket; text painting (imitation of hunting horns, cries, *etc.*).
5.   **Gherardello da Firenze:**   *Tosto che l'alba* (As soon as the dawn appears) (*GEx*, p. 101; *HAM*, No. 52; *PMFC*, v. 7, p. 109; *B* 4, p. 93, Plate I; *B* 15, p. 47; *MSO*, v. 1, p. 28)
6.   **Niccolo da Perugia:**   *Dappoi che'l sole* (The sun was hiding) (*OMM*, p. 180; *AMM*, No. 66; *PMFC*, v. 8, p. 117; *B* 4, p. 30)
7.   **Francisco Landini:**   *Chosi pensoso chom' amor mi ghuida* (*PMFC*, v. 4, p. 219; *B* 4, p. 25; *B* 8b, p. 35; *SSMS*, p. 52)

C.   Ballata
1.   The ballata became the most important secular polyphonic form of the 14th-century Italian composers.
2.   Form
   a.   The ballata is derived from the French *virelai (chanson balladée)*. Originally it was a song for round dances performed by a whole group (refrain, *ripresa*) and a soloist, each part essentially being the same length.
   b.   The poem is of one to three stanzas, each with six lines, preceded and followed by the refrain.
   c.   The music follows the plan: A bba A; open (*aperto*) and closed (*chiuso*) endings are used.
3.   Characteristic features
   a.   French polyphony combined with Italian melody; changes of meter; meters used: 3/1, 4/2, 6/4, 3/2, 9/4, 2/2; the style varies from simple to florid; use of syncopation at the end of the sections; hocket. Texts are sometimes missing in the lower parts.
4.   **Giovanni da Firenze:**   *Io son un pellegrin* (I am a pilgrim) (*HAM*, No. 51)
5.   Anonymous: *Amor mi fa cantar* (Love makes me sing) (*OMM*, p. 169; *PMFC*, v. 11, p. 8); *Medee fu* (Medea was true) (*AMM*, No. 68; *FSC*, v. 2, p. 78; *MFCI*, v. 2, p. 36)
6.   **Francesco Landini** (*AM*, v. 11, p. 12; *MM*, p. 40; *MSO*, v. 1, p. 27)
   a.   *Amor c'al tuo suggetto* (Love to thy subject) (*HAM*, No. 53; *PMFC*, v. 4, p. 183; *B* 15, p. 241; *B* 8b, p. 174)
   b.   *Questa fanciull' amor* (This girl, love) (*AMM*, No. 67; *PMFC*, v. 4, p. 116; *B* 15, p. 234; *B* 8b, p. 285)
   c.   *L'alma mia piange* (My soul weeps) (*OMM*, p. 174; *PMFC*, v. 4, p. 148; *B* 15, p. 219; *B* 8b, p. 232)
   d.   *Angelica biltà* (Angelic beauty) (*GEx*, p. 103; *PMFC*, v. 4, p. 54; *B* 15, p. 204; *B* 8b, p. 48; *GMB*, No. 23)
   e.   *Gram piant' agli ochi* (*GEx*, p. 104; *PMFC*, v. 4, p. 128; *B* 15, p. 224; *B* 8b, p. 222)
7.   **Johannes Ciconia**
   a.   *Con lagrime bagnando me* (With tears bathing my face) (*AMM*, No. 70)

    b.   *Sus une fontayne* (Under a spring) (*OMM*, p. 166), a virelai in "mannered" style.

V.   Technical Features of Trecento Music

A.   Parallel motion is used in moderation.
1.   Unison, fifth, octave, third and rarely the fourth; passing tones used to avoid parallelisms; use of progressions of sixth chords to prolong the time between dissonances and their resolutions.
B.   Dissonances
1.   Triads of two superimposed thirds, also called imperfect consonances, may be major, minor, augmented or diminished. Seconds, fourths and sevenths are used as passing tones. In the **Landini** works (*B* 8b) the second section of No. 106 begins with a dissonance.
C.   Consonances
1.   Unisons, fifths, octaves
    a.   The consonance progresses to the dissonance of a third or triad of two thirds and then returns to the consonance.
2.   There is a strong feeling of tonality in melodic lines in two-part music and, with the development of three-part writing (after 1350), in triads.
3.   The "Landini sixth" (sixth note of the scale) was not invented by **Landini** but was used by all the *Ars nova* composers.
4.   The types of cadences include contrary motion in the outer parts; the root is approached from the tone above; the fifth is approached from a tone or semitone below; the octave is approached from the first or second tone below.
D.   Chromatic notes
1.   C-sharp, F-sharp, G-sharp, B-flat, E-flat and one A-flat are used in the **Landini** works.
2.   B-flat is used in the signature, and E-flat is only rarely used.
E.   Conflicting signatures
1.   Conflicting signatures are used in about one-fifth of **Landini's** music. Often it is an expressive device to create tension between the downward leading B-flat and upward leading B-natural. They are also used to bring out the structure of the music, especially at the cadence. Accidentals in the following **Landini** works (*B* 8b) are read from the top voice downward.
    a.   ♮ (upper voice), ♭ (tenor), pp. 15, 19, 44, 97, 132, 165, 249.
    b.   ♭ (upper voice),   ♮ (tenor), pp. 48, 49, 51, 52, 56, 60, 70, 80, 86, 140, 149, 155.
    c.   ♮ ♮ ♭ , pp. 22, 31, 171, 183, 212, 222, 252.
                                                                d.   ♮ ♭ ♭ p. 229.
    e.   ♭ ♮ ♭ , pp. 202, 249.

VI.   Instrumental Music

A.   Instruments are often pictured in illuminations, on tombstones or described in poems. Included is the *organetto* (14th-century portative organ), psaltery, *viele*, lute and flute. **Landini** was especially famous for his organ playing, but was skilled on many instruments.
B.   Vocal pieces were performed in various ways, with and without instruments. Many pieces are without texts in one or more of the parts. Frequent use of ligatures, lack of texts, wide skips and low range, all found in contratenor and tenor parts, indicate the possibility of the use of instruments. Some of the florid *superius* parts are suitable also for the *organetto* or flute.
C.   Keyboard music
1.   *Estampie* (*HAM*, No. 58)
    a.   The *Robertsbridge Codex* (*c.* 1325), the earliest extant example of keyboard notation and the source of this example, contains dances in Italian style.

   D.   Dance music
1.   The principal instrumental forms are dance music: the *estampie* (*istampita*) and *saltarello*. The *estampie* is mentioned by Boccaccio in his *Decameron* as instrumental music evidently to be listened to rather than to accompany the actual dance.
2.   *Lamento di Tristan* (*HAM*, No. 59a)
    a.   The monophonic dance, an *estampie*, was probably performed on *vieles*. The first section in triple meter (main dance) is made up of three parts (*puncta*), each with first and second endings. The second section in duple meter (*rotta* or after dance) is also in three parts, each with first and second endings. The melodic material of the *rotta* is based on the first section.
3.   *Chominciamento di gioia* (The beginning of joy) (*OMM*, p. 196)
    a. This *estampie* is in five parts, each repeated with open and closed endings.
4.   *Saltarello* in five parts (*OMM*, p. 198)
    a.   The *saltarello* is a sprightly dance with skips and leaps in the repeated phrase form of the *estampie*.
5.   *Estampie* in four parts (*HAM*, No. 59b)
6.   *La Manfredina* (*GMB*, No. 28)

SELECTED BIBLIOGRAPHY

Books and Music

1.   Boccaccio, Giovanni. *Decameron*, tr. Mark Musa and Peter E. Bondanella. New York: W. W. Norton, 1977; tr. Richard Aldington. Garden City, NY: Garden City Publishing Co., 1930.
2.   *Il Canzioniere Musicale del Codice Vaticano Rossi 215*, ed. Giuseppe Vecchi. Bologna, 1966. (*Monumenta Lyrica Medii Aevi Italica*, Ser. III, *Mensurabilia*, v. 2)
3.   Ellinwood, Leonard. *The Works of Francesco Landini*, 2nd ed. Cambridge, MA: The Mediaeval Academy of America, 1945; reprint: New York: Kraus Reprint Co., 1970.
4.   *Fourteenth-Century Italian Cacce*, 2nd ed., ed. W. Thomas Marrocco. Cambridge, MA: The Mediaeval Academy of America, 1961.
5.   *French Secular Compositions of the Fourteenth Century*, 3 vols., ed. Willi Apel. Rome: American Institute of Musicology, 1970. (*CMM*, 53, vols. 1-3)
6.   *French Secular Music in the Late Fourteenth Century*. Cambridge, MA: The Mediaeval Academy of America, 1950.
7.   Hagopian, Viola L. *Italian Ars Nova: A Bibliographic Guide to Modern Editions and Related Literature*, 2nd rev. ed. Berkeley: University of California Press, 1973.
8.   Landini, Francesco
    a. *Works. Polyphonic Music of the Fourteenth Century*, v. 4.
    b. *The Works of Francesco Landini*, ed. Leonard Ellinwood. Cambridge, MA: The Mediaeval Academy of America, 1945; reprint: New York: Krause Reprint Co., 1970.
9.   Marrocco, W. Thomas. "Integrative Devices in the Music of the Italian 'Trecento'," in *L'Ars nova italiana del trecento III: Secondo convegno internazionale, 1969*, pp. 411-429. Certaldo, 1970.
10.   ––––––*The Music of Jacopo da Bologna*. Berkeley: University of California Press, 1954.
11.   *Monumenta lyrica medii aevi Italica*, Ser. III, *Mensurabilia*. Bologna, 1966-
12.   *The Music of Fourteenth Century Italy*, ed. Nino Pirrotta, 5 vols. Amsterdam: American Institute of Musicology, 1954-1964. (*CMM*, 8)
13.   Pirrotta, Nino. *Paola Tenorista*. Palm Springs, CA: E. E. Gottlieb, 1961.
14.   *Polyphonic Music of the Fourteenth Century*, 14 vols., ed. Kurt von Fischer. Monaco: Éditions de L'Oiseau-Lyre, 1959.

15. *Der Squarcialupi Codex*, ed. Johannes Wolf. Lippstadt: Kistner & Siegel, 1955.
16. Streatfield, Richard Alexander. *Masters of Italian Music*. London: Osgood, McIlvanio & Co., 1895.
17. Wolf, Johannes. *Geschichte der Mensural-Notation von 1250-1460*, 3 vols. Leipzig: Breitkopf & Härtel, 1904; reprint: Hildesheim, Georg Olms Verlag, 1965.
18. –––––––*Handbuch der Notationskunde*, 2 vols. Leipzig: Breitkopf & Härtel, 1913-1919.

Articles

1. Apel, Willi. "The Partial Signatures in the Sources up to 1450." *ActaM* 10 (1938), pp. 1-13; 11 (1939), pp. 40-42.
2. Bowles, Edmund A. "Haut and Bas: The Grouping of Musical Instruments in the Middle Ages." *MD* 8 (1954), pp. 115-140.
3. Brown, Samuel E. "A Possible Cantus Firmus among Ciconia's Isorhythmic Motets." *JAMS* 12 (1959), pp. 7-15.
4. Caldwell, John. "The Organ in the Medieval Latin Liturgy, 800-1500." *PMA* 93 (1966-1967), pp. 11-24.
5. Carapetyan, Armen. "A Fourteenth-Century Florentine Treatise in the Vernacular." *MD* 4 (1950), pp. 81-92.
6. Ellinwood, Leonard. "Francesco Landini and His Music." *MQ* 22 (1936), pp. 190-216.
7. –––––––"Origins of the Italian Ars Nova." *PAMS* (1937), pp. 29-37.
8. Fenlon, Iain, and James Haar. "A New Source for the Early Madrigal." *JAMS* 33 (1980), pp. 164-180.
9. Ficker, Rudolf von. "Polyphonic Music of the Gothic Period." *MQ* 15 (1929), pp. 483-505.
10. Fischer, Kurt von. "On the Technique, Origin, and Evolution of Italian Trecento Music." *MQ* 47 (1961), pp. 41-57.
11. Hadaway, Robert. "The Re-creation of an Italian Renaissance Harp." *Early Music* 8 (1980), pp. 59-63.
12. Hughes, Andrew. "New Italian and English Sources of the Fourteenth to Sixteenth Centuries." *ActaM* 39 (1967), pp. 171-182.
13. Johnson, Martha. "A Study of Conflicting Key-Signatures in Francesco Landini's Music." *Hamline Studies in Musicology* 2 (1947), pp. 27-40.
14. Karp, Theodore. "The Textual Origin of a Piece of Trecento Polyphony." *JAMS* 20 (1967), pp. 469-473.
15. Lowinsky, Edward E. "Conflicting Views on Conflicting Signatures." *JAMS* 7 (1954), pp. 181-204.
16. Mace, Dean T. "Pietro Bembo and the Literary Origins of the Italian Madrigal." *MQ* 55 (1969), pp. 65-86.
17. Marrocco, W. Thomas. "The Ballata–a Metamorphic Form." *ActaM* 31 (1959), pp. 32-37.
18. Pirrotta, Nino. "Marchettus de Padua and the Italian Ars Nova." *MD* 9 (1955), pp. 60-71.
19. Schachter, Carl. "Landini's Treatment of Consonance and Dissonance: A Study in Fourteenth-Century Counterpoint." *The Music Forum* 2 (1970), pp. 130-186.
20. Stevens, Denis. "Ceremonial Music in Medieval Venice." *MT* 119 (1978), pp. 321-326.
21. Wolf, Johannes. "Italian Trecento Music." *PMA* 58 (1931), pp. 15-31.

OUTLINE IX

ENGLISH MUSIC FROM 1350 TO 1450

Sources for English Polyphonic Music (1350-1450)
Leonel Power – John Dunstable
Carols and Secular Songs

I. **Sources for English Polyphonic Music (1350-1450)**

A. *Early Bodleian Music* (*M* 4)
   1. Sir John Stainer edited this two volume collection designed to include all the non-liturgical music before 1500 in the Bodleian Library, Oxford. A third volume edited by Edward W. B. Nicholson contains 71 facsimile examples of writing in neumes before 1100. Volume I (transcriptions in Volume II) includes 100 pieces (carols, antiphons, secular songs) in two, three and four parts, dating mostly from 1400-1450. Only three composers are known: **Power, Dunstable** and **Childe**. (Refer to *B* 2)

B. *The Old Hall Manuscript* (*M* 8; *CMM*, 46, vols. 1-3; *B* 2, pp. 34-85)
   1. This important manuscript is called "Old Hall" because it was preserved in Old Hall of St. Edmund's College in Ware. It contains 148 compositions in three volumes. Most of the music was written during the lifetime of King Henry V (1397-1422). The manuscript was assembled about 1420. Volume III has important revisions of Volume I.
   2. It contains grouped settings of the Gloria (including four in canon), Credo, Sanctus and Agnus Dei. Motets and conductus-like pieces are inserted between these groups. Seventy-seven of the compositions are notated in score rather than in separate parts.
   3. Technical devices include division of voices (*OH*, v. 2, p. 8; *CMM*, 46, v. 1, p. 152); alternation of duet passages with four-part writing (*OH*, v. 1, p. 60; *CMM*, 46, v. 1, p. 40; *OH*, v. 2, p. 114; *CMM*, 46, v. 1, p. 210); two-part contrapuntal parts for soloists alternating with three-part sections for chorus (**Thomas Damett**, *Beata Dei genitrix*, *OH*, v. 1, p. 164; *CMM*, 46, v. 2, p. 45; *HAM*, No. 64).
   4. *Cantus firmus* pieces are mostly in conductus style (*OH*, v. 1, p. 156; v. 3, p. 76; *CMM*, 46, v. 1, pp. 138, 357); canonic writing (*OH*, v. 2, p. 101; *CMM*, 46, v. 1, p. 201); melody and accompaniment ("ballade") style (*OH*, v. 3, p. 66; *CMM*, 46, v. 1, p. 350); *ostinato* with upper voices using hocket, canon or short repeated phrases (*OH*, v. 1, p. 92; *CMM*, 46, v. 1, p. 78); *cantus firmus* may appear in different voices in succession (*OH*, v. 3, p. 4; *CMM*, 46, v. 1, p. 314).
   5. Full triads appear in four-part harmony (*OH*, v. 3, p. 76; *CMM*, 46, v. 1, p. 357); some chromaticism and rhythmic variety (*OH*, v. 3, p. 116; *CMM*, 46, v. 1, p. 389); six-four chords at cadences (*OH*, v. 2, p. 1; *CMM*, 46, v. 1, p. 147); frequent use of *gymel* technique (*OH*, v. 1, p. 159; *CMM*, 46, v. 1, p. 141); *fauxbourdon* is rare and there is occasional use of the tritone and augmented fifths.
   6. Isorhythm is frequently used in the upper parts as well as in the tenor (*OH*, v. 1, p. 92; *CMM*, 46, v. 1, p. 78); instruments were probably employed (*GMB*, No. 37).
   7. The notation is often complex (*OH*, v. 2, p. 167; *CMM*, 46, v. 1, p. 245); double coloration (red and blue notation); later compositions frequently use accidentals (*OH*, v. 3, p. 116; *CMM*, 46, v. 1, p. 389).
   8. Composers are conservative English musicians and include **John Cooke** (*fl.* 1402-1433), **John Tyes [Dyes]**, **Nicholas Sturgeon** (*c.* 1389-1454), **Thomas Damett** (*fl.* 1413-1436), **Gervays, Rowland [Rowlard]** (*fl.* 1409-1426), **William Typp[e]** (d. 1438), **Thomas Byttering** (*fl.* 1405-1408), **Pycard [Picart]**, **Leonel Power** (*fl.* 1423-1445), **John**

Forest (*fl.* 1394-1446) and **King Henry IV**, or possibly **Henry V**. The only piece by **John Dunstable** is an anonymous copy of his *Veni Sancte Spiritus* (*OH*, v. 2, p. 66; *CMM*, 46, v. 2, p. 66).

C.   *Seven Trent Codices* (*DTÖ*, vols. 14-15, 22, 38, 53, 61, 76)

1.   Six codices were originally owned by the Cathedral of Trent. In 1891 they were purchased by the Austrian Government and returned to Italy in 1920 as part of the reparations agreement at the end of World War I. The seventh codex was found in 1920.

2.   The original codices contain over 1600 pieces, sacred and secular, by about 75 French, German, Italian, English and Burgundian composers, dating from about 1420 to 1480. There are a number of settings of isolated Mass movements.

3.   English composers include **John Dunstable, Leonel Power, John Forest, Bedingham, Benet** (*NPM*, p. 105, facsimile), **Richard Markham** and others representing a progressive Continental School.

D.   *Egerton Manuscript 3307*, London (*c.* 1435) (*M* 5; *B* 2, pp. 113-175)

1.   The Meaux Abbey collection may be divided into two parts. The first part includes chiefly liturgical pieces for Holy Week, including hymns, versicles, a Missa Brevis (*M5*, pp. 50-54; *MQ* 33 (1947), pp. 39-42) (Gloria and Credo omitted as usual) and the two earliest known polyponic settings of the Passion: St. Matthew (*M5*, pp. 48-50) and St. Luke (*M5*, pp. 54-61; *MQ* 33 (1947), pp. 43-51). No polyphonic music was included for Good Friday. Part II (*MB*, v. 4, pp. 33-62) is made up of the Latin *cantilena* and its English counterpart, the carol.

II.   Leonel Power (d. 1445) (*CMM*, 50)

A.   **Leonel Power** is the first great name in English music. He was associated with Christ Church, Canterbury, from 1423 to his death. Of his 50 or so compositions, all sacred motets and Mass movements, 21 appear in the *Old Hall* manuscript and 30 in continental manuscripts.

1.   The motets may be grouped into three overlapping styles: 1) simple discant, note-against-note counterpoint, 2) "ballade" style in which the upper voice is prominent and 3) motet style in which all voices generally are equal and points of imitation occur.

2.   The compositions may be based on plainsong (*Ave regina coelorum, TECM*, v. 1, p. 110) or, as in his later works, may be completely original.

3.   Techniques include isorhythm and the practice of relating Mass movements by using the same plainsong tenor.

4.   *Sanctus* (*OH*, v. 3, p. 76; *CMM*, 46, v. 1, p. 357; *HAM*, No. 63)

   a.   This early example of four-part writing in discant style uses the plainsong from Mass XVII (*LU*, p. 61) in the tenor.

5.   *Missa super Alma redemptoris mater* (*DPL*, Ser. 1, a., v. 2)

   a.   A three-voice Mass, one of the earliest examples where each movement is based on the same melody in the tenor, the antiphon *Alma redemptoris mater* (*LU*, p. 273).

III.   John Dunstable (*c.* 1370-1453)

A.   **Dunstable**, famous as a mathematician and astronomer, was the outstanding musician of the English School. He was in the employ of John, Duke of Bedford, who was Regent of France (1422-1429) and governor of Normandie (1429-1435). It may be assumed that **Dunstable**, in the employ of the Duke of Bedford, spent time in Burgundy and exerted a strong influence on members of the Burgundian School, especially **Dufay**. **Dunstable** was in turn influenced by **Dufay**. However, the English School did not continue development; leadership passed to the Burgundian School.

B.   About 60 compositions are preserved in continental manuscripts and very few (four) in England.   **Joannes de Tinctoris** (*c.* 1446-1511) describes the influence of **Dunstable** as "the organizer of a new art" (*SR*, p. 195).

C.   The music is original, sonorous and full of melodic invention. Free ornamentation, smooth voice leading and melodies based on triads (*Sancta Maria, MB*, v. 8, p. 121; *DTÖ*, v. 14, p. 197; *HAM*, No. 62) are characteristics. There is an instinctive idea of chordal relationships growing out of chords grouped around the tonic and dominant which lead to functional (tertian) harmony.

D.   Types of motets
1.   English discant
  a.   **Dunstable** (possibly by **John Forest**), *Ascendit Christus* (*DTÖ*, v. 76, p. 53; *MB*, v. 8, p. 148; *CMM*, 46, v. 2, p. 77; *OH*, v. 2, p. xiv)
    1)   The three-voice selections use the melody of *Alma redemptoris mater* (*LU*, p. 273) in the tenor and alternate with two-part writing. Some six-three progressions may be noted.
2.   Ballade style: an original or unborrowed melody is used and the upper part is prominent.
  a.   **Dunstable**, *Sanctus* (*MB*, v. 8, p. 12)
3.   Gymel influence
  a.   Dunstable, *Crux fidelis* (*DTÖ*, v. 14, p. 183; *MB*, v. 8, p. 103; text, *LU*, p. 709)
4.   Isorhythmic motet
  a.   There are twelve examples by **Dunstable**, including four in four voices (*MB*, v. 8, pp. 58-94).
  b.   **Dunstable**, *Veni Sancte Spiritus* (*DTÖ*, v. 14, Plate 203; *OH*, v. 2, Plate 66; *MB*, v. 8, p. 92; *TEM*, p. 91; *TECM*, v. 1, p. 113; *NPM*, p. 124, facsimile of tenor; *RMMA*, p. 415, analysis; *B* 2, p. 63)
    1)   Texts
      a)   First voice: Sequence, *Veni Sancte Spiritus* (*LU*, p. 880)
      b)   Second voice: Trope on *Veni Sancte Spiritus*
      c)   Tenor: Hymn, *Veni Creator Spiritus*, the second and third phrases are used as a *cantus firmus* (*LU*, p. 885).
      d)   Contratenor: Hymn, *Veni Creator Spiritus* (except the last stanza)
    2)   Music
      a)   Considering the three sections, the tenor has two *taleae* (original statement and one rhythmic repetition) in each section. In the second section the time values are reduced one-third and in the third section they are reduced another third (9:6:3 or 3:2:1).
      b)   Isorhythm also appears in the contratenor and the top voice, but very little in the second voice.
5.   Borrowed melody in the top part, ornamented
  a.   **Dunstable**, *Ave Regina celorum* [*sic*] (*MB*, v. 8, p. 99; *DTÖ*, v. 76, p. 50); the text is one of the Antiphons B. V. M. (*LU*, p. 274).
6.   Declamation motet; conductus influence
  a.   The musical rhythm is governed by the rhythm of the spoken word. The equal importance of all parts develops a chordal structure.
  b.   **Dunstable**, *Quam pulchra es* (*MB*, v. 8, p. 112; *DTÖ*, vols. 14-15, p. 190; *TECM*, v. 1, p. 129; *GMB*, No. 34; *AM*, v. 47, p. 35; *SSMS*, p. 60)
    1)   The text is from the *Song of Songs*. (References to measures in the following are from *MB*, v. 8, p. 112)
    2)   Conductus style, except at the cadences. Declamation of the word *"Veni"* (meas. 31-32). The melody is in the upper part and there is frequent use of melodic seconds and thirds.
    3)   Harmonic devices: accented and unaccented passing tones (meas. 6, 36); neighboring tones (meas. 25, 28); escape tone (meas. 7, 14); anticipations (meas. 44); 7-6 and 4-3 suspensions (meas. 21, 42, 52); ornamented *fauxbourdon*, especially

at cadences (meas. 12-14); crossing of parts (meas. 11, 27); syncopation (meas. 21).

    4)   Cadences: the third of the chord is sometimes introduced after the beat (meas. 15); the seventh is softened by a neighboring tone (meas. 8-9); first inversion chord to the fundamental final chord (meas. 14-15); "Landini sixth" (final cadence, meas. 57).

  7.   Double structure

    a.   The motet may be built on two *cantus firmi*, one in the upper voice and one in the tenor, or on two structural elements.

    b.   **John Forest**, *Ascendit Christus* has a freely composed melodic upper voice with the Antiphon *Alma redemptoris* (*LU*, p. 273) in the tenor.

E. *O Rosa Bella* (*MB*, v. 8, p. 133; *DTÖ*, vols. 14-15, p. 229; *HAM*, No. 61)

  1.   A popular secular song to an Italian text. Two manuscripts have three new voices added to the original three-part piece. These can be performed in various ways including all nine parts.

IV. Carols and Secular Part-Songs

A. Carols

  1.   The earliest examples of music for carols date from the first half of the 15th century; they are in two and three parts, in triple meter and frequently move in parallel thirds and sixths reminiscent of earlier *gymel*.

    a.   The texts, many supplied by Franciscans, are generally religious or moralistic in character, in which fragments of religious verse are found.

  2.   Later carols show the influence of the Tudor motet style by adding polyphonic variety, pairing the voices and using duple meter.

  3.   *The merthe of alle this londe* (*MB*, v. 4, p. 112; *GMB*, No. 32a; *EBM*, v. 1, No. LXIX; v. 2, p. 132)

  4.   *Nowel syng we* (*SSMS*, p. 63)

B. *Deo gratias Anglia*, *c.* 1450 (*MB*, v. 4, p. 6; *GMB*, No. 32b; *EBM*, v. 1, No. LXVI; v. 2, p. 128)

  1.   This celebrates the victory of the English over the French at Agincourt in 1415.

    a.   There are three sections: 1) Latin text, two voices, two lines; 2) English text, two voices, six stanzas; 3) Latin text, three voices, repeat of the first two lines of text.

    b.   (The following measure numbers refer to those in *MB*, v. 4, p. 6). Escape tones (meas. 7, 8); appoggiatura (meas. 8); lower neighboring tone (meas. 9); upper neighboring tone (meas. 12); passing tone (meas. 24); 7-6 suspensions (meas. 13, 25).

C. Part-songs

  1.   *I have set my hert so hye* (*c.* 1425) (*EBM*, v. 1, Plate 20; v. 2, p. 51)

    a.   A two-part piece in conductus style. The phrases separated by textless passages suggest the use of instruments.

  2.   *Tappster fille another ale, dryngker* (*c.* 1450) (*EBM*, v. 1, Plate 96; v. 2, p. 177; *HAM*, No. 85)

    a.   A three-part drinking song with textless passages.

  3.   *Go hert [heart] hurt with adversite* (*c.* 1450) (*EBM*, v. 1, Plate 32; v. 2, p. 68)

    a.   This song in ballade style has the text in the upper voice only. Frequent sixths and thirds are used in the lower voices.

D. Chanson: **Dunstable**, *Puisque m'amour* (*GMB*, Nos. 35, 36; *MB*, v. 8, pp. 136, 137)

  1.   This anonymous arrangement for organ was made about 1460.

SELECTED BIBLIOGRAPHY

Books

1. Bukofzer, Manfred. *Geschichte des englischen Diskants und des Fauxbourdons nach den theoretischen Quellen.* Strasbourg: Heitz & Co., 1936.
2. ———————*Studies in Medieval and Renaissance Music.* New York: W. W. Norton, 1950.
3. Davey, Henry. *History of English Music*, 2nd ed. London: J. Curwen, 1921.
4. Farmer, Henry George. *Music in Mediaeval Scotland.* London: William Reeves, 1930.
5. Fellowes, Edmund Horace. *Organists and Masters of the Choristers of St. George's Chapel.* Windsor: Okley & Son, 1939.
6. Galpin, Francis William. *Old English Instruments of Music.* Chicago: A. C. McClurg & Co., 1911.
7. Greene, Richard L. *The Early English Carol.* Oxford: Clarendon Press, 1935.
8. Hamm, Charles. "The Motets of Lionel Power," in *Studies in Music History: Essays for Oliver Strunk*, ed. Harold Powers , pp. 127-136. Princeton: Princeton University Press, 1968.
9. Harrison, Frank Llewelyn. *Music in Medieval Britain*, 4th ed. Buren, Netherlands: Frits Knuf, 1980.
10. Kenney, Sylvia W. "The Theory of Discant," in *Walter Frye and the "Contenance Angloise,"* Chapter 5. New Haven: Yale University Press, 1964.
11. Meyer, Ernst H. *English Chamber Music.* London: Lawrence & Wishart, 1946.
12. Pulver, Jeffrey. *A Biographical Dictionary of Old English Music.* London: Kegan Paul, Trench, Trubner & Co., 1927.
13. ———————*A Dictionary of Old English Music and Musical Instruments.* New York: E. P. Dutton, 1923.
14. Terry, Richard Runciman. *A Medieval Carol Book.* London: B. Oates & Washburn, 1932.
15. Walker, Ernest. *A History of Music in England*, 3rd ed. Oxford: Clarendon Press, 1952.

Articles

1. Andrews, H. K., and Thurston Dart. "Fourteenth-Century Polyphony in a Fountains Abbey Ms. Book." *ML* 39 (1958), pp. 1-12.
2. Apel, Willi. "The Partial *Signatures* in the Sources up to *1450*." *ActaM* 10 (1938), p. 1; 11 (1939), pp. 40-42.
3. Aplin, John. "The Survival of Plainsong in Anglican Music: Some Early English Te-Deum Settings." *JAMS* 32 (1979), pp. 247-275.
4. Bent, Ian. "The English Chapel Royal before 1300." *PMA* 90 (1963), pp. 77-95.
5. Bent, Margaret. "Initial Letters in the Old Hall Manuscript." *ML* 47 (1966), pp. 225-238.
6. ———————"The Old Hall Manuscript." *Early Music* 2 (1974), pp. 2-14.
7. Bent, Margaret and Ian. "Dufay, Dunstable, Plummer—A New Source." *JAMS* 22 (1969), pp. 394-424.
8. Borren, Charles van den. "The Genius of Dunstable." *PMA* 47 (1921), pp. 79-92.
9. Bukofzer, Manfred. "The First English Chanson on the Continent." *ML* 19 (1938), pp. 119-131.
10. ———————"The First Motet with English Words." *ML* 17 (1936), pp. 225-233.
11. ———————"The Gymel, the Earliest Form of English Polyphony." *ML* 16 (1935), pp. 77-84.
12. ———————"John Dunstable and the Music of His Time." *PMA* 65 (1938), pp. 19-43.
13. ———————"The Music of the Old Hall Manuscript." *MQ* 34 (1948), pp. 512-532; 35 (1949), pp. 36-59.
14. ———————"A Newly Discovered 15th-Century Manuscript of the English Chapel Royal." Part II. *MQ* 33 (1947), pp. 38-51. (Part I: refer to Bertram Schofield below)

15. Burstyn, Shai. "Power's *Anima mea* and Binchois' *De plus en plus*: A Study in Musical Relationships." *MD* 30 (1976), pp. 55-72.

16. Caldwell, John. "The 'Te Deum' in Late Medieval English." *Early Music* 6 (1978), pp. 188-194.

17. Davey, Henry. "John Dunstable." *MT* 45 (1904), p. 712.

18. Flood, W. H. Grattan. "Entries Relating to Music in the English Patent Rolls of the Fifteenth Century." *The Musical Antiquary* 4 (1913), pp. 225-235.

19. ──────"The English Chapel Royal under Henry V and Henry VI." *SIMg* 10 (1908), p. 563.

20. ──────"Guild of English Minstrels under King Henry VI." *SIMg* 15 (1913), p. 66.

21. Ford, W. K. "John Dunstable." *MR* 15 (1954), pp. 133-136.

22. Greene, Richard L. "Two Medieval Musical Manuscripts: Egerton 3307 and Some University of Chicago Fragments." *JAMS* 7 (1954), pp. 1-34.

23. Hamm, Charles. "A Catalogue of Anonymous English Music in Fifteenth-Century Continental Manuscripts." *MD* 22 (1968), pp. 47-76.

24. Harrison, Frank Llewellyn. "*Ars Nova* in England: A New Source." *MD* 21 (1967), p. 67.

25. ──────"Faburden in Practice." *MQ* 16 (1962), pp. 11-34.

26. Hoppin, Richard H. "Conflicting Signatures Reviewed." *JAMS* 9 (1956), pp. 97-117.

27. Howlett, D. R. "A Possible Date for a Dunstable Motet." *MR* 36 (1975), pp. 81-84.

28. Hughes, Andrew. "Mass Pairs in the Old Hall and Other English Manuscripts." *Revue belge de musicologie* 19 (1965), pp. 15-27.

29. ──────"Mensural Polyphony for Choir in 15th-Century England." *JAMS* 19 (1966), pp. 352-369.

30. ──────"Mensuration and Proportion in Early Fifteenth-Century English Music." *ActaM* 27 (1965), pp. 48-61.

31. ──────"The Old Hall Manuscript: A Re-appraisal." *MD* 21 (1967), pp. 99-147.

32. Hughes, Andrew, and Margaret Bent. "The Old Hall Manuscript—A Re-appraisal and an Inventory." *MD* 21 (1967), pp. 97-147.

33. Hughes, Dom Anselm. "Background to Roy Henry Music." *MQ* 27 (1941), pp. 205-210.

34. ──────"Music in the Chapel of King Henry VI." *PMA* 60 (1933), pp. 27-37.

35. ──────"Old English Harmony." *ML* 6 (1925), pp. 154-160.

36. Kovarik, Edward. "A Newly Discovered Dunstable Fragment." *JAMS* 21 (1968), pp. 21-33.

37. Lowinsly, Edward E. "Conflicting Views on Conflicting Signatures." *JAMS* 7 (1954), pp. 181-204.

38. Maclean, Charles. "The Dunstable Inscription in London." *SIMg* 11 (1910), p. 232.

39. McPeek, Gwynn S. "Dating the Windsor MS." *JAMS* 3 (1950), pp. 156-157.

40. Meech, Sanford B. "Three Musical Treatises in English from a Fifteenth-Century Manuscript." *Speculum* 10 (1935), pp. 235-269.

41. Montgomery, Franz. "The Musical Instruments in 'The Canterbury Tales'." *MQ* 17 (1931), pp. 439-448.

42. Page, Christopher. "The Myth of the Chekker." *Early Music* 7 (1979), pp. 482-487.

43. Pulver, Jeffrey. "The English Theorists." *MT* 74 (1933), p. 892; 75 (1934), p. 26.

44. Reaney, Gilbert. "John Dunstable and Late Medieval Music in England." *Score* 8 (1953), pp. 22-33.

45. Roper, E. Stanley. "Music at the English Chapels Royal c. 1135-Present Day." *PMA* 54 (1927), pp. 19-33.

46. Sanders, Ernest H. "Cantilena and Discant in 14th-Century England." *MD* 19 (1965), pp. 7-52.

47. Schofield, Bertram. "The Adventures of an English Minstrel and His Varlet." *MQ* 35 (1949), pp. 361-376.

48. ──────"A Newly Discovered 15th-Century Manuscript of the English Chapel Royal." Part I. *MQ* 32 (1946), pp. 509-536. (See No. 14 above)

49. Squire, W. Barclay. "Notes on an Undescribed Collection of English 15th-Century Music." *SIMg* 2 (1901), p. 342.
50. ——————"Notes on Dunstable." *SIMg* 5 (1904), p. 491.
51. Stainer, Cecilia. "Dunstable and the Various Settings of 'O Rosa Bella'." *SIMg* 2 (1900), p. 1.
52. Stevens, Denis. "Communications." *JAMS* 20 (1967), pp. 516-517.
53. ——————"A Recently Discovered English Source of the 14th Century." *MQ* 41 (1955), pp. 26-40.
54. Strunk, Oliver. "The Music of the Old Hall MS—A Postscript." *MQ* 35 (1949), pp. 244-249.
55. Trend, John Brande. "The First English Songs." *ML* 9 (1928), p. 111.
56. Trowell, Brian. "Faburden and Fauxbourdon." *MD* 13 (1959), pp. 43-78.
57. ——————"A Fourteenth-Century Ceremonial Motet and its Composer." *ActaM* 29 (1957), pp. 65-75.
58. Wolf, Johannes. "Early English Musical Theorists." *MQ* 25 (1939), pp. 420-429.

Music

1. *An Anthology of Early Renaissance Music*, ed. Noah Greenberg and Paul Maynard. New York: W. W. Norton, 1975.
2. *An Anthology of English Medieval and Renaissance Vocal Music*, ed. Noah Greenberg. New York: W. W. Norton, 1968.
3. Dunstable, John
   a. *(CE) Complete Works*. (*MB*, v. 8)
   b. *Gloria, Credo* (*DPL*, Ser. I, v. 8)
   c. Pieces in the Trent Codices. (*DTÖ*, vols. 53, 61, 76)
4. *Early Bodleian Music*, 3 vols. Volume I and II, ed. Sir John Stainer; transc. John Frederick Randall Stainer and Cecilia Stainer. London: Novello, 1901; Volume III, ed. Edward Williams Byron Nicholson. London: Novello, 1913; reprint: Farnborough, Hantshire, England: Gregg Press, 1967.
5. *Egerton 3307*, ed. and transc. Gwynn S. McPeek. London: Oxford University Press, 1963; Chapel Hill: University of North Carolina Press, 1963.
6. Harrison, Frank Llewelyn. *Now Make We Merthe* (Medieval and Renaissance Carols), 3 vols. London: Oxford University Press, 1968.
7. *The Old Hall Manuscript*, 3 vols., ed. and transc. Andrew Hughes and Margaret Bent. Rome: American Institute of Musicology, 1969. (*CMM*, 46)
8. *The Old Hall Manuscript*, 3 vols., ed. Alexander Ramsbotham, Anselm Hughes, Henry B. Collins. Burnham, Buckshire, England: The Plainsong and Mediaeval Music Society, 1933, 1935, 1938.
9. Power, Leonel
   a. Pieces in the Trent Codices, vols. 4, 5 (*DTÖ*, vols. 53, 61)
   b. *Missa Alma redemptoris mater* (*DPL*, Ser. I, v. 2)
   c. *Missa Fuit homo missus* (*DPL*, Ser. I, v. 9)
10. *Seven English Songs and Carols of the 15th Century*, ed. James Copley. Leeds: Chorley & Pickersgill, 1940.
11. *Songs and Madrigals by English Composers of the 15th Century*. London: Quaritch, Plainsong and Mediaeval Society, 1891.
12. *Trienter Codices*, v. 1, ed. Guido Adler, Oswald Koller (*DTÖ*, vols. 14-15); v. 2, ed. Guido Adler, Oswald Koller (*DTÖ*, v. 22); v. 3, ed. Oswald Koller, Franz Schegar, Margarethe Loew (*DTÖ*, v. 28); v. 4, ed. Rudolf Ficker, Alfred Orel (*DTÖ*, v. 53); v. 5, ed. Rudolf Ficker (*DTÖ*, v. 61); v. 6, ed. Rudolf Ficker (*DTÖ*, v. 76)
13. Wooldridge, Harry Ellis, and Dom Anselm Hughes. *Early English Harmony*, 2 vols. Volume I, London: Bernard Quaritch, 1897; Volume II, London: Plainsong and Mediaeval Society, 1913.

OUTLINE X

THE BURGUNDIAN SCHOOL

Burgundy – Secular Vocal Music – Church Music
Dance Music

I. **Burgundy**

   A.   The duchy of Burgundy, a part of the kingdom of France, became a political state which included the Low Countries (now Belgium and Holland) and eastern France. It was the center of intellectual and artistic activity in the early 15th century, especially in Dijon at the courts of Philip the Good (reigned 1419-1467) and Charles the Bold (reigned 1467-1477). Most of the Burgundian composers were connected with one or both of these courts. France under Louis XI regained control of Burgundy with the death of Charles the Bold at the Battle of Nancy (1477). Charles' daughter, Mary of Burgundy, who succeeded to the duchy, married Maximilian of Austria and the Germanic element became increasingly strong.

II. **Secular Vocal Music**

   A.   Sources of Burgundian music include about 65 known *chansonniers*.

      1. *Canonici Manuscript misc. 213* (*c*. 1400-1440) (*M* 7; *M* 19)

         a. Now housed in the Bodleian Library, Oxford, England, this manuscript formerly belonged to Matteo Luigi Canonici (1727-1805), a Jesuit of Venice.

         b. It contains 325 vocal compositions in three parts, 27 in two parts, 28 in four parts and two in five parts. Generally written in white note notation, they are mostly secular chansons although motets and Mass movements are fairly common.

         c. Some 60 composers are represented, including **Nicholaus Grenon, Baude Cordier, Hugho** and **Arnold de Lantins**, possibly both from the same family. **Guillaume Dufay** is represented with 52 compositions (45 of them secular) and **Gilles Binchois** has 28, all but one being secular.

      2. *Laborde Chansonnier* (Library of Congress M. 2. i L. 25 Case)

         a. Formerly belonging to the Marquis of Laborde, the manuscript is now in the Library of Congress, Washington, D. C.

         b. It contains 106 pieces mostly in three parts, some in four. Many of the composers represented were at the court of Charles the Bold.

         c. Some of the composers include **Antoine de Busnois, Dufay** and **Hayne van Ghizeghem.**

         d. *Dangier tu m'as tollu* (*NPM*, p. 109, facsimile)

      3. *Mellon Chansonnier* (*M* 15)

         a. The manuscript is named for Paul Mellon who gave it to the Yale University Library.

         b. It contains 57 compositions in three parts and a few in four parts. Most of the composers represented worked at the courts of Philip the Good or Charles the Bold. They include **Dufay** with four compositions, **Binchois** with one, **Busnois** with 15, **Ockeghem** with three, **Philippe (Firmin) Caron,** Hayne van Ghizeghem, **Guillaume Ruby [La Rouge], Tinctoris** and three English composers, **Bedingham, Walter Frye** and **Robert Morton.** Some compositions by anonymous Italian composers are included also.

4. *Dijon Chansonnier, Bibliothèque Publique 517 (M 5)*
   a.   Now in the public library of Dijon, this chansonnier originated at the court of the Dukes of Burgundy about 1470-1475. Its repertoire includes 161 compositions by 31 composers. In addition to **Busnois** with 19 compositions and **Ockeghem** with five, some other composers are **Barbinguant, Loyset Compère, Caron, Hayne van Ghizeghem** and **Johannes Tinctoris**.
5. *Der Kopenhagener Chansonnier (M 10)*
   a.   The Copenhagen Chansonnier, collected near the end of the fifteenth century, contains 33 chansons, mostly in three voices; two are in four voices (*M* 10, pp. 12, 16). Included are four chansons by **Busnois**, three by **Convert** and two by **Ockeghem**, one of which is his three-voice canon *Prenez sur moi vostre exemple amoureux*. Other composers include **Morton** (two compositions), **Hayne van Ghizeghem, Philippe Basiron** (a *bergerette, M* 10, p. 14), **Molinot, Prioris, Michelet** and **Symon**; several chansons are anonymous.

B.   Musical forms
1.   Chanson is a generic term and includes the *formes fixes*: *rondeau, virelai, ballade* and *bergerette*. The rondeau and ballade forms were used most frequently. The chanson was the most popular type of music of the first half of the fifteenth century; it was well adapted to all types of texts, not complex and easy to listen to. The fourteenth-century French secular forms continued with some use of the Italian *caccia* technique and strong influence of English harmonic developments. The occasional use of the term *"chanson"* as a form indicates an a a b form.
   a.   In the following definitions of musical forms, capital letters indicate a refrain and corresponding lower case letters indicate the same music but different text.
2.   Rondeau
   a.   A varying number of lines appear with the standard form: *AB aA ab AB* (only two lines or sections of music occur: *AB*).
   b.   Texts
      1)   Four stanzas of four lines (rondeau quatrain) each: *ABCD ab AB abcd ABCD*.
      2)   Four stanzas of five lines (rondeau quintain) each: *ABCDE abc ABC abcde ABCDE*.
      3)   Four stanzas of six lines (rondeau sixain) is rare.
3.   Virelai
   a.   *A bba A bba A bba A*
4.   Bergerette
   a.   *A bba A*
   b.   The *bergerette*, developed by Burgundian composers, is similar to the *virelai* but with only one stanza.
5.   Ballade
   a.   *ab ab cd EF*

C.   Musical style
1.   Dorian, Ionian, Mixolydian and Aeolian modes are most commonly used.
2.   The rhythms are strong with some syncopation used, but the rhythmical and contrapuntal complexity of the late *Ars nova* has been greatly simplified.
3.   The principal melodic line is in the upper voice (*discantus* or *superius*) with flowing diatonic movement; the melodies are often ornamented triads with the third as the principal interval. The tenor and contratenor are often unvocal with leaps of all intervals; the note values are longer than in the *superius* part and the parts cross frequently.
4.   Before 1450 the range of voices was usually within an octave, and in the high register of men's voices (equal voice writing). The tenor part makes good counterpoint with the *superius* and acts as a real bass. The contratenor rarely makes good counterpoint with either the tenor or the *superius* alone; it was possibly added to complete the other two voices harmonically.

5.   After 1450, in four-part writing, the contratenor was divided into contratenor *altus* (high) and contratenor *bassus* (low). The four normal parts of the mixed chorus appeared. The voice parts became more homogeneous; duple time signatures are frequent; imitation becomes increasingly important; any pair of voices is generally satisfactory.

6.   Cadences

   a.   The ornamental VII$_6$ - I with the "Landini sixth" is the most usual, being known as the "Burgundian cadence." It has two leading tones, one to the fifth and the other to the root.

   b.   In the V - I cadence the parts cross to avoid parallel fifths.

   c.   Other types of cadences, some experimental, are used.

7.   Partial (conflicting) signatures

   a.   B-flat and infrequently E-flat is used in the signature; sharps are never used in the signature.

   b.   In three-part pieces the signatures may be (reading down from the top voice)

   ♮,♮,♭;   ♮,♭,♭;   ♭,♭♭,♭♭, (rare);   ♭,♮,♮ (very rare).

   c.   B-flat in the tenor was often needed for the cadences; probably the main reason for the signature   ♮,♮,♭

   d.   With harmonic development in the later fifteenth century, the signature   ♮, ♭, ♭

became more common.

8.   Consonance and dissonance

   a.   Fifths, octaves and unisons occur on important beats; triads at the beginning and end are rare; the third is common in middle sections and is used in cadences there.

   b.   Non-harmonic devices include accented and unaccented passing tones, cambiata figures, anticipations, suspensions (7-6, 4-3, 9-8) and neighboring tones (usually upper).

9.   Canon, sequence, hocket and repetition is sometimes used. Some repetition of earlier material may occur later in the piece.

10.   Musical settings correspond to the sentiment of the poem as a whole, but within a narrow range of emotional expression.   The text is generally on the subject of love and suggests a certain melancholy.

D.   **Guillaume Dufay** (*c*. 1400-November 27, 1474) (*CMM*, 1, vols. 1-6)

   1.   Possibly born in Hainaut, **Dufay** is first mentioned as a choirboy in the Cambrai Cathedral, and from 1420 to 1426 was in the employ of the Malatesta family of Rimini, Italy. He spent two short tenures in the Papal Choir: in Rome (December 1428 to August 1433) and in Florence (June 1435 to June 1437). Between these two periods he was director of the Chapel at the Court of Savoy.

   2.   In 1436 **Dufay** was appointed Canon of the Cambrai Cathedral, but he was left free to remain in Italy. **Dufay** was highly respected by **Piero** and **Lorenzo de' Medici** and also the Florentine organist, **Antonio Squarcialupi**. He is the chief representative of the Burgundian School and the greatest composer of his time. He continued the tradi-

tions of **Machaut** with the influences of Italian and English styles.

3.   Secular music

a.   Among **Dufay's** 200 surviving works are 84 secular pieces.   They are three-voice French chansons (*rondeau, ballade, virelai*) generally in "ballade style" (melody and accompaniment).   The style is less progressive in the secular than in the sacred works.   The pieces with Italian texts were no doubt composed during his tenure in Italy.

b.   *Adieu m'amour* (Good-by, my love)   (*CMM*, 1, v. 6, p. 91; *HAM*, No. 68; *CW*, v. 19, p. 22)

1)   The music for this late-style *rondeau* is through-composed and divided into two sections; three lines of text comprise the A section and two lines the B section.

2)   The contratenor, without text, is obviously instrumental.

3)   The partial signature in the manuscript has a B-flat for the tenor only.   Compositional devices include canonic imitation (meas. 11-12, superius and tenor; meas. 16-17, tenor and superius), cambiata (meas. 17, contratenor); 7-6 suspensions (meas. 10, 14);   cross relation (meas. 5); "Landini sixth" (meas. 5, 14, 27); fauxbourdon (meas. 2, 13-14); frequent use of triads.

c.   *Mon chier amy* (My dear friend)   (*CMM*, 1, v. 6, p. 30; *HAM*, No. 67)

1)   A three-voice ballade with the normal repeated first section and the longer unrepeated second section.   The instrumental interlude at the end of the first section is repeated at the end.

d.   *Ce jour le doibt* (*CMM*, 1, v. 6, p. 34)

1)   Wrongly printed as *Le jour s'endort* in *GMB*, No. 40 and *DTÖ*, v. 22, p. 85. Several passages of the superius are used in the tenor in longer notes.

e.   *Quel fronte signorille*, a *rotundellus* (*CMM*, 1, v. 6, p. 11; *M 7*, p. 148; *NPM*, p. 103, facsimile)

E.   **Gilles Binchois** (1400-1460)

1.   Born at Mons in Hainaut, **Binchois** served the Burgundian court from *c*. 1430 to 1460 as a chapel master at the court of Philip the Good.   His fame continued into the sixteenth century; his music is sensitive, refined and even in quality.

2.   *Files à marier* (Girls to be married)   (*HAM*, No. 70; *M 16*, p. 46)

a.   Chanson form: A A B.   The use of four voices gives a feeling of modern chord progressions.   The text is used only in the upper voice.   However, the imitation suggests its use also in the second voice.   The two lower voices, tenor and contratenor, are for instruments.

b.   Imitation is frequent in the two voice parts.   There is no key signature but B-flat is often used in the tenor.   Ternary rhythm continues throughout.

3.   *De plus en plus* (More and more)   (*HAM*, No. 69; *GMB*, No. 42; *CW*, v. 22, p. 7; *M 7*, p. 80; *M 3*, p. 15)

a.   The main melody, often triadic, is in the superius and the tenor and contratenor are supporting voices.   The tenor was later used by **Ockeghem** as the basis of his *Missa De plus en plus.*

4.   Chanson: *Adieu m'amour* (Good-by, my love)   (*MM*, p. 48; *CW*, v. 22, p. 5; *M 16*, p. 30; *M 3*, p. 13)

F.   **Hugho de Lantins** (*fl. c.* 1450)

1.   **Hugho**, who probably spent some time in Italy, has 30 works, sacred and secular (*AM*, v. 22, p. 20), surviving.

2.   *Ce ieusse fait* (If I had done)   (*HAM*, No. 72; *NPM*, p. 141, facsimile)

a.   In this three-voice rondeau, the upper two voices in the first section are imitative. The second section, also in ternary rhythm, begins with chords then continues imitatively.

3.   *A madame playsante et belle* (To a pleasant and beautiful lady)   (*GMB*, No. 41; *M 7*, p. 174)

a.   Note the use of free canon between the outer parts, first at the octave and then at the fifth.

G.   **Arnold de Lantins** (*fl. c.* 1450)

1.   The extant works by **Arnold** comprise 30 pieces, sacred and secular. **Arnold**, probably from the town of Lantin in the province of Liège, spent a few months in the Papal Choir in 1431-1432.

2.   *Puisque je voy* (Since I see) (*HAM*, No. 71)

a.   One of his 12 chansons in the Canonici manuscript, this rondeau (*AB aA ab AB*) has a triadic melody supported by two instrumental parts.

H.   **Antoine Busnois [de Busnes]** (*c.* 1440-1492)

1.   The leading composer of the late Burgundian School (1430-1495), **Busnois** was connected with the chapels of Charles the Bold and Mary of Burgundy. A Priest and musician, he was music director at St. Sauveur in Bruges when he died.

2.   Included in his works are 71 chansons, of which 34 are *rondeaux* and 13 *virelais*. Most of the chansons are with French texts. However, there are at least two Italian and one Flemish chansons. Most are in three voices, but some are in four. **Petrucci's** *Odhecaton* includes 45 works by **Busnois**.

3.   *Ja que liu ne s'i attende* (*M*10, p. 60; *M* 15, p. 71)

a.   **Busnois** incorporated the name of his loved one, Jacqueline d'Hacqueville, into several of his texts he set to music as he did this one.

4.   *Mon seul et sangle souvenir* (*DTÖ*, v. 22, p. 74)

5.   *M'a vostre cueur* (*M*10, p. 16)

6.   *Ma plus qu'assez* (*M*10, p. 24)

7.   *Quant vous me ferez plus de bien* (*M*10, p. 44)

I.   Performance

1.   Vocal music with accompaniment was the standard practice up to the sixteenth century and probably later. Paintings, drawings and sculptures of the period show singers together with instrumentalists.

2.   A varying number of voices are set with the same text. The text is usually in the superius, less common in the tenor and rarely in the contratenor. Textless passages for instruments may occur as an introduction, in the middle and at the end of the chanson.

3.   The usual method of performance is with instruments in all three parts, with the superius alone being sung or possibly one other voice being sung. The chanson may also be played as an instrumental composition.

4.   The instruments used at the Burgundian court include the harp, recorder, viol, lute, shawm, portative organ, sackbut (trombone) and *douchaine* (soft double-reed instrument, a cromorne).

a.   Combinations of different types of instruments (mixed consort) were preferred.

5.   Modern performance

a.   Contrasting tone colors with unusual combinations are best. Flute, violin, oboe or English horn for the superius; viola for the tenor; bassoon, lute, gamba (not cello) or trombone for the contratenor.

b.   The vocal style is impersonal; use a steady tone; the voice should be treated as one of the instruments.

6.   Barlines in modern editions show note divisions and not accents; the metrical text determines the stress points.

III.   Church Music

A.   Musical style

1.   Definite Italian influences may be noted in the church music; large numbers of motets and complete Masses (Ordinary), series of Magnificats on the eight tones and cycles of

Hymns for the whole Church Year became common.

2.   Masses

   a.   Early settings of the Mass were individual Mass sections and were grouped together in manuscript collections. Complete settings of the Ordinary were rare before 1450. Attempts were made to unify the settings of the Ordinary and make polyphonic music a part of Church Services. Plainsong was paraphrased (ornamented) in the upper part or used in long notes in the tenor. Secular melodies were at times used in the tenor.

3.   Motets

   a.   Polytextuality and *cantus firmus* tenors were generally abandoned; there is some use of isorhythm in the early motets. Solo motets with instrumental accompaniment developed; the three- and four-part motets developed with the tenor and contratenor forming a harmonic bass.

4.   A real bass, which developed from the contratenor, appears with **Dufay**. A variety in number of parts occurs in various sections and there is some development of the accompanying parts from the principal part. Canon and complex rhythms occur, and fauxbourdon in three-part writing is still used.

B.   **Reginald Liebert** (*c.* 1375)

1.   **Liebert** wrote the earliest known polyphonic setting (three-voice) of both the Ordinary and Proper of the Mass.

2.   *Mass* (*DTÖ*, vols. 14-15, pp. 1-18)

   a.   Since ornamented plainsongs appear in the superius throughout, this is best known as a paraphrase or discant Mass. In contrast to a different borrowed melody for each movement of the Mass, the *cantus firmus* Mass is one in which a single melody forms the basis of the complete Mass.

   b.   The Introit is based on *Salve sancta Parens* (*LU*, p. 1263).

C.   **Jean [Johannes] Brassart** (1400-1470)

1.   **Brassart**, a fine musician, joined the Papal Choir in 1431 and became principal cantor to the German Emperor Frederick III in 1443.

2.   *O flos fragrans* (*DTÖ*, vols. 14-15, p. 102; *DCS*, v. 28)

   a.   This motet appears in several manuscripts; the earlier ones supply the text only to the superius, whereas later ones add the text to all parts. This suggests it may be performed with instruments or, as was becoming more common, *a cappella*.

3.   *Fortis cum quaevis actio* (*DTÖ*, vols. 14-15, p. 97)

   a.   This motet, in honor of St. John the Baptist, is divided into two movements. It opens with an extended duo in the two upper voices, a common practice in sacred music of the early fifteenth century.

4.   *Summus secretarius* (*M* 19, p. 235)

   a.   A motet in honor of a high dignitary of the Pontifical Court.

D.   **Guillaume Dufay** (*c.* 1400-1474)

1.   **Dufay's** church music includes at least 19 motets, 8 complete Masses, some 28 other Mass movements and 51 other liturgical pieces including Antiphons, Hymns (*MSO*, v. 1, p. 30; *AM*, v. 22, p. 18) and Sequences for Masses and Offices (*DCS*, v. 29).

2.   *Missa Se la face ay pale* (*DTÖ*, vols. 14-15, p. 120; *CMM*, 1, v. 3, pp. 1-32; *MM*, p. 45, Kyrie; *AM*, v. 30, p. 51, Sanctus)

   a.   This is based on **Dufay's** ballade (*CMM*, 1, v. 6, p. 36; *M* 7, p. 140) by the same name.

   b.   It represents an early style in which the *cantus firmus* is presented generally in the tenor without elaboration. Another unifying device is the opening motto used at important places.

   c.   Canon is used in the Gloria and Credo.

3.   *Missa L'Homme armé* (*CMM*, 1, v. 3, pp. 33-65)

   a.   The secular melody has been the basis of many cantus firmus Masses: **Ockeghem**,

Obrecht, Busnois, Josquin, Morales, Carissimi and many others.

    b.   The Kyrie (*HAM* No. 66a), in two sections, presents the melody, somewhat ornamented, only once; the opening phrase in a ternary section which returns as a *da capo*, and the middle section in binary rhythm.

    c.   The melody is presented twice in the Gloria and three times in the Credo.

    d.   In the Agnus Dei (*HAM*, No. 66b), in three parts, Agnus Dei I has the melody used complete; in the latter part of Agnus Dei II it is divided between the two lower voices and in Agnus Dei III the theme is presented in the tenor in retrograde, then straight in shorter values.

  4.   *Missa Ave Regina coelorum* (*CMM*, 1, v. 3, pp. 91-121)

    a.   This Mass is based on the same plainsong (*AR*, p. 56) as his Antiphon (*CMM*, 1, v. 5, p. 124; *M* 3, p. 2; *NPM*, p. 119, facsimile) which contains the troped phrase *"Miserere tui labentis Dufay"* (Have mercy on thy dying Dufay).

    b.   Of interest is the anticipation of the "parody" Mass, when in the Agnus Dei II (*CMM*, 1, v. 3, p. 119; meas. 72-83) **Dufay** borrows exactly from his four-voice motet (*CMM*, 1, v. 5, p. 127; meas. 86-96).

  5.   *Missa Sancti Jacobi* (*CMM*, 1, v. 2, pp. 17-44; *GMB*, No. 39, Kyrie; *AM*, v. 22, p. 15, Alleluia)

    a.   In addition to the Ordinary, four sections from the Proper are included. The Communion contains the oldest example of *fauxbourdon* (*CMM*, 1, v. 2, p. 44); in one manuscript a Latin rhyme makes explanation of it.

  6.   *Magnificat* in the Eighth Mode (*CMM* 1, v. 5, p. 81; *DTÖ*, vols. 14-15, p. 174; *DCS*, v. 29)

  7.   Antiphon: *Alma Redemptoris Mater* (*CMM*, 1, v. 5, p. 117; *DTÖ*, v. 53, p. 19; *CW*, v. 19, p. 10; *HAM*, No. 65)

  8.   *Gloria et in terra ad modum tubae* (*CMM*, 1, v. 4, p. 79; *DTÖ*, vols. 14-15, p. 145)

    a.   The upper two parts are in canon; the two lower parts for brass instruments (*"ad modum tubae"*) are also in canon, but in hocket style forming a type of ground bass.

E. **Gilles Binchois** (1400-1460)

  1.   **Binchois'** sacred works include motets (*M* 16, pp. 188-232), hymns (*AM*, v. 12, p. 29), Magnificats and Mass movements (*M* 16, pp. 154-187; *DTÖ*, v. 61, pp. 42-61; (*M* 19, pp. 53-74).

  2.   *Magnificat* on the Second Tone   (*GMB*, No. 43; *M* 16, p. 138)

    a.   The verses are set alternating two and three parts in *fauxbourdon* style.

  3.   Hymn: *A Solis ortus cardine* (*M* 16, p. 188; *DCS*, v. 38)

F. **Hugho de Lantins** (*fl. c.* 1450)

  1.   Three Glorias (*M* 19, pp. 110-122)

    a.   In the first Gloria (*M* 19, p. 110) *fauxbourdon* is common, particularly at cadences.

    b.   In the second Gloria (*M* 19, p. 115) shortness is achieved by overlapping the text among the three voices.

    c.   The third Gloria (*M* 19, p. 118) is in *caccia* style with the tenor singing in canon at the fifth after the superius. In a two-flat signature, two more flats, A and D, are used as accidentals.

IV. Dance Music

A. *Basse danse (bassadanza)* is a dignified ceremonial dance usually in duple meter divisible into three; some are in triple meter; the tempo is moderately slow. It is often followed by a lively *tordion* or *pas de Brabant*.

B. *Manuscript Brussels 9085* is an early source of the music.

  1.   The music is printed with notes of the same value which possibly represented a tenor over which a melody was improvised on a soprano instrument in the proper rhythm of the dance. Under each note are letters indicating the steps to be taken during the dura-

tion of the note: *s = simple, d = double, r = reprisa, b = branle.*

C.   The instruments used were classified as "high" (loud) or "low" (soft); the high instruments generally played from a balcony for festive occasions and the low instruments were located near the dancers in more intimate situations. A typical grouping of high instruments would be two shawms (oboes) and slide trumpet; of low instruments would be harp, lute and recorder. Other instruments might be viols, trombone, fiddle and portative organ.

SELECTED BIBLIOGRAPHY

Books

1.   Brennecke, Jr., Ernest. *John Milton the Elder and His Music.* New York: Columbia University Press, 1938; reprint: New York: Octagon Books, 1973. (*Columbia University Studies in Musicology*, v. 2)

2.   Crane, Frederick. *Materials for the Study of the Fifteenth Century Basse Danse.* Brooklyn: Institute of Mediaeval Music, 1968.

3.   Fischer, Kurt von. "Organal and Chordal Style in Renaissance Sacred Music: New and Little-Known Sources," in *Aspects of Medieval and Renaissance Music: A Birthday Offering to Gustave Reese*, ed. Jan LaRue, pp. 173-182. New York: W. W. Norton, 1966.

4.   Hamm, Charles E. *A Chronology of the Works of Dufay, Based on a Study of Mensural Practice.* Princeton: Princeton University Press, 1964.

5.   Harman, Alec. *Mediaeval and Early Renaissance Music up to c. 1525.* London: Rockliff, 1958.

6.   Heartz, Daniel. "A 15th-Century Ballo: *Rôti Bouilli Joyeax*," in *Aspects of Medieval and Renaissance Music: A Birthday Offering to Gustave Reese*, ed. Jan LaRue, pp. 359-375. New York: W. W. Norton, 1966.

7.   Meyer-Baer, Kathi. *Liturgical Music Incunabula, a Descriptive Catalogue.* London: The Bibliographical Society, 1962.

8.   Pirrotta, Nino. "On Text Forms from Ciconia to Dufay," in *Aspects of Medieval and Renaissance Music: A Birthday Offering to Gustave Reese*, ed. Jan LaRue, pp. 673-682. New York: W. W. Norton, 1966.

9.   Salop, Arnold. "The Early Development of Harmonic Development," in Arnold Salop, *Studies in the History of Musical Style*, pp. 81-102. Detroit: Wayne State University Press, 1971.

10. Sollitt, Edna Richolson. *Dufay to Sweelinck.* New York: I. Washburn, 1933.

11. Thompson, James. *An Introduction to Philippe (?) Caron.* Brooklyn: Institute of Mediaeval Music, 1964.

12. Wright, Craig. *Music at the Court of Burgundy.* Brooklyn: Institute of Mediaeval Music. (*Musicological Studies*, v. 28)

Articles

1.   Aldrich, Putnam. "An Approach to the Analysis of Renaissance Music." *MR* 30 (1969), pp. 1-21.

2.   Apel, Willi. "Imitation Canons on *L'Homme armé*." *Speculum* 25 (1950), p. 367.

3.   ———————"The Partial Signatures in the Sources up to 1400." *ActaM* 10 (1938), p. 1; *A Postscript*, 11 (1939), pp. 40-42.

4.   Bent, Margaret. "The Songs of Dufay." *Early Music* 8 (1980), pp. 454-459.

5.   Borren, Charles van de. "A Light of the Fifteenth Century: Guillaume Dufay." *MQ* 21 (1950), pp. 279-297.

6. Brown, Howard Mayer. "Choral Music in the Renaissance." *Early Music* 6 (1978), pp. 164-169.

7. Bukofzer, Manfred. "The Beginnings of Polyphonic Choral Music." *PAMS* (1940), pp. 23-34.

8. ——————"Changing Aspects of Medieval and Renaissance Music." *MQ* 44 (1958), pp. 1-18.

9. ——————"An Unknown Chansonnier of the 15th Century (*The Mellon Chansonnier*)." *MQ* 28 (1942), pp. 14-49.

10. Burstyn, Shai. "Power's *Anima mea* and Binchois' *De plus en plus*: A Study in Musical Relationships." *MD* 30 (1976), pp. 55-72.

11. Bush, Helen. "The Laborde Chansonnier." *PAMS* (1940), pp. 56-79.

12. Fox, Charles Warren. "Non-Quartal Harmony in the Renaissance." *MQ* 31 (1945), pp. 33-53.

13. Gombosi, Otto. "About Dance and Dance Music in the Late Middle Ages." *MQ* 27 (1941), pp. 289-305.

14. Gossett, Philip. "Techniques of Unification in early Cyclic Masses and Mass Pairs." *JAMS* 19 (1966), pp. 205-231.

15. Kemp, Walter H. "The Manuscript Escorial V. III." *MD* 30 (1976), pp. 97-129.

16. Kennedy, S. S. J., Josepha. "Dufay and Don Pedro the Cruel." *MQ* 61 (1975), pp. 58-64.

17. Kinkeldey, Otto. "Fifteenth-Century Basses Dances." *BAMS*, No. 4 (1940), p. 13.

18. Lang, Paul Henry. "The So-Called Netherlands Schools." *MQ* 25 (1939), pp. 48-59.

19. Lerner, Edward R. "The Polyphonic Magnificat of the 15th-Century." *MQ* 50 (1964), pp. 44-58.

20. Linker, Robert W., and Gwynn S. McPeek. "The Bergerette Form in the Laborde Chansonnier: A Musico-Literary Study." *JAMS* 7 (1954), pp. 113-120. Facsimile of *"O belle Dyanne"* from the Laborde Chansonnier appears between pp. 120-121.

21. Lowinsky, Edward. "The Functions of Conflicting Signatures in Early Polyphonic Music." *MQ* 31 (1945), pp. 227-260.

22. MacClintock, Lander. "Once More on the Pronunciation of Dufay." *ActaM* 37 (1965), pp. 75-78.

23. Marix, Jeanne. "Hayne von Ghizeghem." *MQ* 28 (1942), pp. 276-287.

24. Meyer-Baer, Kathi. "New Facts on the Printing of Music Incunabula." *PAMS* for 1940 (1946), pp. 80-87.

25. Mixter, Keith E. "Isorhythmic Design in the Motets of Johannes Brassart," in *Studies in Musicology: Eassys in the History, Style, and Bibliography of Music in Memory of Glen Haydon*, ed. James W. Pruett, pp. 179-189. Chapel Hill: University of North Carolina Press, 1969.

26. ——————"Johannes Brassart: A Biographical and Bibliographical Study." *MD* 18 (1964), pp. 19-35; 19 (1965), pp. 99-108.

27. Nutting, Geoffrey. "Between Anachronism and Obscurity, Analysis of Renaissance Music." *MR* 35 (1974), pp. 185-216.

28. Perle, George. "The Chansons of Antoine Busnois." *MR* 11 (1950), pp. 89-97.

29. Picker, Martin. "The Cantus Firmus in Binchois's 'Files a Marier'." *JAMS* 18 (1965), pp. 235-236.

30. Planchant, Alejandro Enrique. "Guillaume Dufay's Masses: Notes and Revisions." *MQ* 58 (1972), pp. 1-23.

31. Reaney, Gilbert. "The Manuscript Oxford, Bodleian Library, Canonici Misc. 213." *MD* 9 (1955), pp. 73-104.

32. Sawyer, F. H. "The Use and Treatment of Canto Fermo by the Netherlands School of the Fifteenth Century." *PMA* 63 (1936-1937), pp. 97-116.

33. Seay, Albert. "The Expositio Manus of Johannes Tinctoris." *Journal of Music Theory* 9 (1965), pp. 194-232.

34. Stainer, John Frederick Randall. "Shakespeare and Lassus." *MT* 43 (1902), pp. 100-101.

35.   Treitler, Leo. "Tone System in the Secular Works of Guillaume Dufay." *JAMS* 18 (1965), 131-169.

36.   Van, Guillaume de. "An Inventory of the Mansucript Bologna Liceo Musicale Q 15 (*Olim 37*)." *MD* 2 (1948), pp. 231-257.

37.   ––––––"A Recently Discovered Source of Early Fifteenth-Century Polyphonic Music, the Aosta Manuscript." *MD* 2 (1948), pp. 5-74.

38.   Warren, Charles. "Brunelleschi's Dome and Dufay's Motets." *MQ* 59 (1973), pp. 92-105.

39.   Wright, Craig. "Performance Practices at the Cathedral of Cambrai." *MQ* 64 (1978), pp. 295-328.

Music

1.   Binchois, Gilles
     a.   *Sechzehn weltliche Lieder zu 3 Stimmen*, ed. Willibald Gurlitt. (*CW*, v. 22)
     b.   *Trienter Codices*, vols. 4, 5 (*DTÖ*, vols. 53, 61)
     c.   Chansons, ed. Wolfgang Rehm (*MDm*, v. 2)
     d.   *Missa de angelis* (*DPL*, ser. 1, v. 5)

2.   Brassart, Johannes
     a.   (*CE*) *Opera Omnia*, 2 vols. (*CMM*, 35)
     b.   *Sechs Motetten*, ed. Keith E. Mixter. (*Musik alter Meister*, v. 13). Graz: Akademische Druck- und Verlagsanstalt, 1960.
     c.   *Trienter Codices*, v. 6, ed. Rudolf Ficker (*DTÖ*, v. 76)

3.   *The Burgundian School and the Netherlands School.* New York: Edwin F. Kalmus, 1968.

4.   Busnois, Antoine
     a.   *Anima mea liquifacta est* (*VOTS*, sec. 1, p. 22)
     b.   *Corps digne/Dieu quel mariage* (*VOTS*, sec. 1, p. 27)
     c.   *Kyrie L'Homme armé* (*VOTS*, sec. 1, p. 13)
     d.   *Missa sur L'Homme armé* (*MPL*, ser. 1, v. 1, No. 2)
     e.   *Quant j'ay au cueur* (*VOTS*, sec. 6, p. 185)
     f.   *Regina coeli* (*VOTS*, sec. 1, p. 16)

5.   *Dijon Chansonnier* (*Dijon Bibliothèque Publique Manuscrit 517*), introduction by Dragan Plamenac. Brooklyn: The Institute of Mediaeval Music; reprint: Farnborough, Hantshire, England: Gregg Press, 1966.

6.   Dufay, Guillaume
     a.   (*CE*) *Opera Omnia*, 6 vols., ed. Heinrich Besseler (*CMM*, 1)
     b.   Masses: *CM*, v. 4; *DTÖ*, v. 38; *MPL*, vols. 1, 2, 3, 4; *DPL*, ser. 1, vols. 1, 3, 4, 7, 10
     c.   Motets: *Trienter Codices*, vols. 4, 5, 6 (*DTÖ*, vols. 53, 61, 76)
     d.   *LO*, v. 8
     e.   *Zwölf geistliche und weltliche Werke*, ed. Heinrich Besseler. (*CW*, v. 19)
     f.   *Sämtliche Hymnen*, ed. Rudolf Gerber (*CW*, v. 49)

7.   *Dufay and His Contemporaries*, ed. John Frederick Randall Stainer and Cecilia Stainer. London: 1898; reprint: Irvington-on-Hudson: Capitol Publishing Co., 1951; Amsterdam: Frits A. M. Knuf, 1963.

8.   *Early Fifteenth-Century Music*, 4 vols., ed. Gilbert Reaney. Brooklyn: American Institute of Musicology, 1955-1969.

9.   *Fifteenth Century Basse Dances* (Brussels Bibl. Roy. Ms 9085), ed. James L. Jackman (*WE*, v. 6)

10.   *Der Kopenhagen Chansonnier, MS Thott 291*, ed. Knud Jeppesen. Copenhagen: Der Königlichen Bibliothek. Leipzig: Breitkopf & Härtel, 1927; reprint: New York: Broude Brothers, 1965.

11.   Landini, Francesco
     a.   *The Works of Francesco Landini*, ed. Leonard Ellinwood. Cambridge: The Mediaeval Academy of America, 1939; reprint: New York: Krause Reprint Co. 1970.

12. Lantins, Hugho de
     a. Masses and Mass sections (*DTÖ*, v. 61)
13. Marrocco, W. Thomas. *Fourteenth-Century Italian Cacce*. Cambridge, MA: The Mediaeval Academy of America, 1961.
14. ––––––*The Music of Jacopo da Bologna*. Berkeley: University of California Press, 1954.
15. *The Mellon Chansonnier*, 2 vols., ed. Leeman L. Perkins and Howard Garey. New Haven: Yale University Press, 1979.
16. *Les Musiciens de la Cour de Bourgogne au XVe siècle (1420-1467)*, ed. Jeanne Marix. Paris: Éditions de L'Oiseau-Lyre, 1937.
17. *Musikalische Schrifttafeln*, ed. Johannes Wolf. Leipzig: C. F. W. Siegel, 1922-1923.
18. *Poètes et Musiciens du XVe siècle*, ed. E. Droz. Paris: 1924.
19. *Polyphonia Sacra: A Continental Miscellany of the Fifteenth Century*, ed. Charles van den Borren. University Park: Pennsylvania State University Press, 1963.
20. *Sing und Spielmusik aus älterer Zeit*, ed. Johannes Wolf. Leipzig: 1939.
21. *Der Squarcialupi Codex*, ed. Johannes Wolf. Lippstadt: Kistner & Siegel and Co., 1955.
22. *Trienter Codices*, v. 1, ed. Guido Adler, Oswald Koller (*DTÖ*, vols. 14-15); v. 2, ed. Guido Adler, Oswald Koller (*DTÖ*, v. 22); v. 3, ed. Oswald Koller, Franz Schegar, Margarethe Loew (*DTÖ*, v. 28); v. 4, ed. Rudolf Ficker, Alfred Orel (*DTÖ*, v. 53); v. 5, ed. Rudolf Ficker (*DTÖ*, v. 61); v. 6, ed. Rudolf Ficker (*DTÖ*, v. 76)

11. Conductus from the
Montpellier Codex H 196
(13th century)

12. Psaltery from the *Cantigas de Santa Maria*

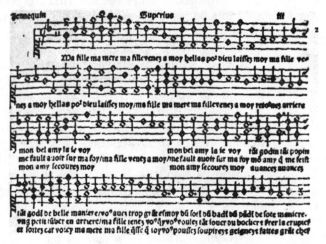

13. A chanson by Clément Janequin
printed in Paris, 1530

FLEMISH – FRENCH – FRANCO-FLEMISH SCHOOLS

**The Renaissance – The Flemish School to Gombert
The French Polyphonic Chanson – Music Printing – French and Flemish Sacred Music
Instrumental Music – Performance of Renaissance Music**

I.   **The Renaissance**

   A.   The Renaissance period in music continued with definite changes from the earlier Bur-
        gundian style. These changes began with the addition of a bass part (about 1450) increas-
        ing the usual number of parts from three to four or more and establishing normal four-
        part polyphony. The use of parallel six-three chords (*fauxbourdon* style) became less fre-
        quent, and new and richer sonorities resulted from a lower range of voices.
   B.   Renaissance style, as realized by **Josquin** and others, had as its features a clear texture,
        smooth-sounding polyphony and homophony, controlled expressiveness; well organized
        principles of composition, including imitation and regulation of dissonances and unusual
        rhythmic flow and complexity (rhythmic counterpoint).
   C.   Secular Renaissance music continued its development, and text-painting became an im-
        portant feature. The use of riddle canons and technical complications were not impor-
        tant features of Renaissance style, although used by many composers. Almost all com-
        posers of the Renaissance wrote Masses, motets, madrigals and chansons, and many
        composed for instruments.

II. **The Flemish School to Gombert** (*c.* 1450-1525)

   A.   **Johannes Ockeghem** (*c.* 1420-1495)
       1.   **Ockeghem** was born in east Flanders and became a choirboy at the Antwerp Cathedral
            (1443-1444). In 1446 he began a two-year tenure as chorister for Duke Charles of
            Bourbon, then in 1454 became first chaplain and composer to Kings Charles VII, Louis
            XI and Charles VIII, as well as master of the King's Chapel in 1465. Later he became
            treasurer of the Abbey of St. Martin in Tours and travelled in Spain (1469-1470) and
            Flanders (1484). **Ockeghem** had a strong influence as a teacher and was called the
            "Prince of Music" by many of his contemporaries.
       2.   **Ockeghem's** output, although not large, is significant; it includes 11 complete Masses,
            a Requiem, 10 motets (*AERM*, p. 76), several other liturgical pieces and 20 chansons.
       3.   He developed the use of imitation. His church style is modal and the polyphony more
            continuous, therefore full cadences are avoided. Full and divided choirs are required.
            Secular *cantus firmi* are used, *L'Homme armé* being one of the most popular. The
            cantus firmi appear in long notes and the other parts are often highly ornamented. The
            chansons are in the Burgundian style. Among his pupils and contemporaries are
            Busnois, Obrecht and **Gaspar van Weerbecke.**
       4.   Masses
           a.   Four types
               1)   *Cantus firmus* in which all movements are based on the same sacred or secular
                    melody, usually in the tenor.
               2)   Plainsong in which each movement uses the melody from the same part of a Gre-
                    gorian Mass.

3)   Parody in which the musical material is borrowed from preexistent pieces, sacred or secular.

4)   Freely composed in which the composer does not rely upon borrowed material.

b.   *Missa Caput* (*CE*, v. 2, p. 37; *DTÖ*, v. 38, p. 59; pp. 49-57, facsimile; *CM*, v. 5, p. 53; *AM*, v. 22, p. 22, Kyrie)

1)   This *cantus firmus* Mass is based on a melody derived from an Antiphon. **Ockeghem** divides each of the main sections into two parts, one in triple and one in duple rhythm.

c.   *Missa Fors seulement* (*CE*, v. 2, p. 37; *DTÖ*, v. 38, p. 59)

1)   The five-voice *cantus firmus* Mass consists only of a Kyrie, Gloria and Credo. At times **Ockeghem** borrows not only the superius from his *rondeau* by the same name but also the tenor. The extension of the range into a lower compass is significant and imitation is common.

d.   *Missa L'Homme armé* (*CE*, v. 1, p. 99; *MPL*, Ser. 1, v. 1, No. 6; *VOTS*, sec. 1, p. 1, Kyrie; *HAM*, No. 73a, b, Kyrie and Agnus Dei; *MSO*, v. 1, p. 32, Kyrie)

1)   The *cantus firmus*, generally without elaboration, is presented throughout in the tenor. Agnus Dei III (*HAM*, No. 73b) makes use of various two-part combinations before all voices come together.

e.   *Missa Prolationum* (*CE*, v. 2, p. 21; Plates II-IX)

1)   This presents a unique study in double canon, some in augmentation. The Mass takes its name from the fact that each voice is in a different prolation. All voices begin together but when the two leader voices arrive at the desired linear separation, all voices move ahead in black notes and complete the movement in double canon. All sections begin with canon at the unison and section by section progress through all intervals to canon at the octave.

a)   Sanctus (*CE* v. 2, p. 31; Plate VII; *MM*, p. 53; *AM*, v. 30, p. 54)

(1)   Double canon at the sixth between superius-contratenor and tenor-bass.

5.   Instrumental motet: *Ut heremita solus* (*GMB*, No. 52), the tenor is an intricate puzzle.

6.   Chansons

a.   Almost all the chansons are in three voices with a text in the superius and the other voices for instruments. Although not characteristic, imitation does appear and the idea of continuous polyphony is strong; there is occasional use of *fauxbourdon*. **Ockeghem's** chansons are generally in duple rhythm.

b.   *O rosa bella* (*DTÖ*, vols. 14-15, p. 233)

1)   **Ockeghem** adds an original voice to a three-voice setting by **Hert**.

c.   *Ma bouche rit* (My mouth laughs) (*HAM*, No. 75; *M* 40c, p. 335; *MMF*, v. 10, p. 60; *Mellon Chansonnier*, p. 113; *EdM*, v. 84, p. 62)

1)   Later **Johannes Martin** used the superius as the basis of a Mass; **Josquin** used it for a chanson.

d.   *D'ung aultre [D'un autre] amer un cueur s'abesseroit* (*VOTS*, sec. 1, p. 12; *Der Kopenhagen Chansonnier*, p. 62); *Ma maîtresse* (*HAM*, No. 74)

7.   Canon: *Fuga trium vocum in epidiatessaron* (Fugue in three voices at the fourth above) (*MSD*, 6, v. 2, p. 532)

a.   Using the text *Prenez sur moi vostre exemple amoureux*, this is a perfect canon notated on one line with a signature of three flats and three sharps; these indicate the accidentals necessary in playing the canon in different modes.

B.   **Jacob Obrecht** (*c.* 1450-1505)

1.   **Obrecht** was born in Bergen-op-Zoom, the Netherlands, on St. Cecilia Day, November 22. He worked in Cambrai (1484-1485), Bruges, Antwerp and at the court of the Estes in Ferrara. He died of the plague in Ferrara.

2.   **Obrecht's** style is less elaborate and more progressive than **Ockeghem's**. He established imitative counterpoint with all voices equally important. His use of the chordal style gives a strong harmonic feeling. The form is generally sectional with clearly defined

cadences (V-I, IV-I).   There is influence of the harmonic Italian frottola and Netherland folk music. **Josquin** was his greatest follower.

3.   **Obrecht's** chansons number about 25; Dutch titles are on 16 of them. His motet-like chansons show a progression away from the *formes fixes*.

4.   The 18 motets, generally polytextual, frequently use a *cantus firmus* in sustained tones, and imitation is rare.

   a.   *O beata Basili* (*HAM*, No. 76a)

     1)   This motet, in honor of St. Basil, is divided into two parts; the first has the *cantus firmus* in the tenor and altus parts and the second part in the tenor and superius.

   b.   Motet: *O vos omnes* (*GMB*, No. 54), is not by **Obrecht** but by **Compère**.

5.   **Obrecht's** Masses show great ingenuity in the use of borrowed melodies. In addition to the standard *cantus firmus* Mass, **Obrecht** also uses the plainsong Mass technique of a different preexistent melody for each section. The borrowed melody may move to any voice (*Missa Caput, CE*, vols. 23, 24). At times **Obrecht** divides the melody into individual phrases and alters the order, but near the end will generally present the melody in its original order (*Missa super Maria zart, CE*, vols. 9-10). Another technique is to borrow countermelody material when it is part of a polyphonic piece. Repetition of a characteristic figure is another means of unification (*Missa sine nomine, CE*, v. 25). The parody technique of borrowing whole segments of a piece becomes increasingly common. (See *ArM*, v. 15, p. 137; *MSD*, 6, v. 2, pp. 303, 305)

   a.   *Missa sine nomine* (*CE*, v. 25; *HAM*, No. 77a, b, Kyrie and Agnus Dei III)

C.   **Heinrich Isaac [Issak, Izak, Yzac, Arrigo Tedesco]** (*c.* 1450-1517)

1.   **Isaac**, an international Flemish musician and composer, wrote Masses and motets, French chansons and German lieder. About 1484 he succeeded **Squarcialupi** at the court of Lorenzo the Magnificent in Florence. In 1494, at the overthrow of the Medicis by Savonarola (1494-1498), **Isaac** fled Florence and in 1497 became court composer to Maximilian I of Vienna. At Innsbruck, another seat for Maximilian, **Isaac** associated with **Paul Hofhaimer**. Still in the employ of Maximilian, **Isaac** was allowed to settle in Florence in 1515 and remained there till his death. **Isaac** played an important part in the development of German music of **Josquin's** time. **Isaac's** secular music will be discussed in Chapter XIV.

2.   *Missa carminum* (*CW*, v. 7)

   a.   The Mass was probably written for a school or private group and makes use of secular German lieder in quodlibet style rather than using chants.

3.   *Missa Ain frelich wesen* (*GMB*, No. 55, Kyrie)

   a.   **Isaac** based this Mass on his own four-voice lied (*DTÖ*, v. 28, p. 62) but also borrowed from a three-voice lied by **Jacobus Barbireau**.

4.   *Choralis Constantinus*, Book I, published in 1550; Books II and III in 1555 (*DTÖ*, vols. 10, 32)

   a.   Commissioned by the Cathedral Chapter of Constance in 1504, this extended three-volume work provides the first complete polyphonic settings for the Proper of the Mass for Sundays and some feast days throughout the complete Church Year. Settings of five Ordinaries and portions of 10 Offices are included in Book III.

   b.   Generally in four parts, the pieces range from two to six parts. The melody is most frequently in the upper voice (discant) in the pieces of Books I and II, but in Book III it appears in the bass. The music is generally continuous except in the strophic sections, the Sequences in particular, where the versicles alternate chant and polyphony. Unfinished when **Isaac** died, **Ludwig Senfl, Isaac's** pupil, completed it.

D.   **Pierre de la Rue** (*c.* 1460-1518)

1.   **La Rue**, probably born at Tournai in Picardy, was employed as a singer by Maximilian. His service to Philip the Handsome (1496-1506) and then Margaret of Austria, regent of the Netherlands under Maximilian, centered in Brussels. Twice **La Rue** visited

Spain and spent his last two years at Courtrai. Although a French composer, he was dominated by the style of **Obrecht**.

2. **La Rue's** works include over 30 Masses (*MMB*, v. 8), several motets (*AM*, v. 22, p. 40; v. 47, p. 46), Lamentations and secular chansons. (See *DCS*, vols. 36, 37)

3. *Requiem* (*CW*, v. 11)

   a. The plainsong is set polyphonically in four or five voices with occasional reduction to only two. Low voices in low registers are unique.

4. *Missa L'Homme armé*

   a. **La Rue** left two Masses on *L'Homme armé*, both of which use canon, one more consistently than the other.

   b. Kyrie I and II (*HAM*, No. 92)

      1) The *cantus firmus* in the lower voice is a mensuration canon which expands into two voices; one in *tempus imperfectum* (duple time) and one in *tempus perfectum* (triple time).

      2) The top voice is free, but the melody also appears in the second voice with irregularities.

E. **Loyset Compère** (*c.* 1450-1518) (*CE = CMM*, 15)

1. **Compère**, a pupil of **Ockeghem** and member of the Franco-Flemish School, was a choirboy at St. Quentin. In 1486 he entered the employ of Charles VIII and later held the post of canon and chancellor at St. Quentin until his death.

2. **Compère** wrote Masses, Mass movements, motets (*AM*, v. 28, p. 25; v. 47, p. 42), Magnificats and chansons. (See *ArM*, v. 13)

3. *Royne du ciel* (*HAM*, No. 79; *MMF*, v. 10, p. 81; *M* 40c, p. 395; *CMM*, 15, v. 5, p. 7)

   a. The motet-chanson, in the form of a *rondeau-quatrain*, presents the two upper voices in imitation. The contratenor, using the opening notes of the Antiphon, *Regina caeli* (*LU*, p. 275), is a sequential ostinato; each of the four sequences begins a note higher.

4. *Le Renvoy* (*DCS*, v. 42, *MMF*, v. 10, p. 84; *M* 40c, p. 381)

   a. The music of line three of this chanson is made up from the music of lines one and two.

5. *Omnium bonorum plena* (*DTÖ*, vols. 14-15, p. 111; *CMM*, 15, v. 4, p. 32)

   a. The text is a supplication for singers including 13 composers' names (**Dufay, Caron, Tinctoris, Ockeghem, Corbet, Faugues, Molinet, Compère**). It is based on the tenor of **Hayne's** chanson by the same name in French, *"De tous bien plaine."*

6. Masses (*CE*, v. 1)

   a. **Compère's** Masses incorporate several melodies borrowed from **Hayne's** chansons (*Missa allez regrets, CE*, v. 1, p. 26). Imitation canon and motivic sequence (*Missa L'Homme armé, CE*, v. 1, p. 1) are characteristics. Series of motets to replace Mass movements make up at least two of **Compère's** "substitution" Masses, involving both the Ordinary and Proper.

F. **Josquin des Prez** (*c.* 1445-1521)

1. Born in Burgundy, **Josquin** went to Italy at an early age and was a singer at the Milan Cathedral (1459-1472). From 1474 to at least 1479 he served as singer at the court of the Sforzas in Milan and then in the Papal Choir (1486-1494) in Rome. **Josquin** was in Ferrara in 1499, later was employed by King Louis XII of France until 1515 and finally settled in Brussels. He was considered by his contemporaries to be the greatest composer of his time and was much admired by **Martin Luther.**

2. **Josquin's** early works are in the ornamented polyphonic style of **Ockeghem.** Under the influence of **Obrecht** he developed a new and varied style with imitative counterpoint carried out in a series of expositions, the so-called "classic" motet. Chordal style is used in alternation with polyphony, and high and low voices also appear in alternation. An early use of the polychoral style is apparent.

3. In **Josquin's** chansons (about 50) there is a great variety of techniques and forms repre-

sented;   other than the *formes fixes*, some forms used are: *aba, aab, aabbc, aa* or through-composed motet-like. Canon, including double and triple canon, is frequently employed and preexistent melodies from other composers or plainsongs are common.

   a.   *Fault d'argent* (Lack of money) (*CE*, v. 5, No. 15; *HAM*, No. 91)

   b.   *A l'heure que je vous* (*CE*, v. 53, p. 12; *GMB*, No. 61), canon (cantus and bass) at the ninth below for four instruments.

   c.   The King's fanfare, *Vive le roy* (*CE*, v. 53, p. 10; *GMB*, No. 62a)

   d.   *Canzone "La Bernardina"* (*CE*, v. 53, p. 14; *GMB*, No. 62b)

4.   In the motets **Josquin** makes his greatest contribution (*CE*, Motets, vols. 1-5; *AM*, v. 22, p. 35; v. 47, p. 44; *DCS*, vols. 25, 43-45; *ArM*, v. 15, p. 86; *AERM*, pp. 108-118).

   a.   The SATB clef signs become standardized although other clefs are used, particularly when the total range is expanded. Polyphonic techniques of canon, including mensuration canon, and imitation are common. However, fugal exposition is becoming increasingly more frequent. A feeling for tonality is gradually developing.

   b.   The *cantus firmus* tenor may appear in long notes or take on the rhythm of the other voices, and the plainsong, though often paraphrased, is still recognized.

   c.   **Josquin** often varies a repetition either melodically or by adding a voice. Alternating pairs of voices and sequence are used to increase the dramatic effect of the motet.

   d.   *Memor esto verbi tui* (Psalm 119:49, Remember thy word unto thy servant) (*CE*, Motets, v. 2, p. 3)

5.   Masses

   a.   **Petrucci** devoted three books (1502, 1505, 1514) to **Josquin's** Masses, a rarity in the first half of the sixteenth century. **Josquin** demonstrates most of the complex contrapuntal techniques of his day.

   b.   *Missa L'Homme armé super voces musicales* (*CE*, v. 10 [Part 1, v. 1], p. 1; *PAM*, v. 6, p. 1; *AM*, v. 30, p. 56, *Agnus Dei*; *MSD*, 6, v. 2, pp. 324, 526, 527)

      1)   The *cantus firmus* not only appears in the tenor but fragments are introduced in other voices. As the Mass proceeds, the melody appears on a new scale step for each movement and is finished soon enough in each part to bring the harmonic feeling to a Dorian cadence. In the *Agnus Dei* the melody continues to the end.

      2)   *Missa L'Homme armé* on the sixth tone (*CE*, v. 14; *ArM*, v. 15, p. 35)

   c.   *Missa Mater Patris* (*CE*, v. 26 [Part I, v. 3], p. 1; *VOTS*, sec. 5, p. 135, *Kyrie*)

      1)   The parody technique is used quite extensively (Kyrie, Gloria, Credo, some in the Sanctus, Agnus Dei I and III) in this Mass based on a three-voice motet by **Antoine Brumel** (*CMM*, 5, v. 5). Other Masses which include some parody are *Missa Malheur me bat* (*CE*, v. 19 [Part 1, v. 2], p. 39; *MSD*, 6, v. 2, p. 528) and *Missa Fortuna desperata* (*CE*, v. 13 [Part 1, v. 1], p. 81; *MSD*, 6, v. 2, p. 469).

   d.   *Missa Pange lingua* (*CE*, v. 33 [Part I, v. 4], p. 1; *CW*, v. 1, p. 5; *DCS*, v. 25)

      1)   Based on the hymn (*LU*, p. 957), the Mass is an outstanding example of a paraphrase Mass. At the opening of the movements the theme, often presented imitatively, is literal but gradually takes on a great variety of paraphrase techniques. Pairing of the voices is common and there is much syllabic writing (*MSO*, v. 1, p. 34, *Gloria*; *MSD*, 6, v. 2, p. 379, *Pleni sunt*)

   e.   *Missa Hercules Dux Ferrariae* (*CE*, v. 17 [Part I, v. 2], p. 19; *ArM*, v. 15, p. 65)

      1)   Composed at least by 1499 in honor of Duke Hercules d'Este I, the Mass *cantus firmus* is made up of the solmization syllables corresponding to the vowels in the title: *re* (d), *ut* (c), *re* (d), *ut* (c), *re* (d), *fa* (f), *mi* (e), *re* (d). **Josquin** dismisses the A in the final diphthong. (See *MSD*, 6, v. 2, pp. 294, 307)

   f.   *Missa La Sol Fa Re Mi* (*CE*, v. 11 [Part I, v. 1], p. 35; *GMB*, No. 59, *Et incarnatus* and *Crucifixus*)

      1)   The Mass is based on a melody (a, g, f, d, e) made up of the solmization syllables which create the pun *"Lascia fare mi"* (Leave it to me).

G.   Among the followers of **Josquin** were many French composers; they include **Antoine de Févin, Elzéar Genet**, called **Carpentras**, and **Jean Mouton**.

1.   **Antoine de Févin** (*c.* 1480-*c.* 1512)

a.   **Glareanus** calls **Févin** a "happy emulator of **Josquin**" (*MMF*, v. 65, p. 354). His works include 9 Masses, 14 motets, other sacred compositions and 17 chansons.

b.   *Missa Mente Tota* (*MMRF*, v. 9, p. 62-123; *HAM*, No. 106, Agnus Dei I, II, III)

1)   **Févin** has borrowed from the fifth part of **Josquin's** motet *Vultum tuum depreca-buntur* (*CE*, Motets, v. 1, p. 117). Agnus Dei II is reduced to two voices, imitation in paired voices in Agnus Dei III and passages in parallel thirds and sixths in Agnus Dei I are all characteristics of the period of **Josquin**.

2.   **Elzéar Genet**, called **Carpentras** (*c.* 1470-1548) (*CMM*, 58)

a.   **Carpentras** spent most of his years in the papal service. In his later life he wrote and published Masses, hymns, Lamentations and Magnificats. The Lamentations remained in the Papal Chapel repertoire for many years.

3.   **Jean Mouton** (*c.* 1460-1522) (*CMM*, 43)

a.   A pupil of **Josquin** and teacher of **Willaert, Mouton** spent most of his life associated with cathedral choral activities at Nesle (1477-1483), Amien (1500) and Grenoble (1501), then at the Royal Chapel of Louis XII and Francis I. Among his compositions are 15 Masses (*CMM*, 28, vols. 1-4; *CW*, v. 70; *MMRF*, v. 9; *MMFR*, v. 12). 120 motets (*CW*, v. 76; *VOTS*, sec. 7, pp. 201-217) and some 20 chansons.

b.   *In illo tempore Maria Magdalene* (*MMRL*, p. 27)

1)   The Easter motet makes use of portions of the Easter Sequence, *Victimae pas-chali,* and canticle, *O filii et filiae.*

c.   *La rouse du moys de may* (The dew of the month of May) (*MMRL*, p. 59)

1)   The six-part chanson uses canon at the fifth in the tenor and alto parts.

III.   The French Polyphonic Chanson

A.   In contrast to the Flemish chanson, the French chanson took on a certain light, elegant, dance-like imitative style interspersed with chordal writing.

1.   Attractive melodies, generally original rather than borrowed, strong lively rhythms and rapidly repeated notes were most often set syllabically. The old *formes fixes* were abandoned and the chanson took new two- and three-part forms with clearly defined sections: ABA, AAB, AABCC. The repeated notes common to the initial subject (♩ ♪ ♪) were carried over into the subsequent instrumental form, the canzona.

2.   Many Italian musicians employed in the French courts contributed to the influence of the Italian *frottola* on the French chanson.

3.   The popularity of these chansons is attested to by the fact that hundreds were published in Italian and German collections arranged for lute or keyboard instruments.

B.   **Clément Janequin** (*c.* 1485-1560)

1.   Born near Poitiers, **Janequin** entered Holy Orders and became active at Bordeaux (*c.* 1529), Anjou and Paris (1548). In 1555 he entered the employ of the king and later became the first to hold the title "composer in ordinary" to the King of France.

2.   **Janequin**, the chief representative of the new sixteenth-century French chanson, wrote 286 chansons, many of which were descriptive or programmatic. (See *MSO*, v. 1. p. 35)

3.   *L'Alouette* (The Lark) (*HAM*, No. 107; *MMRF*, v. 7, p. 105; *CP*, v. 1, p. 99)

a.   The clever combination of light, rhythmic music with witty text, including nonsense syllables, makes this a typical example of a program chanson.

4.   *Les chants des oiseaux* (The songs of the birds) (*MMRF*, v. 7, p. 1; *CP*, v. 1, p. 5)

5.   *Le chasse* (The hunt) (*MMRF*, v. 7, p. 62; *CP*, v. 1, p. 54)

6.   *Les Cris de Paris* (The cries of Paris), 1529 (*FCVR*, v. 3)

a.   The text is composed of slogans heard on the streets of Paris.

7.   *La Guerre* (The war) (*MMRF*, v. 7, p. 31; *CP*, v. 1, p. 23; *AM*, v. 36, p. 7)

    a.   This programmatic chanson, emphasizing rhythm, describes drum-beats, fanfares, rapid alternations of declamatory phrases and hocket to suggest confusion.

C.   **Claudin de Sermisy** (*c.* 1490-1562)

    1.   A composer of Masses (*MLit* v. 1/2) and motets (*MMRF*, v. 12; *MDm*, v. 6) in addition to chansons (*PAM*, v. 23), **Sermisy** was a singer in the Royal Chapel of Louis XII (1508), and later (1533) became a canon in the Sainte Chapelle. Under François I he travelled to Italy (1515) and England (1520).

    2.   **Sermisy's** style is less descriptive and more graceful and polished than that of **Janequin** (*AM*, v. 16, p. 18; v. 41, pp. 13, 16). **Sermisy** also influenced Italian secular music.

    3.   A typical formal pattern for a seven-line chanson would be *ab ab cd EE*.

D.   The prestigious French culture was still being felt beyond the borders of France. During the last half of the sixteenth century the French polyphonic chanson maintained an interest among many composers in France as well as in other countries of Europe (**Arcadelt, Costeley, Caurroy, Le Jeune, Mauduit, Lasso**).

    1.   **Guillaume Costeley** (1531-1606)

        a.   **Costeley** was organist to Charles IX and in 1570 organized the Confraternity of St. Cecilia at Évreux. In 1575 musical contests were added and **Lasso** received the first annual prize.

        b.   **Costeley** does not incorporate the programmatic elements of **Janequin** but uses parlando, repeated sections, lively rhythms and melodies common to the earlier chansons.

        c.   *Musique*, a collection of 60 chansons, was published in 1570 in three volumes: I with 27 pieces (*MMRF*, v. 3); II with 21 pieces (*MMRF*, v. 18); III with 12 pieces (*MMRF*, v. 19).

        d.   *Allon gay, gay, gay bergeres* (*MMRF*, v. 3, p. 65)

        e.   *Las je n'yray plus* (*MMRF*, v. 18, p. 1)

        f.   *Prise de Calaix* (*MMRF*, v. 19, p. 12)

        g.   *J'ayme trop mieux souffrir la mort* (*MMRF*, v. 18, p. 31)

E.   *Musique mesuré – vers mesuré*

    1.   In 1570 Jean Antoine de Baïf, a leader in a group of poets known as the Pléiade, and Joachim Thibaut de Courville established the *Académie de poésie et de musique* to create a stronger bond between poetry and music. Their purpose was to compose, perform and teach *musique mesuré*, music in which the long and short syllables of *vers mesuré* are set to notes of long and short duration; the long notes being twice the length of the short notes. All the voices naturally use the same rhythm, developing a chordal style of music. Among the chief exponents of *musique mesuré* is **Claude Le Jeune.**

    2.   **Claude Le Jeune** (*c.* 1528-1600)

        a.   **Le Jeune** was court composer to Henry IV; he wrote Psalms, motets, French chansons and Italian madrigals. Pierre Ballard, the Parisian printer, in 1608 published 127 *chansons mesurés à l'antique.* (*MISC*, 1)

        b.   *Le Printemps* (Spring) (*MMRF*, vols. 12, 13, 14)

            1)   This is a collection of 39 chansons by Baïf, 33 of which are in *musique mesuré*. Melismatic figures are used to elaborate the long values of the long syllables in the *vers mesuré*.

            2)   The texts are divided into strophes called *"chants"* and refrains called *"rechants"* or *"reprizes."* The music may remain the same or vary for each strophe, and likewise for the *"rechant;"* at times the number of voices is varied to create contrast and variety.

        c.   *D'une coline* (As I walk upon the hill) (*HAM*, No. 138)

        d.   *Octonaires de la vanité et inconstance du monde* (Eight-line poems on the vanity and instability of the world) (Antoine Chandieu) (*MMFR*, v. 5, pp. 1, viii)

        1)   Thirty-six poems in all, there are three on each of the twelve modes, mode I being Ionian (emphasis on major) and not Dorian.

    e.   *La Guerre* (*Airs*, v. 1, pp. 90-117)

  3. **Eustache (François) de Caurroy** (1549-1609)

    a.   *Mélanges*, 1619 (*MMRF*, v. 17)

        1)   *Mélanges* includes some pieces in *musique mesuré* (pp. 56-81), noëls (pp. 26-55) and chansons (pp. 1-25). (See motets in *MMA*, v. 17)

  4. **Jacques Mauduit** (1557-1627)

    a.   *Vous me tuez si doucement* (*MMRF*, v. 10, p. 2; *SSMS*, p. 103)

    b.   *Psaumes mesuré de Jean-Antoine de Baïf* (*FCVR*, v. 7) (See motets in *MMA*, v. 17)

        1)   Psalms 150, 116, 100, 42, 133, 133, 23, 67 in four and five voices.

F. **Roland de Lassus** (Italian, **Orlando di Lasso**) (1532-1594), Flemish

  1. For biographical material see subsequent V. F. 1.

  2. There are extant 148 chansons: one three-part, 69 four-part, 58 five-part, 4 six-part, 5 eight-part and 11 incomplete.

  3. With **Lasso, Mauduit** and **Monte** the evolution of the French chanson was completed. **Lasso's** chansons are typically French and perfectly adapted to the text, many of which were by members of the Pléiade and his favorite, Clément Marot. Several had previously been set by other composers.

  4. **Lasso** did not write descriptive chansons in the style of **Janequin**, but followed the polished lyrical style of **Sermisy**.

  5. About half of **Lasso's** chansons begin with imitation; the others open with chords of free counterpoint. **Lasso** is inspired to give expression to the text in a variety of musical ways.

  6. *Bon Jour mon coeur* (Good day my heart) (*CE*, v. 12, p. 100; *HAM*, No. 145)

  7. *Un jour vis un foulon qui fouloit* (*CE*, v. 12, p. 39; *MMRF*, v. 1, p. 72)

    a.   This chanson was used by Shakespeare in his *Henry IV*, Part II, Act V, Scene 3; several new texts have been used with the music.

G. **Philippe de Monte** (1521-1603)

  1. **Monte** wrote only a few chansons (*CE*, v. 20; *AM*, v. 28, p. 43); they demonstrate a complete mastery of the genre. Rich harmonies, imitation, motet-like qualities are characteristics. Often in the imitative parts there is a separate independent voice which does not take part in the imitation. When using a borrowed melody, **Monte** avoids its literal use but makes suggestion to it.

  2. *Susanne un jour* (*CE*, v. 20, p. 35)

IV. Music Printing (*c.* 1500)

A. The invention of printing as applied to music produced a revolution in the history of music and made possible the international influence of music.

  1. The *Psalterium*, printed in 1457 by the Gutenberg associates, Johann Fust and Peter Schöffer of Mainz, was the first printed book to include music. In this case the staff of three black lines was printed and the notes and a fourth line in red were added by hand.

  2. The first known example of music printing with movable type was a Roman *Missale* printed by Michael Zoratus in 1476 at Milan, Italy. Shortly thereafter in the same year Ulrich Han in Rome printed another *Missale* using, as Zoratus did also, the double-impression technique (first the staff lines in red, then the plainsong notes in black).

B. **Ottaviano dei Petrucci** (1466-1539)

  1. **Petrucci** in 1498 petitioned for exclusive privilege to print music in Venice for a period of twenty years. Included among some 60 publications were motets, Masses, chansons, frottolas and intabulations by French as well as Italian composers such as **Agricola, Brumel, Josquin, Martini, Févin, La Rue** and others.

2. *Harmonice Musices Odhecaton A*, 1501 (*M* 40c; *MMF*, ser. 1, v. 10, facsimile)
   a. This first printed collection of part music was printed by the double impression process. About 80 of the 96 (not 100 as the title suggests) pieces are French chansons (three and four voices) by the composers of the late fifteenth century. These include **Busnois, Ockeghem, Obrecht, Isaac, Josquin, Brumel, Hayne, Alexander, Tinctoris, Agricola** and others.
   b. Only a few of the pieces have texts, but many of the pieces are in other manuscripts with texts. The layout of the music on the open page is in practical part-book form: the soprano and tenor parts separated on the left page and the alto and bass parts on the right. The pieces were probably intended for either instrumental or, when possible, vocal performance.
3. **Francesco Spinacino,** *Recercare*, p. 39 from *Intabolatura de lauto. Libro primo*, Venice, 1507 (*NPM*, p. 63, facsimile)

C. The costly double impression technique was superseded by single impression printing developed by **Pierre Haultin** (d. 1560) in 1525 in Paris. Single impression printing was also fostered by the Parisian publisher **Pierre Attaingnant** (d. *c.* 1552) whose publications (1528-1549) number about 70 collections. All the leading Franco-Flemish composers of the first half of the sixteenth century are represented: **Josquin, Janequin, Le Jeune, Mouton, Clemens non Papa, Sermisy, Willaert** and others.
   1. *Quatorze livres de Motets parus chez Pierre Attaingnant*, 1534-1535, 1539 (*LMA*)
      a. In these 14 books of motets (*LMA*) **Attaingnant** has collected a vast treasury of 416 motets from some 57 composers of the late fifteenth and early sixteenth centuries. They are in three, four, five, six and eight voices; the majority are in four voices and two motets by **Gombert** are for twelve voices.
D. *Lyons Contrapunctus*, 1528 (*RRMR*, vols. 21, 22)
   1. This is the first printed cycle of polyphonic settings for the Proper of the Mass. There are 13 Masses arranged in the order of the church year; each Mass contains five items: *Introit, Responsory, Alleluia, Offertory* and *Communion*. No composer is identified.

V. Flemish and French Sacred Music (Franco-Flemish School)

A. The Reformation in France
   1. The Protestant Reformation began early (1518) in the sixteenth century and grew rapidly under the influence of Lutheranism. In spite of severe persecution the French Protestant church (Huguenots), based on John Calvin's beliefs, was established by 1559.
   2. Calvin's ideas on music were in direct contrast to those of Luther; he sanctioned the singing of Psalms or other Scripture translations monophonically. The melodies were often adaptations of Lutheran songs.
      a. Calvin's first Psalter was published in Strasbourg in 1539; among the 18 Psalm translations were six by himself, the others were revisions of Clément Marot's translations. Included also were the Creed, the Ten Commandments and the Song of Simeon.
      b. Marot associated with Calvin only two years and completed the translation of 50 Psalms; Théodore de Bèza (1519-1605) completed the translation of the Psalms.
   3. **Louis Bourgeois** (composer, compiler, editor) was the one largely responsible for the accepted form of about 85 tunes for the Psalter completed in 1562. The Genevan Psalter furnished tunes for the Reformed Church in England and the Pilgrims in America (*Ainsworth Psalter*).
      a. Thirteen tunes are taken from the Strasbourg Psalter and at least 32 are from chansons.
      b. In general the texts are set syllabically; a wide variety of rhythms including syncopation occur, and the meter is duple. A single phrase may encompass a fourth to a

sixth; the range of the complete melody may be an octave.

    c.   By 1547 **Bourgeois** had made four-part settings mostly in chordal, syllabic style.
       1)   *Psalm 1* (*HAM*, No. 132)
       2)   *Old Hundredth* (*RMR*, p. 361)

4.   Simple part-settings with the melody in the tenor were made for use at home; these were eventually developed into polyphonic motets by **Goudimel, Mauduit, Le Jeune, Sweelinck** and others.

5.   *Souterliedekens*, Antwerp, 1540
    a.   The "Little Psalter Songs" were Dutch monophonic Psalm settings first printed in Antwerp by Symon Cock and continued through many editions into 1613. The Psalms, set largely to Dutch popular song tunes, were intended for use in the home and social gatherings rather than for church service as were those of the Genevan Psalter.

6.   **Claude Goudimel** (*c.* 1505-1572)
    a.   Born in Bescançon in eastern France, **Goudimel** was in Paris in 1549 and lived in Metz in 1565. His conversion from Catholicism to Protestantism occurred about 1560; he was killed in Lyon in the continuation of the Paris St. Bartholomew's Day massacre.
    b.   Among his music for Catholic service are 5 Masses, 3 Magnificats and several motets.
       1)   The Masses, mostly in four voices, are generally short and frequently chordal.
          a)   *Audi filia* (*MMRF*, v. 9, p. 1)
          b)   *Tant plus ie metz* (*MMRF*, v. 9, p. 45)
       2)   Four festival motets (*CW*, v. 103, pp. 1, 8, 13, 19)
    c.   More significant are **Goudimel's** Psalm settings, about 60 in motet style, from three to six voices (1551-1566).
       1)   Two published collections of the Psalms were expressly intended for home use: the 1564 collection in embellished chordal style and the 1565 collection in simple chordal (note-against-note) style. The latter became very popular in Protestant Germany.
          a)   In the 1564 collection the superius generally contains the Psalm tune, but only 17 Psalm melodies are in the superius in the 1565 edition.
       2)   *Les 150 Psaumes de David mis en rime françoise*, 1565 (*MMRF*, vols. 2, 4, 6)
       3)   *Psalm 35* (*MMRF*, v. 2, p. 51; *HAM*, No. 126a) (See *TEM*, p. 126; *SR*, p. 349)

7.   **Claude Le Jeune** (*c.* 1528-1600)
    a.   **Le Jeune** rivaled **Goudimel** with four-part settings of the Psalms; the tenor contained the Psalm melody. Other settings in three to seven voices have the melody phrases in various voices. Not only did **Goudimel** use the Genevan tunes and texts but also the Psalm settings in *vers mesuré* of Baïf (*MMRF*, vols. 20-22; *MMFR*, v. 8).
    b.   *Dodécacorde* (*MMRF*, v. 11)
       1)   This series of twelve motets are elaborate arrangements of the Psalms divided into several sections and have a varying number of voices, from two to seven. The Genevan Psalm tunes serve as *cantus firmi*; they are based on the 12 modes also used by **Glareanus**.

B.   **Nicholas Gombert** (*c.* 1490-*c.* 1560) (*CMM*, 6)
   1.   **Gombert** was born in southern Flanders; he studied with **Josquin** (*c.* 1520) and sang in the Imperial Chapel choir in Brussels (1526). He accompanied Emperor Charles V to Spain, north Italy, Germany and Austria. His last years were spent in Tournai.
   2.   One of the great composers of church music, **Gombert** represents the "classical" Netherlands style. He composed 10 Masses and 169 motets, including 8 Magnificats.
   3.   His style, almost exclusively imitative, is based on the polyphonic techniques of **Ockeghem** and **Josquin**. Imitation, occasionally with tonal rather than real answers, was developed to a high degree of fluency by reworking motives instead of introducing new

ones.   The texture, including the number of voices, generally remains unchanged throughout.

4.   The rhythmic patterns and syncopation are used in a variety of original ways.   In the handling of dissonance **Gombert** anticipates **Palestrina**, although at times strong voice leading creates unusual dissonances.

5.   The use of a *cantus firmus*, rare in the motets, is quite common in the Masses (*CMM*, 6, vols. 1-3).

   a.   *Missa Media vita* (*GMB*, No. 102, *Agnus Dei*; *CMM*, 6, v. 2, p. 26)

6.   **Gombert** often divides the motet into two sections with a change of meter and antici-pates the later Venetian polychoral style.

   a.   *Quem dicunt homines* (*CW*, v. 94; *CMM*, 6, v. 9, p. 166)

   b.   *Homo erat in Jerusalem* (*VOTS*, sec. 7, p. 230; *CMM*, 6, v. 10, p. 9)

   c.   *Super flumina* (*HAM*, No. 114; *CMM*, 6, v. 5, p. 66)

C.   **Jacobus Clemens non Papa [Jacques Clement]** (*c.* 1510-1557) (*CMM*, 4, vols. 1-21)

1.   Evidently "non Papa" was added to the name of **Jacobus Clemens** to avoid confusion with the contemporary poet Jacobus Papa.

2.   **Clemens** was born on the north Netherlands island of Walcheren and his early produc-tive years were spent in Paris.   By 1545 he had returned to the Netherlands and spent his closing years in Ypres and Dixmude.

3.   **Clemens'** sacred works include 15 Masses and 231 motets in addition to his three-voice *Souterliedekens* (*CMM*, 4, v. 2).

4.   The Masses, in from four to six voices, are generally polyphonic in texture, but many chordal passages do occur.   Canon is seldom used; the bass themes are often promi-nent.   **Clemens** uses the parody technique; he often uses expressive melodic materials rather than dissonance to reinforce or symbolize the thoughts of the text.

   a.   *Missa Panis quem ego dabo* (*CMM*, 4, v. 7, p. 85)

     1)   This Mass is based on a motet by **Lupus Hellinck** (d. 1541) (*RMR*, p. 342).   In the Kyrie **Clemens** uses four melodies from **Hellinck's** motet, separately and also combined.   **Palestrina** wrote a five-voice Mass on **Hellinck's** motet also.

5.   In **Clemens'** motets, generally in two parts, many Biblical texts are used; some motets are bi-textual.   The structure of the melodies often incorporates an upward leap fol-lowed by downward stepwise motion; the superius seems to be the most important voice.   The metrical accent of the text influences the rhythm; points of imitation are common; finality is expressed by the authentic cadence.

   a.   *Vox in Rama* (A voice in Rama, Matt. 2:18) (*HAM*, No. 125; *CMM*, 4, v. 9, p. 105)

     1)   This is not based on the plainsong Communion (*LU*, p. 430).

D.   **Philippe de Monte** (1521-1603)

1.   Born in Malines, Belgium, **Monte** took employment in Naples (1540-1554), at the Royal Chapel in Madrid under Philip II (visited England), in Florence (1556), Rome (1568), Vienna and Prague under Maximilian II and Rudolf II (1568-1603).   **Monte** represents with **Lasso** the culmination of the Burgundian and Franco-Flemish poly-phonic art.

2.   **Monte's** output includes 48 Masses, about 300 motets and almost 1200 secular madri-gals and chansons.

3.   A consistent polyphonic style with some influence of his madrigals marks **Monte's** church music.   The texture is usually uniform throughout; the voices generally equal in importance.   Scale passages and filled-in leaps tend to lessen the melodic quality.

   a.   *Missa super Cara la vita mia* (*CE*, v. 21; *HAM*, No. 146b, Sanctus)

     1)   Based on a madrigal by **Giaches de Wert** (1536-1596) (*HAM*, No. 146a), this Mass illustrates **Monte's** frequent use of the parody technique.

E.   **Roland de Lassus [Italian, Orlando di Lasso]** (1532-1594)

1.   **Lasso** was born in Mons, Belgium, and began his early musical experience as choirboy at Saint-Nicolas Church.   Because of his beautiful voice he was abducted three times

and at the age of twelve (1544) his parents let him be taken into the service of Ferdinando Gonzaga, Viceroy of Sicily. During the ensuing years he was in Palermo, Milan, Naples and Rome (appointed choirmaster, St. John Lateran, 1553). After visits to England (1554) and France, **Lasso** settled in Antwerp for two years. In 1556 he accepted employment in the Bavarian court of Duke Albert V in Munich where he remained until his death.

2. An international musician who wrote successfully in many styles, he was the last great Netherland composer of sixteenth-century choral music. He did not create a new style but added Italian and German elements to the Franco-Flemish style of **Gombert** and **Clemens non Papa**.

3. Included in the church music of **Lasso** are 516 motets, 53 Masses in four to six and eight voices, 9 Lamentations (*DCS*, v. 22) and 25 three-voice settings of German Psalms (*DCS*, v. 21).

   a. *Magnum opus musicum* (*CE*, vols. 1, 3, 5, 7, 9, 11, 13, 15, 17, 19, 21; *DCS*, vols. 11, 16), a collection of 516 motets from two to ten and twelve voices.

4. The Masses of **Lasso** do not appear to be on the level of those of **Josquin** and **Palestrina**. The variety in the texts of the motets appears to have been a greater challenge than the unvarying text of the Ordinary. The motets illustrate **Lasso's** unusual creative skills and represent the culmination of the polyphonic ideals of preceding generations.

   a. *Missa de profunctis* (*Introit, HAM*, No. 143)

   b. *Missa Veni sponsa Christi* (*Agnus Dei, MM*, p. 86)

5. More faithful to and influenced by the texts of the motets, **Lasso** is particular about word placement in regard to the music. Although previously there were certain points of word expression depicted in the music, **Lasso** concentrates on making the text more easily understood, thus conveying the pictorial and emotional aspects of the music (*SR*, pp. 325-326).

   a. This brought about a stronger harmonic counterpoint and chordal style favoring syllabic writing, echo effects, division of voices in the choir and modulatory passages.

      1) The bass outlines the harmonic line, often in root position and in root movement by fourths and fifths; chords often have the third in the highest voice.

      2) The use of accidentals may suggest transitions to other modes.

   b. **Lasso** does not rely on existing formal patterns but lets the form evolve freely out of the melodic, motivic and textual content. Strict contrapuntal devices, such as canon, are rare. The influence of the madrigal may be felt in setting a text antiphonally, in short sections of contrasting rhythm and in descriptive passages.

   c. Chromaticism is rare; cross relations occur rather frequently, particularly in change of mode (G major to G minor) or in different chords (D major to F major).

   d. The cambiata figure is used in various rhythms; the dissonant note is usually a major or minor seventh above the root of the chord.

   e. Eighth notes are usually stepwise, but skips to and from an eighth do occur. The eighth note is generally used in groups of two or three, rarely singly, and sometimes up to sixteen, but large groups are rare. Sixteenth notes occur in stepwise groups of two.

VI. Instrumental Music

A. Instruments

1. Music began to be written for specific instruments, particularly those capable of playing polyphonic music. The organ, harpsichord, clavichord and lute became popular. The combination of strings with brass and wind ensembles was used more frequently.

2. Lute

   a. Early makers of the lute were Germans who carried their art to Italy, France and England. The first great lute players and composers were Italian. The lute remained a popular instrument throughout the Renaissance and Baroque periods.

   b.   The lute is a string instrument with a half pear-shaped body and fingerboard divided by frets of catgut and later of wood or brass. The common lute was tuned in six courses: two pairs of perfect fourths separated by a major third (G - c - f - a - d' - g'). For increased volume the two lower courses were generally doubled at the octave and the adjacent three courses were doubled at the unison, thus making an eleven string lute (G - g, c - c', f - f, a - a, d' - d', g). Large lutes were the *archlute*, *theorbo* and *chitarrone*.

3.   Viol

   a.   The viol followed the medieval fiddle (*vielle*) and was in general use from the fifteenth to the eighteenth centuries, especially in England. It was superseded by the prominence of the violin during the seventeenth century.

     1)   Viols were made in three main sizes and tuned like the lute, in two pairs of two perfect fourths each separated by a major third (treble: d, g, c', e', a', d"; tenor: A, d, g, b, e', a'; bass or viola da gamba: D, G, c, e, a, d').

   b.   **Gasparo Bertolotti da Salò** (1540-1609) of Brescia and **Andrea Amati** (*c*. 1520-*c*. 1578) with his two sons, **Antonio** (1550-1638) and **Girolamo** (1556-1630) of Cremona built the first true violins.

4.   Clavichord

   a.   Probably originating in the thirteenth century, the clavichord came into general use in the fifteenth and sixteenth centuries. The clavichord is a rectangular shaped keyboard instrument in which the strings are set in vibration by metal tangents which also divide the strings. Dynamic intensity is varied by pressure of the fingers.

5.   Harpsichord (Italian: *clavicembalo, cembalo*; French: *clavecin*; English: *virginal, spinet*)

   a.   Known from about 1400, the harpsichord became the main string keyboard instrument of the sixteenth and seventeenth centuries; it was used in most of the ensemble music. Dynamic intensity cannot be modified by touch. Strings are plucked by a quill or hard leather point which is raised up by a jack when the key is depressed.

   b.   In the harpsichord of two keyboards the upper keyboard generally had one set of strings at 8' (standard) pitch. The lower keyboard ordinarily had another 8' set of strings and a 4' (octave higher) set. In some cases a fourth set of 16' pitch (octave lower) was added. The upper manual could be coupled to the lower in order to have all sets of strings sound by playing the lower keyboard.

B.   Forms

   1.   Instrumental music has been practiced from earliest times, although the music was not written down until the thirteenth century. Thirteenth century dance music and instrumental motets were followed in the fourteenth century by the Italian *estampie* and arrangements of motets for organ.

   2.   In the fifteenth century chansons were arranged for the organ and independent preludes were composed. Instrumental pieces in imitative polyphonic style (*carmina*) and other types were written by **Isaac, Josquin** and **Hofhaimer**. The *basse danse* was the only stylized dance known in the fifteenth century.

   3.   Sixteenth century composers arranged choral works for keyboard instruments or lute (German: *intabulierung*; Italian: *intavolatura*; English: *intabulation*) with ornaments suited to the instrument. Dance music was brought into the sphere of art music by lutenists and exerted an important influence in the development of instrumental music, particularly in rhythm and regular division of phrases and periods.

   4.   French dances

     a.   **Thoinot Arbeau** (1519-1595) (an anagram of his real name, **Jehan Tabourot**) in his important treatise, *Orchésographie* (1589) gives the earliest description of dances with examples of music.

    1)   Some of the dances included are pavanes, tourdions, galliardes, branles, courantes and allemandes.

  b.   *Basse danse* (1450-1550)

    1)   The *basse danse* is a gliding ceremonial court dance usually in slow triple meter. It is often followed by a *recoupe* and a *tordion* forming an early type of suite (*AM*, v. 26, pp. 18, 22-23; *SSMS*, p. 98).

  c.   *Pavane* and *galliarde* (1500-1550)

    1)   The pavane is a slow dance of Italian (Padua) origin usually in slow triple meter. It is followed by the livelier galliard in compound duple meter (*AM*, v. 26, pp. 13-14).

       a)   After 1550 the faster *passamezzo* and *saltarello* replaced the pavane and galliard as dances; these were used in idealized forms by English virginalists.

    2)   An early suite-type combination is: *pavana - saltarello - piva.*

  d.   Allemande

    1)   The allemande is a German dance in moderate duple time similar to the passamezzo. It is often followed by a jumping dance in triple meter (*tripla, proportz*) and in the seventeenth century by the courante.

  e.   Courante

    1)   The courante originated in the sixteenth century as a lively dance with jumping movements. In the seventeenth century the courante was known in two types: 1) Italian *corrente (coranto)* in quick triple time (3/4 or 3/8) and 2) the French *courante* in a refined moderate 3/2 or 6/4 with occasional shifts to hemiola rhythm.

C. Music

  1. **Pierre Attaingnant** published (1528-1549) music for lute and keyboard, including dances and transcriptions or intabulations of vocal works, such as chansons, Psalms and motets.

    a.   *Dix-huit basses dances . . . avec dixneuf Branles*, 1529

      1)   This is the earliest published collection of French lute music.

    b.   *Sans roch* (*GMB*, No. 90)

  2. **Emanuel Adriaenssen** (*c.* 1545-1604)

    a.   *Pratum Musicum longe amoenissimum*, Antwerp, 1584

      1)   One of three books of lute tablature (1584, 1592, 1600), this is the first lute tablature to be printed in the Netherlands devoted to one composer.

      2)   Five fantasias open the book to be followed with vocal transcriptions and 29 dances (*almande, branle, gailliarde*).

  3. Keyboard music

    a.   **Pierre Attaingnant** in 1531 published seven books of keyboard (*orgues espinettes et manicordion*) compositions; the first four are devoted to transcriptions of chansons and dances (*CMM*, 20); the last three to liturgical pieces and motet transcriptions. These are the first publications of keyboard music in France.

      1)   The transcriptions include works by **Compère, Févin, Obrecht, Brumel, Sermisy** and **Busnois** (*AERM*, p. 210), although the transcriber is not indicated. In some cases, with the chansons in particular, keyboard arrangements of the lute transcriptions are made.

    b.   Thirteen motets and a prelude for organ (*MMA*, Ser. I, v. 5)

    c.   *Deux livre d'orgue* (*MMA*, Ser. I, v. 1)

    d.   *Quatorze Gaillardes, neuf Pavennes, sept Branles et deux Basses Dances*, 1531

      1)   *Pavane* (*Quatorze Gaillardes*, p. 73; *HAM*, No. 104)

      2)   *Branle* (*NPM*, p. 7, facsimile)

  4. Instrumental ensemble

    a.   Little was written for instrumental ensembles other than dances and some *fantasies* (**Le Jeune, Du Caurroy**). In 1530 **Attaingnant** printed in part books two volumes of dances: *basse dances, branles, pavanes* and *gaillardes*. Later, between 1545 and 1557, he published another ten volumes of dances including ones by **Claude Gervaise** and **Étienne du Tertre**, chanson composers.

   b.   The ensembles were made up of a variety of instruments: guitar, lute, theorbo, viol, flute and string keyboard instruments. Doubling of parts seemed to be common.

   c.   *Danceries* in four parts (*LP*, v. 9)

   d.   **Jacob Obrecht** (*c.* 1450-1505)

      1)   Canzona: *T'saat een meskin* (A maiden sat) (*HAM*, No. 78; *M* 40c, p. 407)

   e.   **Claude Gervaise** (*fl.* 1550)

      1)   Three dances: *Basse danse, Pavane* and *Gaillarde, Allemande* (*HAM*, No. 137; *MMRF*, v. 23, pp. 4, 18, 48; *AM*, v. 27, pp. 32, 41)

   f.   **Thoinot Arbeau** (1519-1595)

      1)   *Orchésographie*, 1589

VII. Performance of Renaissance Music

   A.   Pictures of vocal music in churches or the home usually show instrumentalists accompanying the voices. Flexibility is a prominent feature; musical scores were probably considered merely as outlines and full realization was left to the performers. There was little distinction between vocal and instrumental styles; the music was performed by either voice or instruments or by various combinations of both. Therefore, there was no definite grouping of players and singers. *Contrafacta*, that is the replacement of an original text with a new one, particularly the exchange of sacred and secular texts, was common.

   B.   Vocal music was frequently transcribed for keyboard instruments or the lute and was performed with varying degrees of elaboration or embellishment (*diminutio*). Ornaments were added to long notes or used at the cadences; they could be written out or improvised in performance. Many sixteenth-century books systematized various kinds of ornaments as aids to performers. Vocal embellishments were performed by soloists rather than the choirs.

   C.   Reference is made to a performance of a motet by **Lasso** with five *cornetti* (*Zinken*) and two trombones in 1568. Benevenuto Cellini in his *Autobiography* describes the playing of two motets for the Pope. **Hermann Finck** (grand nephew of **Heinrich Finck**), writing in his *Practica musica*, 1556, asks singers not to vary the intensity, but to sing steadily like the organ. Different intensities are suggested by various types of music; sad works are to be sung softly; cheerful ones more loudly; choral music is to be louder than instrumental music.

   D.   Comparatively, the tempos are not slow; the half notes correspond to the quarter notes of today. Ritards are often written into the music by lengthening the note values. In polyphonic music the rhythm of each individual part must be considered; barlines in modern notation do not indicate an accent.

SELECTED BIBLIOGRAPHY

Books

1. Arbeau, Thoinot. *Orchésographie*. London: C. W. Beaumont, 1925; tr. Mary S. Evans. New York: Kamin Dance Publishers, 1948; reprint: ed. Julia Sutton. New York: Dover Publications, 1970.

2. Bradshaw, Murray C. *The Falsobordone. A Study in Renaissance and Baroque Music*. Neuhausen-Stuttgart: Hänssler Verlag, 1978.

3. Brown, Howard Mayer. *Instrumental Music Printed before 1600: A Bibliography*. Cambridge, MA: Harvard University Press, 1965.

4. ———————*Music in the French Secular Theater, 1400-1550*. Cambridge, MA: Harvard University Press, 1963.

5. Casella, Alfredo. *The Evolution of Music Throughout the History of the Perfect Cadence*. London: J. & W. Chester, Ltd., 1924.

6. Chambers, Frank Pentland. *The History of Taste*. New York: Columbia University Press, 1932.

7. Crane, Frederick. *Materials for the Study of the Fifteenth Century Basse Danse*. Brooklyn: Institute of Mediaeval Music, 1968. (*Musicological Studies*, v. 16)

8. Dolmetsch, Mabel. *Dances of England and France, 1450-1600*. London: Routledge & Kegan Paul, 1949.

9. Finscher, Ludwig. *Loyset Compère (c. 1450-1518), Life and Works*. Rome: American Institute of Musicology, 1964. (*Musicological Studies and Documents*, v. 12)

10. Garside, Jr., Charles. *Zwingli and the Arts*. New Haven: Yale University Press, 1966.

11. Glareanus, Henricus. *Dodecachordon*. Basel, 1547; facsimile, New York: Broude Brothers, 1967. (*MMF*, ser. 2, v. 65)

12. ———————*Dodecachordon*, ed. Clement A. Miller. Rome: American Institute of Musicology, 1965. (*Musicological Studies and Documents*, v. 6, parts I and II)

13. Haar, James, ed. *Chanson and Madrigal, 1480-1530; Studies in Comparison and Contrast*. Cambridge, MA: Harvard University Press, 1964.

14. Heartz, Daniel. *Pierre Attaingnant, Royal Printer of Music; A Historical Study and Bibliographical Catalogue*. Berkeley: University of California Press, 1969.

15. Hewitt, Helen. "A *Chanson rustique* of the Early Renaissance: *Bon temps*," in *Aspects of Medieval and Renaissance Music: A Birthday Offering to Gustave Reese*, ed. Jan LaRue, pp. 376-391. New York: W. W. Norton, 1966.

16. Hoerburger, F. *Dance and Dance Music of the 16th Century and Their Relations to Folk Dance and Folk Music*. Budapest: Akadémiai Kiadó, 1965. (*Studia musicologica*, v. 7, pp. 79-83)

17. *Jacques Moderne Publications*. Geneva: S. Pogue, 1969.

18. *Josquin Des Pres. Proceedings of the International Josquin Festival-Conference*, ed. Edward E. Lowinsky. New York: Oxford University Press, 1976.

19. Karp, Theodore. "Modal Variants in Medieval Secular Monophony" in *The Commonwealth of Music in Honor of Curt Sachs*, ed. Gustave Reese and Rose Brandel, pp. 118-129. New York: The Free Press, 1965.

20. Kinkeldey, Otto. *Music and Music Printing in Incunabula*. New York: Bibliographical Society of America, 1932.

21. Lesure, François. *Musicians and Poets of the French Renaissance*, tr. Elio Gianturco and Hans Rosenwald. New York: Merlin Press, 1955.

22. ———————*Musique et Musiciens Français du XVIᵉ Siècle*. Paris: Éditions de Paris, 1950, 1969; reprint: Geneva: Minkoff Reprint, 1976.

23. ———————"Some Minor French Composers of the 16th Century," in *Aspects of Medieval*

and Renaissance Music: A Birthday Offering to Gustave Reese, ed. Jan LaRue, pp. 538-544. New York: W. W. Norton, 1966.

24. Lowinsky, Edward E. *Secret Chromatic Art in the Netherlands Motet*. New York: Columbia University Press, 1946.

25. Marix, Jeanne. *Histoire de la musique et des musiciens de la cour de Bourgogne sous le règne de Philippe le Bon (1420-1467)*. Strasbourg: Heitz & Co., 1939; reprint: Baden-Baden: Verlag Valentin Koerner, 1974.

26. Merritt, A. Tillman. "A Chanson Sequence by Fèvin," in *Essays on Music in Honor of Archibald Thompson Davison, by his Associates*, pp. 91-99. Cambridge, MA: Department of Music, Harvard University, 1957.

27. –––––– "Janequin: Reworkings of Some Early Chansons," in *Aspects of Medieval and Renaissance Music: A Birthday Offering to Gustave Reese*, ed. Jan LaRue, pp. 603-613. New York: W. W. Norton, 1966.

28. Mitchell, William J. "The Prologue to Orlando di Lasso's Prophetiae Sibyllarum," in *The Music Forum*, ed. William J. Mitchell and Felix Salzar, v. 2, pp. 264-273. New York: Columbia Univserity Press, 1970.

29. Novack, Saul. "Fusion of Design and Tonal Order in Mass and Motet, Josquin Desprez and Heinrich Isaac," in *The Music Forum*, ed. William J. Mitchell and Felix Salzar, v. 2, pp. 187-263. New York: Columbia University Press, 1970.

30. Parks, Edna. *The Hymns and Hymn Tunes Found in the English Metrical Psalters*. New York: Coleman-Ross, 1966.

31. Pidoux, Pierre. "Polyphonic Settings of the Genevan Psalter: Are They Church Music? " in *Cantors at the Crossroads: Essays on Church Music in Honor of Walter E. Buszin*, ed. Johannes Riedel, pp. 65-74. St. Louis: Concordia Publishing House, 1967.

32. Pogue, Samuel F. *Jacques Moderne, Lyons Music Printer of the Sixteenth Century*. Geneva: Droz, 1969.

33. Pratt, Waldo Selden. *The Music of the French Psalter of 1562*. New York: Columbia University Press, 1939.

34. Reaney, Gilbert. "The Performance of Medieval Music," in *Aspects of Medieval and Renaissance Music: A Birthday Offering for Gustave Reese*, ed. Jan LaRue, pp. 704-722. New York: W. W. Norton, 1966.

35. Reese, Gustave. "Printing and Engraving of Music," in Oscar Thompson. *The International Cyclopedia of Music and Musicians*, 10th ed., pp. 1720-1722. New York: Dodd, Mead, 1975.

36. Rosenberg, Marianne. "Symbolic and Descriptive Text Settings in the Works of Pierre de la Rue (c. 1460-1518)," in *Miscellanea Musicologica* (Adelaide Studies in Musicology), v. 1, pp. 225-248. Adelaide: University of Adelaide, 1966.

37. Salop, Arnold. "Two 'Insignificant' Motets by Josquin des Prez," in Arnold Salop. *Studies in the History of Musical Style*, pp. 103-132. Detroit: Wayne State University Press, 1971.

38. Sollitt, Edna Richolson. *Dufay to Sweelinck*. New York: I. Washburn, 1933.

39. Sparks, Edgar H. *Cantus Firmus in Mass and Motet, 1420-1520*. Berkeley: University of California Press, 1963.

40. Spiess, Lincoln B. "Inconstancy of Meaning in Certain Medieval and Renaissance Musical Terms," in *Cantors at the Crossroads: Essays on Church Music in Honor of Walter E. Buszin*, ed. Johannes Riedel, pp. 25-32. St. Louis: Concordia Publishing House, 1967.

41. Stein, Edwin Eugene. *The Polyphonic Mass in France and the Netherlands, c. 1525 to c. 1560*. Rochester, NY: University of Rochester Press, 1954.

42. *Tielman Susato Publications*. Berlin: U. Meissner, 1967.

43. Wangermée, Robert. *Flemish Music and Society in the Fifteenth- and Sixteenth-Centuries*, tr. Robert Erich Wolf. New York: Praeger, 1968.

44. Winternitz, Emanuel. *Musical Instruments of the Western World*. New York: McGraw, 1967.

45.   Yates, Frances A. *The French Academies of the Sixteenth Century*. London: Warburg Institute, University of London, 1947.

Articles

1.   Apel, Willi. "Imitation Canons on *L'Homme armé*." *Speculum* 25 (1950), p. 367.
2.   Arnold, Denis. "The Grand Motets of Orlandus Lassus." *Early Music* 6 (1978), pp. 170-181.
3.   Bernstein, Lawrence F. "Claude Gervaise as Chanson Composer." *JAMS* 18 (1965), pp. 359-381.
4.   Blackburn, Bonnie J. "Johannes Lupi and Lupus Hellinck: A Double Portrait." *MQ* 59 (1973), pp. 547-583.
5.   Bowles, Edmund A. "Musical Instruments in Civic Processions during the Middle Ages." *ActaM* 33 (1961), pp. 147-161.
6.   Brown, Howard Mayer. "The Chanson rustique: Popular Elements in the 15th- and 16th-Century Chanson." *JAMS* 12 (1959), pp. 16-26.
7.   ———————"The 'Chanson spirituelle,' Jacques Buus, and Parody Technique." *JAMS* 15 (1962), pp. 146-173.
8.   ———————"Music of the Strozzi Chansonnier." *ActaM* 40 (1968), pp. 115-129.
9.   Bukofzer, Manfred. "On the Performance of Renaissance Music." *MTNAPro* 65 (1941), pp. 225-235.
10.   Carpenter, Nan Cooke. "Music in the Medieval Universities." *Journal of Research in Music Education* 3 (1955), pp. 136-144.
11.   Clive, H. P. "The Clavecinist Attitude to Music, and Its Literary Aspects and Sources." *Bibliothèque d'humanisme et renaissance* 19 (1957), pp. 80-102, 294-319; 20 (1958), 79-107.
12.   Crane, Frederick. "The Derivation of Some Fifteenth-Century Basse-Danse Tunes." *ActaM* 37 (1965), pp. 179-188.
13.   Crawford, David. "Reflections on Some Masses from the Press of Moderne." *MQ* 58 (1972), pp. 82-91.
14.   Croll, Gerhard. "Gaspar van Weerbecke, An Outline of His Life and Works." *MD* 6 (1952), pp. 67-81.
15.   Cunningham, Caroline M. "Estienne du Tertre and the Mid-Sixteenth Century Parisian Chanson." *MD* 25 (1971), pp. 127-170.
16.   Cuyler, Louise E. "The Sequences of Isaac's *Choralis Constantinus*." *JAMS* 3 (1950), pp. 3-16.
17.   Davison, Nigel. "The Motets of Pierre de la Rue." *MQ* 48 (1962), pp. 19-35.
18.   Dent, Edward J. "The Musical Form of the Madrigal." *ML* 11 (1930), pp. 230-240.
19.   Douglas, Fenner, and Maarten Albert Vente. "French Organ Registration in the Early 16th Century." *MQ* 51 (1965), pp. 614-635.
20.   Einstein, Alfred. "Narrative Rhythm in the Madrigal." *MQ* 29 (1943), pp. 475-484.
21.   Falck, Robert. "Parody and Contrafactum: A Terminological Clarification." *MQ* 65 (1979), pp. 1-23.
22.   Ferand, Ernest T. " 'Sodaine and Unexpected' Music in the Renaissance." *MQ* 37 (1951), pp. 10-27.
23.   Finscher, Ludwig. "Loyset Compère and His Works." *MD* 12 (1958), pp. 105-143; 13 (1959), pp. 123-154; 14 (1960), pp. 135-157; 16 (1962), pp. 93-113.
24.   Goldthwaite, Scott. "Rhythmic Pattern Signposts in the 15th-Century Chanson." *JAMS* 11 (1958), pp. 177-188.
25.   Gottwald, Clytus. "Johannes Ghiselin—Janne Verbonnet. Some Traces of His Life." *MD* 15 (1961), pp. 105-111.
26.   Graham, Victor E. "Music for Poetry in France (1550-1580)." *Renaissance News* 17 (1964), pp. 307-317.

27. Graziano, John. "Lupus Hellinck: A Survey of Fourteen Masses." *MQ* 56 (1970), pp. 247-269.

28. Heartz, Daniel. "The Basse Dance; Its Evolution circa 1450-1550." *AnM* 6 (1958-1963), pp. 287-340.

29. ———"A New Attaingnant Book and the Beginning of French Music Printing." *JAMS* 14 (1961), pp. 9-23.

30. ———"Parisian Music Publishing under Henry II: A Propos of Four Recently Discovered Guitar Books." *MQ* 46 (1960), pp. 448-467.

31. ———"Typography and Format in Early Music Printing, with Particular Reference to Attaingnant's First Publications." *Notes* 23 (1966-1967), pp. 702-706.

32. Hoekstra, Gerald R. "An Eight-Voice Parody of Lassus." *Early Music* 7 (1979), pp. 367-373.

33. Hudson, Barton. "Antoine Brumel's *Nativitas unde gaudia*." *MQ* 59 (1973), pp. 519-530.

34. Kahmann, B. "Antoine de Fèvin. A Bio-bibliographical Contribution." *MD* 4 (1950), pp. 153-162; 5 (1951), pp. 143-155.

35. Karp, Theodore. "A Lost Medieval Chansonnier." *MQ* 48 (1962), pp. 50-67.

36. Kempers, K. Ph. Bernet. "Bibliography of the Sacred Works of Jacobus Clemens Non Papa. A Classified List with a Notice on His Life." *MD* 18 (1964), pp. 85-150.

37. ———"A Composition by Clemens non Papa in a 16th-Century Painting." *MD* 8 (1954), pp. 173-175.

38. ———"Jacobus Clemens non Papa's Chansons in Their Chronological Order." *MD* 15 (1961), pp. 187-197.

39. Krenek, Ernst. "The Treatment of Dissonances in Ockeghem's Masses as Compared with the Contrapuntal Theory of Johannes Tinctoris." *Hamline Studies in Musicology* 2 (1947), pp. 1-26.

40. Lenaerts, René B. "The XVIth-Century Parody Mass in the Netherlands." *MQ* 36 (1950), pp. 410-421.

41. Leichtentritt, Hugo. "Orlando di Lasso." *MC* 105 (Sep 17, 1932), pp. 6-7.

42. ———"The Renaissance Attitude Towards Music." *MQ* 1 (1915), pp. 604-622.

43. Lesure, François, and Geneviève Thibault. "Bibliographie des Éditions Musicales publiées par Nicolas du Chemin (1549-1576)." *AnM* 1 (1953), pp. 269-373.

44. Levitan, Joseph S. "Ockeghem's Clefless Compositions." *MQ* 23 (1937), pp. 440-464.

45. Levy, Kenneth J. "Costeley's Chromatic Chanson." *AnM* 3 (1955), pp. 213-263.

46. ———" 'Susanne un jour,' The History of a 16th Century Chanson." *AnM* 1 (1953), pp. 375-408.

47. Litterick, Louise. "Performing Franco-Netherlandish Secular Music of the Late Fifteenth Century." *Early Music* 8 (1980), pp. 474-485.

48. Lowinsky, Edward E. "The Concept of Physical and Musical Space in the Renaissance." PAMS (1941), pp. 57-84.

49. MacClintock, Carol. "The Giaches Fantasias in MS Chigi Q VIII 206: A Problem in Identification." *JAMS* 19 (1966), pp. 370-382.

50. ———"Some Notes on the Secular Music of Giaches de Wert." *MD* 10 (1956), pp. 106-141.

52. Main, Alexander. "Maximilian's Second-Hand Funeral Motet." *MQ* 48 (1962), pp. 173-189.

51. Maniates, Maria Rika. "Mannerist Composition in Franco-Flemish Polyphony." *MQ* 52 (1966), pp. 17-36.

52. Mattfeld, Jacquelyn A. "Some Relationships Between Texts and Cantus Firmi in the Liturgical Motets of Josquin des Pres." *JAMS* 14 (1961), pp. 159-183.

53. Miller, Clement A. "The *Dodecachordon*: Its Origins and Influence on Renaissance Musical Thought." *MD* 15 (1961), pp. 156-166.

54. ———"Jerome Cardan on Gombert, Phinot and Carpentras." *MQ* 58 (1972), pp. 412-419.

55. Miller, Clement A.   "The Musical Source of Brumel's *Missa Dringhs*." *JAMS* 21 (1968), pp. 200-204.
56. Mullally, Robert.   "The Polyphonic Theory of the *Basse Danse*." *MR* 38 (1977), pp. 241-248.
57. Murray, Bain.   "Jacob Obrecht's Connection with the Church of Our Lady in Antwerp." *Revue belge de musicologie* 11 (1957), pp. 125-134.
58. ———"New Light on Jacob Obrecht's Development. A Biographical Study." *MQ* 43 (1957), pp. 500-516.
59. Noblitt, Thomas.   "Problems of Transmission in Obrecht's *Missa Je ne demande*." *MQ* 63 (1977), pp. 211-223.
60. Page, Christopher.   "French Lute Tablature in the 14th Century." *Early Music* 8 (1980), pp. 488-491.
61. Picker, Martin.   "The Chanson Albums of Marguerite of Austria: Mss. 228 and 11239 of the Bibliotèhque [*sic*] Royale de Belgique, Brussels." *AnM* 6 (1958-1963), pp. 145-285.
62. ———"The Unidentified Chansons by Pierre de la Rue in the *Album de Marguerite d'Austriche*." *MQ* 46 (1960), pp. 329-343.
63. Plamenac, Dragan.   "A Postscript to Volume II of the *Collected Works of Johannes Ockeghem*." *JAMS* 3 (1950), pp. 33-40.
64. Pratt, Waldo Selden.   "The Importance of the Early French Psalter." *MQ* 21 (1935), pp. 25-32.
65. Reese, Gustave.   "The First Printed Collection of Part-Music: The Odhecaton." *MQ* 20 (1934), pp. 39-76.
66. ———"The Polyphonic Magnificat of the Renaissance as a Design in Tonal Centers." *JAMS* 13 (1960), pp. 68-78.
67. Rubsamen, Walter H.   "The Earliest French Lute Tablature." *JAMS* 21 (1968), pp. 286-299.
68. ———"Some First Elaborations of Masses from Motets." *BAMS* 4, pp. 6-9.
69. Sachs, Curt.   "Chromatic Trumpets in the Renaissance." *MQ* 36 (1950), pp. 62-66.
70. Salop, Arnold.   "Jacob Obrecht and the Early Development of Harmonic Polyphony." *JAMS* 17 (1964), pp. 288-309.
71. Seay, Albert.   "Poetry and Music in the French Chanson of the Renaissance." *Consort* 20 (Jul 1963), pp. 152-165.
72. Southern, Eileen.   "Some Keyboard Basse Dances of the Fifteenth Century." *ActaM* 35 (1963), pp. 114-124.
73. Tischler, Hans.   "The Earliest Lute Tablature." *JAMS* 27 (1974), pp. 100-103.
74. Titcomb, Caldwell.   "The Josquin Acrostic Re-Examined." *JAMS* 16 (1963), pp. 47-60.
75. Todd, R. Larry.   "Retrograde, Inversion, Retrograde-Inversion, and Related Techniques in the Masses of Obrecht." *MQ* 64 (1978), pp. 50-78.
76. Truron, Walterus.   "The Rhythm of Metrical Psalm-Tunes." *ML* 9 (1928), pp. 29-33.
77. Wagner, Lavern J.   "Flemish Musicians at the Court of Philipp II." *Caecilia* 86 (1959), pp. 107-114.
78. Walker, D. P., and François Lesure.   "Claude Le Jeune and *Musique mesurée*." *MD* 3 (1949), pp. 151-170.
79. Walker, D. P.   "Some Aspects and Problems of Musique Mesurée à l'Antique. The Rhythm and Notation of Musique Mesurée." *MD* 4 (1950), pp. 163-186.
80. Winternitz, Emanuel.   "On Angel Concerts in the 15th Century: A Critical Approach to Realism and Symbolism in Sacred Painting." *MQ* 49 (1963), pp. 450-463.
81. Woodward, Rev. G. R.   "The Genevan Psalter of 1562; Set in 4-Part Harmony by Claude Goudimel." *PMA* 44 (1918), pp. 167-192.
82. Wooldridge, Harry Ellis.   "The Treatment of the Words in Polyphonic Music." *The Musical Antiquary* 1 (1910), pp. 73-92.
83. Wright, Craig.   "Tapissier and Cordier: New Documents and Conjectures." *MQ* 59 (1973), pp. 177-189.

84. Yates, Frances A. "Dramatic Religious Processions in Paris in the Late Sixteenth Century." *AnM* 2 (1954), pp. 215-270; pictures, Plates I-XX.
85. Young, William. "Keyboard Music to 1600." *MD* 17 (1963), pp. 163-193.

Music

1. Adriaenssen, Emanuel. *Pratum Musicum longe amoenissimum*, Antwerp, 1584; facsimile reprint: Buren, Netherlands: Fritz Knuf, 1977.
2. Attaingnant, Pierre
    a. Chansons, ed. Robert Eitner (*PAM*, v. 23)
    b. Thirty chansons for three and four voices from Attaingnant's collections, ed. Albert Seay (*CM*, v. 2)
    c. Transcriptions of chansons for keyboard, ed. Albert Seay (*CMM*, 20)
    d. *Trente et une chansons musicales*, ed. Henry Expert (*MMRF*, v. 5)
    e. *Die Orgel in Kirchenjahr III*, ed. Eberhard Kraus (*CO*, v. 12)
    f. *Danseries à 4 parties*, ed. Raymond Meylan (*LP*, v. 9)
    g. *Deux livres d'orgue édités par Pierre Attaingnant*, ed. Yvonne Rokseth (*MMA*, ser. 1, v. 1)
    h. *Trieze motets et un prélude réduits en la tablature des orgues*, ed. Yvonne Rokseth (*MMA*, v. 5)
    i. *Trieze livres de motets parus chez Pierre Attaingnant en 1534 et 1535*, ed. Albert Smijers and A. Tillman Merritt. Monaco: Éditions de L'Oiseau-Lyre, 1963.
    j. *Quatorzième Livre de motets composés par Pierre de Manchicourt, parus chez Pierre Attaingnant* (1539), ed. A. Tillman Merritt. Monaco: Éditions de L'Oiseau-Lyre, 1964.
3. Barbireau, Jacobus. (*CE*) *Opera Omnia*, 2 vols., ed. Bernhard Meier (*CMM*, 7)
4. Bourgeois, Loys. *Vingt-quatre Psaumes* (4 voices) (*Schweizerische Musikdenkmäler*, v. 3)
5. Brassart, Johannes. (*CE*) *Opera Omnia*, 2 vols., ed. Keith E. Mixter (*CMM*, 35)
6. Brown, Howard Mayer. *Theatrical Chansons of the Fifteenth and Early Sixteenth Centuries*. Cambridge, MA: Harvard University Press, 1963.
7. Brumel, Antoine. (*CE*) *Opera Omnia*, 6 vols., ed. Barton Hudson (*CMM*, 5)
8. Caurroy, Eustache de (François)
    a. *Anthologie du motet latin polyphonique en France*, ed. Denise Launay (*MMA*, ser. 1, v. 17)
    b. *Mélanges*, ed. Henry Expert (*MMRF*, v. 17)
    c. Motets, ed. Henry Expert (*MMFR*, v. 12)
9. *The Chanson Albums of Marguerite of Austria*, ed. Martin Picker. Berkeley: University of California Press, 1965.
10. *Chansonnier du XVIe Siècle*, ed. A. M. Charles Bordes. Paris: Schola Cantorum, 1905.
11. Clemens non Papa, Jacobus
    a. (*CE*) *Opera Omnia*, 21 vols., ed. K. Ph. Bernet Kempers (*CMM*, 4)
    b. *AC*, part 2, v. 2
    c. *CO*, v. 12
    d. Three motets, ed. Bernhard Meier (*CW*, v. 72)
12. Compère, Loyset
    a. (*CE*) *Opera Omnia*, 5 vols., ed. Ludwig Finscher (*CMM*, 15)
    b. *Weltliche Lieder*, ed. Friedrich Blume (*CW*, v. 3)
    c. *Missa Alles regrets*, ed. Ludwig Finscher (*CW*, v. 55)
    d. *VOTS*, sec. 4, pp. 113, 116, 119, 121
13. Costeley, Guillaume
    a. *Arreste un peu*, ed. Henry Expert (*FCVR*, v. 4)
    b. *Musique*, ed. Henry Expert, part 1 (*MMRF*, v. 3); parts 2-3 (*MMRF*, vols. 18-19)
14. Crecquillon, Thomas. (*CE*) *Opera Omnia*, 4 vols., ed. Nani Bridgman and Barton Hudson (*CMM*, 63)

15. *Dutch Keyboard Music of the 16th and 17th Centuries*, ed. Alan Curtis. (*MMN*, v. 3)
16. *Early French Keyboard Music*, ed. Howard Ferguson. New York: Oxford University Press, 1966.
17. Févin, Antoine de
    a. Lamentations, ed. Günther Massenkeil (*MDm*, v. 6)
    b. *Missa Mente tota*, ed. Henry Expert (*MMRF*, v. 9)
    c. Motet: *Benedictus Dominus Deus* (*CMM*, 43, v. 1)
18. Gervaise, Claude. *Six Livres de Danseries*, 6 vols., ed. Bernard Thomas. London: London Pro Musica Edition, 1972-1976; facsimile reprint: Geneva: Minkoff Reprint, 1977.
19. Genet, Elzéar (Carpentras). (*CE*) *Collected Works*, 5 vols., ed. Albert Seay (*CMM*, 58)
20. Ghiselin-Verbonnet, Johannes. (*CE*) *Opera Omnia*, 4 vols., ed. Clytus Gottwald (*CMM*, 23)
21. Gombert, Nicholas
    a. (*CE*) *Opera Omnia*, 12 vols., ed. Joseph Schmidt-Görg (*CMM*, 6)
    b. Motets: *Quem dicunt homines* (*CW*, v. 94); *Homo erat in Jerusalem* (*VOTS*, sec. 7, p. 230)
22. Goudimel, Claude
    a. (*CE*) *Collected Works*, 10 vols., ed. Luther Dittmer and Pierre Pidoux. Brooklyn: Institute of Medieval Music.
    b. Masses in four voices (*MMFR*, v. 9)
    c. Four Festival Motets (*CW*, v. 103)
    d. *150 Psaumes de David*, parts 1-3 (*MMRF*, vols. 2, 4, 6)
    e. *The Psalm Motets of Claude Goudimel*, ed. Eleanor McChesney Lawry. Ann Arbor: University Microfilm, 1955.
23. Hayne van Ghizeghem (*CE*) *Opera Omnia*, ed. Barton Hudson (*CMM*, 74)
24. Isaac, Heinrich
    a. (*CE*) *Opera Omnia*, 5 vols., ed. Edward R. Lerner (*CMM*, 65)
    b. *Choralis Constantinus*, Book I (*DTÖ*, v. 10); Book II (*DTÖ*, v. 32)
    c. *Choralis Constantinus Book III*, tr. Louise Cuyler. Ann Arbor: University of Michigan Press, 1950.
    d. Introits (*CW*, v. 81)
    e. *Missa carminum* (*CW*, v. 7)
    f. Four Masses, ed. Fabio Fano (*Archivium musices metropolitanum Mediolanense*, v. 10)
    g. Motets (*VOTS*, sec. 6, pp. 182, 186, 189, 190, 191, 195, 197); (*AC*, part 1, v. 1; part 2, v. 1)
    h. Keyboard works, ed. Gregor Klaus (*LO*, v. 8)
    i. Six instrumental pieces (*HM*, v. 29)
    j. *Weltliche Werke* (*DTÖ*, vols. 28, 32, 72)
25. Jachet of Mantua. (*CE*) *Collected Works*, 4 vols., ed. Philip Jackson and George Nugent (*CMM*, 54)
26. Janequin, Clément
    a. *Chansons polyphoniques*, vols. 1-4, ed. A. Tillman Merritt, François Lesure
    b. Chansons (*MMRF*, v. 7); (*CW*, v. 73)
    c. *Chantons, sonnons, trompetes* . . . (*FCVR*, v. 1)
    d. *Les cris de Paris* (*FCVR*, v. 3)
27. Josquin des Pres
    a. (*CE*) *Werken*, ed. Albert Smijers. Amsterdam: Alsbach, 1925-
    b. *Missa Pange Lingua*, ed. Thomas Warburton. Chapel Hill: University of North Carolina Press, 1977.
    c. Masses (*CW*, vols. 1, 20, 42); (*PAM*, v. 6)
    d. Other sacred works (*VOTS*, sec. 5, pp. 131, 135, 140, 146, 155, 156, 158); (*CW*, vols. 18, 23, 30, 33, 57, 64)

e. Keyboard works (*CO*, vols. 4, 6, 8; *LO*, v. 8)

f. Secular songs (*CW*, v. 3)

28. La Rue, Pierre de

a. Lamentation (*MDm*, v. 6)

b. Masses (*MDa*, v. 18; *MMB*, v. 8; *MMRF*, v. 8; *DPL*, ser. 1, a., v. 1; *CW*, v. 7)

c. Other sacred works (*CW*, v. 11; *VOTS*, sec. 4, pp. 123, 127; sec. 5, p. 129; *CW*, v. 91)

d. *Weltliche Lieder* (*CW*, v. 3)

29. Lasso, Orlando di

a. (*CE*) *Sämtliche Werke*, 21 vols., ed. Franz Xaver Haberl, Adolf Sandberger.

b. Sacred works (*MDa*, v. 9; *AC*, part 1, vols. 3-4; *CW*, v. 14)

c. Secular works (*AC*, part 2, v. 3; *CW*, v. 13; *FCVR*, v. 2)

d. *Busstränen des heiligen Petrus*, 3 parts (*CW*, vols. 34, 37, 41)

e. *Prophetiae Sibyllarum* (*CW*, v. 48)

f. *Meslanges*, part 1 (*MMRF*, v. 1)

g. Keyboard works (*CO*, vols. 1, 2, 6, 9)

h. Instrumental works (*HM*, vols. 2, 18, 19)

30. Le Jeune, Claude

a. *Airs*, 4 vols., ed. D. P. Walker. Rome: American Institute of Musicology. *Miscellanea*, ser. 1

b. *Le printemps*, ed. Henry Expert (*MMRF*, vols. 12-14)

c. *Meslanges*, ed. Henry Expert (*MMRF*, v. 16)

d. *Psaumes mesurez à l'antique*, ed Henry Expert (*MMRF*, vols. 20-22)

e. *Dodécorde*, ed. Henry Expert (*MMRF*, v. 11)

f. *Missa ad placitum*, ed. Michel Sanvoisin (*LP*, v. 2)

g. *Octonaires de la vanité et inconstance du monde*, Nos. 1-12, ed. Henry Expert (*MMFR*, vols. 1, 8)

h. *Las! ou vas-tu sans moy*, ed. Henry Expert (*FCVR*, v. 6)

31. Manchicourt, Pierre de. (*CE*) *Collected Works*, ed. John D. Wicks and Lavern Wagner (*CMM*, 55)

32. Mauduit, Jacques

a. *Anthologie du motet latin polyphonique en France*, ed. Denise Launay (*MMA*, v. 17)

b. *Chansonettes mesurée*, ed. Henry Expert (*MMRF*, v. 10)

c. *Psaumes mesurés à l'antique*, ed. Henry Expert (*FCVR*, v. 7)

33. *Missae Caput*, ed. Alejandro Enrique Planchart. New Haven: Yale University Press, 1964.

34. Monte, Philippe de

a. (*CE*) *Opera*, ed. Charles van den Borren. Bruges: Desclée, 1927-1939.

b. *Philippi de Monte Opera*. New Complete Edition, ed. René Bernard Lenaerts. Leuven: Leuven University Press, 1977-

c. Madrigals, ed. Alfred Einstein (*DTÖ*, v. 77)

35. Mouton, Jean

a. (*CE*) *Opera Omnia*, 10 vols., ed. Andrew Minor (*CMM*, 43)

b. Masses (*CW*, v. 70; *MMRF*, v. 9; *MMFR*, v. 12)

c. Motets (*CW*, v. 76; *VOTS*, sec. 7, pp. 201, 209)

36. *Musica Divina*, 8 vols., ed. Karl Proske; *Selectus novus missarum*, 2 vols., ed. Karl Proske. Ratisbon: 1855; reprint in 8 vols., New York: Johnson Reprint, 1973.

37. *Les Musiciens de la cour de Bourgogne au XVe siècle*, ed. Jeanne Marix. Paris: Editions de L'Oiseau-Lyre, 1937.

38. Obrecht, Jacob

a. (*CE*) *Werken*, ed. Johannes Wolf. Leipzig: Breitkopf & Härtel, 1908-1921.

b. *Opera Omnia*, ed. Albert Smijers and M. van Crevel. Amsterdam: G. Alsbach & Co., 1953-

    c. *Missa Caput*, ed. Alejandro Enrique Planchart (*CM*, v. 5)

    d. Ten Flemish songs (*VOTS*, sec. 3); three Kyries (*VOTS*, sec. 2, pp. 51, 54, 58)

39. Ockeghem, Johannes

    a. (*CE*) *Collected Works*, ed. Dragan Plamenac. American Musicological Society, 1947-1959.

    b. Masses: *Trienter Codices*, v. 3, ed. Oswald Koller, Franz Schegar, Margarethe Loew (*DTÖ*, v. 38)

    c. *Missa Mi-Mi*, ed. Heinrich Besseler (*CW*, v. 4)

    d. *Missa Caput*, ed. Alejandro Enrique Planchart (*CM*, v. 5)

    e. *Missa L'Homme armé*, ed. Laurentius Feininger (*MPL*, ser. 1, v. 1, No. 6)

    d. Other works (*VOTS*, sec. 1, pp. 1, 3, 12)

40. Petrucci, Ottaviano

    a. *Canti B Numero Cinquanta*, Venice, 1501/1502; facsimile reprint: New York: Broude Brothers, 1975.

    b. *Harmonice Musicae Odhecaton A*, Venice, 1504; facsimile reprint: New York: Broude Brothers, 1973. (*MMF*, ser. 1, v. 10)

    c. *Harmonice Musice Odhecaton A*, ed. Helen Hewitt. Cambridge, MA: Mediaeval Academy of America, 1942; reprint: New York: Da Capo Press, 1978. (*Studies and Documents*, v. 5)

41. Sermisy, Claudin de

    a. (*CE*) *Opera Omnia*, ed. Gaston Allaire and Isabelle Cazeaux (*CMM*, 52)

    b. Chansons, ed. Robert Eitner (*PAM*, v. 23)

    c. *Duos*, ed. Henry Expert (*FCVR*, v. 8)

    d. Lamentations, ed. Günther Massenkeil (*MDm*, v. 6)

    e. *Missa pro defunctis*, ed. Robert Snow (*MLi*, v. 1/2)

    f. Motets, ed. Henry Expert (*MMFR*, v. 12)

42. Slim, H. Colin. *A Gift of Madrigals and Motets*, 2 vols. Chicago: University of Chicago Press, 1972. (music in volume 2)

43. *Trois Chansonniers Français de XVe Siècle*. Paris: E. Droz, 1927; reprint: New York: Da Capo Press, 1978.

44. Watkins, Glenn Elson. *Three Books of Polyphonic Lamentations of Jeremiah*. Rochester, NY: University of Rochester Press, 1954.

14. Painting by Hans Memling (late 15th century)
showing the straight trumpet, folding trumpet,
portative, harp and viol

OUTLINE XII

ITALY

Fifteenth Century – Early Madrigal – Classic Madrigal – Late Madrigal
Madrigal Comedy – Popular Songs
Roman School of Church Music – Venetian School
Music Theory – Instrumental Music

I. **Fifteenth Century**

    A.   There is a comparatively small amount of Italian music of the early fifteenth century, although a number of native and adopted composers are known. Among these are **Johannes Ciacona, Bartolomeo Brolo** and **Nicola Zacharia** (*fl. c.* 1420-1435). Secular pieces in the French style (*rondeau, virelai, ballade*), sacred motets and separate parts of the Ordinary were written. Many Burgundian (**Dufay**) and early Flemish composers (**Isaac, Obrecht, Josquin**) travelled in Italy. Late in the fifteenth century the polyphonic *frottola* was developed into the madrigal by Flemish composers.

        1. **Johannes Ciconia** (*c.* 1340-1411)

           a. Active in Liège, his birthplace, from 1372-1385, **Ciconia** then went to Italy where he spent the remainder of his life.

           b. *O rosa bella* (*DTÖ*, v. 14, p. 227)

           c. *Cacciando un giorno* (A day of hunting) (*JRBM*, 1 (1946), supplement p. 3)

        2. **Bartolomeo Brolo** (*fl. c.* 1430-1440)

           a. *O celestial Lume* (O heavenly light) (see *Outline*, p. 104, *M* 7, p. 83), a *rondeau*.

           b. *Et in terra pax* (*DTÖ*, v. 61, p. 28)

           c. *Der entrepris*, from *Glogauer Liederbuch* (*EdM*, v. 4, p. 80), a three-voice instrumental piece.

    B.   Pre-madrigal forms

        1. Polyphonic *laude*

           a. *Laude* are Italian hymns of praise and devotion, and appeared in a variety of forms. Popular melodies were adapted to religious texts and early French *chanson* tunes were used. Although ranging from two to four voices, the four-voice *laude* became the standard by 1500. The upper voice was the most important and the other voices were freely composed; borrowed melodies were not used in the tenor. The note-against-note style at times had declamatory repeated notes as in the *chansons* of **Dufay**.

           b. **Giacomo [Jacobo] Fogliano** (1473-1548)

              1) *Ave Maria* (*HAM*, No. 94; see *ISM*, v. 1)

           c. **Giovanni Animuccia** (*c.* 1500-1571)

              1) **Animuccia** succeeded **Palestrina** as *maestro de cappella* at the Julian Chapel of the Vatican in 1555 and remained there till his death. Thereupon **Palestrina** resumed his former position. In 1570 **Animuccia** became the music director of St. Philip Neri's Oratory at San Girolamo and brought out two collections including *laude*.

                a) *Il Primo Libro delle Laudi Spirituali*, Rome, 1563

                  (1) *Ben venga amore* (*GMB*, No. 120)

                b) *Il Secondo Libro delle Laudi Spirituali*, Rome, 1570

                  (1) In this collection of 28 pieces, 18 are *laude* of two to eighteen voices.

                c) Six Masses: four *a 4*, one *a 5*, one *a 6*. *Missa Conditor alme siderum: Kyrie* and *Gloria* (*AMI*, v. 1, p. 159); *Missa Ave maris stella* (*PVSP*, v. 1).

2. *Frottole* (late fifteenth and early sixteenth centuries)
   a.   The *frottola* is a popular secular form in three or four voices in chordal style. The main melody is in the upper voice; the bass moves in skips of fourths and fifths; the inner voices merely fill in the harmonies. Inverted pedal points are common.
      1)   The *frottola* is often performed as a solo song with the lower parts played on instruments (*SCMA*, v. 4).
   b.   The music is in several short sections repeated in various ways.
      1)   Music: A B a a b A B (typical form)
      2)   Text: r r s s s r r (r equals two lines of refrain; s equals two lines of stanza)
   c.   **Ottaviano Petrucci** published 11 books of *frottole*, 1504-1514; they contain 579 pieces by 37 known composers (*PäM*, Jg. 8).
   d.   **Giovanni Brocco**: *Ite, caldi sospiri*, from **Petrucci**, *Frottole*, Book III, 1504 (*GMB*, No. 70)
   e.   **Marchetto Cara** (d. *c.* 1530) *Sonno che gli animali* (*SCMA*, v. 4, p. 3; see others in *SCMA*, v. 4; *SSMS*, p. 83; *TEM*, p. 97)
   f.   **Michele Pesenti**, *Dal lecto me levava* (*CW*, v. 43, p. 7)
   g.   **Bartolomeo Tromboncino** (*fl.* 1500; d. *c.* 1535), *Non val aqua* (Water avails not) (*HAM*, No. 95a; see also *SCMA*, v. 4)
   h.   **Josquin des Prez** (*c.* 1445-1521)
      1)   **Josquin** was known in Italy as **Jusquin d'Ascanio** since he served Cardinal Ascanio Sforza (*c.* 1479). He wrote a few *frottole*; one is the macaronic *In te Domine speravi* which also appeared in a Spanish collection (*HAM*, No. 95b; *MME*, v. 5, p. 110).

II.   Early Madrigal (sixteenth century)

   A.   The Italian madrigals at first followed the general style of the *frottola*. The more serious type developed into the madrigal, whereas the less serious, lighter type of *frottola* developed into the *villanesca*.
      1.   The texture is basically homophonic and through composed with some imitative counterpoint used to express the text or to expand the individuality of the voices. The text is of literary quality and restrained expression. The superius, as the most important voice of the *frottola*, gradually lost its prominence and the individual voice parts became more equal.
      2.   The madrigals developed through the efforts of Netherland composers in Italy (**Verdelot, Arcadelt, Willaert**). The first madrigals were published in 1530 (*Madrigali de diversi musici libro primo*) and included madrigals by **Philippe Verdelot** and **Costanza** and **Sebastiano Festa**. The madrigal became very popular and hundreds of volumes were published.
   B.   Composers (members of the Venetian School are represented here only by their madrigals)
      1.   **Bernardo Pisano** (*CMM*, 32, v. 1)
         a.   *Musica de messer Bernardo pisano sopre le Canzone del patrarcha*, Florence, 1520
            1)   This is the first collection of secular music and the first music by any Florentine to be published. It includes canzonets, ballatte, madrigals and two sets of responsories written for the cathedral choir of Florence.
      2.   **Adrian Willaert** (*c.* 1485-1562) (*CMM*, 3) (See below: VIII. B. 1.)
         a.   In 1527 **Willaert** became choir master at St. Mark's Cathedral in Venice; his reputation spread and many students wanted to study with him; among them were **Cipriano de Rore, Gioseffo Zarlino** and **Nicolò Vicentino**.
         b.   **Willaert** was one of the earliest composers of madrigals; his early madrigals are generally chordal with occasional polyphonic passages. The superius is the most important voice melodically; clear-cut phrases are obvious (*RRMR*, v. 30).

    c.   In later madrigals the phrases tend to overlap in motet style; all the voices, conceived in a more polyphonic texture, are equally important and chordal writing is used for expressive purposes.

    d.   *Musica nova*, 1559 (*CMM*, 3, v. 13)

      1)   This large collection of 27 motets and 25 madrigals edited by **Francesco Viola**, a pupil of **Willaert**, is the only one published during **Willaert's** time exclusively devoted to him.

      2)   *Liete, e pensose, accompagnate, e sole* (*CMM*, 3, v. 13, p. 108; *IM*, v. 3, p. 63)

        a)   This seven-voice setting of a Petrarch sonnet demonstrates a variety of vocal registrations; the first quatrain is set in four voices, the second in the remaining three voices; the closing sestet is in four, five and finally seven voices. Each of the last three lines is repeated but in each case the music is different.

  3.   **Philippe Verdelot** (*c.* 1490-*c.* 1545) (*CMM*, 28)

    a.   Active in Florence and Venice, **Verdelot** published three books of four-voice madrigals (1536-1537), four books of five-voice (1535-1540) and one book of six-voice madrigals (1541). Other composers' works were also included. In addition to madrigals, **Verdelot** wrote Masses and hymns (*CMM*, 28, v. 1) and many motets (*CMM*, 28, vols. 2, 3; *M* 31, v. 2, pp. 65-172).

    b.   **Verdelot's** style may be chordal and syllabic or considerably imitative. In general his style is more homophonic with a liberal use of polyphony.

    c.   *Primo libro de Madrigal*, Venice, 1537 (see *M* 31, v. 2, pp. 319-431; *CW*, v. 5)

      1)   *Madonna qual certezza* (My lady, what certainty) (*IM*, v. 3, p. 23; *NOH*, v. 4, p. 42; *M* 31, v. 2, p. 379), homophonic.

    d.   *Madonna, per voi ardo* (My lady, I burn with love) (*GMB*, No. 98; *M* 31, v. 2, p. 353)

    e.   *Madonna'l tuo bel viso* (*IM*, v. 3, p. 29), imitative.

  4.   **Costanza Festa** (*c.* 1495-1545) (*CMM*, 25)

    a.   **Festa**, a prolific composer, was the first Italian composer of madrigals; he entered the Papal Chapel choir in 1517 and later became the *maestro di cappella* at the Vatican.

    b.   *Quando ritrova* (When I find my shepherdess) (*HAM*, No. 129)

      1)   Homophonic in style, each phrase is clearly defined. The last phrase is repeated.

    c.   *Cosi suav' è'l foco* (*IM*, v. 3, p. 36)

      1)   Polyphonic throughout, this opens with paired imitation.

  5.   **Jacques Arcadelt** (*c.* 1504-after *c.* 1567) (*CMM*, 31)

    a.   **Arcadelt**, a Flemish composer, was the leading madrigal composer in Florence, *c.* 1535. In 1539 he was in Rome first as a member of the Julian Chapel and then the Sistine Chapel. In 1539 four books of his four-voice madrigals were published; two more books of madrigals were published, one each in three and four voices in 1542 and 1544 respectively (see *MSO*, v. 1, p. 36; *SSMS*, p. 100).

    b.   *Voi ve n'andat' al cielo* (Ye go heavenward) (*HAM*, No. 130; *CW*, v. 5, p. 16)

      1)   Typical of the style of **Arcadelt** is his use of simple polyphony alternating with chordal passages.

    c.   *Io mi rivalgo indietro a ciascun passo* (*IM*, v. 3, p. 38; *CMM*, 31, v. 3, p. 3)

      1)   On a text by Petrarch, this madrigal makes use of simple polyphony.

    d.   *Voi mi ponesti in foco* (*CMM*, 31, v. 7, p. 183; *GMB*, No. 100)

    e.   Four four-voice *chansons* (*PAM*, v. 23, pp. 1-8; *CMM*, 31, v. 8, pp. 6, 18, 27, 32; *SCMA*, v, 5, pp. 1, 4)

III. Classical Madrigal

  A.   The number of parts increased to six with five parts as the usual number. The style became more polyphonic and imitative; more text-painting is evident. The spiritual madrigal for devotional use was developed.

B.   Composers
   1.   **Cipriano de Rore** (1516-1565) (*CMM*, 14, vols. 2-5)
      a.   Born in Antwerp, **Rore** spent most of his life in Italy. He was a pupil of **Willaert** and about 1547 served at the court of the Duke of Ferrara; later (1561) he was employed by Duke Ottavio Farnese of Parma. In 1563 he succeeded **Willaert** at St. Mark's in Venice but soon (1564) returned to the service of Duke Farnese. **Rore** was one of the finest musicians of his time and represents the last of the Netherlanders in Italy.
      b.   When **Rore** occasionally uses chromaticism, it is to effectively underscore the text. The form is no longer dependent upon the text. Devoting himself generally to serious texts, such as those of Petrarch, **Rore** developed the madrigal toward the more dramatic, using a well-structured polyphony.
      c.   *Anchor che col partire* (Whene'er we part) (*CMM*, 14, v. 4, p. 31; *IM*, v. 3, p. 112; *SCMA*, v. 6, p. 45)
      d.   *Da le belle contrade* (From the beautiful region of the East) (*CMM*, 14, v. 5, p. 96; *HAM*, No. 131; *CW*, v. 5, p. 24)
         1)   In this five-voice madrigal, note the exclamations in measures 30-31 and the chromatic change in measure 41 ("Ah, cruel love").
      e.   *Calami sonum ferentes* (Reeds bearing sound) (*CMM*, 14, v. 6, p. 108), using a chromatic theme.
      f.   Madrigals (*SCMA*, v. 6)
         1)   Thirty eight madrigals: 26 madrigals for four voices, Book I; 9 madrigals for four voices, Book II, and 3 three-voice madrigals.
      g.   *Amor, ben mi credevo* (Love, methought you had bound me) (*CMM*, 14, v. 4, p. 28; *SCMA*, v. 6, p. 47; *CW*, v. 5, p. 21)
   2.   **Andrea Gabrieli** (c. 1510-1586)
      a.   In 1564 **Gabrieli** became an organist at St. Mark's in Venice; in 1585 he was advanced to first organist. There is no direct evidence that he was a pupil of **Willaert**. Among his students were his nephew **Giovanni** and **Hans Leo Hassler**.
      b.   **Gabrieli's** early madrigals follow the contrapuntal motet style.
         1)   *O beltà rara o santi* (O rare beauty) (*IM*, v. 3, p. 178)
      c.   The later madrigals make use of a variety of choral registrations, dialogue between choral groups, strong rhythms, syllabic writing and increased use of chromatic changes.
         1)   *Tirsi morir volea* (Tirsi wishing to die) (*IM*, v. 3, p. 190)
         2)   *A le guancie di rose* (To the rosy cheeks) (*AMI*, v. 2, p. 129)
   3.   **Orlando di Lasso** (1532-1594) (*CE*)
      a.   **Lasso** wrote madrigals to Italian, French and German texts in the musical styles of those countries. He used polyphony mixed with homophonic passages, text-painting, chromaticism and is often humorous and satirical. His use of imitation is sparse.
      b.   *Le voglie e l'opre mie* (*CE*, v. 6, p. 18)
   4.   **Giovanni Pierluigi Palestrina** (1525-1594) (*CE; PWerke*)
      a.   **Palestrina** composed about 100 madrigals, mostly spiritual. His style is reserved yet expressive; he does not use the "modern" techniques but rather imposes the techniques of his sacred music on the madrigals.
      b.   *Alla rivo del Tebro* (On the bank of the Tiber) (*CE*, v. 31, p. 47; *HAM*, No. 142)
   5.   **Philippe de Monte** (1521-1603) (*CE*)
      a.   A Flemish composer by birth, **Monte** spent many years in Italy. After 1554 he issued many books of madrigals, about 1220 madrigals in at least 40 volumes.
      b.   The madrigals are of the finest quality and are often more unified, polyphonic and of closer texture than madrigals of Italian composers. The occasional extraordinary technique may disturb the smoothness, although the total effect created always

          demonstrates a sensitive feeling for the text.

    c.   Basically contrapuntal, his style includes most every technique of the day used in a serious way: text-painting, chromaticism, contrast of rhythms and vocal registrations, scale passages in single, parallel, contrary or rhythmically altered forms and imitation, strict, inverted, or modified and in pairs.

    d.   *In qual parte del ciel* (In that part of the sky) (*CE*, v. 25, p. 40)

    e.   *Carlo ch'en tenerella acerba etade* (*DTÖ*, v. 77, p. 1), in five voices

    f.   *Quella fera son'io* (*DTÖ*, v. 77, p. 75), in seven voices

    g.   *Sottile e dolce ladra* (*IM*, v. 3, p. 297)

  6.   **Giaches de Wert** (1535-1596) (*CE* = *CMM*, 24)

    a.   A Netherlander, **Wert** spent most of his life in Italy. He was a choirboy to the Marchesa of Padulla; from 1565 to his death **Wert** was *maestro di cappella* at the Mantuan court. **Wert** produced 11 books of four- and five-voice madrigals from 1538 to 1595.

    b.   **Wert** followed the general style of his contemporaries. Unusual intervals, extended range and elaborate text-painting are characteristic of his later madrigals.

    c.   *Io non son però morto*, Book VIII, 1586 (*CMM*, 24, v. 8, p. 1; *IM*, v. 3, p. 301)

    d.   *Cruda Amarilli*, Book XI, 1595 (*CMM*, 24, v. 12, p. 43)

  7.   *Musica Transalpina*, London, 1588

    a.   The "Music from across the Alps," compiled by Nicholas Yonge, is the first printed collection of Italian madrigals with English texts. Of the 57 madrigals, 16 are by **Alfonso Ferrabosco**, 10 by **Marenzio**, 5 by **Palestrina** and 4 by **Monte**. **William Byrd** is represented with two madrigals; twelve other composers are included.

      1)   The English translations are quite literal and generally well set to the notes.

    b.   A second *Musica Transalpina*, published by Yonge in 1597, contains only 24 madrigals; some new composers are represented but **Ferrabosco** and **Marenzio** remain the two composers with more madrigals, 6 and 3 respectively.

IV. Late Madrigal

  A.   The style is elaborate and experimental with text-painting, chromaticism, declamatory monody, dramatic effects and solo virtuosity. With **Monteverdi** the madrigal developed from a polyphonic *a cappella* style to an accompanied solo with *basso continuo*. The solo madrigal leads to the seventeenth-century aria.

  B.   Composers

  1.   **Luca Marenzio** (1553-1599)

    a.   **Marenzio** was born near Brescia. He served Cardinal Luigi d'Este in Rome (1579-1586) and later Tasso's protector Cardinal Cinzio Aldobrandini. For a time he was in the service of Poland's King Sigismund III (1596-1598) and also the court at Ferrara; he died in Rome. **Marenzio** represents the culmination of the Italian madrigal; his mastery of the genre gave to the madrigal a superiority and vitality that surpassed all others.

    b.   **Marenzio's** style is expressive, dramatic, flexible, highly refined and follows the poetic content of the text. Alternating polyphonic and homophonic passages, use of chromaticism and modern tonalities are all devices of the style.

    c.   **Marenzio** had a strong influence on **Gesualdo**, **Monteverdi** and the late English madrigal school. Like most other madrigalists, he wrote some sacred music.

    d.   **Marenzio** wrote over 400 madrigals; they were published in 17 books including 9 books of five-voice madrigals, 6 books of six-voice madrigals, one book of *"spirituali madrigali"* and one book of four-, five- and six-voice madrigals.

    e.   *Già torna* (*PäM*, Jg. 4, v. 1, p. 82)

      1)   This madrigal is a detailed example of translating words into music: *"torna"* (return), an ascending fifth followed by a descending minor third; *"rallegrar"*

(make happy), a cheery, quick-moving motive; *"mar"* (sea), the melodic line is like waves; *"s'acqueta"* (calm), slower motion and an octave leap suggest the contrast of the rolling and calm sea; later the singing of birds is suggested by a melisma.

    f.   *Il vago e bello Armillo* (The desirable and beautiful Armillo) (*AMI*, v. 2, p. 215)

        1)   The gentle roll of the waves (*"onde"*), then the dashing against the rock are realistically portrayed.

    g.   *Madonna mea gentil* (My gentle lady) (*HAM*, No. 155; *PäM*, Jg. 4, v. 1, p. 25)

        2)   The suggestion of the ascending scale (concluding five measures) accompanying the word *"paradiso"* is obvious.

    h.   *Solo e pensoso* (*GMB*, No. 165); *S'io parto, i'moro* (*MM*, p. 100)

2. **Carlo Gesualdo** (*c.* 1560-1613) (*CE*)

    a.   **Gesualdo**, the Prince of Venosa, was an outstanding lutenist and patron of the arts in Naples. He wrote about 150 madrigals published in 7 books.

    b.   **Gesualdo** is the most radical member of the chromatic school which includes **Rore** and **Vincentino**. His later madrigals are daring, original, with strong contrasts, new and bold harmonic progressions and skillful use of dissonance. The portrayal of the dramatic and poetic meaning of the text frequently results in a disconnected series of tonal pictures. An unusual effect of tone-color develops through the use of different voice registers. **Gesualdo's** harmonic style is based largely on consecutive unrelated triads producing cross relations and chromaticsm.

        1)   His faster rhythmic devices and complex harmonic techniques are not used at the same time but rather separately. Strong Baroque tendencies are apparent in his style.

    c.   *Io pur respiro* (I still breathe) (*CE*, v. 6, p. 44; *HAM*, No. 161)

    d.   *Moro lasso* (*CE*, v. 6, p. 74; *MSO*, v. 1, p. 37)

        1)   The third relationship chords suggest Wagnerian progressions.

    e.   *Dolcissima mia vita* (Very sweet is my life) (*CE*, v. 5, p. 23; *AMI*, v. 4, p. 9)

    f.   Five madrigals (*AMI*, v. 4, pp. 1-20; *CE*, v. 3, p. 43; v. 5, pp. 19, 23; v. 6, p. 92; v. 3, p. 71)

3. **Claudio Monteverdi** (1567-1643) (*CE*)

    a.   *Il primo* (1587), *Il secondo* (1590), *Il terzo* (1592), *Il quarto* (1603) *libro de madrigali* (*CE*, vols. 1-4)

        1)   The madrigals of **Monteverdi's** first four books are all in five parts and represent his transition from the homophonic-contrapuntal *a cappella* style to the new freedom of expression of the Baroque found in his *continuo* madrigals beginning in Book V (1605). Books I and II contain 21 madrigals each and Books III and IV contain 20 madrigals each.

        2)   *Ohimè, se tanto amate* (*CE*, v. 4, p. 54; *HAM*, No. 188)

            a)   This five-voice madrigal from Book IV represents the culmination of the Italian *a cappella* madrigal.

4. **Orazio Vecchi** (1550-1605)

    a.   **Orazio Vecchi** should not be confused with the *maestro di cappella* of Santa Maria della Scala, **Orfeo Vecchi** (*c.* 1550-1604). **Orazio** wrote several collections of madrigals in which the traditional style is represented as well as the mixed styles of the late madrigal.

        1)   *Il bianco e dolce cigno* (The soft white swan), 1589

            a)   This five-voice madrigal is based on **Arcadelt's** four-voice madrigal by the same name (*SSMS*, p. 100). It is written in the same key but the beginning is transposed down an octave. The tonality is basically major, the writing florid with scale passages in thirds and sixths and imitation in the two soprano parts. The theme of the last section of **Arcadelt's** madrigal is used in diminution.

        2)   *Convito musicale* (Musical banquet), 1597 (*CP*, v. 8; see *M* 18, p. 76)

V.   The Madrigal Comedy

A.   In the latter part of the sixteenth century there developed a considerable repertoire of light humorous entertainment music known as madrigal comedies; these were intended for the stage. The madrigal comedy is a series of madrigals or similar polyphonic vocal music bound together with a dramatic plot.

B.   The principal composers of the madrigal comedy were **Giovanni Croce, Orazio Vecchi, Alessandro Striggio**, the elder, and **Adriano Banchieri.**

   1.   **Alessandro Striggio** (*c.* 1535-*c.* 1595)

      a.   *Il cicalamento delle donne al bucato* (The chattering of the women at the laundry), 1567 (*Rivista musicale italiana*, vols. 12, 13)

         1)   Among the earliest madrigal comedies is this one divided into a prologue in four voices and four scenes in seven voices; it presents scenes of women at the local laundry. Talk about lovers, a story of a ghost, a quarrel and laughter are interwoven with popular songs, complex counterpoint and choral dialogue.

   2.   **Orazio Vecchi** (1550-1605)

      a.   *Il Amfiparnasso* (The lower slopes of Parnassus), 1597 (*PAM*, v. 26; *CP*, v. 5; *AMI*, v. 4, p. 148; *NOH*, v. 4, pp. 75-80)

         1)   The dramatic comedy plot in a prologue and three acts is presented in a series of 15 madrigals mostly in five voices. The characters, masks in the Bavarian court, include the Bolognese Doctor Gratiano, the Venetian merchant Pantalone, lovers Lucio and Isabella, the Spanish Captain Cardon and others. The characters use their native dialects. A broad range of musical techniques are incorporated.

         2)   Act I, scene 1 (*CP*, v. 5, p. 10; *GMB*, No. 164)

         3)   *Tich, tach, toch* (*SSMS*, p. 133)

VI.   Popular Songs

A.   Along with the madrigals there were many lighter forms written by composers of serious madrigals and intended for the same audience as the madrigal. In general these pieces were dance-like, chordal, rhythmical and strophic.

   1.   The *villanella* superseded the former term *"villanesca."*

      a.   Many composers wrote *villanelle*: **Lasso, Marenzio, Palestrina.** Parallel fifths in three-part writing is a common characteristic.

         1)   **Orlando di Lasso,** *Sto core mio* (*CE*, v. 10, p. 69)

         2)   **Giovane Domenico da Nola,** *Canzoni Villanesche,* 1541 (*CW*, v. 43, pp. 13-17)

      b.   Various types of *villanelle* include the *greghesca* with a mixture of Venetian and Greek in the text, the *mascherata* to be sung during a masked ball, the *giustiana* whose text ridicules the stuttering old, senile Venetian men, the *moresca* which represents slaves of southern Italy and the *tedesche* mimicking German accent in Italian.

         1)   *Moresca: Chichilichi-cucurucu* (*IM*, v. 3, p. 83; **Lasso,** *CE*, v. 10, pp. 86-127)

         2)   *Mascherata: Chi la gagliarda donna vo imparare* (*IM*, v. 3, p. 80)

         3)   *Tedesche* (**Lasso,** *CE*, v. 10, p. 93)

   2.   The *villota* generally includes a popular street song and makes use of change of duple and triple meter, dance-like rhythms, nonsense syllables and a rapid section to close.

      a.   *Poi che volse de la mia stella* (*IM*, v. 3, p. 77)

   3.   The *balletto* is a strophic song with each section repeated and each section ending with a fa-fa-la refrain. **Gastoldi's** *Balletti,* 1591 (*LP*, v. 10), were the model for **Morley's** *Balletts,* 1595 (*EM*, v. 4). The *balletti* appeared later in Germany and Italy as instrumental pieces.

      a.   **Giovanni Gastoldi,** *L'acceso: Più d'ogn'altr'o Clori* (More than any other, Chloris) (*LP*, v. 10, p. 51; *HAM*, No. 158); *Lo schernito* (The ridiculous) (*LP*, v. 10, p. 20; *IM*, v. 3, p. 246)

4. *Canti carnascialeschi*   (Carnival songs)
    a. These part songs in which punning was comon were sung by masked singers standing in open carriages in a procession at a court carnival. They represented various guilds: *canto per scriptores* (scribes) (*HAM*, No. 96; *CW*, v. 43, p. 6), *de' profumieri* (perfumers), *de' sartori* (tailors), *etc.* Several carnival songs are included in the secular works of the Florentine composers **Alessandro Coppini** and **Giovanni Serragli** (*CMM*, 32, v. 2; see *SSMS*, p. 86).

VII. **Roman School of Church Music**

A. **Palestrina** is the chief representative of church music in the Roman school, a school which denotes a tradition of *a cappella* music. But it should be kept in mind that in the principal cities of Italy other than Rome there also were church musicians writing Masses, motets and other sacred music following the principles dictated by the Council of Trent.
    1. The Council of Trent met during the years 1545-1563 and recommended that church music be written in a clear, dignified polyphonic and harmonic style. The use of secular melodies for *cantus firmi* was not banned but discouraged. **Palestrina** was not the "saviour of church music," but his style fully represents the ideals of the council.
B. **Giovanni Pierluigi da Palestrina** (*c.* 1525-1594) (*CE*; *PWerke*; Masses: *PVSP*, vols. 3, 4, 6; *SR*, pp. 323-324)
    1. **Palestrina** was one of the choirboys at the Cathedral in Palestrina (1532-1534); he later studied in Rome. In 1544 he was appointed organist and choirmaster at the Cathedral of Palestrina and in 1551 returned to Rome where he held the position of chapelmaster and composer in the Julian Chapel at St. Peter's Basilica. In 1555 he transferred to St. John Lateran, then to Santa Maria Maggiore in 1561. Ten years later he returned to the Julian Chapel at St. Peter's (1571) where he remained the rest of his life. Shortly before his death, **Palestrina** planned to return to service in the cathedral of his birthplace.
    2. Included among his works are 105 Masses, 265 motets, 13 Magnificats, 4 Psalms, 66 Offertories, 9 Lamentations (*ISM*, v. 3, p. 172), 9 Litanies, 41 hymns, 52 spiritual madrigals and a few secular songs (see *M* 32). His Masses represent his greatest achievement.
    3. **Palestrina** was the creator of a pure, diatonic, modal church style, but it does not necessarily represent a culmination of Renaissance music. His style is based on Flemish modal counterpoint and some influence of the Venetian double choir style is apparent. Under the influence of the madrigal his music became more expressive, having qualities of joy, sadness and mysticism.
    4. Characteristics of **Palestrina's** style of modal counterpoint. (The references in the following are from **Palestrina's** *Missa Papae Marcelli, M* 28e; *CE*, v. 4, p. 167).
        a. Melody
            1) There is a free flow of melody similar to plainsong. The ascending and descending lines often counterbalance each other. The "expressive" type of melody is avoided.
            2) Melodic intervals
                a) Perfect fourths, perfect fifths, perfect octaves, up or down.
                b) Major and minor seconds and thirds, up or down.
                c) Minor sixths, up only; major sixths are rare and up only.
                d) Other intervals are not used except as "dead" (after rests and at the ends of phrases) intervals.
        b. Time units
            1) The half-note (minim) is usually the time unit, but at times the whole note is the unit.
                a) Four half notes to the measure (4/2 time)

        (1)   The first and third beats are strong.
      b)   Three whole notes to the measure (3/1 time)
        (1)   The first, third and fifth half-note beats are strong.
        (2)   In rapid tempi there are three whole-note beats to the measure.
      c)   Three half notes to the measure (3/2 time)
        (1)   Only the first beat is strong.

c.   Harmony
  1)   Consonances form the basic harmonic background.
    a)   Perfect unisons, perfect fifths and perfect octaves are consonant.
    b)   Major and minor thirds and sixths are consonant.
    c)   There is generally one harmony to a beat.
    d)   Consonances are approached or left by skips; dissonances are approached or left by step.
    e)   The fourth between the bass and any upper part is treated as a dissonance, except in the so-called dissonant fourth. It is consonant between the upper parts.

d.   Dissonances
  1)   Passing notes
    a)   Unaccented passing tones may be used ascending and descending; accented passing tones are only descending.
  2)   *Nota cambiata* (changing note) (p. 5, meas. 1-2; p. 10, meas. 2-3)
    a)   The *cambiata* figure is a group of four notes, the second of which is taken by step and left by skip of a third (both downward) and followed by an upward step. The second note is usually dissonant and the third note is usually consonant.
  3)   Suspensions (always counted from the lowest voice)
    a)   In two parts: 7-6, 2-3, 4-3 (rare)
    b)   In more than two parts: 7-6 (p. 1, meas. 4); 4-3 (p. 1, meas. 8); 2-1 (p. 14, meas. 11); 9-8 (p. 15, meas. 2); 2-3 (p. 24, meas. 16)
    c)   The discord occurs on the strong beats; the preparation and resolution occur on weak beats.
    d)   In 3/1 time (fast), the suspensions are prepared on the first beat, taken on the second and resolved on the third whole-note beat.
    e)   3/2 time follows the rules for 3/1 time except that the preparation is very rarely taken on the first half-note beat.
    f.   6/5 chord (added sixth) where the fifth and sixth are present together (p. 2, meas. 6, 7, 9).
    g)   Consonant fourth (p. 40, meas. 4) is introduced stepwise on the weak beat over a sustained bass tone, tied over to the next strong beat and becomes a stronger dissonance on that beat by adding the fifth of the chord. It resolves on the next weak beat.
  4)   Neighboring tones (p. 1, meas. 6)
  5)   Anticipations (p. 1, meas. 4; p. 1, meas. 8)

e.   Rhythm
  1)   Stresses do not follow the barlines of modern editions. The rhythm has some of the flexibility of plainsong and a definite rhythmic pulse is avoided.
  2)   Barlines were used in sixteenth century tablatures but rarely in vocal music.
  3)   Collective rhythm with regular alternation between accented and unaccented half notes.
    a)   *Macro* (greater) rhythm
      (1)   This rhythm concerns the piece as a whole and defines the strong (first and third) and weak (second and fourth) beats.

b)   *Micro* (partial) rhythm
   (1)   This rhythm represents the rhythm of the individual parts and follows the stresses of the text.

5.   *Sicut cervus* (As the hart panteth), Psalm 42:1-3 (*CE*, v. 11, p. 42; *PWerke*, v. 5, p. 148; *HAM*, No. 141)
   a.   The melody of this motet (one of 68 in four voices) illustrates the balance of the so-called "**Palestrina** curve." Dividing the motet into two parts is quite common practice particularly when the text expresses parallelism, as is the case frequently with the texts from the Psalms.

6.   *Exaltabo te Domine* (*CE*, v. 17, p. 167; *M* 32, p. 177)
   a.   The collection of 66 *Offertories*, all in five parts, was published in 1593. The text is from the Offertory for Ash Wednesday (*LU*, p. 528). The transposed Ionian mode is used; a series of six expositions in motet style is formed by the imitative treatment of each phrase of the text: 1) *Exaltabo te Domine*; 2) *quoniam suscepisti me*; 3) *nec delectasti*; 4) *inimicos meos super me*; 5) *Domine clamavi ad te*; 6) *et sanasti me*.

C.   **Marc'Antonio Ingegneri** (*c*. 1545-1592)
   1.   A pupil of the Netherlander **Rore** and teacher of **Monteverdi, Ingegneri** spent his productive years in Cremona. In 1578 he entered the service of the Cremona Cathedral and later became the *magistro musice capelle* of the cathedral.
   2.   Included in his works are two books of Masses, 1573 and 1587, three books of motets, eight books of madrigals and 27 *Responsoria* (see *M* 32, pp. 214-225) once ascribed to **Palestrina** and appearing in **Palestrina's** *CE*, v. 32, *opera dubia*.
   a.   *Tenebrae factae sunt* (*M* 32, p. 29) from the *Responsoria*.

D.   The **Palestrina** style continued with the incorporation of the Venetian polychoral style by conservative musicians in Rome. **Nanini, Felice Anerio** and others composed some liturgical music based on the principles of the **Palestrina** period as well as in the so-called "colossal style" (very large scores with choruses, soloists and orchestra). The *Missa Papae Marcelli* by **Palestrina** was arranged by **Giovanni Anerio** as a polychoral work in Venetian style.
   1.   **Giovanni Maria Nanini [Nanino]** (*c*. 1543-1607)
      a.   **Nanino**, a member of the musicians' society *Compagnia dei Musici di Roma* (now the *Accademia di Santa Cecilia*), was a tenor in the Papal Choir in 1571. He was a pupil of **Palestrina** and succeeded him as music director at Santa Maria Maggiore in 1571. In 1604 he became director of the Sistine Chapel. (See *RRMR*, v. 5, 14 liturgical works)
      b.   *Motetti*, 1586
         1)   This collection of 30 canonic motets in three, four and five voices is based on a single *cantus firmus*. Against the long note *cantus firmus* the remaining voices appear in canon in a variety of intervals.
            a)   In *Cantate Domino* (*AMI*, v. 2, p. 18) two voices create a mirror canon at the second with the *cantus firmus* between.
            b)   *Hic est beatissimus* (*MDaP*, v. 2, p. 57; *HAM*, No. 152) has canon at the octave in the two outside voices with the *cantus firmus* between.
            c)   In the five-part *Qui vult venire post me* (*AMI*, v. 2, p. 20) three voices are in canon, one voice is free and the *cantus firmus* is in the top voice.
   2.   **Felice Anerio** (*c*. 1564-1614)
      a.   For six years beginning in 1568 **Anerio** was a choirboy under **G. M. Nanino** at Santa Maria Maggiore and from 1575 to 1579 he sang in the Julian choir under **Palestrina**. In 1594 he became composer to the Papal Choir; he was also a member of the *Compagnia*.

VIII.   Venetian School

A.   The Venetian School developed through the efforts of Flemish and Italian composers working in Venice.   They developed new ideas and, with Florentine monody, prepared the way for the seventeenth century Baroque.   Some of these new ideas were: chromaticism (**Willaert**), free modulation, experiments with quarter-tones and a six-manual harpsichord with 31 tones to the octave (**Vincentino**, *c*. 1550), development of the *toccata* (**A. Gabrieli, Merulo**), Zarlino's theories.   The "Venetian" style of **Giovanni Gabrieli** made use of polychoral treatment, broad sonorities, echo effects and instruments.   German composers, such as **Gallus, Schütz, Heironymous Praetorius, Hassler** and **Michael Praetorius** carried on the Venetian style.

B.   **Adrian Willaert** (*c*. 1485-1562) (*CE = CMM*, 3)

  1.   Born in Flanders, **Willaert** was sent to Paris (*c*. 1514) to study law at the University of Paris but changed to music and became a pupil of **Jean Mouton**.   In 1552 he was employed by the Duke of Ferrara and then briefly (1525) by the duke's brother, Archbishop of Milan.   In December, 1527, **Willaert** was appointed *maestro di cappella* at St. Mark's in Venice where he remained throughout his life.   There he established the "Venetian school of composition" which attracted some of the greatest musicians of his time.

  2.   The two organs and two choirs at St. Mark's inspired him to write for double choir, a style he perfected to a high degree.   Among his works are several Masses, three collections of motets in four to six voices (*CMM*, 3, vols. 1-4), several books of Psalms (*CMM*, 3, v. 6) and hymns (*CMM*, 3, v. 7).   *Musica nova*, 1559 (*CMM*, 3, vols. 5, 13), contains both motets and madrigals.

  3.   *Victimae paschali laudes*, from *Musica nova*, 1559 (*CMM*, 3, v. 5, p. 164; *HAM*, No. 113)

    a.   The six-voice motet is based on the plainsong and shows the Franco-Netherlandish technique firmly established.   It is closely woven polyphony with the initial phrase of the *cantus firmus* in the sextus and then the entire chant in the quintus (meas. 17).

  4.   *Ave Regina coelorum, Mater Regis* (*CMM*, 3, v. 2, p. 34; *LMA*, v. 2, p. 134)

    a.   Unlike the above motet in two sections, this one is continuous throughout.   **Willaert** writes the two upper voices in canon at the fifth below.

C.   **Philippe Verdelot** (*c*. 1490-*c*. 1545) (*CMM*, 28) (Refer earlier to II. A. 3.)

  1.   Masses and hymns (*CMM*, 28, v. 1)

  2.   Motets (*CMM*, 28, vols. 2, 3; *M* 31, v. 2, pp. 65-172)

D.   **Andrea Gabrieli** (*c*. 1510-1586)

  1.   Although limited in number, **Gabrieli's** sacred works are no less distinctive.   He wrote Masses, a volume each of four- and five-voice motets and a book of Psalms.

  2.   *Motecta . . . tuna viva voce, tum omnis generis Instrumentis cantatu commodissimae* (Motets . . . most suitable to be performed sometimes by the living voice, sometimes by all kinds of instruments), 1565

    a.   *Cantate Domino* (Sing to the Lord) (*IMAMI*, v. 1, p. 1)

    b.   *O sacrum conuiuium*, from *Sacrae Cantiones* (*AMI*, v. 2, p. 117)

  3.   *Salmi Davidie*, 1583

    a.   **Gabrieli** suggests, as in the motets, that instruments may be added in various combinations.   St. Mark's was famous for its use of instruments and organs.

    b.   *Deus misereatur nostri* (*ICMI*, v. 5, p. 71)

      1)   This requires three four-voice choirs which sing in a variety of contrasting groups and combinations.   At one place a soprano part is heard above a four-voice male chorus.   (For other polychoral works see *CW*, v. 96)

    c.   *De profundis clamavi* (Psalm 130) (*IMAMI*, v. 1, part 2, p. 13; *GMB*, No. 130)

E.   **Giovanni Gabrieli** (1557-1612) (*CE = CMM*, 12; *CW*, vols. 10, 67)
  1.   **Giovanni Gabrieli**, a famous organist and teacher, was the culminating figure of the Venetian School. Born in Venice, he lived in Munich and in 1584 succeeded **Merulo** as first organist at St. Mark's. He was the first to write vocal music with accompaniments of various groups of instruments (concerted music) anticipating the early Baroque style.
  2.   Included in his works are three books of motets, generally in polychoral style: *Concerti* (6-16 voices), 1587; two books of *Sacrae symphoniae*, Book I, 1597; Book II, published posthumously in 1615.
    a.   *Angelus ad Pastores ait* (*CMM*, 12, v. 1, p. 34; *AMI*, v. 2, p. 177) for two six-voice choirs
    b.   *In ecclesiis* (*CMM*, 12, v. 5, p. 32; *HAM*, No. 157) for two four-part choirs
      1)   In the *stile concertato* of the early Baroque, this motet makes use of instruments and organ, two choirs and solo parts in various arrangements.
F.   Other members of the Venetian School included **Vincenzo Bell'Haver** (d. 1587) (*AMI*, v. 1, pp. 399, 405, 417); **Gioseffo Guami** (1540-1611); **Jacques Buus** (d. 1565) and **Annibale Padovano** (1527-1575).
  1.   **Buus** was first organist at St. Mark's, 1541-1550, and published 21 four-voice motets in 1549. **Padovano** was second organist at St. Mark's, 1552-1564.

IX.   Music Theory

A.   **Johannes Tinctoris** (*c*. 1435-1511) (*CSM*, 22)
  1.   Although born and educated near Brussels, **Tinctoris** spent most of his productive life in Italy (Naples, *c*. 1475; Rome, *c*. 1492). His main contribution to music is a collection of 12 treatises encompassing the important subjects relative to music theory. The first treatise is a dictionary (*Diffinitorium*) of 300 musical terms (*MMF*, Ser. 2, v. 26), 2) is on solmization, 3) on modes in plainsong and polyphony (*CMT*, v. 2), 4-8) on mensural notation, 9) on counterpoint, 10) on proportional notation, 11) on the effects of music, and 12) on singing and instruments.
    a.   The important treatise No. 9, *Liber de arte contrapuncti* (*MSD*, 5; *CSM*, 22, v. 2, p. 11) gives eight rules for composing counterpoint (*RMR*, p. 144; *SR*, pp. 197-199).
    b.   Introduction: *Proportionale Musices* (No. 10) (*CSM*, 22, v. 2a, p. 9; *SR*, p. 193)
B.   **Franchino Gafori [Franchinus Gaffurius]** (1451-1522)
  1.   Born in Lodi, **Gafori** spent time in Mantua (1473) and Verona. In Naples (1477) he held public debates with **Tinctoris** and in 1484 moved to Milan where he taught and became choirmaster at the cathedral.
  2.   Among **Gafori's** five theoretical works (*BMB, Teoria*, vols. 5-7; *MMF*, Ser 2, vols. 21, 96-100) is his most important contribution, the *Practica Musicae*, dealing with contemporary styles and practices. **Gafori** also wrote Masses (*CMM*, 10, vols. 1, 2; *ArM*, vols. 1-3), motets (*ArM*, v. 5), Magnificats (*ArM*, v. 4) and several other liturgical pieces (*ArM*, v. 15).
  3.   *Practica Musicae*, Milan, 1496 (*MMF*, Ser. 2, v. 99; *MSD*, v. 20; *B* 11)
    a.   This includes a discussion on mensural proportions and **Gafori's** eight rules for counterpoint. **Gafori** states that the *tactus*, equal to a semibreve, is normally the rate of "pulse beat of a quietly breathing man," that is between 60 to 80 beats per minute.
C.   **Gioseffo Zarlino** (1517-1590)
  1.   **Rore** succeeded **Willaert** (1563) at St. Mark's and in 1565 **Zarlino** succeeded **Rore** as *maestro di cappella*; both were students of **Willaert**.
  2.   The theoretical writings of **Zarlino** are included in three treatises.
    a.   *Istituzioni armoniche [Institutione harmoniche]*, Venice, 1558 (*MMF*, Ser. 2, v. 1; *SR*, pp. 228-261)
      1)   **Zarlino's** most famous treatise is divided into four books and was translated into French, German and Dutch. Book III (*YMTT*, v. 2) deals principally with the laws

of counterpoint, the possible intervals between two voices, and major and minor harmonics.

    b) In Book IV he discusses the twelve modes like **Glareanus** does, but changes the order: Ionian and Hypoionian, modes I and II; Aeolian and Hypoaeolian, modes XI and XII. **Zarlino** also discusses the importance of setting a text expressively and how to underlay the text in polyphonic music.

  2) *Dimostrationi armoniche*, Venice, 1571 (*MMF*, Ser. 2, v. 2)

    a) Written in the form of dialogues among five friends, **Zarlino** discusses the modes, proportions of intervals and the divisions of the monochord. The major triad evolved from the overtone series (partials 4, 5 and 6); the minor triad evolved from an inversion of the harmonic series. Simple consonances involved a successive number of ratios up to six: 1:2, octave; 2:3, perfect fifth; 3:4, perfect fourth; 4:5, major third; 5:6, minor third.

  3) *Sopplimenti musicali*, Venice, 1588

    a) In Book IV **Zarlino** discusses a system of equal temperament and gives discourses on the organ, including particulars about early organs.

X. Instrumental Music

A. Forms
1. Ricercar
  a. Imitative instrumental ricercar (after 1540)
    1) The ricercar is a contrapuntal piece in motet style which probably developed out of the *carmina* and other early instrumental pieces. The earliest ensemble compositions called *"ricercar"* occured in *Musica nova*, 1540, and among pieces by **Willaert, Jacques Buus, Annibale Padovano** and others.
      a) Frequent points of imitation and crossing of parts are characteristics. There is some indication (*"per cantar et sonar"*) that these could be vocalized as well as played on instruments such as viols and recorders.
  b. Imitative organ ricercar
    1) The organ ricercar is distinct from the ensemble ricercar in that the organ ricercar has only a small number of themes, each extensively developed contrapuntally and brought to a complete close. In some cases the entire ricercar is based on a single theme (monothematic), and becomes the predecessor of the fugue.
      a) Other characteristics include toccata-like passages, coloraturas, particularly at a cadence, and free voice writing. Augmentation, diminution, double counterpoint, inversion and combining themes are also traits that occur.
  c. Non-imitative ricercars for lute, organ, viols and voices appear in free prelude and toccata styles but are unrelated to the motet.
2. Canzona
  a. The canzona developed from the Franco-Flemish chansons of the sixteenth century which appeared in Italy as *"canzon francese."* Arranged for lute, organ and instrumental ensemble, the canzona tends toward a harmonic counterpoint in a variety of treatments: sectional, harmonic contrasted with imitative, triple meter alternating with duple.
  b. Instrumental canzona
    1) Several types of canzonas are apparent. A conservative canzona modeled on the chanson is generally contrapuntal with little contrast. The brilliant polychoric canzona has contrasting sections of imitation and homophony; this evolved into the Baroque sonata.
  c. Keyboard canzona
    1) Like the instrumental canzona, the canzona for keyboard maintained a variety of contrasting elements in sectional development. The sectional quality distin-

guishes it from the ricercar and later the fugue, but the lively and individual thematic design had a strong influence on the fugue. One unifying quality was the frequent use of repeated notes in the opening theme.

3. Prelude
   a. The prelude is unique in that it is the earliest type of idiomatic keyboard music in contrast to types based on pre-existing models. In contrast to contrapuntal vocal styles, the prelude is short (up to 25 measures) and in free style mixing chords and passage work.
   b. The lute prelude is similar to the keyboard prelude but often more extended.
4. Toccata
   a. The toccata is a keyboard piece in free style using full chords and running passages. It may include sections in imitative style alternating with free sections.

B. Lute music
1. From 1550 into the early part of the seventeenth century there was a large number of lute books published in Italy. These included lute transcriptions of vocal works, dance pieces, dance suites, ricercars and fantasies. Soon after 1600 the lute became less important and the violin became the main instrument of performance.
2. **Joan Ambrosio Dalza**
   a. *Intabulatura di Lauto*, 1508, printed by **Petrucci**
      1) *Ricercar* (*HAM*, No. 99a; *AERM*, p. 236)
         a) **Dalza** introduces this piece by saying *"Tastar de corde con li soi recercar dietro"* (Sounding of the strings with the ricercar afterward). The ricercar is introduced with a short "warming up" piece mainly of chords and scale passages.
3. **Felice Anerio** (1560-1614)
   a. *Al suon* (At the sound) (*HAM*, No. 106b), a song arranged for lute and harpsichord
4. **Giovanni Anerio** (1567-1621)
   a. *Gagliarde* (*GMB*, No. 181)

C. Keyboard music
1. **Marco Antonio Cavazzoni** (*c.* 1490-after 1569)
   a. *Recerchari, motetti, canzoni, Libro I*, 1523 (*MMF*, Ser. 1, v. 12; *ICMI*, v. 1, pp. 1-55; *M* 21, pp. 35*-82*; *NPM*, p. 5)
      1) The ricercars are improvisational pieces which show early development of a motif along with the usual passage work and some suggestion of imitation.
2. **Girolamo Cavazzoni** (*c.* 1520-*c.* 1577)
   a. *Intavolatura cioè Recercari, Canzoni, Hinni, Magnificati*, 1542 (*ICDMI*, v. 6)
      1) These ricercars are the standard motet-like polyphonic compositions.
      2) *Ricercar* (*HAM*, No. 116; *ICDMI*, v. 6)
      3) *Missa Apostolorum [Missa Cunctipotens]* (*HAM*, No. 117; *MOP*, p. 192)
         a) This is a polyphonic setting for organ of the Ordinary of the Mass; plainsong alternates with the organ paraphrases.
      4) *Falte d'argens* (*HAM*, No. 118; *ICDMI*, v. 6)
         a) This organ *canzona francese* is based on themes from **Josquin's** *chanson* by the same name.
      5) *Ad coenam agni providi*, Easter hymn for organ (*GMB*, No. 103; *ICDMI*, v. 6)
3. **Giacomo Fogliano** (1473-1548)
   a. *Ricercari* (*ICMI*, v. 1)
4. **Jacques Buus** (d. 1565)
   a. *Ricercari*, 1547
      1) The collection contains the earliest monothematic ricercar.
5. **Andrea Gabrieli** (1510-1586)
   a. *Intonazione* (*HAM*, No. 135; *AMI*, v. 3, p. 77)
      1) The "intoning piece" is an improvisational prelude for liturgical use to set the pitch for the choir or cantor.

b. *Canzona francese deta Pour ung plaisir* (*MM*, p. 64), on a *chanson* by **Thomas Crequillon** (d. 1557).
c. *Fantasia allegra* (*AMI*, v. 3, p. 67)
6. **Claudio Merula** (1533-1604)
a. *Toccate*, Book I, 1598; Book II, 1604
b. *Toccate* (*HAM*, No. 153; *AMI*, v. 3, pp. 91, 99; *AMO*, v. 10, pp. 53, 61, 116; *GMB*, No. 149)
7. **Girolamo Diruta** (1557-1612)
a. *Il Transilvano*, Part I, 1593; Part II, 1608
1) This is the first method book to differentiate between harpsichord and organ performance practices. Hand position, fingering, ornaments and general rules for registration are discussed. Etudes are composed to illustrate various technical problems. Included are works by **Merulo**, the **Gabrielis, Luzzaschi, Bell'Haver** and **Gioseffo Guami**.
D. Music for instruments
1. During the *cinquecento* instruments were used for a variety of functions, public, private and in the churches and courts. City bands enhanced festivities. Instrumental groups were portrayed in paintings by many of the great Renaissance painters and contemporary writings praise the skill of many instrumentalists. The viols were especially prominent in chamber groups; instruction methods for various instruments began to be written.
2. **Adrian Willaert** (*c*. 1485-1562)
a. *Fantasie, Ricercari, Contrapunti*, 1559
1) *Ricercar decimo* (*HAM*, No. 115; *GMB*, No. 105)
3. **Silvestro di Ganassi** (*fl.* 1535-1545)
a. *Opera intitulata Fontegara* (The book entitled Fontegara), Venice, 1535 (*M* 16a)
1) This is a treatise on the art of playing the recorder and of free ornamentation.
b. *Regola Rubertina*, 1543-1543 (*M* 16b)
1) This is one of the earliest instruction methods for the viol; it also contains *ricercari* in tablature.
2) Two ricercars (*HAM*, No. 119), note the double stops.
4. **Andrea Gabrieli** (*c*. 1510-1586)
a. *Madrigali et ricercari*, 1589 (*IMAMI*, v. 1, p. 86)
1) *Ricercare del 12° tono* (*HAM*, No. 135)
b. *Battaglia per strumenti da fiato* (Battle for wind instruments) (*IMAMI*, v. 1, p. 177)
5. **Annibale Padovano** (1527-1575)
a. *Battaglia per strument da fiato* (*IMAMI*, v. 1, p. 93)
1) At one time this was performed with an ensemble of 40 instruments: 8 *tromboni*, 8 *viol da arco*, 8 *grandi flauti*, one *strumento da penna*, one *laute* and voices.
6. **Fiorenza Maschera**
a. *Canzoni da sonare*, 1593 (*AIM*, pp. 1, 2; *HAM*, No. 201)
7. **Giovanni Gabrieli** (1557-1612)
a. *Sacra symphoniae*, Book I, 1597 (*IMAMI*, v. 2; *CMM*, 12, vols. 1, 2)
1) Included are 14 canzonas and 2 sonatas.
2) *Sonata pian' e forte* (*HAM*, No. 173; *IMAMI*, v. 2, p. 64; *GMB*, No. 148; *AIM*, p. 7; *MSO*, v. 1, p. 63)
a) The sonata is the earliest known piece to contrast *"piano"* and *"forte"* and to give the exact instrumentation. It is scored for two instrumental choirs: 1) *cornetto (Zink)* and 3 trombones; 2) *violino* (viola) and 3 trombones.
3) *Canzon per sonar* (*AIM*, p. 4)

SELECTED BIBLIOGRAPHY

Books

1. Arnold, Denis. *Marenzio*. New York: Oxford University Press, 1965.
2. Bernstein, Melvin. "The Hymns of Giaches de Wert," in *Studies in Musicology: Essays in the History, Style, and Bibliography of Music in Memory of Glen Haydon*, ed. James W. Pruett, pp. 190-210. Chapel Hill: University of North Carolina Press, 1969.
3. Berquist, Peter. "Mode and Polyphony around 1500: Theory and Practice," in *The Music Forum*, ed. William J. Mitchell and Felix Salzar, v. 1, pp. 99-161. New York: Columbia University Press, 1970.
4. Boetticher, Wolfgang. "New Lasso Studies," in *Aspects of Medieval and Renaissance Music: A Birthday Offering to Gustave Reese*, ed. Jan LaRue, pp. 17-26. New York: W. W. Norton, 1966.
5. Bradshaw, Murray C. *Origin of the Toccata*. Rome: American Institute of Musicology. (*MSD*, v. 28)
6. Brown, Howard Mayer. "Chansons for the Pleasure of a Florentine Patrician: Florence, Biblioteca del conservatorio di musica, MS Basevi 2442," in *Aspects of Medieval and Renaissance Music: A Birthday Offering to Gustave Reese*, ed. Jan LaRue, pp. 56-66. New York: W. W. Norton, 1966.
7. Clerex, Suzanne. *Johannes Ciconia, un musicien liégeois et son temps*, 2 vols. Bruxelles: Palais des académies, 1960.
8. Coussemaker, Charles Edmond Henri. *Scriptorum de Musica medii aevi nova series*, v. 4 (facsimile: Tinctoris, 11 treatises). Hildesheim: Georg Olms Verlagbuchhandlung, 1963.
9. Crozier, Catharine. *The Principles of Keyboard Technique in Il Transilvano by Girolamo Diruta*. University of Rochester, Eastman School of Music Thesis, 1941.
10. Einstein, Alfred. *The Italian Madrigal*, 3 vols, tr. Alexander H. Krappe, Roger Sessions, Oliver Strunk. Princeton: Princeton University Press, 1949.
11. Gafori, Franchino [Franchinus Gaffurius]. *Practica Musicae*. Milan, 1496; facsimile reprint: Farnborough, Hantshire, England: Gregg Press, 1967; tr. Clement A. Miller. Rome: American Institute of Musicology, 1968 (*MSD*, v. 20); tr. Irwin Young. Madison: The University of Wisconsin Press, 1969.
12. Gray, Cecil, and Philip Heseltine. *Carlo Gesualdo, Prince of Venosa, Musician and Murderer*. London: K. Paul, Trench, Trubner & Co., 1926.
13. Hagopian, Viola L. *Italian Ars Nova Music: A Bibliographic Guide to Modern Editions and Related Literature*, 2nd ed. Berkeley: University of California Press, 1973.
14. Gombosi, Otto. "About Organ Playing in the Divine Service circa 1500," in *Essays on Music in Honor of Archibald Thompson Davison, by His Associates*, pp. 51-68. Cambridge, MA: Department of Music, Harvard University, 1957.
15. Haigh, Andrew C. "Modal Harmony in the Music of Palestrina," in *Essays on Music in Honor of Archibald Thompson Davison, by His Associates*, pp. 111-120. Cambridge, MA: Department of Music, Harvard University, 1957.
16. Hess, Albert Günter. *Italian Renaissance Paintings with Musical Subjects; A Corpus of Such Works in American Collections, with Detailed Descriptions of the Musical Features*, 2 vols. New York: Libra Press, 1955.
17. Horsley, Imogene. "Fugue and Mode in 16th-Century Vocal Polyphony," in *Aspects of Medieval and Renaissance Music: A Birthday Offering to Gustave Reese*, ed. Jan LaRue, pp. 406-422. New York: W. W. Norton, 1966.
18. Jeppesen, Knud. *Counterpoint, the Polyphonic Vocal Style of the Sixteenth Century*, tr. Glen Haydon. Englewood Cliffs, NJ: Prentice-Hall, 1947.
19. ————*The Style of Palestrina and the Dissonance*, tr. Margaret Hamerik. Copenhagen: E. Munksgaard, 1946.

20. Jeppesen, Knud. "An Unknown Pre-Madrigalian Music Print in Relation to Other Contemporary Italian Sources (1520-1530)," in *Studies in Musicology: Essays in the History, Style, and Bibliography of Music in Memory of Glen Haydon*, ed. James W. Pruett, pp. 3-17. Chapel Hill: University of North Carolina Press, 1969.

21. Kaufmann, Henry W. *The Life and Works of Nicola Vicentino (1511-c. 1576)*. Rome: American Institute of Musicology, 1966. (*MSD*, v. 11)

22. Kenney, Sylvia M. "In Praise of the Lauda," in *Aspects of Medieval and Renassiance Music: A Birthday Offering to Gustave Reese*, ed. Jan LaRue, pp. 489-499. New York: W. W. Norton, 1966.

23. Kinkeldey, Otto. "A Jewish Dancing Master of the Renaissance (Guglielmo Ebreo)," in *Studies in Jewish Bibliography and Related Subjects, in Memory of Abraham Solomon Freidus (1867-1923)*. New York: The Alexander Kohut Memorial Foundation, 1929.

24. Lockwood, Lewis. "On 'Parody' as Term and Concept in 16th-Century Music," in *Aspects of Medieval and Renaissance Music: A Birthday Offering to Gustave Reese*, ed. Jan LaRue, pp. 560-575. New York: W. W. Norton, 1966.

25. –––––––"A Sample Problem of *Musica ficta*: Willaert's *Pater noster*," in *Studies in Music History: Essays for Oliver Strunk*, ed. Harold Powers, pp. 161-182. Princeton: Princeton University Press, 1968.

26. Lowinsky, Edward E. *Tonality and Atonality in Sixteenth Century Music*. Berkeley: University of California Press, 1962.

27. –––––––"Echoes of Adrian Willaert's Chromatic 'Duo' in Sixteenth- and Seventeenth-Century Compositions," in *Studies in Music History: Essays for Oliver Strunk*, ed. Harold Powers, pp. 183-204. Princeton: Princeton University Press, 1968.

28. –––––––"Problems in Adrian Willaert's Iconography," in *Aspects of Medieval and Renaissance Music: A Birthday Offering to Gustave Reese*, ed. Jan LaRue, pp. 576-594. New York: W. W. Norton, 1966.

29. MacClintock, Carol. *Giaches de Wert (1935-1596). Life and Works*. New York: American Institute of Musicology, 1966. (*MSD*, v. 17)

30. –––––––"Two Lute Intabulations of Wert's *Cara la vita*'," in *Essays in Musicology: A Birthday Offering for Willi Apel*, ed. Hans Tischler, pp. 93-100. Bloomington: Indiana University School of Music, 1968.

31. Mason, Wilton. "The Architecture of St. Mark's Cathedral and the Venetian Polychoral Style: A Clarification," in *Studies in Musicology: Essays in the History, Style, and Bibliography of Music in Memory of Glen Haydon*, ed. James W. Pruett, pp. 163-178. Chapel Hill: University of North Carolina Press, 1969.

32. Masson, Paul-Marie. *Chants de Carnaval Florentins*. Paris: Édition Maurice Senart, 1913.

33. Ness, Arthur J. *The Lute Music of Francesco Canova da Milano (1497-1543)*, 2 vols. Cambridge, MA: Harvard University Press, 1970.

34. Plamenac, Dragan. "The Recently Discovered Complete Copy of A. Antico's *Frottole intabulate* (1517)," in *Aspects of Medieval and Renaissance Music: A Birthday Offering to Gustave Reese*, ed. Jan LaRue, pp. 683-692. New York: W. W. Norton, 1966.

35. Riemann, Hugo. *History of Music Theory*, Books I & II: *Polyphonic Theory to the Sixteenth Century*, tr. Raymond H. Haggh. Lincoln: University of Nebraska Press, 1962.

36. Roche, Jerome. *The Madrigal*. New York: Charles Scribner's Sons, 1972.

37. Rokseth, Yvonne. *Musical Instruments in the Fifteenth Century Church*. Cambridge: Bois de Boulogne, 1968.

38. Schrade, Leo. *Monteverdi, Creator of Modern Music*. New York: W. W. Norton, 1950; London: Gollancz, 1951.

39. Shirlaw, Matthew. *The Theory of Harmony*, 2nd ed. De Kalb, IL: B. Coar, 1955.

40. Soderlund, Gustave Fredric. *Direct Approach to Counterpoint in 16th Century Style*. New York: Appleton-Century-Crofts, 1947.

41. Tinctoris, Johannes. *Ten Treatises in Manuscript Sources*, 2 vols., ed. Albert Seay. Rome: American Institute of Musicology. (*CSM*, 22)

42. Tinctoris, Johannes. *Concerning the Nature and Propriety of Tones (De natura et proprietate tonorum)*, tr. Albert Seay. Colorado Springs: Colorado College Music Press, 1967. (*CMT*, v. 2)

43. ———*Dictionary of Musical Terms. An English Translation of "Terminorum Musicae Diffinitorium" Together with the Latin Text*, tr. Carl Parrish. New York: Free Press of Glencoe, 1963.

44. Ward, John. "Parody Technique in 16th-Century Instrumental Music," in *The Commonwealth of Music in Honor of Curt Sachs*, ed. Gustave Reese and Rose Brandel, pp. 208-228. New York: The Free Press, 1965.

45. Watkins, Glen E. *Gesualdo: The Man and His Music*. Chapel Hill: University of North Carolina Press, 1974.

46. Woodworth, G. W. "Texture Versus Mass in the Music of Giovanni Gabrieli," in *Essays on Music in Honor of Archibald Thompson Davison, by His Associates*, pp. 129-138. Cambridge, MA: Department of Music, Harvard University, 1957.

47. Zarlino, Gioseffo. *The Art of Counterpoint; Part Three of "Le Istitutioni Harmoniche," 1588*, tr. Guy A. Marco and Claude V. Palisca. New Haven: Yale University Press, 1968.

Articles

1. d'Alessi, Giovanni. "Precursors of Adriano Willaert in the Practice of Coro Spezzato." *JAMS* 5 (1952), pp. 187-210.

2. Anthon, Carl. "Some Aspects of the Social Status of Italian Musicians During the Sixteenth Century." *JRBM* 1 (1946), pp. 111-123; 222-234.

3. Apel, Willi. "The Early Development of the Organ Ricercar." *MD* 3 (1949), pp. 139-150.

4. Arnold, Denis. "Music as a Confraternity in the Renaissance." *ActaM* 37 (1965), pp. 62-72.

5. ———"Toward a Biography of Giovanni Gabrieli." *MD* 15 (1961), pp. 199-207.

6. Bedbrook, Gerald S. "The Genius of Giovanni Gabrieli (1557-1612)." *MR* 8 (1947), pp. 91-101.

7. Bobbitt, Richard. "Harmonic Tendencies in the *Missa Papae Marcelli*." *MR* 16 (1955), pp. 273-288.

8. Boyd, Malcolm. "Structural Cadences in the Sixteenth-Century Mass." *MR* 33 (1972), pp. 1-13.

9. Bukofzer, Manfred. "Two Mensuration Canons." *MD* 2 (1948), pp. 165-171.

10. Burns, Joseph A. "Antonio Valente, Neapolitan Keyboard Primitive." *JAMS* 12 (1959), pp. 133-143.

11. Carapetyan, Arman. "The Concept of the 'Imitazione della natura' in the Sixteenth Century." *JRBM* 1 (1946), pp. 47-67.

12. ———"The *Musica Nova* of Adriano Willaert." *JRBM* 1 (1946), pp. 200-221.

13. Collins, Michael B. "The Performance of Sesquialtera and Hemiola in the 16th Century." *JAMS* 17 (1964), pp. 5-28.

14. Crocker, Richard L. "A New Source for Medieval Music Theory." *ActaM* 39 (1967), pp. 161-171.

15. Egan, Patricia. " 'Concert' Scenes in Musical Paintings of the Italian Renaissance." *JAMS* 14 (1961), pp. 184-195.

16. Einstein, Alfred. "The Greghesca and the Giustiniana of the Sixteenth Century." *JRBM* 1 (1946), pp. 19-32.

17. ———"The Madrigal." *MQ* 10 (1924), pp. 475-484.

18. "Facsimile of the Codex Faenza, Bibliotheca Comunale, 117." *MD* 13 (1959), pp. 79-107; 14 (1960), pp. 65-104; 15 (1961), pp. 63-104, music.

19. Ferand, Ernest T. "Improvised Vocal Counterpoint in the Late Renaissance and Early Baroque." *AnM* 4 (1956), pp. 129-174.

20.   Ferand, Ernest T. "Two Unknown Frottole." *MQ* 27 (1941), pp. 319-328.

21.   Garden, Greer. "François Roussel: A Northern Musician in Sixteenth-Century Rome." *MD* 31 (1977), pp. 107-133.

22.   Ghisi, Federico. "Carnival Songs and Origins of Intermezzo Giocoso." *MQ* 25 (1939), pp. 325-333.

23.   ──────"The Perugia and Pistoia Fragments of the Lucca Codex, and Other Unpublished Early Fifteenth Century Sources." *JRBM* 1 (1946), pp. 173-191.

24.   Harrán, Don. " 'Mannerism' in the Cinquecento Madrigal? " *MQ* 55 (1969), pp. 521-544.

25.   ──────"Vicentino and His Rules for Text Underlay." *MQ* 59 (1973), pp. 620-632.

26.   Haydon, Glen. "The Hymns of Costanza Festa. A Style Study." *JAMS* 12 (1959), pp. 105-117.

27.   Helm, Everett B. "Heralds of the Italian Madrigal." *MQ* 27 (1941), pp. 306-318.

28.   Horsley, Imogene. "Improvised Embellishment in the Performance of Renaissance Polyphonic Music." *JAMS* 4 (1951), pp. 3-19.

29.   ──────"The Solo Ricercar in Diminution Manuals: New Light on Early Wind and String Techniques." *ActaM* 33 (1961), pp. 29-40.

30.   ──────"Wind Techniques in the Sixteenth and Early Seventeenth Centuries." *Brass Quarterly* 4 (1960), pp. 49-62.

31.   Hudson, Frederick. "Giovanni Gabrieli's Motet a 15, *In ecclesiis*." *MR* 24 (1963), pp. 130-133.

32.   Hunt, Edgar. "The Renaissance Recorder." *The Consort* 19 (Jul 1962), pp. 116-121.

33.   Jeppesen, Knud. "Cavazzoni-Cabezón." *JAMS* 8 (1955), pp. 81-85, 148.

34.   ──────"A Forgotten Master of the Early 16th Century: Gaspar de Albertis." *MQ* 44 (1958), pp. 311-328.

35.   Kaufmann, Henry W. "The Motets of Nicola Vicentino." *MD* 15 (1961), pp. 167-185.

36.   ──────"Vicentino and the Greek Genera." *JAMS* 16 (1963), pp. 325-346.

37.   Kenton, Egon F. "The Late Style of Giovanni Gabrieli." *MQ* 48 (1962), pp. 427-443.

38.   Kristeller, Paul Oskar. "Music and Learning in the Early Italian Renaissance." *JRBM* 1 (1946), pp. 255-274.

39.   Leichtentritt, Hugo. "The Reform of Trent and Its Effect on Music." *MQ* 30 (1944), pp. 319-328.

40.   Lockwood, Lewis. "A Dispute on Accidentals in Sixteenth-Century Rome." *Analecta Musicologica* 2 (1965), pp. 24-40.

41.   ──────"Jean Mouton and Jean Michel: French Music and Musicians in Italy, 1505-1520." *JAMS* 32 (1979), pp. 191-246.

42.   ──────"Vincenzo Ruffo and Musical Reform After the Council of Trent." *MQ* 43 (1957), pp. 342-371.

43.   Lowinsky, Edward E. "Early Scores in Manuscript." *JAMS* 13 (1960), pp. 126-173.

44.   ──────"The Medici Codex. A Document of Music, Art, and Politics in the Renaissance." *AnM* 5 (1957), pp. 61-178.

45.   Longyear, Rey M. "Some Aspects of 16th-Century Instrumental Terminology and Practice." *JAMS* 17 (1964), pp. 193-198.

46.   Luoma, Robert G. "Aspects of Mode in Sixteenth-Century Magnificats." *MQ* 62 (1976), pp. 395-408.

47.   ──────"Relationship Between Music and Poetry (Cipriano de Rore's *Quando signor lasciaste*)." *MD* 31 (1977), pp. 135-154.

48.   Manzetti, Leo P. "Palestrina." *MQ* 14 (1928), pp. 320-328.

49.   Marrocco, W. Thomas. "The Newly-Discovered Ostiglia Pages of the Vatican Rossi Codex 215: The Earliest Italian Ostinato." *ActaM* 39 (1967), pp. 84-91.

50.   Marshall, Robert L. "The Paraphrase Technique of Palestrina in His Masses Based on Hymns." *JAMS* 16 (1963), pp. 347-372.

51.   Miller, Clement A. "Erasmus on Music." *MQ* 52 (1966), pp. 332-349.

52.   Nuffel, J. van. "Philippe de Monte." *PMA* 57 (1931), pp. 99-118.

53. Pirrotta, Nino. "Music and Cultural Tendencies in 15th-Century Italy." *JAMS* 19 (1966), pp. 127-161.

54. Plamenac, Dragan. "A Note on the Rearrangement of Faenza Codex 117." *JAMS* 17 (1964), pp. 78-81.

55. Pope, Isabel. "Musical and Metrical Form of the Villancico." *AnM* 2 (1954), pp. 189-214.

56. Radcliffe, Philip F. "The Relation of Rhythm and Tonality in the Sixteenth Century." *PMA* 57 (1930-1931), pp. 73-97.

57. Sartori, Claudio. "Organs, Organ-Builders and Organists in Milan, 1450-1476. New and Unpublished Documents." *MQ* 43 (1957), pp. 57-67.

58. Schrade, Leo. "The Organ in the Mass of the 15th Century." *MQ* 28 (1942), pp. 329-336; 467-487.

59. Sherr, Richard. "Notes on Two Roman Manuscripts of the Early Sixteenth Century." *MQ* 63 (1977), pp. 48-73.

60. Silbert, Doris. "Melancholy and Music in the Renaissance." *Notes* 4 (1947), pp. 413-424.

61. Strunk, W. Oliver. "Guglielmo Gonzaga and Palestrina's *Missa Dominicalis*." *MQ* 33 (1947), pp. 228-239.

62. Sutherland, Gordon. "The Ricercari of Jacques Buus." *MQ* 31 (1945), pp. 448-463.

63. Thomas, Bernard. "Renaissance Music in Modern Notation." *Early Music* 5 (1977), pp. 4-11.

64. Walker, D. P. "Musical Humanism in the 16th and Early 17th Centuries." *MR* 2 (1941), pp. 1-13, 111-121, 220-227, 288-308; 3 (1942), pp. 55-71.

65. Ward, Tom R. "The Polyphonic Office and the Liturgy of Fifteenth-Century Italy." *MD* 26 (1972), pp. 161-188.

66. Weaver, Robert L. "Sixteenth Century Instrumentation." *MQ* 47 (1961), pp. 363-378.

67. Wilkins, Nigel. "The Codex Reina: A Revised Description." *MD* 17 (1963), pp. 57-73.

68. Young, William. "Keyboard Music to 1600." *MD* 17 (1963), pp. 163-193.

Music

1. Anerio, Felice. *Canzonette a quattro voci, Libro I*, ed. Camillo Moser. Padova: G. Zanibon, 1968.

2. Anerio, Giovanni
   a. *Missa della Battaglia*, ed. Karl Gustav Fellerer (*MDa*, v. 11)
   b. Three spiritual concerts (*CS*, v. 14)

3. Animuccia, Giovanni
   a. Sacred and secular vocal works (*AMI*, v. 1)
   b. *Missa Ave maris stella* (*PVSP*, v. 1)

4. Arcadelt, Jacob
   a. (*CE*) *Opera Omnia*, 9 vols., ed. Albert Seay (*CMM*, 31)
   b. Italian madrigals (*CW*, vols. 5, 58; *SCMA*, v. 5; *VOTS*, sec. 7, p. 227)
   c. Chansons (*PAM*, v. 23)
   d. Motet (*CW*, v. 54)

5. Brolo, Bartolomeo. Mass and Mass movements (*DTÖ*, v. 61)

6. Cavazzoni, Girolamo. Keyboard pieces (*CO*, v. 4; *AMI*, v. 3)

7. Ciconia, Johannes. Mass and Mass movements (*DTÖ*, v. 61)

8. Diruta, Girolamo
   a. Organ pieces (*CO*, v. 12)
   b. *Il Transilvano* (*MMF*, ser. 2, v. 88; *BMB*, sec. 2, Teoria, v. 33)

9. *An Early Fifteenth-Century Italian Source of Keyboard Music* (Faenza Codex). Rome: American Institute of Musicology, 1961. (*MSD*, v. 10)

10. *Early Italian Keyboard Music*, ed. Howard Ferguson. New York: Oxford University Press, 1968.

11. Festa, Costanza
    a. *(CE) Opera Omnia*, ed. Alexander Main *(CMM*, 25)
    b. *Sacrae cantiones*, ed. Edvardus Dagino *(Monumenta Polyphoniae Italicae*, v. 2)
    c. *Hymni per totum annum*, ed. Glen Haydon *(Monumenta Polyphoniae Italicae*, v. 3)

12. Fogliano, Giacomo
    a. *Ricercari* *(ICMI*, v. 1); sacred works *(ISM*, v. 1)

13. Gabrieli, Andrea
    a. Sacred works *(CW*, v. 96; *ICMI*, v. 5; *IMAMI*, vols. 1, 2; *AMI*, v. 2)
    b. Organ works *(CO*, v. 2; *AMI*, v. 3)

14. Gabrieli, Giovanni
    a. *(CE) Opera Omnia*, 10 vols., ed. Denis Arnold *(CMM*, 12)
    b. Instrumental music *(IMAMI*, old ser. vols. 1-2; *HM*, v. 70)
    c. Motets *(CW*, vols. 10, 67; *AMI*, v. 2)
    d. Organ works *(CO*, v. 2)

15. Gafurio, Franchino
    a. *(CE) Opera Omnia*, 2 vols., ed. Ludwig Finscher *(CMM*, 10)
    b. Masses and motets *(ArM*, vols. 1-5)
    c. *Liber Capella Ecclesie Maioris Quarto Codice di Gaffurio*, facsimile *(ArM*, v. 15)

16. Ganassi, Sylvestro di
    a. *Opera intitulata Fontegara*, ed. Hildemarie Peter.   Berlin-Lichterfelde: Robert Lienau, 1959.
    b. *Regola Rubertina*; *Prattica di sonare il violone* *(BMB*, sec. 2, Teoria, vols. 19, 20)

17. Gesualdo, Carlo
    a. *(CE) Sämtliche Werke*, 10 vols., ed. Wilhelm Weismann, Glenn A Watkins. Hamburg: Ugrino.
    b. Madrigals *(AMI*, v. 4; *Instituto Italiano per la Storia della Musica*, ser. 2, v. 1)

18. *The Golden Age of the Madrigal*, ed. Alfred Einstein. New York: G. Schirmer, 1942.

19. Ingegneri, Marc Antonio. Madrigals *(IMAMI*, old ser. v. 6)

20. *Italia Sacra Musica*, 3 vols., ed. Knud Jeppesen. Copenhagen: Wilhelm Hansen, 1962.

21. *Die Italienische Orgelmusik am anfang des Cinquecento*, ed. Knud Jeppesen. Copenhagen: Einar Munksgaard, 1943.

22. *The Madrigal Collection 'L'Amorosa Ero,'* Brescia, 1588, ed. Harry B. Lincoln. Albany: State University of New York Press, 1968.

23. Marenzio, Luca
    a. *(CE) Opera Omnia*, 4 vols., ed. Bernhard Meier and Roland Jackson *(CMM*, 72)
    b. *Sämtliche Werke*, ed. Alfred Einstein *(PäM*, Jg 4:1, vols. 1,2)
    c. Keyboard works *(CO*, v. 6; *LO*, vols. 1-2)
    d. Vocal works *(AMI*, v. 2)
    e. *The Secular Works*, 2 vols., ed. Steven Ledbetter and Patricia Myers. New York: Broude Brothers, 1977.

24. Merulo, Claudio
    a. *Sacred Works*, 8 vols., ed. James Bastian *(CMM*, 51)
    b. Keyboard works *(CO*, v. 2; *AMI*, v. 3)
    c. Vocal works *(AMI*, v. 1)

25. Monte, Philippe de
    a. *(CE) Opera*, 31 vols, ed. Charles Van den Borren, Georges van Doorslaer. Bruges: Desclée. 1927-1939.
    b. *New Complete Edition*, ed. Piet Nuten, Milton Steinhardt.   Leuven, Belgium: Leuven University Press, 1978-

26. *Music of the Florentine Renaissance*, 9 vols., ed. Frank D'Aconne *(CMM*, 32)

27. *Monuments of Renaissance Music*, 6 vols., ed. Edward E. Lowinsky. Chicago: University of Chicago Press, 1964-

28. Palestrina, Giovanni
    a. *(CE) Le opere complete*, 31 vols. Rome: Fratelli Scalera, 1939-1965.
    b. *(PWerke) Werke*, 33 vols. Leipzig: 1892-1907; reprint: New York: Broude Brothers.
    c. Masses *(PVSP*, vols. 3, 4, 6; *Monumenta Polyphoniae Italicae*, v. 1)
    d. Organ works *(CO*, vols. 1, 6)
    e. *Pope Marcellus Mass. An Authoritative Score, Backgrounds and Sources, History and Analysis, Views and Comments*, ed. Lewis Lockwood. New York: W. W. Norton, 1975.
29. Pallovicino, Benedetto. *(CE) Opera Omnia*, 7 vols., ed. Peter Flanders and Kathlyn Bosi Monteath *(CMM*, 89)
30. Rore, Cipriano de
    a. *(CE) Opera Omnia*, 8 vols., ed. Bernhard Meier *(CMM*, 14)
    b. Madrigals *(CW*, v. 5; *SCMA*, v. 6)
31. Slim, H. Colin. *A Gift of Madrigals and Motets*, 2 vols. Chicago: University of Chicago Press, 1972.
32. Soderlund, Gustave Fredric. *Examples of Gregorian Chant and Works by Orlandus Lassus, Giovanni Pierluigi Palestrina and Marco Antonio Ingegneri*. New York: Appleton-Century-Crofts, 1943.
33. Tromboncino, Bartolomeo. *Lamentations (MDm*, v. 6)
34. Vecchi, Orazio
    a. *L'Amfiparnaso*, tr. Cecil Adkins. Chapel Hill: University of North Carolina Press, 1977.
    b. *L'Amfiparnasso (PAM*, v. 26; *CP*, v. 5; *AMI*, v. 4)
    c. *Missa in resurrectione Domini (CW*, v. 26)
    d. *Convito musicale (CP*, v. 8); *Le veglie de Siena (CP*, v. 2)
    e. Sacred and secular vocal works *(AMI*, v. 2)
35. Verdelot, Philippe
    a. *(CE) Opera Omnia*, 3 vols., ed. Anne-Marie Bragard *(CMM*, 28)
    b. Madrigals *(CW*, v. 5; *PAM*, v. 3)
36. Vicentino, Nicola. *(CE) Collected Works*, ed. Henry H. Kaufmann *(CMM*, 26)
37. Wert, Giaches de
    a. *(CE) Opera Omnia*, 17 vols., ed. Carol MacClintock, Melvin Bernard *(CMM*, 24)
    b. *The 5-part Madrigals of Giaches de Wert*, ed. Carol Cook MacClintock. Ann Arbor: University Microfilms, 1955.
    c. *Three Motets*, ed. Bernard Bailly de Surcy. University Park: The Pennsylvania State University Press, 1969.
38. Willaert, Adrian
    a. *(CE) Opera Omnia*, 14 vols., ed. Hermann Zenck, Walter Gerstenberg, Helga and Bernhard Meier *(CMM* 3)
    b. Madrigals *(CW*, vols. 5, 8)
    c. Motets *(CW*, vols. 54, 59)

Early Renaissance – Instrumental Music
Sacred Choral Music – Madrigals – Portugal – Latin America

I. **Early Renaissance**

A. Until recently the knowledge of Spanish music has been limited. Between *c*. 1300 and *c*. 1450 Spanish music was influenced by musicians from France and Italy, both politically and through the church. In the late 15th century during the more stable reign (1474-1516) of *los Reyes Católicos* Ferdinand (1452-1516) and Isabella (1451-1504), many distinguished musicians, vocalists and instrumentalists, were employed at the court for performance of music, particularly sacred music. Some Spanish musicians appeared in the Papal Choir in Rome (**Antonio de Ribera, Juan Escribano, Cristóbal de Morales, Francisco de Peñalosa**). Various Flemish composers (**Ockeghem**, 1469; **La Rue**, 1502, 1503; **Alexander Agricola**, 1502, 1505-1506) spent short tenures in Spain.

B. *Cancioneros* (song [Spanish, *canción*] collections)

1. Collections of pieces, mostly *villancicos*, from the late fifteenth and early sixteenth centuries. Some pieces appear in more than one collection.

   a. The texts show a great variety of themes (love, history, the church) and many suggest use in dancing.

   b. The earlier examples are in the style of the Burgundian *chanson*, French *ballade* and *virelai*. The *virelai* form was later modified and used by composers who called these pieces *villancicos* (rustic songs).

      1) The *villancico* is a popular form imitated by courtly and religious poets; its artistic use dates from about 1450 in secular and religious drama. During the sixteenth century it was used as a solo song with lute or vihuela accompaniment; it was also used in religious services. After 1600 it became extended into a large work on a religious text with chorus, soloists and orchestra.

         a) The traditional sixteenth century *villancico* consists of two music sections: the first section A, called *estribillo* and the second section B, *vuelto*, in the repeat plan A B B A. The text, however, is continuous except for the last line which is a repeat of the last line of the first section, thus serving somewhat as a refrain.

         2) After the *villancico*, the *romance* (ballad), is the next most popular form; it sometimes has a refrain.

   c. Many composers are identified: **Alonso de Córdoba, Juan del Encina, Juan Escobar, Juan de León, Francisco de la Torre** and others.

2. *Seville Manuscript 7-1-28* (contents in *MME*, v. 1, pp. 104-106)

   a. Among the earliest of *cancioneros*, a copy of this collection was secured by Ferdinand, the son of Christopher Columbus, in 1534.

   b. It contains 95 pieces, mostly in three voices, including two in French, 12 in Latin and the remaining in Castilian.

3. *Cancionero de Palacio, c.* 1500 (*MME*, vols. 5, 10)

   a. In addition to the extant 463 pieces, 92 pieces have been lost. These court songs are in two to four parts with instrumental accompaniment; a few instrumental pieces are included.

    b.   Mostly *villancicos* with the superius containing the melody, the style makes use of strong rhythms and is basically chordal (homophonic) with occasional points of imitation, sometimes in pairs of voices. Languages used include Latin, Portuguese, Italian, French and mostly Castilian.

  4.   *O Cancioneiro Musical*

    a.   This Portuguese *cancioneiro* contains 65 pieces which appear to be less complex than those of Spain. Generally chordal and short, the pieces are in three parts or less.

  5.   *Cancionero de Upsala*, Venice, 1556 (*M* 3)

    a.   Included are 54 pieces for two to five voices; these show a frequent use of imitation. The only composer indicated is **Gombert** who was attached (1526) to the court of Charles V (1516-1556), successor to Ferdinand.

C.   Composer and music

  1.   **Juan del Encina** (*c*. 1468-*c*. 1529)

    a.   The most distinguished poet and musician during the reign of Ferdinand and Isabella, **Encina** was born near Salamanca and was employed by the Duke of Alba. In 1496 he went to Rome, was ordained in 1519 and after 1523 resided in León where he died.

    b.   Most of his pieces included in the *cancioneros* were written early in his life and are on the subject of love. In addition to the *romance*, he wrote some pastoral plays frequently incorporating a four-part ensemble piece (see *SSMS*, p. 89; *TEM*, p. 94).

    c.   *Congoxa mas que cruel* (Anguish worse than cruel) (*HAM*, No. 98a), form: ABBA

    d.   *Pues que jamas olvidaros* (Since now my heart) (*HAM*, No. 98b), form: ABBA

    e.   *Mas vale trocar* (Better exchange) (*HAM*, No. 98c), form: ABBA

    f.   *Triste España sin ventura* (*AERM*, p. 195)

II.   Instrumental Music and Accompanied Songs

A.   The Spanish master of the sixteenth century were preeminent in the field of sacred vocal music, music for organ, vihuela and guitar, *villancicos* and *romances* for solo voices with vihuela accompaniment and secular music (madrigals).

B.   Vihuela

  1.   The term *"vihuela"* was used for both viols and guitars, therefore it could be bowed (viol), played with a plectrum or with the fingers (guitar).

  2.   The vihuela has a flat back rather than the half-pear shaped body of the lute, common throughout most of Europe. In general the vihuela has six strings tuned in pairs of fourths separated by a major third (G - c - f - a - d' - g'). **Bermudo** suggests that to convert a vihuela into a guitar, delete the first and sixth strings of the vihuela.

    a.   The four-course guitar was used by peasants in city and country while the six-course vihuela was preferred by musicians of the court.

  3.   Spanish vihuela tablature is the same as the Italian lute tablature. The lines of the tablature staff represent the strings of the vihuela; the highest line being the lowest string G. Each fret progressing by semitones is indicated by a figure from O (open) to 9 on the appropriate line of the tablature. Rhythmic signs are used to indicate note values; however, when two different values appear as a unison, only the shortest value is indicated in simultaneous notes.

C.   Composers and music

  1.   **Luis Milán** (*c*. 1500-1561)

    a.   *Libro de Música de Vihuela de Mano intitulado El Maestro* (Book of music for the vihuela entitled The Instructor), Valencia, 1535, 1536 (*PäM*, v. 2; *M* 14, pp. 2-69; *B* 5, pp. 53-69; *MMF*, ser. 1, v. 30)

      1)   This is the first printed Spanish tablature book; principally for beginners, the music is arranged from simple to more complex. In this book the tablature staff

is inverted so the highest line represents the highest string g'.

2) It gives directions for tuning the instrument and reading tablature. It contains instrumental pieces (40 *fantasia*, 6 *pavanas*, 4 *tientos*) and songs (12 *villancicos*, 6 *sonetas*, 4 *romances*).

3) The free improvisational elaborations of the double *villancicos* and other songs give evidence of considerable development of instrumental practices in Spain.

4) **Milán** and **Narváez** include some of the earliest known tempo indications.

5) *Fantasia*, No. 17 (*PäM*, v. 2, p. 42; *HAM*, No. 121; *M* 12b, p. 76; *MMF*, Ser. 1, v. 30)

  a) **Milán** expects a freedom of tempo in the fantasias: chordal sections slow, ornamental passages fast.

6) *Romance: Durandarte* (*MME*, v. 10, p. 193; *M* 14, p. 2; *M* 12b, p. 124; *GMB*, No. 96a; *MMF*, Ser. 1, v. 30)

7) *Villancico: Falai mina amor* (Portuguese) (*M* 12b, p. 120; *GMB*, No. 96b)

8) *Agora viniesse un viento* (That a wind would now come), a *villancico* (*PäM*, v. 2, p. 74; *M* 14, p. 12; *M* 12b, p. 115; *NOH*, v. 4, p. 136; *MMF*, ser. 1, v. 30)

2. **Luis de Narváez** (*fl.* 1538) (*M* 14, pp. 72-93; *B* 5, pp. 70-81)

  a. *Los seys libros del Delphin de músic* (Six books of the Delphin of music), Valladolid, 1538 (*MME*, v. 3)

1) These books contain arrangements of vocal pieces (**Gombert, Josquin**), lute songs, 14 *fantasias* and several sets of variations (*diferencias*). The *fantasias* are contrapuntal in the style of the motet or ricercar.

2) **Narváez**, more than **Milán**, develops a regular style by combining the chordal and polyphonic elements into a more unified structure.

3) *Diferencias sobra O Gloriosa Domina* (*MME*, v. 3, music p. 44; *HAM*, No. 122)

  a) Based on a hymn melody, the set of variations is among the earliest examples of the variation form.

3. **Alonsa de Mudarra** (*fl.* 1545)

  a. *Tres libros de música en cifra*, Seville, 1546 (*MME*, v. 7; *M* 14, pp. 96-129; *B* 5, pp. 82-85)

1) Among the 77 pieces there are some intabulations of motets (**Josquin**) and chansons in addition to *villancicos, sonetos, pavanas, gallardas* and *canciónes*. There are also six pieces for the four-course guitar.

2) The seond book includes groups of pieces (a *tiento* and two *fantasias*) organized in each of the eight church modes.

4. **Enríquez de Valderrábano**

  a. *Libro de música de vihula intitulado Silva de Sirenas*, Valladolid, 1547 (*MME*, vols. 22, 23; *M* 14, pp. 132-173; *B* 5, pp. 86-100)

1) This contains 97 pieces and includes many intabulations (**Gombert, Morales, Willaert, Josquin**), some arranged for two vihuelas, 33 *fantasias*, 27 *sonetos*, 4 *romances*, 9 *canciónes* and several sets of *diferencias*. One set of *diferencias* (*MME*, v. 23, p. 82) contains no less than 74 variations.

2) *Diferencias sobre Guárdame las vacas* (*MME*, v. 23, p. 72; *HAM*, No. 124)

  a) Seven variations on the "Romanesca" tune of a descending four-note pattern common in the early Italian Baroque (**Frescobaldi, Trabaci**).

5. **Miguel de Fuenllana** (*fl.* 1550)

  a. *Orphénica lira: Libro de música para vihuela*, Seville, 1554 (*M* 14, pp. 196-225)

1) Like other collections this contains many intabulations (motets and Mass movements), some paired with his own *fantasias*. In two to four voices and using one or more themes, the *fantasias* show a variety of forms and a richness of polyphonic texture.

2) *Fantasia sobre una passado forçado*

  a) The theme is introduced 29 times, including diminution and augmentation.

        3)   *Paseábase el rey moro* (*HAM*, No. 123; *M* 14, p. 196)

6.   **Diego Pisador** (*c.* 1508-1557)

    a.   *Libro de música de vihuela*, Salamanca, 1552 (*M* 14, pp. 176-193)

       1)   Five of the seven books are intabulations of vocal music; Book V contains eight complete Masses by **Josquin.**

       2)   Among the *fantasias* (Book III) red letters are introduced to indicate the theme.

       3)   Since exact pitches are notated in the vihuela tablatures and by comparing the original with the intabulation, valuable information on performance practices of the period may be discovered.

7.   **Esteban Daza**

    a.   *Libro de música en cifras para vihuela intitulado el Parnaso*, Valladolid, 1576 (*M* 14, pp. 230-252)

       1)   *El Parnaso*, similar in content to the previous collections, is the last work published specifically for six-course vihuela. After this the four-course "Spanish" guitar became popular and the vihuela was rarely mentioned.

D.   Organists and theorists

  1.   The Spanish word *tecla* means keyboard, which could have been organ, harpsichord or clavichord. In the treatises other instruments are discussed, particularly the *harpa*, although no music is extant for it specifically. Ensemble music, in addition to vihuela duets, is discussed and includes groups of viols and brass instruments.

    a.   The music played includes *fantasias, tientos,* hymns, Psalms, *romances* and *villancicos*. In addition, ornamenting of the melody or a cadence and simple variation figures developed a form of diminution called *glosas*. More elaborate or extensive variations, by contrast, were known as *diferencias*.

    b.   The Spanish keyboard tablature makes use of numbers on a staff of three to five lines, each line representing a voice part. Numbers ranging from 1 to 7 represent the notes of the diatonic scale beginning on f. Higher and lower octaves are indicated by special signs attached to the numbers; the comma indicates a tie and the diagonal line a rest.

  2.   **Bartolomé Ramos de Pareja** (*c.* 1440-*c.* 1492)

    a.   **Ramos**, a lecturer on music theory, left Salamanca by 1472, published his *Musica practica* in Bologna (1482) where he lectured and later went to Rome.

    b.   *De Musica Tractatus sive Musica Practica*, Bologna, 1482 (*BMB*, Series 2, *Teoria*, v. 3; *SR*, pp. 201-204)

       1)   Topics discussed in *Musica practica* include a new system of solmization thus dispensing with that of **Guido**, a discussion of the ratios of 4:5 (major third), 5:6 (minor third), 3:5 (major sixth) and 5:8 (minor sixth), a twelve-tone scale approaching equal temperament, imitation as used in canon and fugue, *musica ficta* and instruments.

  3.   **Fray Juan Bermudo** (*fl.* 1550)

    a.   *Declaración de Instrumentos Musicales*, Osuna, 1549, 1555 (*DM*, Ser. 1, v. 11)

       1)   This student treatise deals with theory in detail, instruments, their technical problems, tuning and repertoire, and performance practices.

  4.   **Luis Venegas de Henestrosa**

    a.   *Libro de cifra nueva tecla, harpa e vihuela*, Alcala, 1557 (*MME*, v. 2)

       1)   **Henestrosa** includes *glosas*, as well as *fantasias, tientos, fabordones, himnos, villancicos, salmos, romances, entrads* and *canciones* in the large collection of 138 compositions. Pieces by many of the famous organists of the time are included.

  5.   **Tomás de Sancta [Santa] María** (d. 1570)

    a.   *Libro llamado Arte de tañer fantasia assí para tecla como para vihuela*, Valladolid, 1565 (*MMF*, Ser. 2, v. 124)

       1)   In his treatise **Sancta María** considers the art of instrumental performance, particularly that of the clavichord and organ. Significant are his directions for playing

fantasias and the practice of improvisation. Original compositions give examples of the text.

    2)   Fantasias on the eight tones (*LO*, v. 3, pp. 44-51)

  6.   **Antonio de Cabezón** (1510-1566)

    a.   **Cabezón**, blind, was court organist and harpsichordist to Charles V and Philip II. He accompanied Philip through Italy, Germany and Holland (1548-1555) and to England and Holland (1554-1556) where he influenced various composers (**Sweelinck**).

    b.   **Cabezón's** music, published posthumously by his son **Hernando**, includes 32 organ hymns, 29 *tientos* (preludes in ricercar style), 9 sets of variations (*diferencias*) and many other pieces for church use. The music of **Cabezón** is often favorably compared to that of **Johann Sebastian Bach**.

    c.   *Obras de música para tecla, harpa y vihuela*, Madrid, 1578   (*B* 5, pp. 110-121)

      1)   Most of **Cabezón's** compositions are included in this work.

      2)   *Versos del sexto tono* (*HAM*, No. 133; *HSMS*, v. 3, p. 27; *LO*, v. 3, p. 11)

      3)   *Diferencias sobre el canto de Cavallero* (*HAM*, No. 134; *HSMS*, v. 8, p. 3)

      4)   *Fuga al contrario* (*GMB*, No. 113; *HSMS*, v. 4, p. 59)

  7.   **Francisco de Salinas** (1513-1590)

    a.   Blind, **Salinas** studied at the University of Salamanca, went to Rome with Cardinal Compostela, became palace organist for the Duke of Alba in Naples and returned to Spain in 1561. He later taught at the University of Salamanca, 1566-1587.

    b.   *De musica libri septem*, Salamanca, 1577 (*DM*, v. 13; *MMF*, Ser. 2, v. 121)

      1)   This theoretical work explains mean-tone temperament based on four slightly flat fifths thus giving a perfect 5:4 ratio for the major third. This proved satisfactory for simple keys up to no more than two or three sharps or flats, but there is almost a quarter-tone difference between enharmonic tones (g-sharp and a-flat).

      2)   The latter part of the work deals with rhythm illustrated with examples of Spanish folksongs of the day. Therefore it is the earliest collection of Spanish folk music.

      3)   *Que me quereis caballero* (*B* 5, p. 91)

E.   Viols and other instruments

  1.   **Diego Ortiz** (*fl.* 1550-1570)

    a.   *Tratado de glosas sobre claúsulas y otros generos de puntos en la música de violones*, Rome, 1553 (*M* 18)

      1)   Consisting mainly of music examples, the treatise gives rules for ornamentation, improvisation over *bassi ostinati* and variation technique with some of the earliest examples of instrumental variations (for bass viol and *cembalo*). The instrumental style is shown by the use of short note values, sequential patterns and wide leaps.

III.   **Sacred Choral Music**

A.   The political stability of Spain during *el siglo de oro* (the golden age) of the reign of Ferdinand and Isabella favored and encouraged the production of much sacred music. Among highly regarded musicians were **Juan de Anchieta** and **Francisco de Peñalosa**. These were followed by the main figures of the Spanish Renaissance: **Morales** (*HSMS*, v. 1), **Victoria** and **Guerrero** (*HSMS*, v. 2)

  1.   **Juan de Anchieta** (*c*. 1462-1523)

    a.   *Missa de Nuestra Senora* (*MME*, v. 1, music p. 25)

      1)   In this Mass, as in others, **Anchieta** draws frequently on plainsong. The *Sanctus* and *Agnus Dei* are by **Escobar**.

  2.   **Francisco de Peñalosa** (*c*. 1470-1528)

    a.   *Missa Ave Maria* (*MME*, v. 1, music p. 62)

3. **Cristóbal de Morales** (*c.* 1500-1553) (*MME*, vols. 11, 13, 15, 17, 20, 21, 24)
   a. **Morales**, the first important master of the Late Renaissance, was director of cathedral music in Avila (1526-1530) and joined the Papal Choir in Rome in 1535. He returned to Spain in 1540 and again in 1545 to become music director at Toledo.
   b. His works comprise mostly sacred compositions: 2 Masses, 16 Magnificats and at least 50 motets.
   c. Masses (*MME*, vols. 11, 15, 21, 24)
      1) The majority of Masses are based on Gregorian melodies or composed motets (**Mouton, Gombert, Verdelot**). However, eight of them are based on secular melodies: two on *L'Homme armé* (*MME*, v. 11, p. 193; v. 21, p. 67) and two on Spanish folksongs (*Desilde al cavallero; Tristezas me matan*) in which Spanish texts combine with the Latin liturgical texts (*MME*, v. 24, pp. 58, 83).
      2) A variety of techniques are used, such as canon (*Missa Ave, Maris Stella, MME*, v. 11, p. 104), imitation, at times in pairs, and chordal passages. The melodies may be paraphrased, but the plainsong melodies generally maintain their regular contour.
   d. Motets (*MME*, vols. 13, 20)
      1) As in the Magnificats, plainsong often alternates with polyphony. The voices often sing in pairs or small groups rather than all the time. A frequent practice in the motets is to use two texts simultaneously, for example the Ash Wednesday response *Emendemus*.
         a) *Emendemus in melius – Memento homo* (Let us make amends – Remember, man) (*HAM*, No. 128; *HSMS*, v. 1, p. 29)
            (1) In this case, "Remember, man, that dust thou art" as an ostinato fifth voice dramatically punctuates the text "Let us make amends for our sins" (meas. 13, 28, 43, 58, 73, 88), which is presented in typical motet fashion.
   e. *Magnificats*, Venice, 1545 (*MME*, v. 17)
      1) Generally in four voices, there are eight each written polyphonically on the odd- and even-numbered verses.
         a) *Magnificat*, Tone 8 (*MME*, v. 17, p. 126; *HSMS*, v. 1, p. 20)
4. **Tomás Luis de Victoria** (Italian is **Vittoria**) (1548-1611) (*CE*; *M* 25b)
   a. An outstanding Spanish composer of the Roman School, **Victoria** entered the Jesuit Collegium Germanicum in Rome in 1565 and probably studied under **Palestrina**; he succeeded **Palestrina** as *maestro di cappella* of the Roman Seminary in 1571. In 1575 **Victoria** was ordained a priest. Entering the service of Empress Maria, he returned to Spain serving as priest, choirmaster and organist from 1586 to his death.
   b. Generally of high quality, **Victoria's** works, all religious, numbering almost 180 compositions, include 20 Masses, 45 motets (4-6, 8 voices), Psalms, 32 four-voice hymns (1581) for the liturgical year and many other pieces for church use including 16 Magnificats and Sequences.
   c. **Victoria's** style is based on Franco-Flemish polyphony, but is more simple, smooth, expressive and colorful, full of tenderness and with a devotional feeling.
      1) **Victoria's** contrapuntal style is similar to that of **Palestrina** but with more freedom, especially in handling dissonance. There is some use of cross relations, chromaticism and rarely augmented seconds. Nearly half of the movements in quarter notes begin on accented beats; there is a free treatment of the *cambiata*. Escape tones left by a skip of a fourth are frequent, although rare in **Palestrina**. The treatment of passing tones is similar to that of **Palestrina** and more dotted-quarter and eighth-note rhythms are used.
   d. The organ is used to sustain the parts of chorus I in the antiphonal compositions for two and three four-part choruses, as well as in works for four- and five-part antiphonal choruses (*CE*, v. 7, pp. 1, 20, 17, 43, 53, 63, 73, 85, 95). The use of instruments was not unusual in Spanish music of the sixteenth century.

    e.   Motets (*CE*, v. 1)
1) Although **Victoria** wrote no madrigals, various madrigal techniques appear in his motets, such as text painting and word delineation.
- a) The theme ascends through an octave, *Ascendens Christus*, meas. 1-4 (*CE*, v. 1, p. 53; *MME*, v. 26, p. 44)
- b) Descending in thirds, *Descendit angelus*, meas. 1-2 (*CE*, v. 1, p. 77; *MME*, v. 31, p. 56)
- c) Grief expressed by the ascending diminished fourth, *Sancta Maria, succurre*, meas. 17-18 (*CE*, v. 1, p. 19; *MME*, v. 31, p. 19)
- d) Octave leap for dramatic intensity, *Veni, sponsa Christi (CE*, v. 1, p. 50)

2) Other techniques include canon, double canon (*Trahe me post te, CE*, v. 1, p. 140) and harmonic sequence (*Domine, non sum dignus, CE*, v. 1, p. 39; *MME*, v. 31, p. 12).

3) *O vos omnes* (Lamentations 1:12) (*CE*, v. 1, p. 27; *MME*, v. 26, p. 17; *HAM*, No. 149)

4) *O magnum mysterium* (*SSMS*, pp. 108, 111), a Mass is based on this motet.

    f.   Masses (*CE*, v. 2, 4, 6, 8)
1) Almost no secular melodies occur in **Victoria's** Masses (*Missa pro victoria, CE*, v. 6, p. 26, on **Janequin's** *La Guerre*); 11 are parodies on his own motets; one Mass *Missa Surge propera* (*CE*, v. 2, p. 119) is based on a motet by **Palestrina** (*CE*, v. 3, p. 57; *PalW*, v. 5, p. 47); **Victoria's** *Missa Gaudeamus* (*CE*, v. 4, p. 1) is based on **Morales'** *Jubilate Deo* (*MME*, v. 13, p. 184). In the four-voice *Missa Simile est regnum coelorum* (*CE*, v. 2, p. 21), based on a motet by **Francisco Guerrero**, four additional voices sing the final *Agnus Dei* in quadruple canon.

2) In addition to regular polyphony and canon, **Victoria** frequently adds one or two voices and a continuing tendency toward chordal writing and short time values is apparent.

3) Several Masses are based on plainsongs.

5. **Francisco Guerrero** (1528-1599)
- a. Probably a more completely Spanish composer than **Morales** or **Victoria**, **Guerrero** published (mostly abroad) 8 Magnificats (Louvain, 1563), 18 Masses (Book I, Paris, 1566; Book II, Rome, 1582) and 2 Passions (St. Matthew and St. John, 1585) (*HSMS*, v. 2, pp. 24, 38), in addition to a book of Psalms (Rome, 1559), two books of motets in four, five, six and eight voices (Venice, 1570, 1589) and more motets totalling about 115 and many other sacred works (*MME*, vols. 16, 19).
- b. Since Marian compositions are common in his output, **Guerrero** is often called *el cantor de Maria*.
- c. *Salve Regina*, antiphon B. V. M. (*HSMS*, v. 2, p. 48; *HAM*, No. 139)
  1) Polyphonic sections are sung *alternatim* with the plainsong melody. The opening notes of *"Salve"* are repeated at the entrance of each voice in the first imitative section that follows.

IV. Madrigals

A. Various terms beside *"villancico"* were applied to part songs of the period; *estrambote* is the Spanish equivalent of the Italian *frottola*. *Ensaladas* (musical salads) combine popular songs with liturgical melodies, religious texts with comic and dramatic verse, mixing Latin, Italian, Spanish and French in the nature of textual and melodic *quodlibets*. The term "madrigal" was not commonly used and those published show mostly an Italian influence.

1. The use of imitation, text painting, alternation of polyphonic and homophonic writing were all common devices used in the Spanish madrigals.

B.   The secular music of Spain is generally overshadowed by the sacred; nevertheless, secular music, both polyphonic and melody with accompaniment, was composed by several different composers.

1.   **Juan Vasquez** (*fl.* 1550-1560)

   a.   *Recopilación de sonetos y villancicos a quatro y a cinco*, Seville, 1560 (*MME*, v. 4)

      1)   Included are 45 *sonetos, villancicos* and *canciones* in four and five voices with points of imitation alternating with chordal passages.

      2)   In the *villancicos* **Vasquez** often modifies melodically or rhythmically the repeated refrains. Popularity of his pieces is confirmed by the many transcriptions for solo voice and vihuela accompaniment.

      3)   *Agora que soy nina* (*MME*, v. 4, p. 150)

2.   **Joan Brudieu** (d. 1591)

   a.   *Els marigals*, 1585 (*BC*, v. 1)

      1)   These 16 madrigals, generally in four part (SSAT), make use of melodic modification (*BC*, v. 1, p. 1), dissonance (*BC*, v. 1, p. 215) and programmatic elements which recall **Janequin** (*BC*, v. 1, pp. 55-108).

3.   A unique six-voice *ensalada, Por las sierras* (*MME*, v. 10, p. 75) by **Peñalosa**, uses four *villancicos* simultaneously with free outer voices, the lowest one being the text *"Loquebantur variis linguis magnalia dei"* (They spoke in various tongues the wonderful works of God), possibly a paraphrase of Acts 2:11.

4.   Other madrigalists, most of whom spent much time outside of Spain, include **Pedro Alberch Vila** (1517-1582), one of the finest Spanish musicians of his time; **Mateo Flecha** the Younger (*c.* 1520-1604) (*BC*, v. 16, *Las ensaladas*) who resided in Prague and Vienna and had a madrigal collection appear in Venice in 1568; **Pedro Valenzuela [Valenzola]**, whose madrigals were published in Venice in 1578; **Sebastian Raval** who was active in Rome and Palermo and **Pedro Ruimonte [Rimonte]** whose madrigals, printed in 1614, are the only ones with Spanish texts exploiting the later chromatic techniques of the madrigals.

V.   Portugal

A.   Early sixteenth century

1.   Sacred vocal music continued prospering during the reign of John III (1521-1557), an artistic tradition having been established under Alfonso V (1438-1481). The positive influence of the counter-reformation no doubt had its effect.

   a.   **Damiao de Góis [Goes]** (1502-1574) is represented by a three-voice motet in the *Dodecachordon* (1547) of **Glareanus**.

      1)   *Ne laeteris inimica mea* (*PAM*, v. 16, p. 211)

   b.   **Heliodoro de Paiva** (d. 1552), a canon at the Monastery of Santa Cruz where composition was studied, composed Masses, motets and Magnificats.

2.   Secular vocal music was mainly *vilancicos* which correspond to the Spanish *villancicos*. The most common form is A B B A.

   a.   **Gil Vicente** (*c.* 1465-*c.* 1536), an outstanding composer, dramatist and founder of the Portuguese theatre, interpolated *vilancicos* and choral songs in his tragi-comedies.

B.   Late sixteenth and early seventeenth centuries

1.   Portuguese polyphony of the "golden age" developed a little later than that of Spain and Italy. Two important schools developed: one in the Colégio da Claustra and the cathedral in Evora under the leadership of **Manuel Mendes** (d. 1605), and the other a little later by a distinguished pupil of **Mendes, Duarte Lobo** at the Lisbon Cathedral.

   a.   **Gines da Morata** (*MME*, v. 8, pp. 57, 63, 66, 72, 78, 91, 117)

      1)   **Morata** was director of chapel music for the Dukes of Braganza.

    b.   **Duarte Lobo** (*c.* 1560-1646)

       1)   **Lobo**, director of the Lisbon Cathedral music for more than forty years, is considered Portugal's most important composer. Among his published works are a book of responsories and an eight-voice Mass (1602), two books of Masses (1621, 1639) and a book of Magnificats (1605) from Antwerp and others from Lisbon.

    c.   **John IV**, King of Portugal (1604-1656)

       1)   A patron of music, composer and writer on music, he amassed one of the finest libraries in the world; it was destroyed in the Lisbon earthquake, 1755.

          a)   *Defensa de la música moderna*, Lisbon, 1649

          b)   *Respuestas a las dudas que se pusieron a la missa 'Panis quem ego dabo' de Palestrina*, Lisbon, 1654

    d.   **Felipe de Megalhaes** (*fl.* 1614-*c.* 1650)

       1)   Master of the royal chapel (1623-1641) and another pupil of **Mendes**, **Megalhaes** in turn was the teacher of the Spanish-born **Estevao Lopez Morago** (*PortM*, v. 3A), who became director of cathedral music at Viseu (1599-1628) near Coimbra, the seat of another school of music and the University.

    e.   **Manuel Cardoso** (*c.* 1569-1650)

       1)   **Cardoso's** works, published by Craesbeck in Lisbon, include Magnificats (1613), three books of Masses (1625, 1636, 1636) and a book of motets (1648); these suggest the style of **Palestrina**.

       2)   He served the court of and was highly respected by **John IV** and the Spanish kings.

       3)   Motets: *Cum audisset* (*ProskeDMa*, Ser. 1, v. 11, p. 12); *Angelis suis* (*ProskeDMa*, Ser. 1, v. 11, p. 98)

       4)   *Liber primus missarum* (*PortM*, v. 5−6A)

  C.   Instrumental music

    1.   The viola is the Portuguese guitar corresponding to the Spanish vihuela.

      a.   The forms of guitar music include *glosas* and *diferencias* (variations) written in dance forms such as *folia* and *chacona*, possibly of Portuguese origin.

    2.   The organ music of **Coelho** is discussed in *Music Literature Outlines*, Series II, *Music in the Baroque*, third edition, p. 62.

    3.   **André de Escobar** in 1550 settled in the Indies and wrote a method for the shawm.

VI. **Latin America** (sixteenth century)

  A.   European music was introduced into Mexico, Brazil, Peru and the River Plate region by Catholic missionaries (Franciscans, Dominicans, Jesuits) in the sixteenth century. Schools were established for teaching rudiments of music, singing, composition and playing and construction of instruments. The first teacher of European music in the New World was **Pedro de Gante** (1480-1572), a Franciscan missionary; he was in Mexico from 1523-1572.

  B.   The first book containing music printed in the western hemisphere was an *Ordinarium* published in Mexico City in 1556, 142 years before the appearance of the first *Bay Psalm Book* edition containing music (1698).

    1.   **Hernando Franco** (1532-1585)

      a.   **Franco** arrived in Guatemala in 1554, then in 1575 became *maestro de capilla* at the Mexico City Cathedral, a position first held by **Juan Xuárez** in 1539.

      b.   His extant music includes 7 Magnificats, 2 *Salve* settings and various responsories, hymns and Psalms.

       1)   Some of his works use translations of the text into the native Indian language.

    2.   **Juan Navarro** (*c.* 1550-*c.* 1610)

      a.   A Spanish composer, **Navarro** emigrated to Mexico and in 1604 published his 105-page *Liber in quo quatuor Passiones Christi Domini continentur*. This contains four Passions set monodically, a set of Lamentations and other religious works.

SELECTED BIBLIOGRAPHY

Books

1. Anglés, Higinio. "Early Spanish Musical Culture and Cardinal Cisneros's Hymnal of 1515," in *Aspects of Medieval and Renaissance Music: A Birthday Offering to Gustave Reese*, ed. Jan LaRue, pp. 3-16. New York: W. W. Norton, 1966.
2. Bermudo, Juan. *Declaraciòn de instrumentos musicales*, ed. Macario Santiago Kastner. Kassel: Bärenreiter. (*Documenta musicologica*, ser. 1, v. 11)
3. Chase, Gilbert. *The Music of Spain*. New York: W. W. Norton, 1941; 2nd rev. ed.: New York: Dover Publications, 1959.
4. Donovan, Richard B. *The Liturgical Drama in Medieval Spain*. Toronto: Pontifical Institute of Mediaeval Studies, 1958.
5. Jacobs, Charles. *Tempo Notation in Renaissance Spain*. Brooklyn: Institute of Mediaeval Music, 1964. (*Musicological Studies,* v. 8) (Examples of Milán, pp. 53-69; Narváez, pp. 70-81; Mudarra, pp. 82-85; Valderrábano, pp. 86-100; Cabezón, pp. 103-121)
6. Livermore, Ann. *A Short History of Spanish Music*. New York: Vienna House, 1972.
7. Plamenac, Dragan. "The Two-Part Quodlibets in the Seville Chansonnier," in *The Commonwealth of Music in Honor of Curt Sachs*, ed. Gustave Reese and Rose Brandel, pp. 163-181. New York: The Free Press, 1965.
8. Ramos de Pareja, Bartolomé. *Musica practica*, ed. Johannes Wolf. Leipzig: Breitkopf & Härtel, 1901.
9. Reese, Gustave. "The Repertoire of Book II of Ortiz's *Tratado*," in *The Commonwealth of Music in Honor of Curt Sachs*, ed. Gustave Reese and Rose Brandel, pp. 201-207. New York: The Free Press, 1965.
10. St. Amour, Sister Mary Paulina. *A Study of the Villancico*. Washington, D. C.: The Catholic University Press, 1940.
11. Spiess, Lincoln B. "Instruments in the Missions of New Mexico," in *Essays in Musicology: A Birthday Offering for Willi Apel*, ed. Hans Tischler, pp. 131-136. Bloomington: Indiana University School of Music, 1968.
12. Starkie, Walter F. *Spain: A Musician's Journey through Time and Space*, 2 vols. Geneva: Edisli-at Editions Rene Kister, 1958.
13. Stevenson, Robert. *Music in Mexico, A Historical Survey*. New York: Crowell, 1952.
14. ――――――*Spanish Cathedral Music in the Golden Age*. Berkeley: University of California Press, 1961.
15. ――――――*Spanish Music in the Age of Columbus*. The Hague: Martinus Nijhoff, 1960; reprint: 1964.
16. Trend, John Brande. *Luis Milán and the Vihuelistas*, vols. 2-4. London: Oxford University Press, 1925.
17. ――――――*The Music of Spanish History to 1600*. London: Oxford University Press, 1926; reprint: New York: Krause Reprint Corp., 1965.

Articles

1. Apel, Willi. "Accidentals and the Modes in 15th and 16th Century Sources." *BAMS* No. 2 (June, 1937), p. 6.
2. ――――――"Early Spanish Music for Lute and Keyboard Instruments." *MQ* 20 (1934), pp. 289-301.
3. ――――――"The Importance of Notation in Solving Problems of Early Music." *PAMS* (1938), pp. 51-61.
4. ――――――"Neapolitan Links between Cabezón and Frescobaldi." *MQ* 24 (1938), pp. 419-437.
5. Bal, Jesús. "Fuenllana and the Transcription of Spanish Lute Music." *ActaM* 11 (1939), pp. 16-27.

6. Chase, Gilbert. "Barbieri and the Spanish Zarzuela." *ML* 20 (1939), pp. 32-39.

7. ———"Guitar and Vihuela: A Clarification." *BAMS* 6 (1942), pp. 13-14.

8. ———"Juan del Encina: Poet and Musician." *ML* 20 (1939), pp. 420-430.

9. ———"Origins of Lyric Theater in Spain." *MQ* 25 (1939), pp. 292-305.

10. Dart, Thurston. "Cavazzoni and Cabezón." *ML* 36 (1955), pp. 2-6.

11. Dodge, Janet. "Lute Music of the 16th and 17th Centuries." *PMA* 34 (1908), p. 123.

12. ———"Ornamentation as Indicated by Signs in Lute Tablature." *SIMg* 9 (1907-1908), p. 318.

13. Fox, Charles Warren. "Accidentals in Vihuela Tablatures." *BAMS* No. 4 (Sep 1940), p. 22.

14. Gerson-Kiwi, Edith. "On the Musical Sources of the Judeo-Hispanic *Romance*." *MQ* 50 (1964), pp. 31-43.

15. Grebe, Maria-Ester. "Modality in Spanish Vihuela Music and Archaic Chilean Folksongs: A Comparative Study." *Ethnomusicology* 11 (1967), pp. 326-342.

16. Guzmán-Bravo, José-Antonio. "Mexico, the Home of the First Musical Instrumental Workshops in America." *Early Music* 6 (1978), pp. 350-355.

17. Hill, Arthur G. "Medieval Organs in Spain." *SIMg* 14 (1912-1913), p. 487.

18. Howell, Jr., Almonte C. "Cabezón: An Essay in Structural Analysis." *MQ* 50 (1964), pp. 18-30.

19. ———"Paired Imitation in 16th-Century Spanish Keyboard Music." *MQ* 53 (1967), pp. 377-396.

20. Morrow, Michael. "The Renaissance Harp." *Early Music* 7 (1979), pp. 499-510.

21. Pope, Isabel. "The Musical Development and Form of the Spanish Villancico." *PAMS* (1940), pp. 11-22.

22. Randel, Don M. "Sixteenth Century Spanish Polyphony and the Poetry of Garcilaso." *MQ* 60 (1974), pp. 61-79.

23. Salazar, Adolfo. "Music in the Primitive Spanish Theatre Before Lope de Vega." *PAMS* (1938), pp. 94-108.

24. Sharp, G. B. "Antonio de Cabezón, 1510-1566." *MT* 107 (1966), pp. 955-956, 1053-1055.

25. Simpson, Glenda, and Barry Mason. "The 16th-Century Spanish Romance: A Survey of the Spanish Ballad as Found in the Music of the Vihuelists." *Early Music* 5 (1977), pp. 51-57.

26. Spell, Lota M. "The First Music-Books Printed in America." *MQ* 15 (1929), pp. 50-54.

27. ———"Music in the Cathedral of Mexico in the Sixteenth Century." *Hispanic American Historical Review* 26 (1946), pp. 293-319.

28. Stevenson, Robert. "Cristóbal de Morales (*ca.* 1500-53), A Fourth-Centenary Biography." *JAMS* 6 (1953), pp. 3-42.

29. ———"Anuario Musical." *ML* 36 (1955), pp. 287-291.

30. Tiby, Ottavio. "Sebastián Raval—A 16th-Century Spanish Musician in Italy." *MD* 2 (1948), pp. 217-223.

31. Trend, John Brande. "Cristóbal Morales." *ML* 6 (1925), pp. 19-34.

32. ———"Salinas: a Sixteenth Century Collector of Folk Songs." *ML* 8 (1927), pp. 13-24.

33. Ward, John. "The Editorial Methods of Venegas de Henestrosa." *MD* 6 (1952), pp. 105-113.

Music

1. Brudieu, Joan. *Els Marigals i la Missa de defunto*, ed. Felipe Pedrell and Higini Anglés (*BC*, v. 1)

2. Cabezón, Antonio de
   a. (*CE*) *Collected Works*, ed. Charles Jacobs (*The Institute of Medieval Music. Collected Works*, v. 4)

Cabezón (continued)
    b. *Obras de musica para tecla, arpa, vihuela* (*MME*, vols. 28-29; *MMF*, ser. 1, v. 3)
    c. Organ works (*LO*, v. 3)
3. *Cancionero de Upsala*, ed. Rafael Mitjana. Pánuco: El Colegio de Mexico, 1944.
4. *Cancionero musical de los siglos XV y XVI*, ed. F. Asenjo Barbieri. Madrid: Tip. de los Huérfanos, 1890.
5. *Cancionero musical popular espanol*, 4 vols., ed. Felipe Pedrell. Barcelona: Casa Editorial de Música Boileau, 1919-1920.
6. Cardoso, Frei Manuel. *Liber primus missarum*, ed. José A. Alegria (*PortM*, vols. 5-6A)
7. Coelho, Manuel Rodriquez. *Florés de musica pera o instrumento de tecla & harpa*, 2 vols., ed. Macario Santiago Kastner (*PortM*, vols. 1A, 3A)
8. Flecha, Mateo. *Las ensaladas*, ed. Higini Anglés (*BC*, v. 16)
9. *The Franco Codex of the Cathedral of Mexico*, ed. Steven Barwick. Carbondale: Southern Illinois University Press, 1965.
10. Guerrero, Francisco. *Opera Omnia*, ed. M. Querol-Gavaldá (*MME*, vols. 16, 19)
11. *Hispaniae schola musica sacra*, 8 vols., ed. Felipe Pedrell. Barcelona: Juan Bta. Pujol; Leipzig: Breitkopf & Härtel, 1894-1898.
12. Milán, Luis
    a. *Libro de musica de vihuela de mano initualado El maestro* (*MMF*, ser. 1, v. 30; *PAM*, v. 2, ed. Leo Schrade)
    b. *Luis de Milán: El Maestro*, ed. Charles Jacobs. University Park: Pennsylvania State University Press, 1971.
13. Morales, Cristóbal de
    a. (*CE*) *Opera Omnia*, 7 vols., ed. Higini Anglés (*MME*, vols. 11, 13, 15, 17, 20, 21, 24, 34)
    b. *Missa de beata virgine* (*Musica Hispana*, ser. B., v. 1); Organ pieces (*CO*, v. 6)
14. Morphy, Guillermo. *Les Luthistes Espagnols de XVIᵉ Siècle*, 2 vols. Leipzig: Breitkopf & Härtel, 1902; reprint: New York: Broude Brothers, 1967.
15. Mudarra, Alónso de. *Tres libros de musica*, ed. Emilio Pujol (*MME*, v. 7)
16. *La musica en la corte de los reyes católicos*, ed. Higini Anglés (*MME*, vols. 1, 10, 14); *Cancioneros musical de Palacio*, 2 vols. (*MME*, vols. 10, 14)
17. Narváez, Luys de. *Los seys libros del delphin de musica,* ed. Emilio Pujol (*MME*, v. 3)
18. Ortiz, Diego. *Tratado de glosae sobre clausulas y otros generos de puntos en la musica de violones*, ed. Max Schneider. Kassel: Bärenreiter, 1967.
19. Ramos de Pareja, Bartolomé. *Musica practica* (*BMB*, sec. 2, v. 3; ed. Johannes Wolf. *Internationale Musikgesellschaft*, sec. 2, ser. 1, v. 2)
20. Salinas, Francisco de. *De musica libri septem* (*MMF*, ser. 2, v. 121; *DM*, v. 13)
21. Santa Maria, Tomás de.
    a. *Libro llamado art de taner fantasia* (*MMF*, ser. 2, v. 124)
    b. Organ pieces (*LO*, v. 3)
22. *Spanish Organ Music after Antonio de Cabezón*, ed. Willi Apel (*CEKM*, v. 14)
23. Valderrábano, Enriques de. *Libro de musica de vihuela, intitulado Silva de serenas*, ed. Emilio Pujol (*MME*, vols. 22-23)
24. Vega, Lope de. *Treinta Canciones de Lope de Vega*. Madrid: "Residencia," 1935.
25. Victoria, Tomás Luis de
    a. (*CE*) *Opera Omnia*, 8 vols., ed. Felipe Pedrell. Leipzig: Breitkopf & Härtel, 1902-1913; reprint: Ridgewood, NJ: Gregg Press, 1966.
    b. *Opera Omnia*, ed. Higini Anglés (*MME*, vols. 25, 26, 30)
    c. Organ pieces (CO, v. 6)
    d. *Missa pro defunctis cum responsorio Libera me Domine* (*MDa*, v. 15)

OUTLINE XIV

GERMANY

Polyphonic Lieder – Instrumental Music
Music of the Reformation – Protestant and Catholic Church Music
Musical Theory – Meistersinger
Music in Poland

I.   **Polyphonic Lieder**

A.   Polyphonic music in Germany began development later than it did in the other countries of Europe. About the beginning of the fifteenth century, **Oswald von Wolkenstein** (*c.* 1377-1445) and many of his successors often borrowed compositions from France and the Low Countries and adapted them to new German texts.
   1.   The earliest polyphonic settings of German *lieder* come from **Oswald von Wolkenstein** (*DTÖ*, v. 18) and **Hermann, Münch der Salzburg** (Monk of Salzburg) (*fl.* end of the fourteenth century).
   2.   Several early examples appear in various manuscripts but the larger number of early polyphonic *lieder* have been preserved in three main collections: the Lochamer, Schedel and Glogau song books.
      a.   *Christ ist erstanden* (*DTÖ*, vols. 14-15, pp. 260-264) in three- and four-voice settings in the Trent Codex, v. 1.
B.   The *Liederbücher*, which contain many foreign compositions, nevertheless include representative compositions of a German style which is gradually emerging.
   1.   Sections of uneven length are clearly defined in contrast to the continuous flow of the Flemish style.
   2.   The *cantus firmus* in three-voice pieces is generally in the middle voice, unified with the discant. The countertenor is generally used to fill in the harmony. The *cantus firmus*, which has the text, is sung and the other parts may be performed on instruments.
   3.   Imitation is quite common in the Schedel and Glogau song books.
   4.   The common forms are the *bar* form (a a b) and through composed, frequently in duple time.
   5.   **Conrad Paumann** is the only German composer of reputation included in these song books. Several of the melodies have been used more recently by **Johannes Brahms, Robert Franz** and **Arnold Schoenberg**.
C.   Early *Liederbücher* in manuscript
   1.   *Lochamer Liederbuch, c.* 1458 (*DTB, Sonderband*, v. 2; *M* 26)
      a.   This contains 47 anonymous pieces, 44 of which have German texts, and 3 monophonic songs are in Latin. Of the ones with German texts, 35 are monophonic, 2 are two-voice and 7 are three-voice songs.
         1)   Eight of the monophonic songs are marked "tenor" or "discant" which suggests they have been borrowed from polyphonic settings.
         2)   In a variety of settings, there appears the first use of the German folksong in polyphony.
      b.   *Mit ganczem Willen* (With my entire will) (*HAM*, No. 81a; *M* 26, p. 136)
      c.   *Der Wald hat sich ent laubet* (*GMB*, No. 45; *DTB, Sonderband*, v. 2, p. 47; *M* 26, p. 118; *AC*, Part 2, v. 1, p. 1)
      d.   *Elend, du hast umfangen mich* (*GMB*, No. 47; *DTB, Sonderband*, v. 2, p. 16; *M* 26, p. 97; *AC*, Part 2, v. 1, p. 1)

2. *Schedelsches Liederbuch, c.* 1460-1470 (*EdM*, v. 84 (facsimile); vols. 74, 75 (transcriptions)

    a. The *Liederbuch* of Dr. Schedel is also known as *Münchener, Waltersches,* or *Jüngeres Nürnberger Liederbücher*.

    b. Written down by the doctor, historian, **Hartmann Schedel** (1440-1514), the song book contains a variety of pieces: 68 polyphonic and 2 monophonic *Lieder*, 20 *chansons*, 18 Latin songs, 2 Italian songs and 18 textless compositions, 128 in all.

    c. Among the composers represented are **Dunstable, Ockeghem, Dufay, Busnois, Walter Frye, John Bedingham** and **Conrad Paumann**.

3. *Glogauer [Berliner] Liederbuch, c.* 1477-1488 (EdM, vols. 4, 8)

    a. The extensive collection (294 pieces) is in three volumes, each a different part (*discantus, tenores, contratenores*), possibly the first examples of part books.

        1) It consists of 158 Latin pieces (hymns, antiphons, sequences, responsories), 70 *Lieder*, 3 *quodlibets* (perhaps the earliest), one Italian and one Slavic song and 61 instrumental compositions.

    b. The composers represented include **Dufay, Ockeghem, Tinctoris, Busnois** and **Caron**.

    c. *O rosa bella* (*HAM*, No. 82a; *EdM*, v. 4, p. 40; v. 84, p. 39)

        1) This early example of the *quodlibet* makes use of 22 fragments of German *Lieder* in the tenor.

    d. The *quodlibet* (as you please) may be separated into at least three different types; it is a composition in which different melodies or texts are combined.

        1) The polyphonic *quodlibet* uses different melodies simultaneously, often each melody with its own text.

        2) The successive *quodlibet* presents various melodies or fragments successively. The tenor of *"O rosa bella"* is an example in which 22 melodic fragments are combined successively.

        3) The textual *quodlibet* makes use of a combination of various borrowed texts irregardless of their melodies.

        4) As in the example of *"O rosa bella,"* some compositions may make use of all three types; the superius and the tenor make use of the textual type as well as the simultaneous melodic *quodlibet*; the tenor alone uses the successive type with the 22 fragments.

D. The secular polyphonic *Lied* continued development in the early fifteenth century; the number of voices frequently included an alto as a fourth voice; many of the voices took on greater melodic independence and imitation became more frequent, especially at the beginning of a piece.

    1. **Erhard Öglin**, *Liederbuch*, Augsburg, 1512 (*PAM*, v. 9)

        a. The first collection of part songs to be completely in four voices, the *Liederbuch* contains 43 German *Lieder,* sacred and secular, and 7 pieces with Latin texts. No composers are indicated but pieces by **Isaac, Senfl** and **Hofhaimer** have been identified.

    2. **Peter Schöffer**, *Liederbuch*, 1513 (*CW*, v. 29 includes 15 of the pieces)

        a. As in the **Öglin** song book, most of the texts are given only in the tenor book.

        b. In this collection of 62 German *Lieder*, 26 compositions are identified by composer, among them **Jörg Schönfelder, Malchinger, Sebastian Virdung** and **Johannes Sies**.

    3. **Heinrich Finck**, *c.* 1445-1527 (*PAM*, v. 8; *DTÖ*, v. 72; *EdM*, v. 57)

        a. **Finck** spent considerable time at the Polish court in Cracow; was employed by Duke Ulrich at Stuttgart (1509-1513); became *Kapellmeister* at the Salzburg Cathedral and spent his last years as music director at the Imperial Court in Vienna.

        b. *Schöne auszerlesene lieder,* 1536

            1) Published in part books, there are 55 compositions, the first 30 by **Finck** (*PAM*, v. 8, pp. 1-65).

            2) *Ich sund an einem morgen* (I stood one morning) (*DTÖ*, v. 72, p. 21)

a)   Note the pairs of voices in parallel motion and the imitation, both common traits with **Finck**.

4.   **Heinrich Isaac** (*c*. 1450-1517)

a.   **Isaac**, with **Hassler** and **Senfl**, is one of the great composers of secular songs. Many of his songs appeared in various publications for thirty years after his death.

b.   These show advancing development which incorporates a variety of melodic, rhythmic, homophonic and polyphonic techniques.

c.   *Isbruck [Insbruck] ich muss dich lassen* (Innsbruck, I now must leave thee) (*DTÖ*, v. 28, p. 15; *AC*, v. 2, p. 4; *AERM*, p. 178; *GD*, fifth edition, v. 4, p. 546)

1)   This predominantly homophonic setting with melody in the superius anticipates, because of its strong sectional character, the later **Bach** chorale.   It appears in Book I of **Forster's** *Frische teutsche Liedlein*, 1539;   in 1598 **Johann Hesse's** hymn text *"O welt ich muss dich lassen"* and in 1633 another text, *"Nun ruhen alle Wälder,"* were set to the melody.   **Bach** harmonized it several times and used it in his *St. Matthew Passion*; **Brahms** wrote two organ chorales on it.

d.   *Zwischen perg [Berg] und tieffe tal* (Between the mountain and the deep valley) (*DTÖ*, v. 28, p. 26; *PAM*, v. 9, p. 5; *MSO*, v. 1, p. 33)

1)   The part song, based on a folksong, is polyphonic in style.   Canon at the octave occurs in the bass and tenor.

e.   *Mein Müterlein* (*DTÖ*, v. 28, p. 18)

1)   In this imitative setting where the melody is in the tenor, there is more than customary alteration of the melody, both melodically and rhythmically.

f.   *Es het ein Baur ein Töchterlein* (*DTÖ*, v. 28, p. 7)

1)   In this song chordal sections alternate with contrapuntal sections in which the melody moves from one voice to another polyphonically, rather than remaining in one voice.

5.   **Paul Hofhaimer** (1459-1537)

a.   In a style similar to that of **Finck, Hofhaimer's** secular part songs have the melody in the tenor and are generally sectional with simultaneous cadences in all voices (21 songs in *DTÖ*, v. 72, pp. 31-45; see *SSMS*, p. 91).

b.   *Meins traurens ist* (My sorrow is) (*HAM*, No. 93; *DTÖ*, v. 72, p. 41)

1)   The structure is that of the *bar* form: a a b.

6.   **Georg Forster** (*c*. 1510-1568)

a.   *Frische teutsche Liedlein*, 1539-1556

1)   In five parts, this is a collection of 380 *Lieder* including 37 by **Forster** himself. Part I: *EdM*, v. 20; Part II (1540): *EdM*, v. 60; *PAM*, v. 29; Part III: *EdM*, v. 61; 10 selections from Parts III-V in *CW*, v. 63.

7.   **Johann [Hans] Ott** (*fl.* 1530-1545)

a.   **Ott** was a publisher and book salesman in Nuremberg, an important center of music publishing.   He had high respect for **Josquin** whom he called the hero of his art; **Senfl** and **Isaac** were next.

b.   Of the 236 songs in his two collections, 146 are by **Senfl**.   Composers represented are **Isaac, Stoltzer** and others.

c.   *121 Neue Lieder*, Nuremberg, 1534

1)   *Ewiger Gott* (*GMB*, No. 84)

d.   *Ein Hundert Fünfzehn weltliche und einige geistliche Lieder*, published in 1544 by **Johann Ott** (*PAM*, vols. 1-3)

1)   *O Elslein, liebstes Elslein mein* (*PAM*, vols. 1-3, p. 45; *GMB*, No. 85)

8.   **Orlando di Lasso [Roland de Lassus]** (1532-1611) (*CE*)

a.   **Lasso** published 93 examples of German *Lieder* in three to six parts, some with religious texts (1566-1590).   Characteristics of the *villanella* (homophonic style), madrigal (motet-like polyphony, chromaticism and text–painting) and *chanson* (*parlando*) all are apparent.

    b.   The secular texts include the subjects of love, humor, drinking, reflective and popular songs. Many of the songs are in the *bar* form.

    c.   "To sing and to use on all kinds of instruments" is an indication **Lasso** used on his song collections.

    d.   *Vatter unser im Himmelreich* (*CE*, v. 18, p. 1)

        1)   The first and last phrases of the melody appear in the tenor, but the other melody phrases are used imitatively in the other four voices.

    e.   *Ich waiss mir ein meidlein* (I know a maiden) (*CE*, v. 20, p. 44)

        1)   The humorous repetition of syllables and words is effectively illustrated in this four-voice song.

  9. **Johann Eccard** (1553-1611)

    a.   *Newe geistliche und weltliche Lieder*, Königsberg, 1589 (*PAM*, v. 21)

        1)   Of the 25 pieces in four and five voices, 15 are secular.

    b.   *Preussiche Festlieder*, Ebling, 1642, with **Eccard** and his pupil **Johann Stobäus** (1580-1646)

        1)   *Wach auf, du werte Christenheit* (*GMB*, No. 159)

 10. **Hans Leo Hassler** (1564-1612)

    a.   *Neue teutsche Gesäng nach Art der welschen Madrigalien und Canzonetten mit 4. 5. 6. unnd 8. Stimmen* (New German songs which resemble madrigals and canzonettes), 1596 (*CE*, v. 2, pp. 62-201; *DTB*, vols. 8-9)

        1)   These 24 pieces are generally chordal and in well defined sections rather than of the typical contrapuntal madrigal style.

    b.   *Lustgarten neuer teutscher Gesäng, Balletti, Galliarden und Intraden*, Nuremberg, 1601 (*CE*, v. 9; *PAM*, v. 15)

        1)   Included are 32 German *Lieder* in four to eight voices in addition to 7 other vocal pieces and 11 instrumental compositions (10 *intrada* and one *gagliarda*). In general **Hassler** places the main melody in the top voice.

        2)   *Mein Gmüth ist mir verwirret* (My mind is completely confused by an obstinate maiden) (*CE*, v. 9, p. 53; *PAM*, v. 15, p. 24)

           a)   The melody of this five-voice secular song had added to it (in 1613) the religious text *"Herzlich thut mich verlangen"* (My heart is filled with longing) and also became the chorale with **Paul Gerhardt's** text *"O Haupt voll Blut und Wunden"* (O sacred head now wounded) used by **Bach** in his *St. Matthew Passion.*

        3)   *Ach Schatz* (Alas, my love) (*CE*, v. 9, p. 13; *PAM*, v. 15, p. 5; *DTB*, v. 9, p. 112; *HAM*, No. 165)

        4)   *Ach, süsse Seel'* (*CE*, v. 9, p. 65; *PAM*, v. 15, p. 31; *GMB*, No. 152)

  E. Many other composers published collections of polyphonic *Lieder*. Among those of the last quarter of the sixteenth century was **Jakob Regnart** (d. *c.* 1600), a Dutchman who served at various German courts and whose *lied* publications were very popular. In his *Kurzweilige teutsche Lieder zu dreyen stimmen nach art der Neapolitanen oder Welschen Villanellen*, 1583, Italian characteristics may be noted, even as suggested by the title. **Antonio Scandello** published the first Italian song collection in Germany (Nuremberg, 1566).

II.   Instrumental Music

  A. The organs of the Renaissance are generally represented by three different sizes: 1) the portative organ, 2) the positive and 3) the larger organ permanently installed in a church.

    1.   The portative organ (Italian *organetto*) was widely used during the time of **Landini** (fourteenth century). A purely melodic instrument, the portative with a small keyboard was played with the right hand; the bellows were pumped with the left hand or arm.

2. The positive organ was an independent self-contained organ which could easily be moved. Often used as an accompaniment instrument, it was customarily placed in the chancel of a church or used in a small room. It had a keyboard, but no pedalboard nor large pipes.

3. The positive organ by 1400 had developed into a larger stationary instrument of considerable size. In the fourteenth century a primitive pedalboard was introduced in Germany (Halberstadt, 1361) and later in France and Spain. In Italy pedals were rarely used in the sixteenth century and in England the pedalboard did not become common until after **Handel's** time (c. 1780). The sixteenth-century organ on the continent, particularly in Germany, had two or three keyboards (manuals), a fairly complete pedalboard and a considerable number and variety of stops (principals, flutes, reeds and mixtures). These organs were particularly suitable for playing polyphonic music.

4. **Arnolt Schlick** (c. 1460-after 1517)
   a. *Spiegel der Orgelmacher und Organisten* (Mirror of Organ Builders and Players), Heidelberg, 1511
      1) The *"Spiegel"* is the first printed work on organ construction in Germany; it gives a detailed description of the early Renaissance organ in Germany. Chapters include discussion on registers (principals, flutes, reeds, mixtures), materials, tuning and particularly pitch.

5. Until after 1750 music for keyboard instruments (clavichord, harpsichord and even organ) was often designated by the term *"clavier"* without specifying which instrument was intended.

B. Early books on instruments and tablatures
   1. **Sebastian Virdung**, *Musica getutscht*, Basel, 1511 (*PAM*, v. 11)
      a. "Music rendered into German," so-called because it was written in German rather than Latin, is the earliest printed treatise on instruments and tablatures. Written as a dialogue, it discusses string (chordophones), wind (aerophones) and percussion (membranophones) instruments, including the "virginal," and illustrates them with wood cuts. Explanations and examples of tablature and transcribing vocal music for instruments are also given.
      b. Other versions of this work were published: a Latin version by the German **Luscinius [Ottmar Nachtgall]** and an anonymous French version of the second part was published in Antwerp under the title *Livre plaisant et tres utile*.
   2. **Martin Agricola** (1486-1556), *Musica instrumentalis deudsch*, 1528 (*PAM*, v. 20)
      a. This book is based on **Virdung's** work; the text is presented in rhymed verse form.

C. Tablature (*NPM*, pp. 21-81)
   1. Tablature is music for lute, guitar, viol, flute, keyboard and some other instruments written in a specific system of notation. It indicates by letters, numerals and other signs the string, fret, fingerhole or key to be touched.
   2. There are two types of keyboard tablature (German and Spanish) and three types of lute tablature (French, German and Italian). Italian lute tablature was used in Spain for the *vihuela* and the French tablature was commonly used everywhere after 1600.
   3. The German keyboard tablature before 1550 used a staff with notes for the upper part and letters for the lower parts. The time values were indicated with rhythmic symbols. After 1550 the notation on the staff was gradually discarded and the tablature used letters and rhythmic symbols exclusively.

D. Composers and music
   1. The oldest examples of German organ music are a Sagen manuscript from about 1425 (incomplete *Gloria*), a manuscript of **Ludolf Wilkin** of Winsem from about 1430 (some organ versets for the Mass and arrangements of German songs) and a Munich manuscript (some liturgical fragments) from about 1435.
   2. *Adam Ileborgh Tablature*, 1448 (*CEKM*, v. 1, pp. 28-32)
      a. Copied by **Adam Ileborgh**, Rector of Stendal, the tablature contains the first

preludes in idiomatic keyboard style found in tablatures of the fifteenth and early sixteenth centuries. The collection consists of five preludes (3 in two voices, 2 in three voices) and three long pieces based on the tenor *Frowe al myn hoffen* (2 in three voices).

b.   The right hand plays a fantasie-like, rhythmically varied melody notated on a staff, whereas the left hand part, indicated by letters, is generally constructed of long sustained single or pairs of notes.

c.   *Praeambula* (*CEKM*, v. 1, p. 28, No. 36; *HAM*, No. 84b) (*CEKM*, v. 1, p. 28, No. 33; *HAM*, No. 84a)

3.   **Conrad Paumann** (1410-1473)

a.   *Fundamentum organisandi* (Foundations of composition), 1452 (*M* 26, pp. 177-224)

1)   Developed as an instruction book, the *Fundamentum* contains 13 pieces; it demonstrates how to add a melody to a diatonic bass (up or down) or by progressions of thirds up to sixths; cadence formulas and repeated notes are discussed.

2)   Included also are several arrangements of German *Lieder*. Their melodies are all presented in the *Lochamer Liederbuch* in which manuscript the *Fundamentum* is contained.

3)   *Mit ganszem Willen* (With all my will) (*M* 26, pp. 204, 136; *HAM*, No. 81b; *MOP*, pp. 102, 297)

4)   *Elend, du hast umfangen mich* (*M* 26, pp. 208, 97; *GMB*, No. 48)

4.   *Das Buxheimer Orgelbuch, c.* 1460 (*DM*, Ser. 1, v. 1, facsimile; *EdM*, vols. 37-39, transcription; see also *CO*, vols, 4, 8, 12 for excerpts)

a.   The Buxheim Organ Book with its 250 pieces written in German organ tablature is the most comprehensive collection of German organ music in the fifteenth century. It includes 15 preambles and the other pieces are arrangements of songs (*Intabulierung* [intabulations]), many of them Burgundian *chansons* (**Dufay, John Bedingham, Walter Frye, Guillaume Legrant, Touront [Tauranth]**); many are included in the *Schedelesches* (25) and *Lochamer* (36) *Liederbücher*.

b.   The indications for pedal in these and the Ileborgh tablature confirm this to be real organ music.

c.   *Praeambula* (*HAM*, Nos. 84c, 84d)

5.   **Arnoldt Schlick** (*c.* 1460-after 1517)

a.   *Tabulaturen etlicher lobgesang und lidlein uff die orgeln und lauten* (Tablatures of several songs of praise and little songs for the organ and lute), Mainz, 1512

1)   This is the oldest printed collection of keyboard music; it contains 14 organ pieces in three and four parts, 3 pieces for lute and 12 songs with lute accompaniment. Most of the organ pieces are based on Gregorian plainsongs.

2)   *Maria zart von edler Art* (Gentle Mary of noble mein) (*MOP*, p. 206)

a)   The three-part contrapuntal setting uses a folk-like sacred song melody in the upper part. The other two voices introduce points of imitation (*vorimitation*) with the upper voice; it suggests a later treatment of organ chorales.

3)   *O Pia* from *Salve regina* (*MOP*, p. 198)

4)   *Salve regina* (*HAM*, No. 100)

a)   The *Salve regina* melody, one of four antiphons B. V. M., is introduced in the tenor and the other three voices enter in imitation.

6.   **Paul Hofhaimer** (1459-1537), a famous organist and composer, left only a small amount of organ music. He was made a nobleman in the court of Maximilian I, Emperor of Austria; he gathered around himself a loyal group of students who called themselves "Paulomimes;" they held important positions throughout the empire. Among these were **Leonhard Kleber** at Gröppinger in Württemberg, **Hans Kotter** at Freiburg and Berne in Switzerland, **Johann Buchner** at Constance, **Dionisio Memmo** at St. Gall in Switzerland and St. Mark's in Venice and **Luscinius** at Strasbourg.

      a.   **Hans Kotter** (*c*. 1485-1541)
         1) **Kotter's** manuscript is a collection of 67 pieces dated 1513 and includes compositions by **Isaac** and **Josquin**, as well as **Hofhaimer** and **Buchner**.
            a) *Nach willen dein* (*SSMS*, p. 92)
      b.   **Leonhard Kleber** (*c*. 1490-1556)
         1) Possibly not a "Paulomime" even though his tablature includes **Hofhaimer** compositions. His tablature (1524) in two parts contains 112 compositions; the first part for keyboard, the second part requiring pedal.
         2) Preludes in various keys: in *mi* (*HAM*, No. 84e); in *re* (*HAM*, No. 84f; *MOP*, p. 180)
      c.   **Hans [Johann] Buchner** (1483-*c*. 1538) (*EdM*, vols. 54, 55)
         1) *Fundamentum* (published posthumously, 1551), a collection of secular songs, sacred pieces (many on the Mass) and a Latin treatise, is the oldest preserved manuscript that explains theoretically the principles of keyboard playing and composition. One example of music with fingering is given.
            a) *Quem terra, pontus,* with original fingering (*GMB*, No. 83; *EdM*, v. 54, p. 10)
   7. Colorist School
      a.   In the latter part of the sixteenth century, composers applied colorations, stereotyped ornamentation, to vocal compositions for keyboard performance, and thus gave the name to this school. Many of their tablature books include examples of ornaments to be used to fill in various intervals. Dance music also occupies a major portion of these tablature books.
      b.   Mensural notation disappeared and all the parts are written in letters.
      c.   Among the most important "colorists" are **Elias Nicolaus Ammerbach, Bernhard Schmidt** the Elder (1522-1592) and the Younger (b. 1548) (*MMF*, Ser. 1, v. 20), **Jakob Paix** (1556-after 1617) and **Augustus Nörmiger**.
      d.   **Elias Nicolaus Ammerbach** (*c*. 1530-1597)
         1) *Orgel oder Instrument Tabulatur* (1571; second edition, 1583)
            a) In the preface **Ammerbach** explains tablature transcription, ornamentation and, of great importance, fingering. The second edition is considerably enlarged with 142 compositions in all, including a large repertory of dances. Many of the principal composers of the time are identified.
            b) *Passamezzo antico* (*HAM*, No. 154); *Die Megdlein sind von Flandern* (a German dance) (*GMB*, No. 135)
   8. **Hans Leo Hassler** (1564-1612)
      a.   Keyboard pieces (*DTB*, v. 7; *CO*, v. 2, p. 20; v. 12, p. 23)
 E. Lute
   1. The early sixteenth century in Germany saw the beginning of a prolonged interest in the lute, particularly for home use. Most of the lute tablatures are simple and often for the instruction of amateurs.
   2. German lute tablature
      a.   The normal tuning of the lute is that of two pairs of conjunct fourths separated by a major third (G – c – f – a – d' – g').
      b.   The tablature was originally designed in the fifteenth century for a five-course lute with c as the lowest string. Numbers 1 to 5 designated the open strings and letters designated the particular fret on the string. Stems, often tied together in groups, designated the rhythmic values.
         1) In the sixteenth century the tablature was expanded to be used with a six-course lute which added the lowest string G.
   3. The repertory consists largely of dance pieces, transcriptions of polyphonic vocal pieces, both sacred and secular, foreign and native German, preludes and fantasias.
      a.   In contrast to the "colorists" in organ music, the lutenists used limited ornamentation. Generally chordal in style, rapid passage-work and some points of imitation

contribute interest.

    b.   The German dances often appear in two parts: the *Tantz* in duple time followed by the *Nachtanz* (after dance), generally a repetition, at times elaborate, of the main dance in triple time (*Proportz*). About 1550 there is some indication of various dances being grouped together as a suite.

    4.   Composers and music

        a.   **Arnolt Schlick** (*c.* 1460-after 1517)

           1)   *Tabulaturen etlicher lobgesang und lidlein uff die orgeln und lauten* (Tablatures for some songs of praise and little songs for the organ and lute), Mainz, 1512

              a)   Included are 3 pieces for lute and 12 songs with lute accompaniment.

        b.   **Hans Judenkünig** (*c.* 1450-1526)

           1)   *Ain schöne kunstliche Underweisung*, Vienna, 1523   (*DTÖ*, v. 37, pp. 2-14)

        c.   **Hans Neusiedler [Newsidler]** (1508-1563)

           1)   **Neusiedler** published three books (1536, 1540, 1544, the latter in two parts) for lute (*DTÖ*, v. 37, pp. 15-37; 38-43; 44-59)

              a)   *Hoftanz* (Court dance) (*HAM*, No. 105a; *DTÖ*, v. 37, p. 34)

              b)   *Der Juden Tanz* (The Jew's dance) (*HAM*, No. 105b; *DTÖ*, v. 37, p. 58)

                  (1)   Note the strong dissonances (suggesting bitonality): e against e-sharp; b against b-sharp.

        d.   **Hans Weck** (*fl.* 1510)

           1)   *Spanyöler Tancz* (*HAM*, No. 102b)

        e.   *Der Prinzen-Tanz; Proportz, c.* 1550 (*MM*, p. 76)

        f.   **Sixt Kargel** (sixteenth century)

           1)   Fantasia for lute from *Lautenbuch viler newerleseren*, Strassburg, 1586 (*GMB*, No. 138)

  F.   Music for instruments

    1.   The *Glogauer Liederbuch* (*c.* 1460) contains some of the earliest truly instrumental music.

        a.   Instrumental piece (*HAM*, No. 83a; *EdM*, v. 4, p. 49)

        b.   *Der neue Bauernschwanz* (The new peasant dance) (*HAM*, No. 83b; *EdM*, v. 4, p. 87)

    2.   **Heinrich Isaac** (*c.* 1450-1517)

        a.   *Canzona* (*HAM*, No. 88; *DTÖ*, v. 28, p. 119)

        b.   *Canzona "La Martinella"* for organ or two instruments and organ (*GMB*, No. 56; *DTÖ*, v. 28, p. 86)

    3.   **Johann Walter** (1496-1570)

        a.   *Sechs und zwentzig Fugen auff die acht Tonos*, 1542

        1)   Canon for three wind instruments (*GMB*, No. 81)

    4.   **Ludwig Senfl** (*c.* 1492-*c.* 1555)

        a.   *Fortuna ad voces musicales*, from Glareanus, *Dodecachordon* (*MMF*, Ser. 2, v. 65, p. 222; *GMB*, No. 86; *EdM*, v. 15 [**Senfl**, *Werke*, v. 4], p. 20)

    5.   **Hans Leo Hassler** (1564-1612)

        a.   *Lustgarten neuer teutscher Gesäng, Balletti, Galliarden und Intraden*, Nuremberg, 1601 (includes 10 *intradas*)

        1)   *Intrada* (*PAM*, v. 15, p. 64; *GMB*, No. 153; *CE*, v. 9, p. 122)

III. Music of the Reformation

  A.   **Martin Luther** (1483-1546)

    1.   **Luther**, a German theologian and amateur musician, was a player of the lute, did some composing and had been trained in Gregorian chant; he admired the music of **Josquin** ("a master of the notes"), **Senfl** and other sixteenth century composers (**La Rue, Heinrich Finck**). He was instrumental in developing the unison chorale with German text

as an important means of reaching the people, who were encouraged to participate in the Services.

2.   The chorale

a.   There are two main sources from which the music of the Lutheran Church is derived: 1) the plainsongs of the Catholic Church and 2) pre-Reformation religious songs, mostly German.

1)   Many plainsongs, with texts translated into German, were introduced into the Lutheran liturgy.   Sometimes the plainsong melody was modified and at other times a completely new melody was used (*PCM*, p. 15).

   a)   *Veni redemptor gentium* became *Nun komm' der Heiden Heiland; Veni creator spiritus* became *Komm Gott Schöpfer, heiliger Geist.*

2)   The second category may itself be divided into four groups: 1) non-liturgical Latin pieces, 2) pre-Reformation German religious songs, 3) *contrafacta, i. e.* old pieces using new texts and 4) newly written songs especially for the Lutherans.

   a)   Non-liturgical Latin songs: *Puer natus in Bethlehem* became *Ein Kind geborn zu Bethlehem* (A Child is born in Bethlehem) and *Dies est laetitiae* became *Der Tag der ist so freudenreich* (All hail this joyous day).

   b)   Pre-Reformation German songs: the Easter song *Christ ist erstanden* (Christ is arisen) and *Nun bitten wir den heiligen Geist* (Now we pray for the Holy Ghost).

   c)   *Contrafacta* texts were rewritten for use among Lutherans, often a sacred text replacing a secular one.   *Vom himmel hoch, da homm ich her* (From heaven above to earth I come) was adapted from *Aus fremden Landen komm ich her* (From a foreign country I come).

      (1)   In the sixteenth century about 175 *contrafacta* were adopted by the Lutheran Church.

   d)   The original songs by **Luther** include *Ein feste Burg*.   Among the 36 texts by **Luther**, some are original, some translations from Latin and some are based on or paraphrases of previous texts.   From **Luther's** time, there are about 50 melodies to be used with the 36 texts.

b.   The melodies were sung in unison by the congregation; later the choir sang in parts and by the seventeenth century organ accompaniments were added.

c.   Early chorale books

1)   The period of 1523 to 1545 produced many song books edited by **Martin Luther** or in direct relationship with him.   The three earliest collections of monophonic music date from 1524.

   a)   *Etlich Christlich lider Lobgesang und Psalm (Achtliederbuch)*, Nuremberg, 1523-1524, published by **Jobst Gutknecht**, contains 8 monophonic songs, four by **Luther**, three by **Speratus** and one anonymous.

   b)   Two *Enchiridia*, Erfurt, 1524, one published by **M. Maler**; the other published by **J. Loersfelt** (monophonic).

   c)   *Die zwei ältesten Königsberger Gesangbücher von 1527*

   d)   *Enchiridion*, Leipzig, 1528 or 1529, published by **Michael Blum**, contains 25 hymns, 18 of them by **Luther**.

   e)   **Valentin Babst**, *Geystliche Lieder*, Leipzig, 1545

      (1)   This contains 128 hymns, including **Luther's** hymns and his German and Latin Litanies.   Each 16 pages (8 on each side of the folio) use the same series of woodcuts.

IV. Protestant and Catholic Church Music

A.   Many collections of polyphonic *Lieder* were published for use by children, the schools and adults in singing societies.   Two of these collections were important models for succeeding publications, one by **Walter** and one by **Rhau [Rhaw]**.

1.   **Johann Walter** (1496-1570) *Wittenberger Geystliche gesangk Buchleyn*, 1524 (*PAM*, v. 7; *CE*, v. 3; *SR*, pp. 341-344)

   a.   Especially written for youth, this is the first polyphonic music based on Protestant chorales.

   b.   In all there are 43 pieces, 38 of which are German songs and 5 are Latin motets; 23 of the texts are by **Luther**. Four-part writing with the melody in the tenor predominates, but 12 pieces are in five parts and two are in three parts.

   c.   Two styles are apparent: 1) the polyphonic *Lieder* style of **Hofhaimer, Issac** and **Finck** (see *TEM*, p. 120) and 2) the chordal style which ultimately leads to the standard four-part chorale.

   d.   *Aus tiefer Not* (Out of the depths) (*HAM*, No. 111a; *PAM*, v. 7, p. 10)

   e.   *Christ lag in Todesbanden* (Christ lay in the bonds of death) (*GMB*, No. 80; *PAM*, v. 7, p. 18)

2.   **Georg Rhau** (1488-1548), *Newe deudsche geistliche Gesenge für die gemeinen Schulen*, Wittenberg, 1544 (*DdT*, v. 34)

   a.   This collection by a friend of **Luther** has 123 pieces and represents a rather comprehensive cross section of styles common to the early Protestants. Included among the composers are several Catholics.

   b.   **Ludwig Senfl**, *Da Jakob nu das Kleid ansah* (When Jacob now saw the coat) (*CE*, v. 6, p. 32; *DdT*, v. 34, p. 180; *HAM*, No. 110; *AERM*, p. 147)

B.   **Heinrich Finck** (1445-1527)

1.   Among his limited extant works are 3 Masses, several motets and some hymns.

2.   *Missa [In summis]* (*CW*, v. 21; *EdM*, v. 57)

   a.   This is a brilliant pre-Reformation Mass probably composed while **Finck** was in the employ of Duke of Ulrich (1509-1513). Generally written in six or seven parts, considerable imitation and some chordal work is apparent; **Finck** borrows liturgical melodies.

3.   Hymns (*CW*, vols. 9, 32; *AERM*, p. 140)

4.   *Quodlibet: Veni sancte spiritus – Veni creator spiritus* (*HAM*, No. 80; *CW*, v. 32, p. 19)

   a.   These two plainsongs for use on Whitsunday are incorporated into this five-part composition; the Sequence (*LU*, p. 800) in the alto and the Hymn (*LU*, p. 885) in the tenor.

C.   **Thomas Stol[t]zer** (*c.* 1470-1526)

1.   A prolific German composer, **Stolzer** was a member of the Royal Chapel of Hungary from 1490 to his death in the battle of Mohacs, 1526.

2.   About 150 pieces and some 60 fragments include Masses, motets (*EdM*, v. 22), responsories, antiphons, 11 German songs and 19 German Psalms and hymns (*EdM*, v. 66). His songs are represented in the songbooks of **Schöffer** (1536), **Forster** (1539) and **Ott** (1544) (*AC*, Part 1, pp. 20-25; Part 2, pp. 33-39).

3.   *Christ ist erstanden* (*DdT*, v. 34, p. 26; *HAM*, No. 108)

   a.   The melody appears in the tenor and *vorimitation* introduces each phrase.

   b.   *Christ ist erstanden*, which resembles the Easter Sequence *Victimae paschali laudes* (*LU*, p. 780) is one of the oldest sacred German folk tunes from the twelfth century. It is included in **Babst's** *Geystliche Lieder*, 1545 (No. LIX) along with *Christ lag in Todesbanden* (No. VIII) which **Luther** called *Christ ist erstanden gebessert* (improved).

D.   **Ludwig Senfl** (*c.* 1492-1555)

1.   Born in Zürich, **Senfl** was a friend of **Hofhaimer**, became a student of **Isaac** at Constance and was appointed court composer to Maximilian I (1515). In 1520 he completed **Isaac's** *Choralis Constantinus* in Augsburg and later was associated with the Bavarian court in Munich.

    2.   Included in his works are 7 Masses, motets (*CE*, v. 11; *DTB*, v. 5, pp. 79-170; *CW*, v. 62) and German *Lieder* (*EdM*, vols. 10, 15; *CE*, vols. 2, 4, 5) from various collections including **Ott's** *Liederbuch* of 1534, testifying to his sympathy with **Luther** and his cause (*AC*, Part 1, pp. 56-64; Part 2, pp. 65-83; *MSD*, 6, v. 2, pp. 295, 410, 523).

    3.   *Liber selectarum cantionum*, Augsburg, 1520

        a.   This is the first printed collection of Latin motets to contain German works by German composers (**Josquin**, 8; **Senfl**, 7; **Isaac**, 5; others).

    4.   *Missa dominicalis super L'Homme armé* (*CE*, v. 1 [*EdM*, v. 5], p. 3)

        a.   The combining of a double *cantus firmus*, plainsong and a *chanson* tune, throughout the four-voice Mass is rather unusual at this time.

    5.   Motet: *Quinque Salutationes Domini nostri Jesu Christi; Salutatio prima: Ave domine Jesu Christe* (*CE*, v. 11, p. 87; *DTB*, v. 5, p. 103; *HAM*, No. 109)

E.   **Arnold von Bruck** (*c*. 1500-1554)

    1.   **Bruck** served as chief *Kapellmeister* in Vienna from 1541 to 1545. His extant works do not include any Masses but his German songs are represented in various songbooks of the period, including **Ott's** *121 neue Lieder*, Nuremberg, 1534 (*DTÖ*, v. 72) and 17 are in **Rhau's** *Newe deudsche geistliche Gesenge*, Wittenberg, 1544 (*PAM*, v. 2; *AC*, Part 1, pp. 66-75; Part 2, pp. 84-87).

    2.   *Aus tiefer Not* (Out of the depths) (*HAM*, No. 111b; *DdT*, v. 34, p. 104)

F.   **Jakob Handl** [Latinized to **Jacobus Gallus**], real name is **Jakob Petelin** (1550-1591)

    1.   A devout Catholic, **Handl** sang in the Vienna Court Chapel choir (1574) and in 1586 was employed in the court at Prague where he also was cantor at St. John's Church.

    2.   His compositions include 19 Masses, mostly parody Masses, many motets, a Passion and some 47 additional contrapuntal pieces in five, six and eight parts. His works show the influence of the Venetian polychoral style and the contrapuntal imitative style of the Netherland composers. Root movement of a major third is common (*AC*, Part 1, p. 154; *DCS*, vols. 31-33).

    3.   *Opus musicum*, Prague, 1586-1591 (*DTÖ*, vols. 12, 24, 30, 40, 48, 51-52)

        a.   The *Opus*, published in four books, is a monumental collection of 374 motets in four to twenty-four voices for the entire church year.

        b.   The motets show great variety; imitation and text-painting are common; voice combinations in from one to four choruses, *e. g.* in the multiple chorus works the treble chorus may alternate with a bass chorus, or equal choruses may alternate; echo is also used.

        c.   *Ecce quomodo moritur justus* (Behold, the righteous perish) (*DTÖ*, v. 24, p. 171; *HAM*, No. 156; *GMB*, No. 131)

        d.   *Tribus miraculis* (*DTÖ*, v. 12, p. 110), for three equal four-voice choruses

    4.   *Moralia*, Part I, 1589; Part II, 1596 (*RRMR*, vols. 7, 8)

        a.   Included in Part I are 53 secular Latin pieces in four to eight voices; Part II contains 47 pieces in five, six and eight voices.

G.   **Johannes Eccard** (1553-1611)

    1.   Born in Mülhausen, **Eccard** studied with **Lasso** in Munich (1571), was employed by the Fugger family in Augsburg (1578) and became *Kapellmeister* in Königsberg in 1604. He spent the last three years of his life in Berlin (see *AC*, Part 1, pp. 164-175; Part 2, pp. 196-204).

    2.   *Geystliche Lieder auff den Choral*, Königsberg, 1597

        a.   In these 52 five-voice chorales, **Eccard** breaks from the purely chordal style to an independent polyphonic quality for each voice. The Lutheran chorale appears in the top voice (*Vom himmel hoch, AC*, Part 1, p. 165).

    3.   *Preussiche Festlieder*, published posthumously in two parts, 1642, 1644

        a.   These 27 pieces, **Eccard's** last, are more in the style of the motet. A continuous melody is lacking; free treatment with emphasis on expressing the text contributes to the power exploited in double choruses, eight-voice settings, or to the spiritual content of the texts.

H.   **Leonhard Lechner**   (1553-1606)   (*CE*; *PAM*, v. 19; *AC*, Part 1, pp. 156-163; Part 2, pp. 150-160)

1.   Born in the south Tyrol into a Catholic family, **Lechner** turned Protestant in 1571 at the age of eighteen; he was *Kapellmeister* at the court of Hohenzollern-Hechingen and eventually at the court in Stuttgart. **Lechner** was the most significant composer of his time.

2.   **Lechner's** Masses (*CE*, v. 8), Magnificats (*CE*, v. 4) and Latin motets (*CE*, v. 1) show strong influence of **Lasso** but his German works use many techniques common to Italian madrigals, dissonance, the rhythm following the text and textual expression.

3.   *Newe teutsche Lieder*, 1577 (*CE*, v. 3), in four and five voices.

4.   *Neue gaistliche [sic] und weltliche deutsche Lieder*, 1589 (*CE*, v. 13)

   a.   *Deutsche Sprüche von Leben und Tod* (*CE*, v. 13, p. 20)

      1)   This is a series of 15 short (often only one page) pieces in a variety of styles: homophonic (*CE*, v. 13, p. 27), free imitation (*CE*, v. 13, p. 28) and polyphonic (*CE*, v. 13, p. 35).

I.   **Hans Leo Hassler**   (1564-1612)

1.   The son of an organist, **Hassler** was the first great German composer to study in Italy (1584). He became a pupil of **Andrea Gabrieli** and was strongly influenced by the Venetian polychoral style. In 1585 he returned to Germany where he was appointed organist to Octavian II Fugger; in 1602 he became chief town *Kapellmeister* of Nuremberg and organist at the Frauenkirche. In 1608 **Hassler** was appointed organist and music librarian to the Elector of Saxony.

2.   **Hassler's** larger sacred works include Masses and motets; many of the motets are usable either in Catholic or Protestant Services.

   a.   The Masses (*CE*, v. 4 [*DdT* v. 7]) are in four, five and six voices; one is for two four-part choruses and one is for three four-part choruses.

3.   **Hassler's** style is simple, direct and clear.

   a.   Duple time and the Ionian mode predominate.

   b.   There is much antiphonal writing between pairs of voices or between two or four parts. Polyphonic writing is characterized by imitation of short motives at the fifth and octave; very little canon or counterpoint is used.

   c.   Homophonic style predominates in much of **Hassler's** work. The chords are mostly in root position or first inversion; root movement is by fifths.

   d.   Non-harmonic tones include passing tones, anticipations, suspensions, portamentos and added sixths. There are very few cross relations.

   e.   The texts are generally treated syllabically.

4.   *Cantiones sacrae*, 1591 (*CE*, v. 1)

   a.   A collection of 31 motets in four to twelve voices.

   b.   *Quia vidisti me, Thoma* (Because thou hast seen me, Thomas) (*CE*, v. 1 [*DdT*, v. 2], p. 31; *HAM*, No. 164)

5.   *Psalmen und Christliche Gesäng*, 1607 (*CE*, v. 7)

   a.   These 52 motet-like pieces are based on 29 chorale melodies and have each phrase of the chorale successively developed in free imitation.

6.   *Kirchengesäng: Psalmen und geistliche Lieder*, 1608 (*CE*, v. 8)

   a.   There are 67 pieces in a more simple, note-against-note style suggesting congregational use. To close, there are two songs, one with three separately set verses, set for two four-part choruses in a more elaborate style.

V.   **Music Theory**

A.   **Henricus Glareanus [Heinrich Glarean; in reality Heinrich Loris]**   (1488-1563)

1.   **Glareanus**, born in the canton of Glarus in Switzerland, was a music theorist and teacher who taught in Basel, Paris and Freiburg. His most significant contribution is the *Dodecachordon*.

2. *Dodecachordon* (Twelve strings), Basel, 1547 (*MMF*, Ser. 2, v. 65; *PAM*, v. 16; *MSD*, 6; *HM*, v. 181; *SR*, pp. 219-227)

    a. In addition to the traditional eight church modes, **Glareanus** describes four new independent modes which long before had been brought about by the use of b-flat in the Lydian and Dorian modes. The major mode becomes Ionian and Hypoionian modes (modes XI and XII) and the natural minor becomes Aeolian and Hypoaeolian modes (modes IX and X). **Glareanus** considered the modes on B (XIII and XIV) impractical because the mode could not be divided into a conjunct perfect fifth and perfect fourth. These he called "Hyperaeolian" and "Hyperphrygian."

       1) **Glareanus** also discusses and gives examples of the music of various fifteenth- and sixteenth-century composers such as **Ockeghem** (3 examples), **Obrecht** (4) and **Josquin** (29); some lesser known composers included are **Nicolas Crain [Craen]** (*MSD*, 6, v. 2, p. 404), **Gregor Meyer** (*MSD*, 6, v. 2, pp. 352, 389, 416, 419), **Jean Mouton** (*MSD*, 6, v. 2, pp. 372, 401, 538-540), **Sixtus Dietrich** (*MSD*, 6, v. 2, pp. 348, 407, 421-423) and **Bertrandus Vaqueras** (*MSD*, 6, v. 2, p. 308).

VI.   Meistersinger, 1450-1600

A. The *Meistersinger*, organized into town guilds in Germany, were middle-class poet-musicians who earned their livelihood as tradesmen.

    1. Although the *Meistersinger* considered themselves the successors to the *Minnesinger*, by way of contrast, the *Minnesinger* were professional musicians, many of noble birth, and produced a quality music. The *Meistersinger* were amateurs whose music was circumscribed with rules.

    2. The *Meistersinger* guilds held weekly meetings after church on Sundays, promoted competitions with prizes, created a system of promotions for its members and developed schools. Regulating each school and the contests was a *Tabulatur* which detailed the rules and penalties.

       a. The members were promoted according to their achievements.

          1) A *Schüler* (pupil) was an apprentice; he had not learned the *Tabulatur*.

          2) A *Schulfreund* (friend) was one who had learned the *Tabulatur*.

          3) A *Sänger* (singer) had learned four or six *"Töne"* (tunes).

          4) A *Dichter* (poet) wrote poems to existing *"Töne."*

          5) A *Meister* (master) was one who created new melodies (*Weisen* or *Töne*).

    3. A rapid decline in the schools took place in the seventeenth century but certain schools continued through the eighteenth century. The guild at Ulm was terminated in 1839.

B. Characteristics of *Meistersinger* songs

    1. The subject matter is often Biblical with the chapter and verse being mentioned in the poem.

    2. A pedantic and uninspired style resulted from the observation of rigid and detailed rules of composition included in the *Tabulatur*.

    3. The poems were sung to standard melodies (*Töne*); their titles frequently referred to the composers or to some other characteristic.

       a. The lines could not exceed 13 syllables since each line had to be sung with one breath.

C. Musical form

    1. The *bar* form (a a b), used traditionally by the *Meistersinger*, was used for most songs.

       a. No instruments were used by the *Meistersinger*.

    2. The melodies were written in a notation (*Hufnagelschrift*) similar to that of plainsong. The rhythm was free, dependent on the text.

    3. The melodies often make use of coloraturas called *"Blumen."*

    4. **Richard Wagner** in his *Die Meistersinger von Nürnberg* (Act I, scene 3 and Act III, scene 2) describes the form and rules. The "Prize Song" follows the *bar* form. The

fanfare in the "Overture" is based on the first few notes of **Heinrich von Mügling's** "*Langeton*".

D.   Composers and music
1.   **Michel Behaim** (1416-1474)
   a.   **Behaim** was probably the first significant *Meistersinger*;   he was in the service of princes in Hungary, Denmark and Germany.
   b.   *Her winter lass ab dein geblei* (*AM*, v. 2, p. 64)
2.   **Muscatblut** (early fifteenth century)
3.   **Conrad Nachtigall**
4.   **Hans Sachs** (1494-1576)
   a.   **Sachs**, who lived in Nuremberg, was a prolific composer;   some 4000 of his 6000 extant works are *Meisterlieder* (see *TEM*, p. 105).
   b.   *Silberweisse* (Silver melody) (*GMB*, No. 78; *AM*, v. 2, p. 64)
   c.   *Der Gülder Ton* (The Golden melody) (*HAM*, No. 24)
   d.   *Klingende Ton* (*AM*, v. 2, p. 65)
5.   **Hans Folz** (*c*. 1560)
   a.   *Kettenton* (The Necklace melody) (*GMB*, No. 79)
6.   **Adam Puschmann** (1532-1600)
   a.   **Puschmann** was one of the greatest of the later *Meistersinger*. In his book *Gründlicher Bericht des deutschen Meistergesangs* (A thorough commentary on German master songs), 1571, he discusses the *Meistersinger* and their songs.

VII.   **Music in Poland**

A.   During the fifteenth century sacred music continued to be promoted by the church. A limited number of manuscripts show French and Italian influences which suggest that Polish musical developments more or less paralleled those of western Europe.
1.   The University of Cracow, established in 1364, became a prominent musical center.
2.   In the later fifteenth century, *organum* style in two to four voices produced the line of development which led into the sixteenth century style, a style influenced by Franco-Netherlandish imitation. The influence of **Palestrina** was felt particularly during the late sixteenth century.
3.   Composers wrote motets, Masses and Psalms; the use of plainsong *cantus firmi* was common. Many note-against-note Psalm settings appeared in collections.
4.   Many of the prominent Polish composers of the last half of the sixteenth century were indebted to the *Collegium Rorantistarum* founded in 1543 at the court chapel of King Sigismund and his successor, Sigismund Augustus, at Cracow.
   a.   **Waclaw Szamotulczyk** (*c*. 1533-*c*. 1568), composer to the king.
      1)   *In te Domine speravi*, 1554 (*M* 30, p. 234)
      2)   *Daylight declines*, 1556 (*M* 30, p. 228)
      3)   *Christ, the day of our lightness*, 1556 (*M* 30, p. 231)
   b.   **Marcin Lwowczyk** [Latin is **Leopolita**] (1540-1589), influenced by the Roman and Flemish schools.
      1)   *Missa Paschalis: Kyrie* (*M* 30, p. 252); *Benedictus* (*M* 30, p. 256)
   c.   **Nicholas Gomólka** (*c*. 1539-1609)
      1)   **Gomólka** remained in the employ of the Royal Chapel until 1563; he composed four-part note-against-note settings of the 150 Psalms (1580) in the style of **Goudimel** but with more frequent use of dissonance.
      2)   *Psalms 45, 47, 108, 137*, 1580 (*M* 30, pp. 261-271)
B.   In addition to vocal composition, the construction of instruments and instrumental writing became prominent in Poland. Two large organ tablatures show the influence of instrumental music of western Europe. They are written in a keyboard tablature similar to that of this period in Germany.

1.   **Jan of Lublin**, *Tabulatura Joannis de Lublin Canonicorum Regularium de Crasnyc*, 1540 (*CEKM*, 6, vols. 1-6)
   a.   This 520-page organ tablature includes many intabulations of vocal works (Masses, motets, hymns) by **Janequin, Verdelot, Sermisy** and others; **Cavazzoni** is represented with one keyboard piece. Other than vocal transcriptions, there are 21 four-part *praeambula* (the pedal is mentioned) in the style of **Kotter** and 36 dances.
   b.   The *Lublin tablature* also includes a treatise on composition with special rules governing imitation.
2.   *Cracow tablature*, 1548
   a.   The *Cracow tablature* includes intabulations of vocal works by **Josquin, Janequin, Senfl, Gombert, Finck** and others. A composition indicating pedal is also included.
3.   *Organ Tablature of the Warsaw Musical Society*, *c*. 1580 (*AMP*, v. 15)
   a.   Included in the 74 compositions are 8 Magnificats, one on each tone, 4 Kyries and 47 Introits. Seven compositions are by Polish composers, including one by **Marcin Lwowczyk**; no other composer is identified.
4.   *Pelplin Organ Tablature*, *c*. 1620 (*AMP*, vols. 1-10)
   a.   The *Pelplin tablature* represents the last development of German organ tablature in Poland. There are in the six volumes 911 compositions, mostly intabulations of vocal compositions; a few are by Polish composers. Among the representative group of 111 composers from throughout Europe are **Johannes Eccard, Hans Leo Hassler, Peter Philips, Thomas Morley, Giovanni Croce, Orfeo Vecchi, Jacob Handl** and **Luca Marenzio**.
      1)   *AMP* volumes 2-7 contain the facsimile of the tablature; volumes 8-10 the transcriptions. Volume 1 is a descriptive introduction to the tablature.

SELECTED BIBLIOGRAPHY

Books

1.   Ameln, Konrad. "Leonhard Lechner in His Time," in *Cantors at the Crossroads: Essays on Church Music in Honor of Walter E. Buszin*, ed. Johannes Riedel, pp. 75-86. St. Louis: Concordia Publishing House, 1967.
2.   Bell, Clair Hayden. *Georg Hager: a Meistersinger of Nürnberg, 1552-1624*. Berkeley: University of California Press, 1947.
3.   Cuyler, Louise. *The Emperor Maximilian I and Music*. London: Oxford University Press, 1973.
4.   ––––––"Musical Activity in Augsburg and Its *Annakirche*, ca. 1470-1630," in *Cantors at the Crossroads: Essays on Church Music in Honor of Walter E. Buszin*, ed. Johannes Riedel, pp. 33-44. St. Louis: Concordia Publishing House, 1967.
5.   Fellerer, Karl Gustav. "Sixteenth-Century Musicians in Matheson's *Ehrenpforte*," in *Studies in Musicology: Essays in the History, Style, and Bibliography of Music in Memory of Glen Haydon*, ed. James W. Pruett, pp. 72-79. Chapel Hill: University of North Carolina Press, 1969.
6.   Geiringer, Karl. "*Es ist genug, so nimm Herr meinen Geist*: 300 years in the History of a Protestant Funeral Song," in *The Commonwealth of Music in Honor of Curt Sachs*, ed. Gustave Reese and Rose Brandel, pp. 283-292. New York: The Free Press, 1965.
7.   Glareanus, Henricus. *Dodecachordon*. (*MMF*, ser. 2, v. 65; German tr., Peter Bohn, *PAM*, v. 16; tr. Clement A. Miller, *MSD*, v. 6)
8.   Jenny, Markus. "The Hymns of Zwingli and Luther: A Comparison," in *Cantors at the Crossroads: Essays on Church Music in Honor of Walter E. Buszin*, ed. Johannes Riedel, pp. 45-64. St. Louis: Concordia Publishing House, 1967.

9.   MacClintock, Carol. "New Light on Giaches de Wert," in *Aspects of Medieval and Renaissance Music: A Birthday Offering to Gustave Reese*, ed. Jan LaRue, pp. 595-603. New York: W. W. Norton, 1966.

10. Mattfeld, Victor. *Georg Rhaw's Publications for Vespers*. Brooklyn: Institute of Mediaeval Music. (*Musicological Studies*, v. 11)

11. Parker, Robert L. "The Polyphonic Lieder of Adam Rener: A Postscript to Recent Studies of the Composer's Works," in *Paul A. Pisk. Essays in His Honor*, ed. John Glowacki, pp. 38-56. Austin: University of Texas, 1966.

12. Schlick, Arnolt. *Spiegel des Orgelmacher*, ed. Paul Smets. Mainz: Rheingold-Verlag, 1959; ed. Ernst Flade. Kassel: Bärenreiter, 1951.

13. Southern, Eileen. "Basse-Dance Music in Some German Manuscripts of the 15th Century," in *Aspects of Medieval and Renaissance Music: A Birthday Offering to Gustave Reese*, ed. Jan LaRue, pp. 738-755.

14. Virdung, Sebastian. *Musica getutscht* (*PAM*, v. 11)

15. White, John R. "Original Compositions and Arrangements in the Lublin Keyboard Tablature," in *Essays in Musicology: A Birthday Offering for Willi Apel*, ed. Hans Tischler, pp. 83-92. Bloomington: Indiana University School of Music, 1968.

Articles

1.   Apel, Willi. "Early German Keyboard Music." *MQ* 23 (1937), pp. 210-237.

2.   ———————"A Remark About the Basse Danse." *JRBM* 1 (1946), pp. 139-143.

3.   Buszin, Walter E. "Luther on Music." *MQ* 32 (1946), pp. 80-97.

4.   Gleason, Harold. "Arnold Schlick, Organ Expert and Composer." *BAMS* 1 (1936), p. 8.

5.   ———————"The Cracow Tablature of 1548." *BAMS* 3 (1939), p. 14.

6.   Grew, Eva Mary. "Martin Luther and Music." *ML* 19 (1938), pp. 67-78.

7.   Jachimecki, Zdzislaw. "Polish Music." *MQ* 6 (1920), pp. 553-572.

8.   Knotts, Eugene Porter. "Music of the Reformation. The Influence of Martin Luther." *MC* 108 (Apr 21, 1934), pp. 6, 15; (Apr 28, 1934), pp. 6, 19.

9.   Lenneberg, Hans H. "The Critic Criticized. Sebastian Virdung and His Controversy with Arnold Schlick." *JAMS* 10 (1957), pp. 1-6.

10. Lerner, Edward R. "The 'German' Works of Alexander Agricola." *MQ* 46 (1960), pp. 56-66.

11. Lowinsky, Edward E. "On the Use of Scores by Sixteenth-Century Musicians." *JAMS* 1 (1948), pp. 17-23.

12. Miller, Clement A. "The *Dodecachordon*: Its Origins and Influence on Renaissance Musical Thought." *MD* 15 (1961), pp. 155-166.

13. Moser, Hans Joachim. "Lutheran Composers in the Hapsburg Empire, 1525-1732." *MD* 3 (1949), pp. 3-24.

14. Naylor, Edward W. "Jacob Handl (Gallus) as Romanticist." *SIMg* 11 (1909), pp. 42-54.

15. Rubsamen, Walter H. "The International 'Catholic' Repertoire of a Luthern Church in Nürnberg (1574-1597)." *AnM* 5 (1957), pp. 229-327.

16. Schrade, Leo. "The Organ in the Mass of the 15th Century." *MQ* 28 (1942), pp. 329-336; 467-487.

17. Siebert, F. Mark. "Mass Sections in the *Buxheim Organ Book*: A Few Points." *MQ* 50 (1964), pp. 353-366.

18. Southern, Eileen. "Foreign Music in German Manuscripts of the 15th Century." *JAMS* 21 (1968), pp. 258-285.

19. Sternfeld, Frederick W. "Music in the Schools of the Reformation." *MD* 2 (1948), pp. 99-122.

20. Van, Guillaume de. "A Recently Discovered Source of Early Fifteenth Century Polyphonic Music." *MD* 2 (1948), pp. 5-74.

21.   White, John R. "The Tablature of Johannes of Lublin (Ms 1716 of the Polish Academy of Sciences in Cracow)." *MD* 17 (1963), pp. 137-163.
22.   Wienpahl, Robert W. "Modal Usage in Masses of the Fifteenth Century." *JAMS* 5 (1952), pp. 37-52.
23.   Wiora, Walter. "The Origins of German Spiritual Folk Song: Comparative Methods in a Historical Study." *Ethnomusicology* 8 (1964), pp. 1-13.
24.   Woodward, G. R. "German Hymnody (from the Twelfth to the Middle of the Seventeenth Century)." *PMA* 32 (1905-1906), pp. 73-99.

Music

1.   Agricola, Martin
    a.   *Musica instrumentalis deudsch*, ed. Robert Eitner (*PAM*, v. 20)
    b.   *Newe deudsche geistliche Gesange*, ed. Johannes Wolf (*DdT*, v. 34)
    c.   *Rudimenta musices* (*MMF*, ser. 2, v. 34)
2.   Ammerbach, Nicolas Elias
    a.   *Orgel oder Instrument Tabulatur*, 1571 (*MMF*, ser. 1, v. 34)
    b.   Organ music (*CO*, v. 11)
    c.   Warren Becker. *A Transcription of Elias Nikolaus Ammerbach's Orgel oder Instrument Tabulatur*, 1588. University of Rochester dissertation, 1963.
3.   *Antiquitates Musicae in Polonia*, 15 vols., ed. Hieronim Feicht. Warsaw: Warsaw University Press, 1963-
4.   Bruck, Arnold von
    a.   Latin motets (*DTÖ*, v. 99)
    b.   Sacred songs (*DdT*, v. 34; *AC*, pt. 1, v. 3)
5.   Buchner, Johann. *Fundamentum*, ed. Wilibald Nagel (*Monatshefte für Musikgeschichte*, v. 23)
6.   *Das Buxheimer Orgelbuch*, facsimile ed. Bertha Antonia Wallner. Kassel: Bärenreiter, 1955 [*DM*, ser. 2, v. 1] ; *Monatshefte für Musikgeschichte*, supplement 20; ed. Eileen Southern. Brooklyn: Institute of Mediaeval Music, 1963 (*Musicological Studies*, v. 6); transcription (*EdM*, vols. 37-39); excerpts (*CO*, vols. 4, 8, 12)
7.   Craen, Nicolaas. *Si ascendero in caelum* (*VOTS*, v. 4, p. 111)
8.   Dietrich, Sixtus
    a.   Geistliche gesange (*EdM*, v. 23; *DdT*, v. 34; *AC*, pt. 1, v. 1; *PäM*, Jg. 3, v. 2)
    b.   *Novum ac insigne opus musicum 36 antiphonarum*, ed. Walter Buszin. Kassel: Bärenreiter, 1955- (*Rhau, Georg, Musikdrucke*, v. 7)
9.   *Early German Keyboard Music*, ed. Howard Ferguson. New York: Oxford University Press, 1970.
10.   Eccard, Johann. *Neue geistliche und weltliche Lieder*, ed. Robert Eitner (*PAM*, v. 21; *AC*, pt. 1, v. 3; pt. 2, v. 4)
11.   *Eyn Enchiridion oder Handbüchlein*. Erfurt: J. Loersfelt, 1524; Kassel: Bärenreiter, 1929.
12.   *Etlich Christliche lider Lobgesang vnd Psalm (Achtliederbuch)*. Nuremberg, 1523. Kassel: Bärenreiter, 1957.
13.   Finck, Heinrich
    a.   *Lieder* (*DTÖ*, v. 72; *PAM*, v. 8; *CW*, vols. 9, 32; *AC*, pt. 1, v. 1)
    b.   Masses and motets (*CW*, v. 21, *Missa In summis*; *EdM*, v. 57)
    c.   Organ works (*CO*, v. 8)
14.   Finck, Hermann
    a.   *Practica musica* (*BMB*, sec. 2, Teoria, v. 21)
    b.   *Lieder* (*PAM*, v. 8)
15.   Forster, Georg. *Frische teutsche Liedlein* (*EdM*, v. 20; *PAM*, v. 29; *CW*, v. 63)
16.   Glareanus, Henricus. *Bicinien* from *Dodecachordon* (*HM*, v. 187)

17.   *Glogauer Liederbuch* (*EdM*, vols. 4, 8; *AC*, pt. 1, v. 1; pt. 2, v. 1; *CO* v. 8)
18.   Handl, Jakob
    a.   *Opus musicum* (*DTÖ*, vols. 12, 24, 30, 40, 48, 51-52)
    b.   Masses (*DTÖ*, vols. 78, 94-95, 117)
    c.   Vocal works (*AC*, pt, 1, vols. 3-4)
19.   Hassler, Hans Leo
    a.   (*CE*) *Sämtliche Werke*, ed. J. Russell Crosby. Wiesbaden: Breitkopf & Härtel, 1961.
    b.   *Canzonette und Neue Teutsche Gesang*, ed. Rudolf Schwartz (*DTB*, vols. 8-9)
    c.   *Madrigale* (*DTB*, v. 20)
    d.   *Cantiones sacrae* (*DdT*, v. 2)
    e.   *Sacri concentus* (*DdT*, vols. 24-25)
    f.   Masses (*DdT*, v. 7)
    g.   Motet (*CW*, v. 14)
    h.   *Lustgarten* (*PAM*, v. 15; *HM*, v. 73, Intradas)
    i.   Organ works (*CO*, vols. 2, 12)
20.   Hofhaimer, Paul
    a.   Choral works (*AC*, pt. 2, v. 2; *DTÖ*, v. 72)
    b.   Keyboard works (*CO*, v. 11; *LO*, v. 8)
    c.   *Harmoniae poeticae*, ed. C. Massei (*Corpus Mensurabilis More Antiquo Musicae*, v. 3)
21.   Isaac, Heinrich
    a.   Masses (*ArM*, v. 10; *VOTS*, v. 6; *CW*, v. 7, *Missa carminum*)
    b.   Motets (*AC*, part 1, v. 1)
    c.   *Choralis Constantinus* (*DTÖ*, vols. 10, 32)
    d.   Secular choral works (*AC*, part 2, v. 1; *DTÖ*, vols. 28, 32, 72)
    e.   Instrumental pieces (*HM*, v. 29); Keyboard works (*LO*, v. 8)
22.   Jan of Lublin. Tablature of keyboard music (*CEKM*, ser. 6, vols. 1-6)
23.   Judenkönig, Hans. Lute music (*DTÖ*, v. 37)
24.   Lasso, Orlando di
    a.   (*CE*) *Sämtliche Werke*, ed. Franz Xaver Haberl, Adolf Sandberger. Leipzig: Breitkopf & Härtel, 1894-
    b.   (*SW*) *Sämtliche Werke, neue Reihe*. Kassel: Bärenreiter.
    c.   *Busstränen des heiligen Petrus*, ed. Hans J. Therstappen (*CW*, vols. 34, 37, 41)
    d.   Madrigals and chansons (*CW*, v. 13; *FCVR*, v. 2; *MMRF*, v. 1; *AC*, pt. 2, v. 3)
    e.   Masses (*MDa* v. 9; *Kirchenmusicalisches Jahrbuch*, v. 5)
    f.   Motets (*CW*, v. 14; *AC*, pt. 1, vols. 3-4)
    g.   Instrumental pieces (*HM*, v. 2, Bicinien; vols. 18, 19, Fantasies)
    h.   Organ pieces (*CO*, vols. 1, 2, 6, 9)
25.   Lechner, Leonhard
    a.   (*CE*) *Werke*, ed. Konrad Ameln. Kassel: Bärenreiter, 1954-
    b.   *Neue deutsche weltliche Lieder*, 1577. Kassel: Bärenreiter, 1954.
    c.   Five-voice lieder (*PAM*, v. 19; *AC*, pt. 2, v. 3)
    d.   *Deutsche Sprücke von Leben und Tod*, ed. Walther Lipphardt and Konrad Ameln. Kassel: Bärenreiter, 1929.
    e.   *Das Hohelied Salomonis*, ed. Walther Lipphardt and Konrad Ameln. Kassel: Bärenreiter, 1928.
26.   *Das Locheimer Liederbuch nebst der Aus Organisandi von Conrad Paumann*, ed. Friedrich Wilhelm Arnold. Wiesbaden: Dr. Martin Sändig oHG, 1969.
27.   Luther, Martin. *Deutsche Messe und Ordnung Gottes Diensts*, ed. Johannes Wolf (*Veröffentlichungen der Musik-Bibliothek*, ed. Paul Hirsch, ser. 1, v. 11)
28.   *Meistersinger*, ed. Friedrich Gennrich (*AM*, v. 2)
29.   Merian, Wilhelm. *Der Tanz in den deutschen Tabulaturbüchern . . . des 16. Jahrhunderts.*

Leipzig: Breitkopf & Härtel, 1927.

30. *Music of the Polish Renaissance*, ed. Józef M. Chomiński and Zofia Lissa. Cracow: National Printing Works, 1955.

31. Newsidler, Hans. Lute music, ed. Adolf Koczirz (*DTO*, v. 37)

32. *Erhart Oglin's Liederbuch*, ed. Robert Eitner and Julius J. Maier (*PAM*, v. 9)

33. Ott, Hans

    a. *Ein hundert fünfzehn weltliche und einige geistliche Lieder*, ed. Robert Eitner, Ludwig Erk and Otto Kade (*PAM*, vols. 1-4)

    b. *Lieder* from Ott's *Liederbuch*, ed. Arnold Geering, Wilhelm Altwegg (*EdM*, v. 15)

34. Paumann, Conrad. *Das Locheimer Liederbuch nebst der Aus Organisandi von Conrad Paumann*, ed. Friedrich Wilhelm Arnold. Wiesbaden: Dr. Martin Sändig oHG, 1969.

35. Rhau, Georg, publisher

    a. *Rhau, Georg, Musikdrucke aus den Jahren 1538 bis 1545*, 7 vols., ed. Hans Albrecht. Kassel: Bärenreiter, 1955-

    b. *Sacrorum hymnorum liber primus*, ed. Rudolf Gerber (*EdM*, vols. 21, 25)

    c. *Newe deudsche geistliche Gesange für die gemeinen Schulen*, ed. Johannes Wolf (*DdT*, v. 34)

    d. *Enchiridion utriusque Musicae practicae I*, ed. Hans Albrecht. (*DM*, ser. 1, v. 1)

    e. *Georg Rhaw's publications for vespers*, ed. Victor Mattfeld (*Musicological Studies*, v. 11)

36. *Schedelsches Liederbuch* (facsmilie, *EdM*, v. 84; transcription, *EdM*, vols. 74, 75)

37. Schmidt, Bernhard the Elder. Organ works (*CO*, vols. 1, 6, 9)

38. Schmidt, Bernhard the Younger

    a. *Tabulatur Buch* (*MMF*, ser. 1, v. 20; *BMB*, v. 52)

    b. Organ works (*CO*, vols. 6, 7, 12)

39. *Schatz des liturgischen Chor- und Gemeindegesangs*, 3 vols. 1865-1872.

40. *Peter Schöffer's Liederbuch*, fifteen German songs (*CW*, v. 29)

41. Senfl, Ludwig

    a. (*CE*) *Sämtliche Werke*, 7 vols. Wolfenbüttel: Möseler-Verlag. (vols. 1-4 are *EdM*, vols. 5, 10, 13, 15)

    b. *Werke*, v. 1, ed. Theodor Kroyer and Adolf Thürlings (*DTB*, v. 5)

    c. Sacred and secular songs (*PAM*, vols. 1-3; *AC*, pt. 2, v. 2)

    d. Sacred songs (*DdT*, v. 34; *AC*, pt. 1, v. 1; motets (*CW*, v. 62)

    e. Organ works (*CO*, v. 12; *LO*, v. 8)

42. Stolzer, Thomas

    a. Masses and motets (*EdM*, v. 22; *CW*, v. 74, Easter Mass; *CW*, v. 6, Paslm 37)

    b. *Sämtliche lateinische Hymnen und Psalmen* (*DdT*, v. 65)

    c. Sacred songs (*DdT*, v. 34; *AC*, pt. 1, v. 1); Secular songs (*AC*, pt. 2, v. 1)

43. Vaqueras, Bertrandus

    a. (*CE*) *Opera Omnia*, ed. Richard Sherr (*CMM*, 78)

    b. *Missa L'Homme armé* (*MPL*, ser. 1, v. 10)

44. Walter, Johann

    a. (*CE*) *Sämtliche Werke*, ed. Otto Schröder. Kassel: Bärenreiter.

    b. Canons (*HM*, v. 63)

    c. Sacred choral works (*AC*, pt. 1, v. 2); secular choral works (*AC*, pt. 2, v. 1)

    e. *Wittembergisch geistliche Gesangbuch*, ed. Otto Kade (*PAM*, v. 7)

45. Wolkenstein, Oswald von. *Geistliche und weltliche Lieder*, ed. Josef Schatz and Oswald Koller (*DTÖ*, v. 18)

OUTLINE XV

ENGLAND

Sacred Vocal Music – Secular Vocal Music – Instrumental Music

I. Sacred Vocal Music

A. The great era of English music begins with the Tudor period (1485-1603). The name comes from Owen Tudor, a Welsh nobleman, who married the widow of Henry V. The rulers of this period were Henry VII (reigned 1485-1509); Henry VIII (1509-1547), a Romanist at heart, who nevertheless established an independent church with himself as head; Edward VI (1547-1553), Protestant son of Henry VIII, who reigned under a regency from age ten (Thomas Cranmer, Archbishop of Canterbury, was one of the regents); Mary I [Mary Tudor] (1553-1558), a Catholic daughter of Henry VIII; and Elizabeth I (1558-1603), a Protestant daughter of Henry VIII. James I (1566-1625; reigned 1603-1625), son of Mary, Queen of Scots, was the first of the Jacobian rulers of the House of Stuart (1603-1714, except during the Commonwealth).

  1. After the break with Rome (1534) and during the reigns of Henry VI and Mary I until Elizabeth's ascent to the throne, English composers of church music went through a period of disorder and skepticism. With monasteries destroyed and schools and choirs disbanded, musicians were left without employment.

     a. One of the basic requirements of reform was that the Service should be in the vernacular. For a period of time until English became the official language of the Anglican Service, Latin continued to be used and therefore did not indicate for which Service, Catholic or Anglican, a composition was intended.

  2. When Elizabeth ascended the throne, the Anglican Church was Protestant; English church music in the form of Anthems and Services had its beginning with **Tye** and **Tallis**, even though these composers had written Latin polyphonic music earlier.

     a. About 1560 the anthem with English text developed from the Latin motet; it was syllabic and more harmonic than the motet; the phrases were shorter, the rhythm regular and emphasis was on the text.

     b. Settings for the "Service" included Morning Prayer (*Venite, Te Deum, Benedictus* or *Benedicite, Jubilate Deo*), Evening Prayer (*Magnificat, Nunc dimittis, Cantate Domino, Deus Miseratur*) and Communion (*Kyrie, Gloria, Credo, Sanctus, Benedictus, Agnus Dei*).

     c. The "Great" Service made use of the elaborate polyphonic motet style with phrase repetition in contrast to the "Short" Service which utilized a short, simple, syllabic style. Settings for the "Full" Service usually included all three Services.

B. Early Tudor composers are represented in the Eton manuscript which established the musical link between **Dunstable** and **Fayrfax** (*c*. 1450-*c*. 1500).

  1. The Eton Manuscript (*MB*, vols. 10-12)

     a. The choirbook originally contained 97 pieces representing 24 composers; only 54 pieces remain, not all in good condition. Included in the remaining pieces are 38 antiphons, 6 out of 24 Magnificats (*MB*, v. 12, pp. 63-111), a portion of a Passion by **Richard Davy** (*MB*, v. 12, p. 112) and **Robert Wylkynson's** 13-part setting of the Apostles' Creed (*MB*, v. 12, p. 135).

     b. The compositions may represent three periods or stages of the development of a florid style.

    1)   In stage I five-part writing in non-imitative polyphony is common. The full five-part sections often alternate with sections of a lesser number of voices. Compositions by **William Horwood, Gilbert Banester** and **Richard Hygons** represent the first stage.

        a)   **Richard Hygons,** *Salve regina* (*MB*, v. 11, p. 39)

    2)   Stage II, represented by **John Browne, Walter Lambe** and **Richard Davy,** shows frequent use of imitation, more dramatic setting of the text, greater variety of parts, more frequent use of plainsong *cantus firmi* and occasional use of simultaneous cross relations.

        a)   **John Browne,** *Stabat Mater* (*MB*, v. 10, p. 43)

    3)   The third stage, represented by **Cornysh** and **Fayrfax,** shows a more conservative style, frequent points of imitation, lack of plainsong *cantus firmi* and use of simpler vocal lines.

        a)   **William Cornysh,** *Ave Maria mater Dei* (*MB*, v. 12, p. 57; *TECM*, v. 1, p. 150; *Magnificat*: *EECM*, v. 4, p. 49)

C.   In pre-Reformation England, Masses may be divided into two groups which correspond to the Great and Short Services of the Anglican Church of a later period. The idea, fostered by the Council of Trent, called for a *Missa brevis*, a shorter, simpler type of Mass in contrast to the large polyphonic Masses which were composed particularly for festive occasions in large churches.

D.   Tudor composers

  1.   **Robert Fayrfax** (*c.* 1460-1521) (*CE* [*CMM*, 17])

    a.   The most representative of early Tudor composers, **Fayrfax** was organist at St. Albans Abbey, received the Doctor of Music degree at Cambridge University (1504) and the first similar degree at Oxford University (1511).

    b.   Included in his sacred works are 6 Masses (*CE*, v. 1), 2 Magnificats and 12 motets (*CE*, v. 2); several secular songs are in *CE*, v. 3.

    c.   In the Masses, **Fayrfax** relies on several *cantus firmi, e. g. Regali ex progenie* (*CE*, v. 1, p. 104) and *Tecum principium* (*CE*, v. 1, p. 137; *CW*, v. 97) on antiphons (*LU*, pp. 1626 and 412 respectively). *O bone Jesu* (*CE*, v. 1, p. 1) is a parody Mass on his own Magnificat (*CE*, v. 2, p. 12). *Albanus Mass* (*CE*, v. 1, p. 33) uses the nine notes which set the word *"Albanus"* in the antiphon for the feast of St. Albans.

      1)   In general **Fayrfax** uses an *incipit* of the *cantus firmus* to open each movement of his festival Masses.

    d.   The motets consist generally of several sections sung by a varying number of voices.

      1)   *Ave Dei Patris Filia* (*CE*, v. 2, p. 36)

      2)   *Magnificat: Regale* (*CE*, v. 2, p. 1; *TECM*, v. 1, p. 154) also varies the vocal texture by changing the number of voices.

  2.   **John Taverner** (*c.* 1494-1545) (*TCM*, vols. 1, 3)

    a.   As a boy **Taverner** was a member of the choir at Collegiate Church at Tattershall; in 1524 he became Master of the Choristers. From 1525 to 1530 he was organist at Wolseys Cardinal College, now Christ Church, Oxford. By this time he had become a master of the Franco-Flemish polyphonic style. In 1530 he joined the Reformation movement and spent the remainder of his life promoting religious persecution; he wrote no more music.

    b.   **Taverner** wrote 8 Masses in four, five and six (*EECM*, v. 20) voices, 3 Magnificats, one each in four, five and six voices (*TECM*, v. 1, p. 197) and about 30 motets in three to six voices.

    c.   **Taverner's** Masses omit the Kyrie and the texts of the Credos have a variety of deletions. In his larger works, imitation, sequence, canon and ostinato all contribute to a well-balanced florid texture. Long melismas and alternating polyphony and chant are common. In the shorter works **Taverner** uses less elaborate procedures; he relies on chordal, imitative and antiphonal writing.

1)   Two-part canon is used in the six-voice *O Michaell* Mass (*EECM*, v. 20, p. 170; *TCM*, v. 1, p. 194).

   a)   Canon occurs in the Gloria: *qui tollis, TCM*, v. 1, p. 197; Credo: *filium Dei*, p. 204; Sanctus: *Gloria tua*, p. 214; Benedictus: *Benedictus*, p. 216; Agnus Dei: *Agnus Dei* (III), p. 222.

2)   The *Gloria tibi Trinitas* Mass (*EECM*, v. 20, p. 1; *TCM*, v. 1, p. 126) is based on plainsong (*LU*, p. 914).

   a)   Many instrumental pieces named *"In nomine"* are based on the antiphon *Gloria tibi Trinitas* even though the words do not appear in the text of the antiphon. In reality, the text *"In nomine"* does appear as a part of the *Benedictus* of this Mass and the instrumental transcriptions of the passage (*TCM*, v. 1, p. 148) in the **Taverner** Mass have caused the two to be associated for a long time.

  d.   *The Western Wynde* Mass (*TCM*, v. 1, p. 3)

   1)   Based on an English folk tune (*HAM*, No. 112a), the Mass consists of 36 variations, nine in each of the four movements; many variation techniques are used.

   2)   *Benedictus* (*HAM*, No. 112b; *TCM*, v. 1, p. 20)

   3)   *Agnus Dei* (*TECM*, v. 1, p. 188; *TCM*, v. 1, p. 23)

3. **John Merbecke** [Marbeck] (1523-*c.* 1585)

  a.   **Merbecke** was organist at St. George's, Windsor, from 1541 to his death. After barely escaping execution for Calvinistic interests (1544), he espoused Protestantism, wrote no more Latin church music and applied himself to theological endeavors; he wrote the first concordance to the complete English Bible and the *Book of Common Prayer noted.*

  b.   *Booke of Common Praier noted,* 1550

   1)   This is the first complete musical setting (*"noted"*) of the *Book of Common Prayer,* 1549. Designed for unison congregational singing without accompaniment, the melodies, some originally composed, are in general simple adaptations of familiar plainsongs.

   2)   **Merbecke** applied a system of rhythmic values to the melodies; therefore they are not purely mensural nor are they true plainsong. Accommodating the accentuation of English text, the melodies are set syllabically throughout and incorporate many leaps.

  c.   In 1552 the second Book of Common Prayer of Edward VI was issued without **Merbecke's** music. Not until the Oxford movement of 1833 and its resulting activities later in the century was **Merbecke's** contribution revived for use. Choral settings for the Service, beginning with **Tye** and **Tallis**, replaced **Merbecke's** work.

  d.   Motets: *Ave Dei Patris* (*TCM*, v. 10, p. 215); *Domine Jesu Christe* (*TCM*, v. 10, p. 200)

  e.   *Missa Per arma justitiae* (*TCM*, v. 10, p. 165)

4. **Christopher Tye** (*c.* 1500-1573)

  a.   **Tye** grew up as a singer in the choir of King's College, Cambridge. For twenty years (1541-1561) he was Master of the Choristers of Ely Cathedral. Later he became rector of Doddington on the Isle of Ely and died there.

  b.   His Latin church music includes 4 Masses (*EECM*, v. 24) and 20 motets (*RRMR*, v. 14).

   1)   *Missa The Western Wynde* (*RRMR*, v. 13, p. 69), like that of **Taverner**, uses the variation idea; the tune is repeated 29 times in the alto.

   2)   *Missa Euge bone* (*OEE*, v. 10; *RRMR*, v. 13, p. 17)

   a)   The Sanctus opens with fermata chords (*OEE*, v. 10, p. 32) and later the superius divides into *gymel* and the three lowest voices rest (*OEE*, v. 10, p. 35).

  c.   **Tye's** English church music includes 15 anthems and *Acts of the Apostles.* His anthems are generally polyphonic in style, with chordal passages distributed among free imitative sections.

1)   *I will exalt thee* (*EECM* v. 19, p. 125)
2)   *Acts of the Apostles*, 1553 (*EECM*, v. 19, pp. 274-315;   *B* 16, pp. 343-373)
   a)   Chapters of the Book of Acts are set in 14 four-part settings in simple style, incorporating some imitation.

5.   **Thomas Tallis** (*c*. 1505-1585)
  a.   **Tallis** was organist at Waltham Abbey until its termination (1540). He then served in the Royal Chapel until his death. In 1575 Queen Elizabeth granted him and **William Byrd** a 21-year monopoly for printing music, the first of its kind.
  b.   **Tallis'** Latin church music includes 2 Masses, Office hymns, Lamentations, 2 Magnificats and some 30 motets. **Tallis** and **Byrd** published 19 of the motets in their *Cantiones sacrae*, 1575, the first printed English music with Latin texts.
    1)   The style is rather uneven and lacks uniformity; at times there are frequent short sections and changes in the number of voices; there is little continuous imitation. **Tallis'** structural and polyphonic high point is his 40-voice (8 five-part choruses) *Spem in alium* (*TCM*, v. 6, p. 299), in which the opening consists of 20 imitative entrances of the same theme.
    2)   *Audivi vocem* (I heard a voice) (*TCM*, v. 6, p. 90; *HAM*, No. 127)
    3)   *In manus tuas, Domine* (Psalm 31:6) (*TCM*, v. 6, p. 202; *GMB*, No. 129)
  c.   **Tallis'** English church music includes 17 anthems (*EECM*, v. 12, pp. 1-54) which, in general, follow the simple, syllabic style suggested by Archbishop Cranmer. In addition there is service music (*EECM*, v. 13) and several motets which have had the Latin texts replaced with English words (*EECM*, v. 12, pp. 55-94); in these cases the anthems show more of the traditional polyphonic, imitative style.
    1)   *Blessed be Thy name* (*EECM*, v. 12, p. 55) is adapted from *Mihi autem nimis* (*TCM*, v. 6, p. 204).
  d.   Other English church music includes 2 Services, one a four-voice Short Service in Dorian mode (*M* 51, v. 1, p. 1) and the other a five-voice Full Service, 3 sets of Psalms (10 in all), Preces, Responses, Litanies and 8 Psalm tunes printed in Archbishop Matthew Parker's *The whole Psalter translated into English metre*, 1567, but never sold.
6.   **Robert White** (*c*. 1530-1574) (*TCM*, v. 5)
  a.   **White**, the son-in-law of **Tye**, succeeded **Tye** at Ely Cathedral and about 1570 became organist of Westminster Abbey.
  b.   Most of **White's** extant works are sacred pieces; included are 20 Latin motets and 4 English anthems.
    1)   *Lamentations* for five voices (*TCM*, v. 5, p. 14)
7.   **William Byrd** (1543-1623) (*CE*)
  a.   **Byrd**, a pupil of **Tallis**, was the greatest composer of the English Renaissance. Although he held positions in the Anglican Church, he remained a Catholic throughout his life. From 1563 to 1572 he was organist at Lincoln Cathedral and in 1570 was employed by the Chapel Royal; from 1572 to **Tallis'** death (1585), **Tallis** shared the position of chapel organist with him. When **Tallis** died **Byrd** became the sole owner of the printing monopoly.
  b.   **Byrd**, a versatile musician, wrote all types of music (choral, vocal solo, virginal and chamber music), but was at his best in church music. For the Catholic services he wrote 3 Masses, 2 books of *Gradualia*, his part with **Tallis** of the *Cantiones sacrae* (1575) in addition to 2 other volumes by himself (1589, 1591) and many motets in three to six, eight and nine voices.
    1)   The 3 Masses (in three, four and five voices) (*CE*, v. 1), 1605, make use of the "motto" idea for most of the movements; no *cantus firmus* is identifiable.
    2)   *Cantiones quae ab argumento sacrae vocantur*, 1575 (*CE*, v. 1, p. 119)
     a)   A variety of imitative and canonic techniques is used: crab canon in the eight-voice *Diliges Dominum* (*CE*, v. 1, p. 232; *TCM*. v. 9, p. 149), double canon at

the fourth in the six-voice *Miserere mihi, Domine* (*CE*, v. 1, p. 240; *TCM*, v. 9, p. 129) on the antiphon (*LU*, p. 266) and mirror canon in *Quomodo cantabimus* (*CE*, v. 9, p. 99; *TCM*, v. 9, p. 283).

3) *Cantiones sacrae*, Book I, 1589; Book II, 1591 (*CE*, vols. 2, 3)

    a) Containing a total of 61 compositions, these two books have only two examples of *cantus firmus* technique (*CE*, v. 2, p. 139 [*MAS* v. 6, p. 83]; *CE*, v. 3, p. 150).

    b) A careful setting of words, text painting and interesting uses of melodic intervals are noticeable.

4) *Gradualia*, Book I, 1605; Book II, 1607 (*CE*, vols. 4-7; *TCM*, v. 7; *SR*, pp. 327-330)

    a) The two books contain 109 pieces, not only Graduals but pieces for other parts of Offices and Masses. In from three to six voices, a variety of vocal registrations are used in addition to the normal dispersions: SAATB, SSST, ATB, AATB, TTBB, AATBB.

    b) In Book II particularly, there are interesting examples of text painting.

    c) *Non vos relinquam* (I will not leave thee comfortless) (*CE*, v. 7, p. 66; *TCM*, v. 7, p. 318; *HAM*, No. 150)

c. With **Byrd** we have the first appearance of what is known as a "verse" anthem or Service (Service II, *CE*, v. 10, p. 108; *TCM*, v. 2, p. 99); it consists of solo passages with instrumental accompaniment (organ or viols) alternating with sections for full choir. The "full" anthem is for chorus throughout.

d. Included in **Byrd's** music for the Anglican Church are 4 Services (*CE*, v. 10, pp. 52-252; *TCM*, v. 2, pp. 51-222), many anthems and 3 large collections of 114 pieces in all, both sacred and secular: *Psalmes, Sonets, & songs of sadnes and pietie*, 1588 (*CE*, v. 12; *EM*, v. 14); *Songs of sundrie natures*, 1589 (*CE*, v. 13; *EM*, v. 15); *Psalmes, Songs and Sonnets*, 1611 (*CE*, v. 14); these are for one to six voices, the majority for five voices and some with instrumental accompaniment.

1) *The Great Service* (*CE*, v. 10, p. 136; *TCM*, v. 2, p. 123)

2) *Christ rising again* (*CE*, v. 13, p. 280; *HAM*, No. 151) is a verse anthem published in **Byrd's** *Songs of sundrie natures*.

8. **Thomas Tomkins** (1571-1656)

a. A pupil of **Bryd**, **Tomkins** became organist at Worcester Cathedral about 1596; in 1621 he became a member of the Chapel Royal but continued his responsibilities at Worcester until 1646.

b. Although **Tomkins** lived well into the 17th century, his style is basically polyphonic and adheres to the musical concepts common among composers of the late Renaissance in England.

c. *Musica Deo Sacra et Ecclesiae Anglicanae: or, Musick dedicated to the Honor and Service of God, and To the Use of Cathedral and other Churches of England, Especially of the Chapell-Royal of King Charles the First*, printed posthumously in 1668 (*EECM*, vols. 5, 8, only 25 anthems)

1) This contains 5 Services (*TCM*, v. 8, pp. 17-250), two of which are "short" four-voice Services and two are "verse" Services with rather elaborate organ accompaniments with the solo passages.

2) Also included are 93 anthems, 52 of which are "full" anthems in which **Tomkins** maintains a high quality of polyphonic writing. Forty-one are "verse" anthems.

3) Thirteen anthems (*RRMR*, v. 4)

d. *Songs of 3, 4, 5 and 6 Parts*, 1622 (*EM*, v. 18)

1) A collection of 28 pieces, predominately secular, for three to six voices, this includes canzonets, balletts, madrigals, sacred songs and metrical versions of Scripture. **Tomkins** dedicated each of these compositions to a different person: a relative, friend or colleague.

2) *When David heard that Absolum was dead*, II Samuel 18:33 (*EM*, v. 18, p. 112; *HAM*, No. 191)

9. **Orlando Gibbons** (1583-1625)

   a. **Gibbons** came from a musical family; in 1596 he became a choir boy at King's College, Cambridge; he later became organist at the Chapel Royal (1605) and Westminster Abbey (1623). **Gibbons** is the last great composer of the English Renaissance. He was a master of rhythm, imitation and the melodic line.

   b. **Gibbons** composed secular music for keyboard, instrumental and vocal ensembles and sacred anthems and hymns for the Anglican Church only (*EECM*, vols. 3, 21; *TCM*, v. 4). Of the 40 anthems, 15 are full anthems and, like **Tomkins**, reveal his better work.

   c. *Almighty and Everlasting God* (*TCM*, v. 4, p. 126)

     1) This anthem in motet style was considered "vicious" in **Gibbons'** day; the expositions begin at words 1) "Almighty," 2) "mercifully," 3) "and in all," 4) "Stretch forth," 5) "through Christ." Each of the five themes is rhythmically and melodically individual; the same word is not sung by all four parts until the close; theme 2 appears near the close.

   d. *O Lord, increase my faith* (*TCM*, v. 4, p. 270; *HAM*, No. 171)

     1) **Gibbons** has used the characteristics of the full anthem but developed them in a short, simple way.

   e. *This is the record of John*, John 1:19-23 (*EECM*, v. 3, p. 179; *TCM*, v. 4, p. 297; *HAM*, No. 172)

     1) Reese says "of **Gibbons'** verse anthem, [this] . . . is probably the best." The narrative verse text (solo) is repeated by the full chorus but with different music. The accompaniment to the "verse" sections of **Gibbons'** anthems are often elaborate and at times distracting.

II.   Secular Vocal Music

A. Pre-madrigal composers

   1. Secular polyphony, other than carols, had its beginning in the English Renaissance by many early Tudor composers, among them **King Henry VIII, Robert Fayrfax, William Cornysh, Thomas Farthyng** (*c.* 1475-1520). These are represented in the British Museum Add. Ms. 31922 (*MB*, v. 18), which contains 109 pieces, including 24 instrumental consorts.

     a. **Robert Fayrfax** (*c.* 1465-1521) (*CE* [*CMM*, 17])

       1) *Sum what musying* (*CE*, v. 3, p. 12; *MB*, v. 18, p. 90)

     b. **William [John?] Cornysh** (1465-1523), 11 songs in Ms. 31922 (*MB*, v. 18)

       1) *Adew Adew my hartis lust* (*MB*, v. 18, p. 17; *HAM*, No. 86a)

       2) *Blow Thy horne hunter* (*AERM*, p. 199)

     c. **King Henry VIII** (1491-1547), 22 songs in Ms. 31922 (*MB*, v. 18)

     d. **Robert Cooper** (*fl.* 1494-1516)

       1) *I have bene a foster* (*MB*, v. 18, p. 48; *HAM*, No. 86b)

B. First period of madrigal composers

   1. One of the earliest known true madrigals is **Richard Edwards'** (d. 1566) *In goinge to my naked bedde* (*c.* 1555) (*MB*, v. 1, p. 60; *EM*, v. 36, Part 4, p. 4; *InM*, v. 2, p. 22). Points of imitation and chordal passages alternate; Italian influence is suggested. Other evidence of early madrigals is found in the incomplete *Songes to three, fower, and five voyces*, 1571, 76 songs by **Thomas Whythorne** (12 songs in *M* 52).

   2. The English Madrigal School began seriously in 1588 with the publication of **Byrd's** first book of songs (see 5. b. below), the first printed collection of English madrigals, and *Musica Transalpina*, the first printed collection of Italian madrigals with English translations, 55 by Italian or Italo-Flemish composers and two by **Byrd**.

a.   In 1597 Nicholas Yonge, the compiler of the first *Musica Transalpina*, published
under the same name another collection of 24 Italian madrigals with English translations.

3.   The madrigals are usually in five parts, in imitative polyphonic style with some chordal
writing, similar to the motets of the period. There is a close affinity between the music
and the text and expressive qualities of the text are brought out in the music (text
painting). Diatonicism in both harmony and melody is the norm; a certain tunefulness
is always apparent. The parts are printed in separate part books.

4.   The texts, in general, are light and do not exhibit the strong literary qualities found in
the Italian madrigals. The poetry of significant English writers is lacking.

5.   **William Byrd** (1543-1623)

a.   **Byrd** is the first English composer to realize the importance of the madrigal. He
continued the English tradition with less Italian influence than other madrigalists.

b.   *Psalmes, Sonets, & songs of sadnes and pietie*, 1588 (*CE*, v. 12; *EM*, v. 14)

1)   The 35 five-voice songs are divided into three groups: 1) *Psalms* (Nos. 1-10),
2) *Sonnets and Pastorals* (Nos. 11-26) and 3) *Songs of Sadness and Piety* (Nos.
27-33). Included are two funeral songs by **Sir Philip Sidney** (Nos. 34-35).

2)   **Byrd** explains that these sacred and secular songs, mostly strophic, were originally
composed for solo voice and instruments but now the four instrumental parts
have been arranged for voices. The "first singing part" is distinct from the others.

3)   *Though Amaryllis dance in green* (*CE*, v. 12, p. 60; *EM*, v. 14, p. 60)

a)   The *"Sonet"* in two parts has five stanzas sung to the same music. Unusual
rhythmic independence makes use of 3/2 (measure 1) and 6/4 (measure 2)
rhythm alternately and then together (*hemiola*) (measures 6-7); in the second
section 3/2 rhythm is gradually established. Although contrapuntal in style,
the work is basically harmonic with little imitation and few passing dissonances; there is frequent use of the 4-3 suspension.

c.   *Songs of sundrie natures*, 1589 (*CE*, v. 13; *EM*, v. 15)

1)   The 47 songs range from two to six voices. No. 41, *What made thee Hob?* (*CE*,
v. 13, p. 241; *EM*, v. 15, p. 241) is a dialogue between two shepherds for two
tenors and has string accompaniment.

d.   *Psalmes, Songs, and Sonnets*, 1611 (*CE*, v. 14; *EM*, v. 16)

1)   The last two of these 32 songs are for solo voice with viol accompaniment.

2)   Like the foregoing collection, these songs are for three to six voices (except for
the two solo songs) and are sacred as well as secular.

6.   Other composers who followed the spirit of **Byrd** by composing madrigals in the old
style are **John Mundy** in his *Songs and Psalmes*, 1594 (*EM*, v. 35b; see *InM*, v. 1, p.
51), **Richard Carlton** in his *Madrigals to Five Voices*, 1601 (*EM*, v. 27), **Richard Alison**
in his *An Howre's Recreation in Musicke*, 1606 (*EM*, v. 33) and **Orlando Gibbons** in
his *The First Set of Madrigals and Motetts of 5. Parts: apt for Viols and Voyces*, 1612
(*EM*, v. 5).

7.   **Thomas Morley** (1557-1603)

a.   **Morley's** madrigals follow the general style of the classic Italian madrigal. His five
sets were of strong influence to all succeeding English madrigalists.

b.   *The First Booke of Canzonets to Two Voices*, 1595 (*EM*, v. 1)

1)   **Morley** here borrows many characteristics of the Italian *canzonetta*: a short
piece, light and delicate in texture, generally humorous and witty, sudden alternation of quick and slow sections and short motifs intermingling among the
voices. This book was issued in both English and Italian versions. Most of the
texts are translations of Italian poems.

2)   *Arise gett upp my deere* (*EM*, v. 1, p. 101)

a)   This elaborate madrigal in **Morley's** personal narrative style tells the story of a
country wedding.

    c.   *Madrigalls to Foure Voyces*, 1594 (*EM*, v. 2)

        1)   Similar to the *Canzonets*, these also contain some serious and more narrative madrigals. This is the first collection published in England to be named "madrigals" (see *InM*, v. 2, pp. 6, 9, 16).

    d.   *The First Booke of Balletts to Five Voyces*, 1595 (*EM*, v. 4)

        1)   Particularly successful are the *Balletts* with "fa-la" refrains which are modelled on **Gastoldi's** *Balletti a cinque voci*, 1591 (*LP*, v. 10). The ballets are strongly rhythmical, more homophonic than the madrigals and the "fa-la" refrains are often danced.

        2)   *My bonny lass* (*EM*, v. 4, p. 23; *HAM*, No. 159)

            a)   Compare with **Gastoldi**, *L'Acceso* (*HAM*, No. 158; *LP*, v. 10, p. 51)

    e.   *Canzonets or Little Short Aers to five and sixe Voices*, 1597 (*EM*, v. 3; see *InM*, v. 1, pp. 16, 32)

    f.   *The Triumphes of Oriana*, 1601 (*EM*, v. 32)

        1)   The collection of 25 five- and six-voice pieces by 24 English composers was edited by **Morley** and imitated the collection of Italian madrigals *Il trionfo di Dori*, 1592, published by the Venetian Gardano. In honor of Queen Elizabeth, each madrigal closes with the refrain "Long live fair Oriana," which corresponds to *"Viva la bella Dori"* in Gardano's anthology.

            a)   **Morley's** second entry, *Hard by a crystle fountain* (*EM*, v. 32, p. 238), is his English adaptation of **Giovanni Croce's** *Ove tra l'herb' ei fiori*.

    g.   *Plaine and Easie Introduction to Practicall Music*, 1597; second edition, 1608; third edition, 1771 (*MMF*, Ser. 2, v. 113)

        1)   Written in dialogue form, this is one of the most important sources of information about Elizabethan music and musical life; included are sections on notation, counterpoint and madrigal writing.

C.   Second period of madrigal composers

   1.   The composers of this period developed in the madrigal a more serious composition; they followed the Italian models of **Gesualdo** and particularly **Marenzio**.

   2.   **Thomas Weelkes** (*c.* 1575-1623)

    a.   One of the greatest and most individualistic English madrigalists (94 madrigals), **Weelkes** was strongly influenced by the Italians, **Marenzio** in particular. Chromatic melodic lines, experimental harmonies and dramatic expressiveness develop a subtle and refined style.

    b.   *Madrigals to 3. 4. 5. & 6. voyces*, 1597 (*EM*, v. 9; see *InM*, v. 1, p. 55; v. 2, p. 32)

        1)   These 24 madrigals are relatively light but of sound character.

    c.   *Balletts and Madrigals to five voyces*, 1598 (*EM*, v. 10; *OEE*, vols. 13-15)

        1)   *Hark, all ye lovely saints* (*EM*, v. 10, p. 32; *HAM*, No. 170)

    d.   *Madrigals of 5. and 6. parts, apt for the Viols and voices*, 1600 (*EM*, v. 11)

        1)   *O care thou wilt dispatch mee* (*EM*, v. 11, p. 19)

            a)   In the second part (*EM*, v. 11, p. 26) the text describes a person who, burdened with "cruel care," looks to Music, the "sick man's Jewel," to comfort him.

            b)   This madrigal which represents harmonic experimentation and interesting chord relationships is in two parts; each part is divided into four short sections alternating between slow and fast music according to the text. The second part, "Hence care, thou art too cruel" is even more chromatic than the first part; note the very unusual use of A-sharp (meas. 7). The theme of the second section ("come music") is echoed in diminution in the "fa-las" that follow; the word "sustain" is illustrated by a pedal point.

    e.   *Ayres or Phantasticke Spirites for three voices*, 1608 (*EM*, v. 13; see *InM*, v. 1, pp. 2, 22, 42; v. 3, pp. 4, 16; *OEE*, vols. 16, 17)

        1)   *The Ape, the Monkey and Baboone did meet* (*EM*, v. 13, p. 24; *MMRL*, p. 84)

3.   **John Wilbye** (1574-1638)

a.   **Wilbye's** 65 madrigals are among the finest of English or Continental composers. Having a clear sensitivity to the work of **Marenzio, Wilbye** reset several of **Marenzio's** texts. He is particularly imaginative in setting English text; the text-painting always seems appropriate. The use of sequence and pedal points reinforce the concept of tonality.

b.   *First Set of English Madrigals to 3. 4. 5. and 6. voices*, 1598 (*EM*, v. 6; see *InM*, v. 1, p. 44; v. 2, p. 50)

c.   *Second Set of Madrigales to 3. 4. 5. and 6. parts apt both for Voyals and Voyces*, 1609 (*EM*, v. 7)

1)   *Happy, oh happy he* (*EM*, v. 7, p. 82)

4.   **Orlando Gibbons** (1583-1625)

a.   *The First Set of Madrigals and Mottets of 5. parts: apt for Viols and Voyces*, 1612 (*EM*, v. 5)

1)   *The Silver Swan* (*EM*, v. 5, p. 1)

a)   This is characteristically serious treatment of a fine "moral" text. There are three sections of seven measures each: A B B. Themes are developed in the four lower voices and the chief melody is the upper voice. Techniques included are complete chords, passing tones, suspensions, anticipations, augmented fifth chords (meas. 10, 17, on the word "death").

b.   *Cries of London* (*M* 20) is a fantasie for five strings and voices. Seventy-seven street cries are sung, depicting life in London from early morning until late at night. Different voices sing the cries in succession while the instruments continue playing. The instrumental parts use the *"In nomine"* theme based on the plainsong *Gloria tibi Trinitas*, as a *cantus firmus*.

5.   Other collections of madrigals, canzonets and ballets may be found in *The English Madrigalists*: **John Mundy** (1594), v. 35b; **George Kirbye** (1597), v. 24; **William Holborne** (1597), v. 36; **Giles Farnaby** (1598), v. 20; **Michael Cavendish** (1598), v. 36; **John Farmer** (1599), v. 8; **John Bennett** (1599), v. 23; **Richard Carlton** (1601), v. 27; **Michael East** (1604), vols. 29, 30, 31a, 31b; **Thomas Greaves** (1604), v. 36; **Robert Jones** (1607), v. 35a; **Henry Lichfield** (1613), v. 17; **Francis Pilkington** (1613), vols. 25, 26; **John Ward** (1613), v. 19; **Thomas Vautor** (1619), v. 34; **Thomas Tomkins** (1622), v. 18.

D.   Songs and ayres

1.   The ayres are simple and popular English songs derived from the Italian *canzonet* and *balletto*.

a.   Ayres may be in a variety of styles and textures; strophic or through-composed, homophonic or rhythmic and imitative.

b.   The song is planned for various methods of performance; the upper voice predominates and the lower voices may also be sung or played on the lute or viols. As a practical arrangement, the music of the solo part, text and lute tablature is printed on the left-hand page; the other instrumental or vocal parts are printed on the right-hand page. The barring is irregular and inconsistent.

1)   The bass viol often played the bass line with the lute, and the virginals began to be used for accompaniment.

2.   **John Dowland** (1563-1626)

a.   An original and progressive composer, **Dowland** became the most famous Elizabethan lutenist song writer.

b.   *First Booke of Songes or Ayres*, 1597 (*EL*, Ser. 1, vols. 1, 2; *ELS*, v. 4, No. 14; see *InM*, v. 2, p. 20)

c.   *Second Booke of Songes or Ayres*, 1600 (*EL*, Ser. 1, vols. 5, 6; *ELS*, v. 4, No. 16)

d.   *The Third and Last Booke of Songs or Aires*, 1603 (*EL*, Ser. 1, vols. 10, 11; *ELS*, v. 4, No. 17)

  1) *What if I never speed* (*EL*, Ser. 1, vols. 10-11, p. 18; *HAM*, No. 163; *ELS*, v. 4, No. 17, piece No. IX)

e. *A Pilgrime's Solace* (Fourth Book of Aires), 1612 (*EL*, Ser. 1, vols. 12, 14; *ELS*, v. 4, No. 19)

  1) In addition there are three lute songs included in his son's (**Robert Dowland**) *A Musicall Banquet*, 1610 (*EL*, Ser. 1, vol. 14, pp. 73-84; *ELS*, v. 4, No. 19, pieces No. VIII, IX, X).

f. **Andreas Ornithoparchus [Vogelsang]**, *Musicae activae micrologus*, Leipzig, 1516, was translated into English by **John Dowland** and published in London in 1606 (*B* 34).

3. **John Danyel** (*c*. 1565-1630)

  a. *Songs for lute, viol and voice*, 1606 (*EL*, Ser. 2, v. 8)

  1) *Stay, cruell, stay* (*EL*, Ser. 2, v. 8, p. 18; *HAM*, No. 162; *ELS*, v. 3, No. 13, song No. VII)

4. **Thomas Campion** (1567-1620)

  a. A prolific composer of lute songs, **Campion** wrote four books of aires; two were published in 1613 and two in 1617 (*EL*, Ser. 2, vols, 1, 2, 10, 11; *ELS*, v. 2, Nos. 4, 5). In addition he published another book of aires in conjunction with **Philip Rosseter** in 1601 (*EL*, Ser. 1, vols. 4, 13; *ELS*, v. 9, No. 36)

  b. **Campion** was more distinguished as a poet than as a composer; he wrote the texts for all his aires. His melodies are attractive and the accompaniments are in a simple style (see *InM*, v. 1, p. 4; v. 2, p. 12).

5. Popular music, distinguished from art music, was manifest in catches and ballads sung by minstrels and others unskilled to perform madrigals. For the largest collection of these songs we are indebted to **Thomas Ravenscroft's** (*c*. 1587-*c*. 1635) three printed catch books.

  a. *Pammelia*, 1609 (*M* 36b, c)

  1) The earliest printed collection of catches, it contains 100 rounds and catches of three to ten parts in one, some with sacred text, either Latin or English.

  b. *Deuteromelia*, 1609, subtitled *"Qui canere potest canat"* (Catch, that catch can) (*M* 36c)

  1) This collection of 31 pieces in three and four voices includes, possibly for the first time in print, the famous round *Three Blind Mice* (*M* 36c, p. 74).

  c. *Melismata*, 1611 (*M* 36a, c)

  1) In addition to nine rounds, there are four "conceits" (*M* 36c, pp. 126-135), little non-imitative, homophonic part songs.

6. In addition to the three above publications, two others establish **Ravenscroft** as a unique figure among Elizabethan composers; not only wishing to satisfy the taste of the masses, he was also capable as a serious and educated musician.

  a. *A Brief Discourse of the true (but neglected) use of Charact'ring the Degrees*, 1614 (*MMF*, Ser. 2, v. 22)

  1) Including quotations from various writers on music, such as **Glareanus, Ornithoparchus, Dunstable** and **Morley, Ravenscroft** discusses mensural notation and composed examples for illustration.

  b. *The whole Booke of Psalmes with the Hymnes Evangelicall and Songs Spirituall*, 1621

  1) There are 105 harmonizations (51 by **Ravenscroft**); only 28 had appeared before. Other composers who contributed to the Psalter include **Farnaby, Dowland, Michael Cavendish, John Milton, Tallis, Tomkins** and 14 others.

III. Instrumental Music

A. The English virginal school (1560-1620)

1. More than 600 pieces for virginals are extant; they include dances (pavanes, galliardes, allemandes), variations on popular melodies and ground basses, liturgical organ pieces, preludes, descriptive pieces, fantasies and transcriptions of vocal pieces.

   a. The most prominent members of the school are **Byrd**, **Bull** and **Gibbons**. The early development of the instrumental style incorporated rapid scale passages, repeated chords and ornamentation.

2. The term "virginal" was used for all quilled keyboard instruments; the most common was the rectangular "spinet" type. The term "virginal" appears in **Sebastian Virdung's** *Musica getutscht* (*PAM*, v. 11, pp. B, C iii), 1511, and in **Martin Agricola's** *Musica instrumentalis deudsch* (*PAM*, v. 20, p. 54), 1528. As used in England, "single" or "double" virginals, the term referred to the compass of the instrument; notes below G were designated with "double" letters (FF, EE, *etc*.) and notes above G with "single" letters. The virginals did not employ stops and the double keyboards were used for transposition.

3. The virginal had a normal compass of four octaves, chromatic except for the lowest octave which was often a "short" octave.

   a. The "short" octave, also used on the organ, substituted other notes for the little-used C-sharp, D-sharp, F-sharp and G-sharp: *e. g.* C F F# G G# A B♭ B

   became in the "short" octave C F D G E A B♭ B.

   b. Difficult or impossible stretches in the bass on a regular keyboard are easy on the "short" octave keyboard (*FVB*, v. 1, p. 287).

4. Early collections of music for virginals

   a. *Mulliner Book* (*c.* 1545-*c.* 1585) (*MB*, v. 1) (contents: *GD*, fifth edition, v. 5, pp. 996-998)

      1) Compiled by Thomas Mulliner, this collection contains 120 pieces primarily for organ. It includes settings of plainsong and psalm tunes, dances and vocal transcriptions. Composers included are **Redford** with 35 pieces, **Tallis** (18), **Blithemann** (15), **Shepherd** (8), **Allwood** (5) and several others.

      2) Eleven pieces for cittern and gittern are included.

   b. Hans F. Redlich in the article "Virginal Music, Collections of." (*GD*, fifth edition, v. 9, pp. 4-16) gives the contents of the following early collections.

   c. *My Ladye Nevell's Booke*, 1591 (*M* 30)

      1) Copied out by John Baldwin, this contains 42 pieces by **William Byrd** for his pupil Lady Nevill.

   d. *Fitzwilliam Virginal Book, c.* 1620 (*M* 19)

      1) The 297 compositions represent almost every composer of the period; **Byrd** has 72 pieces; **Bull**, 44; **Farnaby**, 54; **Morley**, 9; **Philips**, 19; **Tallis**, 2; **Gibbons**, 2; and many others.

      a) **Sweelinck** is represented with 4 pieces.

      2) Included are dances, organ pieces, arrangements of popular songs and madrigals, variations on the hexachord, fantasies and preludes.

   e. *Benjamin Cosyn's Virginal Book, c.* 1620 (*M* 46)

      1) The 98 pieces are primarily by **Cosyn, Bull** and **Gibbons**.

   f. *Will. Forster's Virginal Book*, 1624

      1) This contains 78 pieces, almost all of which are by **Byrd**.

   g. *Parthenia or The Maydenhead*, 1611 (*MMF*, Ser. 1, v. 11; *M* 33)

      1) The *Parthenia* is the first printed collection of virginal music; it contains 21 pieces by **Byrd** (8), **Bull** (7) and **Gibbons** (6). The book consists mostly of pavanes and galliards.

5.   Composers and music
    a.   **Hugh Aston** (*c*. 1480-1522)
        1)   *A Hornepype* (*EKMV*, v. 1, p. 4)
           a)   This very early example of variations with a drone bass (V-I) makes use of tech-
niques typical of later virginal music: scale passages, broken chords and recurring rhythmic patterns.
    b.   **Giles Farnaby** (*c*. 1560-1600)
        1)   Forty-four pieces in the *Fitzwilliam Virginal Book* are by **Farnaby**; one of them,
No. 55 (*FVB*, v. 1, p. 202) is a short piece for two virginals.
        2)   *The New Sa-hoo* (*FVB*, v. 2, p. 161)
           a)   This melody, possibly of Dutch origin, occurs in **Hilton's** *Catch that catch can*,
1652, as a catch entitled "Slaves to the World." It was used by several virginalists; later **Sweelinck** used the tune for his *Est-ce Mars?* (**Sweelinck:** *CE*, v. 1,
p. 115) and **Scheidt** for his *Cantio gallica* (*DdT*, v. 1, p. 65).
           b)   There is frequent use of sixteenth and thirty-second notes, mostly in the right
hand; imitation does not occur; the left hand supplies the harmonic background. The left hand skips a seventh (meas. 7) to begin a new octave. The
root movement suggests a fundamental bass.
    c.   **William Byrd** (1543-1623)
        1)   **Byrd** is an outstanding representative of the English Virginal School; more than
120 of his pieces are extant (*CE*, vols. 18-20 [*MB*, vols. 27, 28]).
        2)   Many of his pieces are included in the *Fitzwilliam, Lady Nevill, Will. Forster* and
Parthenia collections.
           a)   *Mr. Bird's Battell* (*MB*, v. 28, p. 174) is a descriptive work which uses the
march as one of its earliest examples as an art form.
    d.   **John Bull** (1563-1628)
        1)   **Bull's** keyboard works number about 130 pieces including many plainsong and
hexachord fantasias and sets of variations on songs.
        2)   The prelude is a short piece made up of chord progressions and figurations; its
primary function is to set the mode or pitch for the choir or cantor. The continued development of the prelude demanded considerable virtuosity. The natural
retardation by gradually lengthening the note values at the end was common.
           a)   *Praeludium* (*M* 19, v. 1, p. 158; *HAM*, No. 178)
        3)   The fantasia with a variety of characteristics is common among virginal composi-
tions. At times one theme may be developed extensively and at other times several themes may be used. Some end in brilliant toccata style, others in chordal
progressions. Free imitation, sequence, broken chords, much ornamentation and
passages in thirds are techniques frequently incorporated.
           a)   *Ut, re, mi, fa, sol, la* (*FVB*, v. 1, p. 183)
           (1)   As one of the hexachord fantasias, the tonic keys through which the modula-
tions move outline two whole-tone scales representing all the notes of the
chromatic scale: G, A, B, D-flat, E-flat, F and A-flat, B-flat, C, D, E, F-
sharp. The piece may well have been played on an instrument approximat-
ing equal temperament.
    e.   **John Mundy [Munday]** (d. 1630)
        1)   *Fantasia* (*FVB*, v. 1, p. 23)
           a)   This 80-bar fantasia describes a storm; the sections are entitled "Faire wether,"
"Lightning," "Thunder," "Calme Wether," "Lightning," "Thunder," "Faire
wether," "Lightning," "Thunder," "A Cleare Day."
        2)   *Goe from my window* (*FVB*, v. 1, p. 153; *HAM*, No. 177)
           a)   The variation form of the virginalists contributed toward an idiomatic harpsi-
chord style (rapid scale passages, parallel thirds and sixths, broken chords, ornamentation, idiomatic accompaniment patterns).

b)   This set of variations, lacking the last variation, is attributed to **Thomas Morley** (*FVB*, v. 1, p. 42). A setting by **Byrd** (*MB*, v. 28, p. 112) may be found in *Cosyn's Virginal Book*, p. 157, and in *Forster's Virginal Book*, p. 324. Another setting appears in lute tablature by **Francis Pilkington**.

  f. **Peter Philips** (*c.* 1560-1633)

    1) Among virginal pieces are many vocal works (secular pieces and motets) transcribed for keyboard with keyboard figurations and ornamentation added. A few such transcriptions are included among **Philips'** 19 pieces in the *Fitzwilliam Virginal Book*, Nos. 70-88 (*FVB*, v. 1, pp. 280-356).

      a) *Bon Jour mon Cueur*, 1605 (*FVB*, v. 1, p. 317; *HAM*, No. 145b) is transcribed from a chanson by **Orlando di Lasso** (*CE*, v. 12, p. 100; *HAM*, No. 145a).

      b) *Chi fara fed'al cielo* (*FVB*, v. 1, p. 312) is transcribed from a madrigal by **Alexander Striggio** (*AMO*, v. 10, p. 153).

B. Organ music

  1. Most of the Renaissance composers in England were organists and wrote pieces with plainsong *cantus firmi*. The hymn-melody settings were intended to alternate with stanzas sung in plainsong (*alternatim*).

  2. **John Redford** (*c.* 1485-1545)

    a. Of the 48 extant liturgical settings, 34 of them appear in *The Mulliner Book* (*MB*, v. 1). (See also *EECM*, vols. 6, 10; *EKMV*, v. 2, p. 11; *CO*, v. 12, p. 3)

    b. *Veni Redemptor* (*MB*, v. 1, p. 40; *HAM*, No. 120a; *EECM*, v. 6, pp. 126, 127)

    c. *Lucem tuam* (*MB*, v. 1, p. 32; *HAM*, No. 120b; *EECM*, v. 6, p. 34)

  3. **Thomas Tallis** (*c.* 1505-1585)

    a. *The Mulliner Book* (*MB*, v. 1) includes 12 of **Tallis'** 17 organ works (see also *EKMV*, v. 2, p. 12).

    b. Two Offertories on *Felix namque* are included in the *Fitzwilliam Virginal Book* (*FVB*, v. 1, p. 427; v. 2, p. 1; *M* 41a, pp. 10, 20)

  4. **William Blithemann** (*c.* 1520-1591)

    a. There are 6 settings of the antiphon (*LU*, p. 914) *Gloria tibi Trinitas* (*MB*, v. 1, pp. 67-72) in *The Mulliner Book*. (See also *EKMV*, v. 2, p. 14; *CO*, v. 12, p. 5)

    b. One setting of *In nomine* appears in the *Fitzwilliam Virginal Book*, v. 1, p. 181.

  5. **William Byrd** (1543-1623)

    a. Among **Byrd's** extensive keyboard works are several fantasies on plainsong melodies probably intended for organ (2 each on *Clarifica me, Pater; Gloria tibi Trinitas; Miserere* and *Salvator mundi*). In addition there are three voluntaries (*LO*, v. 10; *T-W*, v. 8; *MB*, v. 28, pp. 5-13, 74-78).

C. Chamber music

  1. Instruments in common use at the court of Henry VIII include harp, rebec, taboret, viol, drum, fife, lute, trumpet and sackbut. During the first half of the 16th century the dance exerted a strong influence on instrumental music. Much music has the designation "apt for voices or for viols."

  2. Ensemble music for viols and other instruments is divided into two categories: 1) a "whole" consort consists of instruments of the same family and 2) a "broken" consort, instruments of different families. The "whole" consort was the most popular ensemble during the Elizabethan period.

    a. A chest of viols consists of two treble, two tenor and two bass viols. A complete consort, rarely required, consists of 8 different viols.

  3. In addition to dance music, two other types are common among ensemble music: the *In nomine* settings and fancies.

    a. The *In nomine* settings are *cantus firmus* pieces based on the melody from the *Benedictus* of **Taverner's** Mass on *Gloria tibi Trinitas*; the words *"in nomine Domini"* appear in the *Benedictus*.

      1) Composers of these settings include **Tye** (*RRMR*, v. 3, pp. 1-64, 18 settings),

Robert Parsons (*EIM*, v. 2, p. 4), Brewster (*EIM*, v. 2, p. 11), Byrd (*CE*, v. 17, pp. 80-107), Tomkins (*HAM*, No. 176), Weelkes (*MB*, v. 9, p. 93), Gibbons (*MB*, v. 9, pp. 42, 90) and many others (*MB*, v. 9).

4.   Composers
  a.   **Christopher Tye** (*c.* 1500-1573)
    1)   Instrumental ensemble music (*RRMR*, v. 3)
      a)   This includes 21 *In nomine*, 4 *Dum Transisset* and 6 other pieces.
  b.   **Robert White** (*c.* 1530-1574)
    1)   Instrumental music (*RRMR*, v. 12)
  c.   **Anthony Holborne** (*c.* 1570-1602) (*MB*, v. 9)
    1)   *The Cittharn Schoole*, 1597 (*HPM*, v. 5)
      a)   This includes pieces for solo cittern and 25 pieces for cittern and bass viol.
      b)   *The Fruits of Love* for cittern with bass viol.
    2)   *Almayne* (*HPM*, v. 5, p. 118)
    3)   Galliard No. 13, *Heigh Ho Holiday* (*MB*, v. 9, p. 108; *HPM*, v. 1, p. 122)
  d.   **Thomas Morley** (1557-1602)
    1)   *The First Booke of Consort Lessons made by divers exquisite Authors for six Instruments*, 1599
      a)   This contains 25 pieces and specific instruments are indicated.
    2)   *Fifteen Fantasias*
  e.   **William Byrd** (1543-1623)
    1)   Fantasias (*CE*, v. 17, pp. 2-72)
      a)   *Fantasie à 4* (*CE* v. 17, p. 7; *M 16*, v. 2, p. 1)
    2)   *In nomine* (*CE*, v. 17, pp. 80-107)
  f.   **Orlando Gibbons** (1583-1625)
    1)   *Fantasias in three parts*
    2)   *In nomine* (*TEM*, p. 202)
  g.   **John Dowland** (1562-1626) (*EMR*, v. 1; *NagMA*, v. 173)
    1)   *Lachrimae or Seaven Teares figured in Seaven Passionate Pavans, with divers other Pavans, Galiards, and Almands, set forth for the Lute, Viols, or Violons, in five parts*, 1604
      a)   One of the earliest collections of concerted instrumental music printed in England. It includes the *Lachrimae*, followed by six pavans thematically derived from it and one pavan, nine galiards, two almands, and two other pieces. *Lachrymae antiquae* first appeared as a song "Flow, my tears" (*Second Booke of Songs or Ayres*, 1600); many of the *galiards, pavans* and *almands* are named for friends of **Dowland** (*"Mrs. Nichol's Almand"*). Dances are described by **Morley** in his *Plaine and Easie* . . .
      b)   The music was originally published on two pages similar to the lute and voice parts of ayres.
  h.   **Thomas Tomkins** (1573-1656)
    1)   *Fantasia* (*MB*, v. 9, p. 16)

SELECTED BIBLIOGRAPHY

Books

1. Andrews, Herbert K. *The Technique of Byrd's Vocal Polyphony*. New York: Oxford University Press, 1966.
2. Benham, Hugh. *Latin Church Music in England c. 1460-1575*. London: Barrie and Jenkins, 1977.
3. Borren, Charles van den. *The Sources of Keyboard Music in England*. London: Oxford University Press, 1948.
4. Bridge, Sir Frederick. *The Old Cryes of London*. London: Novello, 1921.
5. Brown, David. *Thomas Weelkes; A Bibliographical and Critical Study."* New York: Praeger, 1967.
6. Buetens, Stanley. *Method for the Renaissance Lute*. San Pedro, CA: Instrumenta Antiqua Publications, 1968.
7. Daniel, Ralph T. "Contrafacta and Polyglot Texts in the Early English Anthem," in *Essays in Musicology: A Birthday Offering for Willi Apel*, ed. Hans Tischler, pp. 101-106. Bloomington: Indiana University School of Music, 1968.
8. Davey, Henry. *History of English Music*. London: J. Curwen & Sons, 1895.
9. Dolmetsch, Mabel. *Dances of England and France, 1450-1600*. London: Routledge & Kegan Paul, 1949.
10. Ellinwood, Leonard. "From Plainsong to Anglican Chant," in *Cantors at the Crossroads: Essays on Church Music in Honor of Walter E. Buszin*, ed. Johannes Riedel, pp. 21-24. St. Louis: Concordia Publishing House, 1967.
11. Fellowes, Edmund Horace. *The English Madrigal*. London: Oxford University Press, 1952.
12. ───────*The English Madrigal Composers*. London: Clarendon Press, 1950.
13. ───────*English Madrigal Verse, 1588-1632*, 3rd ed., rev. Frederick W. Sternfeld and David Greer. Oxford: Clarendon Press, 1967.
14. ───────*Orlando Gibbons and His Family; The Last of the Tudor School of Musicians*. New York: Oxford University Press, 1951; Hamden, CT: Archon, 1970.
15. ───────*William Byrd*. London: Oxford University Press, 1953.
16. Frost, Maurice. *English and Scottish Psalm and Hymn Tunes, c. 1543-1677*. New York: Oxford University Press, 1953.
17. Galpin, Francis William. *Old English Instruments of Music; Their History and Character*, 4th ed. New York: Barnes & Noble, 1965.
18. Gorali, Moshe. *The Bible in English Music: W. Byrd–H. Purcell*. Haifa: The Haifa Music Museum, 1970.
19. Illing, Robert. "Tallis's Psalm Tunes," in *Miscellana Musicologica*, v. 2, pp. 21-74. Adelaide: University of Adelaide, 1967.
21. Kastendieck, Miles M. *England's Musical Poet Thomas Campion*. New York: Russel & Russell, 1963.
22. Kerman, Joseph. "Byrd, Tallis, and the Art of Imitation," in *Aspects of Medieval and Renaissance Music: A Birthday Offering to Gustave Reese*, ed. Jan LaRue, pp. 519-537. New York: W. W. Norton, 1966.
23. ───────*The Elizabethan Madrigal; A Comparative Study*. New York: American Musicological Society, 1963. (*MSD*, v. 4)
24. Long, John H. *Shakespeare's Use of Music; A Study of the Music and Its Performance in the Original Production of Seven Comedies*. Gainesville, FL: University of Florida Press, 1965.
25. Mazzaro, Jerome. *Transformations in the Renaissance English Lyric*. Ithaca: Cornell University Press, 1970.
26. Meyer, Ernst H. *English Chamber Music*. London: Lawrence & Wishart, 1951.

27.   Mishkin, Henry G. "Irrational Dissonance in the English Madrigal," in *Essays on Music in Honor of Archibald Thompson Davison, by His Associates*, pp. 139-145. Cambridge, MA: Department of Music, Harvard University, 1957.

28.   Morley, Thomas A. *A Plaine and Easie Introduction to Practicall Musicke*. London: 1597. (*MMF*, ser. 2, v. 113)

29.   ———————*Plaine and Easy Introduction to Practical Music*, ed. R. Alec Harman. London: Oxford University Press, 1953.

30.   Murphy, Catherine M. *Thomas Morley Editions of Italian Canzonets and Madrigals, 1597-1598*. Tallahassee: The Florida State University, 1964.   (*Florida State University Studies*, No. 42)

31.   *Music in English Renaissance Drama*, ed. John H. Long. Lexington: University of Kentucky Press, 1968.

32.   Neighbour, Oliver Wray. *The Consort and Keyboard Music of William Byrd*. Berkeley: University of California Press, 1978.

33.   Noble, Richmond Samuel Howe. *Shakespeare's Use of Song; With the Text of the Principal Songs*. Oxford: Clarendon Press, 1966.

34.   Ornithoparchus, Andreas, and John Dowland. *A Compendium of Musical Practice*. New York: Dover Publications, 1973. (Andreas Ornithoparchus. *Musice active micrologus*, pp. 1-110; John Dowland. *Andreas Ornithoparcus, His Micrologus, or Introduction: Containing the Art of Singing*, pp. 111-212)

35.   Pattison, Bruce. *Music and Poetry of the English Renaissance*, 2nd ed. London: Methuen, 1970.

36.   Pfatteicher, Carl Friedrich. *John Redford, Organist and Almoner of St. Paul's in the Reign of Henry VIII*. Kassel: Bärenreiter-Verlag, 1934.

37.   Poulton, Diana. *John Dowland His Life and Works*. London: Faber & Faber, 1972; Berkeley: University of California Press, 1972.

38.   Pulver, Jeffrey. *A Biographical Dictionary of Old English Music*. New York: E. P. Dutton, 1927; London: Kegan Paul, Trench, Trubner & Co., 1927.

39.   ———————*A Dictionary of Old English Music and Musical Instruments*. London: Kegan Paul, Trench, Trubner & Co., 1923; New York: E. P. Dutton, 1923.

40.   Satterfield, John. "A Catalogue of Tye's Latin Music," in *Studies in Musicology: Essays in the History, Style, and Bibliography of Music in Memory of Glen Haydon*, ed. James W. Pruett, pp. 51-59. Chapel Hill: University of North Carolina Press, 1969.

41.   Stevens, Denis. *Thomas Tomkins, 1572-1656*. London: Macmillan, 1957.

42.   ———————*Tudor Church Music*, 2nd ed. London: Faber & Faber, 1966.

43.   Stevens, John E. *Music and Poetry in the Early Tudor Court*. Cambridge, England: Cambridge University Press, 1961, 1979.

44.   Tuttle, Stephen D. "Watermarks in Certain Manuscript Collections of English Keyboard Music," in *Essays on Music in Honor of Archibald Thompson Davison, by His Associates*, pp. 147-158. Cambridge, MA: Department of Music, Harvard University, 1957.

Articles

1.   Andrews, Herbert K. "Printed Sources of William Byrd's 'Psalms, Sonets and Songs'." *ML* 44 (1963), pp. 5-20.

2.   Andrews, Hilda. "Elizabethan Keyboard Music." *MQ* 16 (1930), pp. 59-71.

3.   Arkwright, G. E. P. "Elizabethan Choirboy Plays and Their Music." *PMA* 40 (1914), pp. 117-138.

4.   Arnold, Denis M. "Thomas Weelkes and the Madrigal." *ML* 31 (1950), pp. 1-12.

5.   Baillie, Hugh. "Nicholas Ludford (c. 1485-c. 1557)." *MQ* 44 (1958), pp. 196-208.

6.   Baines, Francis. "The Consort Music of Orlando Gibbons." *Early Music* 6 (1978), pp. 540-543.

7.   Benham, Hugh. "The Formal Design and Construction of Taverner's Works." *MD* 26 (1972), pp. 189-209.

8. Bergsagel, John D. "The Date and Provenance of the Forrest-Heyther Collection of Tudor Masses." *ML* 44 (1963), pp. 240-248.
9. ——————"An Introduction to Ludford (c. 1485-c. 1557)." *MD* 14 (1960), pp. 105-130.
10. ——————"On the Performance of Ludford's *Alternatim Masses*." *MD* 16 (1962), pp. 35-55. (Seven plates included)
11. Bowers, Roger. "The Performing Pitch of 15th-Century Church Polyphony." *Early Music* 8 (1980), pp. 21-28.
12. Bray, Roger. "More Light upon Early Tudor Pitch." *Early Music* 8 (1980), pp. 35-42.
13. Brett, Philip. "The English Consort Song 1570-1625." *PMA* 88 (1961-1962), pp. 73-88.
14. Brown, David. "Thomas Morley and the Catholics: Some Speculations." *Monthly Musical Record* 89 (1959), pp. 53-61.
15. ——————"The Styles and Chronology of Thomas Morley's Motets." *ML* 41 (1960), pp. 216-222.
16. Caldwell, John. "Keyboard Plainsong Settings in England, 1550-1660." *MD* 19 (1965), pp. 129-153.
17. Carpenter, Nan Cooke. "The Study of Music at the University of Oxford in the Renaissance (1450-1600)." *MQ* 41 (1955), pp. 191-214.
18. Clulow, Peter. "Publication Dates for Byrd's Latin Masses." *ML* 47 (1966), pp. 1-12.
19. Collins, Henry B. "John Taverner's Masses." *ML* 5 (1924), pp. 322-334; 6 (1925), pp. 314-329.
20. Dart, Thurston. "Renaissance Music: Some Urgent Tasks for Scholars." *Renaissance News* 7 (1954), pp. 84-91.
21. ——————"The Cittern and Its English Music." *The Galpin Society Journal* 1 (1948), pp. 46-63.
22. Davison, Nigel. "Structure and Unity in Four Free-Composed Tudor Masses." *MR* 34 (1973), pp. 328-338.
23. Duckles, Vincent. "Florid Embellishment in English Song of the Late 16th and Early 17th Centuries." *AnM* 5 (1957), pp. 329-345.
24. Ellinwood, Leonard. "Tallis' Tunes and Tudor Psalmody." *MD* 2 (1948), pp. 189-203.
25. Fraser, Russell A. "Early Elizabethan Songs, John Hall's *Court of Virtue*, 1565." *MD* 7 (1953), pp. 199-203.
26. Gray, Walter. "Motivic Structure in the Polyphony of William Byrd." *MR* 29 (1948), pp. 223-233.
27. ——————"Some Aspects of Word Treatment in the Music of William Byrd." *MQ* 55 (1969), pp. 45-64.
28. Harrison, Frank Llewelyn. "An English 'Caput'." *ML* 33 (1952), pp. 203-214.
29. ——————"The Eton Choirbook, Its Background and Contents. *AnM* 1 (1953), pp. 151-175.
30. Helm, Everett B. "Italian Traits in the English Madrigal." *MR* 7 (1946), pp. 26-34.
31. Hendrie, Gerald. "The Keyboard Music of Orlando Gibbons." *PMA* 89 (1962), pp. 1-15.
32. Hughes, Andrew. "Continuity, Tradition and Change in English Music up to 1600." *ML* 46 (1965), 306-315.
33. Hughes, Dom Anselm. "An Introduction to Fayrfax." *MD* 6 (1952), pp. 83-104.
34. ——————"The Works of Robert Fayrfax." *ML* 30 (1949), pp. 118-120.
35. Hughes, Charles W. "Peter Phillips, An English Musician in the Netherlands." *PAMS* (1940), pp. 35-48.
36. ——————"Richard Deering's *Fancy for Viols*." *MQ* 27 (1941), pp. 38-46.
37. Izon, John. "Italian Musicians at the Tudor Court." *MQ* 44 (1958), pp. 329-337.
38. Jackman, James L. "Liturgical Aspects of Byrd's 'Gradualia'." *MQ* 49 (1963), pp. 17-37.
39. Jeffrey, Brian. "The Lute Music of Antony Holborne." *PMA* 93 (1966-1967), pp. 25-31.
40. Joiner, Mary. "Another Campion Song." *ML* 48 (1967), pp. 138-139.
41. Kerman, Joseph. "Morley and 'The Triumphs of Oriana'." *ML* 34 (1953), pp. 185-191.
42. Kerman, Joseph. "Byrd's Settings of the Ordinary of the Mass." *JAMS* 32 (1979), pp. 408-439.

43. Kerman, Joseph. "On William Byrd's 'Emendemus in melius'." *MQ* 49 (1963), pp. 431-449.

44. LeHuray, Peter. "The English Anthem 1580-1640." *PMA* 86 (1959), pp. 1-13.

45. Lockwood, Lewis. "A Continental Mass and Motet in a Tudor Manuscript." *ML* 42 (1961), pp. 336-347.

46. Mark, Jeffrey. "Dryden and the Beginnings of Opera in England." *ML* 5 (1924), pp. 247-252.

47. ———"Thomas Ravenscroft, B. Mus." *MT* 65 (1924), p. 881.

48. Marlow, Richard. "The Keyboard Music of Giles Farnaby." *PMA* 92 (1965-1966), pp. 107-120.

49. Mies, Otto Heinrich. "Elizabethan Music Prints in an East-Prussian Castle." *MD* 3 (1949), pp. 171-172.

50. Miller, Hugh M. "Pretty Wayes: For Young Beginners to Looke On." *MQ* 33 (1947), pp. 543-556.

51. Morehen, John. "The English Consort and Verse Anthems." *Early Music* 6 (1978), pp. 381-385.

52. Newton, Richard. "English Lute Music of the Golden Age." *PMA* 65 (1938-1939), pp. 63-90.

53. Page, Christopher. "The Earliest English Keyboard." *Early Music* 7 (1979), pp. 308-314.

54. Parton, Kenton. "On Two Early Tudor Manuscripts of Keyboard Music." *JAMS* 17 (1964), pp. 81-83.

55. Philipps, G. A. "John Wilbye's Other Patrons: The Cavendishes and Their Place in English Musical Life During the Renaissance." *MR* 38 (1977), pp. 81-93.

56. Philips, Peter. "Performance Practice in 16th-Century England." *Early Music* 6 (1978),, pp. 195-199.

57. Pilgrim, Jack. "Tallis' *Lamentations* and the 'English Cadence'." *MR* 20 (1959), pp. 1-6.

58. Richardson, Brian. "New Light on Dowland's Continental Movements." *Monthly Musical Record* 90 (1960), pp. 3-9.

59. Reese, Gustave. "The Origin of the English *In Nomine*." *JAMS* 2 (1949), pp. 7-22.

60. Schofield, Bertram. "The Manuscripts of Tallis's Forty-Part Motet." *MQ* 37 (1951), pp. 176-183.

61. Shaw, Watkins. "William Byrd of Lincoln." *ML* 48 (1967), pp. 52-59.

62. Smith, Alan. "The Gentlemen and Children of the Chapel Royal of Elizabeth I: An Annotated Register." *Royal Music Association Research Chronicle* No. 5 (1965), pp. 13-46.

63. Spector, Irwin. "The Music of Robert White." *Consort* 23 (1966), pp. 100-108.

64. ———"John Taverner and the *Missa Gloria tibi Trinitas*." *MR* 35 (1974), pp. 217-222.

65. Squire, W. Barclay. "On an Early Sixteenth Century MS. of English Music in the Library of Eton College." *Archaeologia* 56 (1898), p. 89.

66. Stevens, Denis. "A Musical Admonition for Tudor School-Boys." *ML* 38 (1957), pp. 49-52.

67. ———"Plays and Pageants in Tudor Times." *Monthly Musical Record* 87 (1957), pp. 4-9.

68. ———"A Unique Tudor Organ Mass." *MD* 6 (1952), pp. 167-175.

69. Stevens, John. "Carols and Court Songs of the Early Tudor Period." *PMA* 77 (1951), pp. 51-62.

70. Stevenson, Robert. "John Marbeck's *Noted Booke* of 1550." *MQ* 37 (1951), pp. 220-233.

71. Trowell, Brian. "A Fourteenth-Century Ceremonial Motet and Its Composer." *ActaM* 29 (1957), pp. 65-75.

72. Warren, Edward B. "Life and Works of Robert Fayrfax." *MD* 11 (1957), pp. 134-152.

73. ———"The Masses of Robert Fayrfax." *MD* 12 (1958), pp. 145-176.

74. ———"Robert Fayrfax: Motets and Settings of the Magnificat." *MD* 15 (1961), pp. 112-143.

75. Weidner, Robert W. "The Instrumental Music of Christopher Tye." *JAMS* 17 (1964), pp. 363-369.
76. –––––––"Tye's *Acts of the Apostles*: A Reassessment." *MQ* 58 (1972), pp. 242-258.
77. Wulstan, David. "The Problem of Pitch in Sixteenth-Century English Vocal Music." *PMA* 93 (1966-1967), pp. 97-112.

Music

1. Alison, Richard. *An Hour's Recreation in Music* (*EM*, v. 33)
2. *An Anthology of Early Renaissance Music*, ed. Noah Greenberg and Paul Maynard. New York: W. W. Norton, 1975.
3. Aston, Hugh. Anthems (*TCM*, v. 10)
4. Blitheman, William. Organ Music (*CO*, v. 12; *MB*, v. 1)
5. Browne, John. Works in the *Eton Choir Book* (*MB*, vols. 10-12)
6. Bull, John. Consort Music (*MB* v. 9); Keyboard Music (*MB*, vols. 14, 19)
7. Byrd, William
    a. (*CE*) *Collected Vocal Works*, 20 vols., ed. Edmund H. Fellowes. London: Stainer & Bell, 1937-1950.
    b. *The Byrd Edition*, vols. 1, 15-17 (new edition). London: Stainer & Bell. (Keyboard music is *MB*, vols. 27, 28)
    c. *Gradualia*, Books 1, 2 (*TCM*, v. 7)
    d. *Forty-five Pieces for Keyboard Instruments*, ed. Stephen D. Tuttle. Paris: Éditions de L'Oiseau Lyre, 1939.
    e. English church music (*TCM*, v. 2); Masses, cantiones and motets (*TCM*, v. 9)
    f. Organ works (*LO*, v. 10; *Tallis to Wesley*, v. 8. London: Hinrichsen)
    g. *Fifteen Pieces*, ed. Thurston Dart. London: Stainer & Bell, 1969.
    h. *My Ladye Nevells Booke of Virginal Music*, ed. Hilda F. Andrews. New York: Dover Publications, 1969.
    i. *Psalms, sonnets and songs* (*EM*, v. 14); *Songs of sundry natures* (*EM*, v. 15); *Psalms, songs and sonnets* (*EM*, v. 16)
8. Campion, Thomas
    a. *The Works of Thomas Campion: Complete Songs, Masques, and Treatises, with a Selection of the Latin Verse*, ed. Walter R. Davis. New York: Doubleday, 1967.
    b. Songs and Aires (*ELS*, ser. 1, vols. 4, 13; ser. 2, vols. 1, 2, 10, 11)
    c. *Campion's Works*, ed. Percival Vivian. Oxford: Clarendon Press, 1909, 1966.
9. Carlton, Richard. *Madrigals to 5 voices* (*EM*, v. 27)
10. Cornysh, William. *Early Tudor Magnificats* (*EECM*, v. 4)
11. Davy, Richard. Music in *Eton Choir Book* (*MB*, v. 11)
12. Dowland, John
    a. *Ayres for 4 voices* (*MB* v. 6); Airs (*ELS*, ser. 1, vols. 1-2, 5-6, 10-11, 12, 14)
    b. *The Complete Lute Fantasias*, ed. Stanley Buetens. San Pedro, CA: Instrumenta Antiqua Publications, 1975.
    c. *John Dowland Lachrimae*, ed. Warwick Edwards. Leeds, England: Boethius Press, 1974. (facsimile: *Early Music Reprinted*, v. 1)
13. *Early English Keyboard Music*, ed. Howard Ferguson. New York: Oxford University Press, 1971.
14. *An Elizabethan Song Book*, ed. Noah Greenberg. Garden City, NY: Doubleday, 1955.
15. *English Lute Songs 1597-1632*, 8 vols., facsimiles, ed. Frederick W. Sternfeld. Menston, England: The Scolar Press, 1970.
16. *English Instrumental Music of the 16th and 17th Centuries from the Manuscripts in the New York Public Library*, ed. Sydney Beck. New York: C. F. Peters, 1954. (Nine Fantasias in Four Parts by Byrd, Bull, Ferrabasco, Jenkins and Ives)

17.   Farnaby, Giles. *Canzonets to 4 voices* (*EM*, v. 20); Keyboard music (*MB*, v. 24)
18.   Fayrfax, Robert
  a.   (*CE*) *Collected Works*, 3 vols., ed. Edwin B. Warren (*CMM*, 17)
  b.   *Early Tudor Magnificats* (*EECM*, v. 4); *Missa Tecum principium* (*CW*, v. 97)
19.   *Fitzwilliam Virginal Book*, ed. John A. Fuller-Maitland and W. Barclay Squire. Leipzig: Breitkopf & Härtel, 1899; New York: Broude Brothers, 1949; New York: Dover Publications, 1979.
20.   Gibbons, Orlando
  a.   *Complete Keyboard Works*, 5 vols., ed. Margaret H. Glyn. London: Stainer & Bell, 1925; Keyboard works (*MB*, v. 20); Organ works (*LO*, v. 10); *Parthenia* (*MMF*, ser. 1, v. 11)
  b.   Sacred works (*TCM*, v. 4); Verse anthems (*EECM*, v. 3)
  c.   *Madrigals and motets of 5 parts* (*EM*, v. 5)
  d.   *London Street Cries*. London: Schott, 1933.
  e.   *Consort music* (*MB*, v. 9)
21.   Henry VIII. *Music at the Court of Henry VIII* (*MB*, v. 18)
22.   Holborne, Anthony. (*CE*) *Complete Works*, ed. Masakata Kanazawa (*HPM*, 1)
23.   Hayes, Gerald R. *The King's Music*. London: Oxford University Press, 1937.
24.   Hunt, J. Eric. *Cranmer's First Litany, 1544. and Merbecke's Book of Common Prayer, 1550.* (facsimile, 1939)
25.   *Invitation to Madrigals*, 4 vols., ed. Thurston Dart. London: Stainer & Bell, 1961-1967.
26.   *Madrigals by English Composers of the Close of the Fifteenth Century*. London: Novello, 1893.
27.   Merbecke, John. Works in *TCM*, v. 10.
28.   Morley, Thomas
  a.   Canzonets, Madrigals, Balletts (*EM*, vols. 1, 2, 3, 4)
  b.   *First book of airs* (*ELS*, ser. 1, v. 16)
  c.   English madrigals (*CW*, v. 99)
  d.   *Triumphs of Oriana* (*EM*, v. 32)
  e.   *A Plaine and Easie Introduction to Practicall Musicke* (*MMF*, ser. 2, v. 113)
  f.   *Morley's Canzonets for Two Voices*, ed. John Earle Uhler. Baton Rouge: Louisiana State University Press, 1954.
29.   Mundy, John. *Psalms and songs of 3, 4, and 5 parts* (*EM*, v. 35b)
30.   *My Ladye Nevells booke*, ed. Hilda F. Andrews. New York: Dover Publications, 1969.
31.   *The Old English Edition*, 25 vols., ed. G. E. P. Arkwright. London: Joseph Williams, 1889; reprint: New York: Broude Brothers, 1968.
32.   *The Oxford Book of English Madrigals*, ed. Philip Ledgar. London: Oxford University Press, 1978.
33.   *Parthenia*, ed. Thurston Dart. London: Stainer & Bell, 1969.
34.   Philips, Peter
  a.   *Trios* (*AMO*, v. 10); some keyboard works (*AMP*, vols. 1-8)
  b.   Consort music (*MB*, v. 9)
  c.   Italian madrigals (*MB*, v. 29)
35.   *Lautenmusik aus der Renaissance*, v. 1, ed. Adalbert Quadt. Leipzig: VEB deutscher Verlag, 1967. (Introduction in German and English)
36.   Ravenscroft, Thomas
  a.   *Melismata, Musicall Phansies, 1611*. New York: Da Capo Press, 1974. (facsimile)
  b.   *Pammelia, Musicks Miscellanie, 1609*. New York: Da Capo Press, 1971. (facsimile)
  c.   *Pammelia, Deutromelia, Melismata*, ed. MacEdward Leach. Philadelphia: The American Folklore Society, 1961. (facsimile)
37.   Redford, John. Organ music (*CO*, vols. 1, 12; *EECM*, v. 6; *LO*, v. 10; *MB*. v. 1)
38.   *The Renaissance Singer*, ed. Thomas Dunn. Boston: E. C. Schirmer, 1976.
39.   *Schott's Anthology of Early Keyboard Music*, 5 vols. London: Schott, 1951.

40.   *Seven Consort Pieces for Strings by Byrd, Cranford, Dering, Forde, Parsons, and Perslye,*
      ed. Richard Runciman Terry. London: Curwen, 1923.

41.   Tallis, Thomas
      a. *Complete Keyboard Works*, ed. Denis Stevens. New York: C. F. Peters, 1953.
      b. *Complete Organ Works*, ed. Denis Stevens. New York: C. F. Peters, 1953.
      c. Church music (*TCM*, v. 6); organ works (*CO*, v. 1)

42.   Taverner, John. Eight Masses (*TCM*, v. 1); motets (*TCM*, v. 3)

43.   Tomkins, Thomas
      a. Consort music (*MB*, v. 9); keyboard music (*MB*, v. 5); organ music (*LO*, v. 10)
      b. *Musica Deo sacra*, parts 1, 2 (*EECM*, vols., 5, 8)
      c. Services (*TCM*, v. 8); thirteen anthems (*RRMR*, v. 4)
      d. *Songs of 3, 4, 5 and 6 parts* (*EM*, v. 18)

44.   *The Treasury of English Church Music*, 5 vols., ed. Gerald H. Knight and William L. Reed.
      London: Blandford Press, 1965.

45.   Trefusis, Lady Mary. *Songs, Ballads and Instrumental Pieces Composed by Henry VIII.*
      Oxford: 1912.

46.   *Twenty-five Pieces for Keyed Instruments from Benjamin Cosyn's Virginal Book*, ed. John
      A. Fuller-Maitland and W. Barclay Squire. London: J. & W. Chester, 1923.

47.   Tye, Christopher. Instrumental music (*RRMR*, v. 3)

48.   Weelkes, Thomas
      a. Collected anthems (*MB*, v. 23)
      b. Airs, Ballets and Madrigals (*EM*, vols. 9-13.

49.   White, Robert. Anthems (*TCM*, v. 5)

50.   Wilbye, John. First and Second Sets of Madrigals (*EM*, vols. 6, 7)

51.   Boyce, William. *Cathedral Music*, 3 vols. London: 1788; reprint facsimile: New York:
      Broude Brothers.

52.   *Oxford Choral Songs from the Old Masters*, ed. Peter Warlock. London: Oxford University Press, 1927.

15. Woodcuts of the harpsichord and virginal from
Sebastian Virdung's *Musica getutscht* (1511)

GENERAL BIBLIOGRAPHY

Books

AnM   1.   **Annales Musicologiques**. Neuilly-sur-Seine: Société de Musique d'Autrefois.

HD   2.   Apel, Willi. **Harvard Dictionary of Music**, 2nd edition. Cambridge, MA: The Belknap Press of Harvard University Press, 1972.

   3.   ————**The History of Keyboard Music to 1700**, tr. Hans Tischler. Bloomington: Indiana University Press, 1972.

NPM   4.   ————**The Notation of Polyphonic Music, 900-1600**. Cambridge, MA: Harvard University Press, 1949.

   5.   Bedbrook, Gerald. **Keyboard Music from the Middle Ages to the Beginnings of the Baroque**. London: Macmillan, 1949.

   6.   Bessaraboff, Nicholas. **Ancient European Musical Instruments**. Cambridge, MA: Harvard University Press, 1941.

PCM   7.   Blume, Friedrich. **Protestant Church Music, A History**. New York: W. W. Norton, 1974.

   8.   Brown, Howard. **Music in the Renaissance**. Englewood Cliffs, NJ: Prentice-Hall, 1976. (Prentice-Hall History of Music Series)

CaMM   9.   Caldwell, John. **Medieval Music**. Bloomington: Indiana University Press, 1978.

  10.   **Cantors at the Crossroads: Essays on Church Music in Honor of Walter E. Buszin**, ed. Johannes Riedel. St. Louis: Concordia Publishing House, 1967.

  11.   Charles, Sidney Robinson. **A Handbook of Music and Music Literature in Sets and Series**. New York: The Free Press, 1972.

  12.   **The Commonwealth of Music in Honor of Curt Sachs**, ed. Gustave Reese and Rose Brandel. New York: The Free Press, 1965.

CSM   13.   **Corpus Scriptorum de Musica**. Rome: American Institute of Musicology, 1950-

  14.   **Essays in Musicology: A Birthday Offering for Willi Apel**, ed. Hans Tischler. Bloomington: Indiana University School of Music, 1968.

  15.   **Essays on Music in Honor of Archibald Thompson Davison, by His Associates**. Cambridge, MA: Harvard University Press, 1957.

  16.   **Essays Presented to Egon Wellesz**, ed. Jack A. Westrup. Oxford: Clarendon Press, 1966.

  17.   Grout, Donald Jay. **A History of Western Music**. New York: W. W. Norton, 1960.

GD   18.   **Grove's Dictionary of Music and Musicians**, 5th edition, 10 vols., ed. Eric Blom. New York: St. Martin's Press, 1959.

  19.   Heyer, Anna Harriett. **Historical Sets, Collected Editions and Monuments of Music**, 2nd edition. Chicago: American Library Association, 1969.

HMM   20.   Hoppin, Richard H. **Medieval Music**. New York: W. W. Norton, 1978.

  21.   Kratzenstein, Marilou. **Survey of Organ Literature and Editions**. Ames, IA: Iowa State University Press, 1980.

  22.   Lang, Paul Henry. **Music in Western Civilization**. New York: W. W. Norton, 1941.

  23.   **Music from the Middle Ages to the Renaissance**, ed. Frederick William Sternfeld. New York: Praeger Publishers, 1973. (Praeger History of Western Music, v. 1)

MTT   24.   **Musical Theorists in Translation**. Brooklyn: The Institute of Medieval Music, 1959-

NGD   25.   **The New Grove Dictionary of Music and Musicians**, 6th edition, 20 vols., ed. Stanley Sadie. London: Macmillan, 1980.

NOH   26.   **New Oxford History of Music**, ed. Jack A. Westrup. London: Oxford University Press, 1960.
         v. 1   Ancient and Oriental Music
         v. 2   Early Medieval Music up to 1300
         v. 3   Ars Nova and the Renaissance (1300-1540)
         v. 4   The Age of Humanism (1540-1630)

OHM   27.   **Oxford History of Music**, ed. Harry Ellis Wooldridge. Oxford: Clarendon Press, 1905.
         vols. 1, 2   The Polyphonic Period of Music, parts 1, 2

NMM   28.   Parrish, Carl. **Notation of Medieval Music**. New York: W. W. Norton, 1957.

  29.   **The Pelican History of Music**, ed. Alec Robertson and Denis Stevens. New York: Penguin Books, 1960.
         v. 1   Ancient Forms to Polyphony
         v. 2   Renaissance to Baroque

30. **Prentice-Hall History of Music Series**, ed. H. Wiley Hitchcock. Englewood Cliffs, NJ: Prentice-Hall.
    v. 1   Albert Seay. **Music in the Medieval World**, 1975.
    v. 2   Howard Brown, **Music in the Renaissance**, 1976.
31. **Readings in the History of Music in Performance**, ed. Carol MacClintock. Bloomington: Indiana University Press, 1979.

RMMA   32. Reese, Gustave. **Music in the Middle Ages**. New York: W. W. Norton, 1940.
RMR   33. ————Music of the Renaissance. New York: W. W. Norton, 1959.
34. Sachs, Curt. **The History of Musical Instruments**. New York: W. W. Norton, 1940.
35. ————The Rise of Music in the Ancient World. New York: W. W. Norton, 1943.
36. Salop, Arnold. **Studies on the History of Musical Style**. Detroit: Wayne State University Press, 1971.

SR   37. **Source Readings**, ed. Oliver Strunk. New York: W. W. Norton, 1950. (also in five volumes, 1965)
    v. 1   Antiquity and the Middle Ages
    v. 2   The Renaissance
    v. 3   The Baroque Era
    v. 4   The Classic Era
    v. 5   The Romantic Era
38. **Studies in Music History: Essays for Oliver Strunk**, compiled by Harold Powers. Princeton: Princeton University Press, 1968.
39. **Studies in Musicology: Essays in the History, Style, and Bibliography of Music in Memory of Glen Haydon**, ed. James W. Pruett. Chapel Hill: University of North Carolina Press, 1969.
40. **Yale Studies in the History of Music**. New Haven, CT: Yale University Press.
YMTT   41. **Yale University, Music Theory Translation Series**, ed. Richard J. Crocker. New Haven, CT: Yale School of Music, 1963-
42. Williams, Peter. **The European Organ, 1450-1850**. London: P. T. Batsford, 1966.
43. ————New History of the Organ: From the Greeks to the Present Day. London: Faber & Faber, 1980.

Music

ACT   1. **Anthologie de Chants de Troubadours**, ed. Jean Maillard. Nice, France: Georges Delrieu & Cie, 1967.
AERM   2. **An Anthology of Early Renaissance Music**, ed. Noah Greenberg and Paul Maynard. New York: W. W. Norton, 1975.
AMM   3. **Anthology of Medieval Music**, ed. Richard H. Hoppin. New York: W. W. Norton, 1978.
AM   4. **Anthology of Music**, ed. Karl Gustave Fellerer. Köln: Arno Verlag, 1960-
AR   5. **Antiphonale sacrosanctae Romanae ecclesiae**. Rome: Vatican Press, 1912
AC   6. **Antiqua Chorbuch**, ed. Helmuth Mönkemeyer. Mainz: B. Schott's Söhne, 1951.
AMP   7. **Antiquitates Musicae in Polonia**, ed. Hieronim Feicht. Warsaw: Warsaw University Press, 1965-
AMO   8. **Archives des Maîtres de l'Orgue des XVIe, XVIIe, et XVIIIe Siècles**, ed. Alexandre Guilmant and André Pirro. Paris: Durand, 1898-1910.
ArM   9. **Archivium musices metropolitanum Mediolanense**, ed. Luciano Magliavacca. Milan: Veneranda Fabbrica del Duomo, 1958-
AMI   10. **L'Arte Musicale Italia**, ed. Luigi Torchi. Milan: Ricordi, 1897-1908.
BC   11. **Biblioteca de Catalunya**. Barcelona: Institut d'estudio Catalans, 1921-
BMB   12. **Bibliotheca musica Bononiensis**. Bologna: Arnaldo Forni.
CO   13. **Cantantibus organis**, ed. Eberhard Kraus. Regensburg: Friedrich Pustet, 1958-
CS   14. **Cantio sacra**, ed. Rudolf Ewerhart. Köln: Edmund Bieler, 1958-
CP   15. **Capolavori polifonici del secolo XVI**, ed. Bonaventura Somma. Rome: Edizioni de Santis, 1940-1953.
ChP   16. **Chansons polyphoniques**, ed. A. Tillman Merritt and François Lesure (Janequin)
CW   17. **Das Chorwerk**, ed. Friedrich Blume. Berlin: Kallmeyer, 1929-
CM   18. **Collegium Musicum**, ed. Leo Schrade. New Haven, CT: Yale University Press, 1955-
CMT   19. **Colorado College Music Press Translations**, ed. Albert Seay. Colorado Springs: The Colorado College Music Press, 1967-

CMM 20. **Corpus Mensurabilis Musicae**, ed. Arman Carapetyan. Rome. American Institute of Musicology, 1947-

CEKM 21. **A Corpus of Early Keyboard Music**, ed. Willi Apel. Rome: American Institute of Musicology, 1963-

DTB 22. **Denkmäler der Tonkunst in Bayern**, ed. Adolf Sandberger. Braunschweig: H. Litolff's Verlag, 1900-1938.

DTO 23. **Denkmäler der Tonkunst in Österreich**, ed. Guido Adler. Vienna: Artaria, 1894-

DdT 24. **Denkmäler deutscher Tonkunst**, ed. Max Seiffert. Leipzig: Breitkopf & Härtel, 1892-1931.

DCS 25. **Dessoff Choir Series**, ed. Paul Boepple. New York: Music Press, 1941-1948.

DM 26. **Documenta Musicologica**. Kassel: Bärenreiter, 1951-

DPL 27. **Documenta polyphoniae liturgiae Sanctae Ecclesiae Romanae**, ed. Laurentius Feininger. Roma: Societas universalis Sanctae Ceciliae, 1947.

EECM 28. **Early English Church Music**, ed. Frank Llewelyn Harrison. London: Stainer & Bell, 1963-

EFM 29. **Early Fifteenth Century Music**, 3 vols., ed. Gilbert Reaney. Rome: American Institute of Musicology, 1947. **(CMM, 11)**

ELS 30. **English Lute Songs 1597-1632**, 8 vols., ed. Frederick William Sternfeld. Menston, England: The Scolar Press, 1970.

EM 31. **The English Madrigalists**, ed. Edmund H. Fellowes. London: Stainer & Bell, 1958-

EL 32. **The English School of Lutenist Song Writers**, ed. Edmund H. Fellowes. London: Winthrop Rogers, Stainer & Bell, 1959-

EdM 33. **Das Erbe deutscher Musik**. Leipzig: Breitkopf & Härtel, 1935-1942, 1954-

GEx 34. **Examples of Music before 1400**, ed. Harold Gleason. New York: Appleton-Century-Crofts, 1945.

FCVR 35. **Florilege du concert vocal de la renaissance**, ed. Henry Expert. Paris: Cite des Livres, 1928-

FSC 36. **French Secular Compositions of the Fourteenth Century**, 3 vols., ed. Willi Apel. Rome: Institute of Musicology, 1970. **(CMM, 53)**

FSM 37. **French Secular Music of the Late Fourteenth Century**, ed. Willi Apel. Cambridge, MA: Mediaeval Academy of America, 1950.

GMB 38. **Geschichte der Musik in Beispielen**, ed. Arnold Schering. Leipzig: Breitkopf & Härtel, 1931.

MOP 39. Gleason, Harold. **Method of Organ Playing**, 6th ed. Englewood Cliffs, NJ: Prentice-Hall, 1980.

GR 40. **Graduale sacrosanctae Romanae ecclesiae**. Rome: Vatican Press, 1907; Solesmes edition, Tournai and Paris: Desclée, 1924.

HPM 41. **Harvard Publications of Music**. Cambridge, MA: Harvard University Press, 1968-

HSMS 42. **Hispaniae Schola Musica Sacra**, ed. Felipe Pedrell. Barcelona: J. B. Pujol y Co., 1894-1898; Leipzig: Breitkopf & Härtel, 1894-1898.

HAM 43. **Historical Anthology of Music**, ed. Archibald T. Davison and Willi Apel. Cambridge, MA: Harvard University Press, 1949.

HM 44. **Hortus Musicus**. Kassel: Bärenreiter, 1936-

ICDMI 45. **I Classici della Musica Italiani**, ed. Gabriele d'Annunzio. Milan: Società Anonima Notari La Santa, 1919-1921.

ICMI 46. **I Classici Musicali Italiani**, ed. Eugenio Bravi. Milan: I Classici Musicali Italiani, 1956-

InM 47. **Invitation to Madrigals**, 4 vols., ed. Thurston Dart. London: Stainer & Bell, 1961-1967.

IMAMI 48. **Istituzione e monumenti dell'arte musicale Italiana**. Milan: Ricordi, 1939, 1956-

ISM 49. **Italia sacra musica**, ed. Knud Jeppesen. Copenhagen: Wilhelm Hansen, 1962-

IM 50. **The Italian Madrigal**, v. 3, ed. Alfred Einstein. Princeton: Princeton University Press, 1949.

LO 51. **Liber Organi**, ed. Ernst Kaller. Mainz: B. Schott's Söhne, 1931-1938, 1954-

LU 52. **Liber Usualis**, ed. Benedictines of Solesmes. Tournai and New York: Desclée Co., 1961.

MMRF 53. **Les Maîtres Musiciens de la Renaissance Française**, ed. Henry Expert. Paris: Alphonse Leduc, 1894-1908.

MM 54. **Masterpieces of Music before 1750**, ed. Carl Parrish and John F. Ohl. New York: W. W. Norton, 1951.

55. **A Medieval Motet Book**, ed. Hans Tischler. New York: Associated Music Publishers, 1973.

MLMI 56. **Monumenta lyrica medii aevi Italica**. Bologna: Arnaldo Forni, 1966-

MMMA 57. **Monumenta monodica medii aevi**, ed. Bruno Stäblein. Kassel: Bärenreiter, 1956-

MMN 58. **Monumenta Musica Neerlandica**. Amsterdam: Nederlandse musiekgescheidenis, 1959-

MMB 59. **Monumenta Musicae Belgicae**. Antwerp: 1932-

MPL 60 **Monumenta Polyphoniae Liturgicae Sanctae Ecclesiae Romanae**, ed. Laurentius Feininger. Rome: Societas universalis Sanctae Ceciliae, 1947.

MME   61.   **Monumentos de la Musica Española**, ed. Higini Anglés. 1941-
MMA   62.   **Monuments de la Musique Ancienne**. Paris: Société Française de Musicologie, 1925-
MMFR   63.   **Les Monuments de la Musique Française au temps de la Renaissance**, ed. Henry Expert. Paris: Maurice Senart, 1924-1930.
MMF   64.   **Monuments of Music and Music Literature in Facsimile**, ser. 1. New York: Broude Brothers, 1964-
MRM   65.   **Monuments of Renaissance Music**, ed. Edward E. Lowinsky. Chicago: University of Chicago Press, 1964.
        66.   **Music History in Examples, From Antiquity to Johann Sebastian Bach**, ed. Otto Hamburg, tr. Susan Hellauer. New York: C. F. Peters, 1973.
MMRL   67.   **Music in Medieval and Renaissance Life**, ed. Andrew Minor. Columbia: University of Missouri Press, 1964.
MFCI   68.   **Music of Fourteenth Century Italy**, ed. Nino Pirrotta. Amsterdam: American Institute of Musicology, 1954. (**CMM**, 8)
MSO   69.   **Music Scores: Omnibus**, ed. William J. Starr and George F. Devine. Englewood Cliffs, NJ: Prentice-Hall, 1964.
MB   70.   **Musica Britannica**. London: Stainer & Bell, 1951-
MDa   71.   **Musica Divina**, ed. Bruno Stäblein. Regensburg: Friedrich Pustet, 1950-
MDaP   72.   **Musica Divina**, ed. Karl Proske. Ratisbon, 1855; reprint: New York: Johnson Reprint, 1973.
MH   73.   **Musica Hispana**. Barcelona: Instituto Español de musicologia, 1952-
MLi   74.   **Musica Liturgica**, ed. Robert J. Snow. Cincinnati: World Library of Sacred Music, 1958-
MSD   75.   **Musicological Studies and Documents**. Rome: American Institute of Musicology, 1951-
MDm   76.   **Musikalische Denkmäler**. Mainz: B. Schott's Söhne, 1955-
OEE   77.   **The Old English Edition**, ed. Godfrey E. P. Arkwright. London: J. Williams, 1889-1902.
OMM   78.   **The Oxford Anthology of Medieval Music**, ed. W. Thomas Marrocco and Nicholas Sandon. New York: Oxford University Press, 1977.
PM   79.   **Paléographie Musicale**, ed. Dom André Mocquereau. Solesmes: Benedictines de Solesmes, 1889-1937, 1955-
PVSP   80.   **Polifonia vocale sacra e profana**, ed. Bonaventura Somma. Rome: Edizioni de Santis, 1940-
PMFC   81.   **Polyphonic Music of the Fourteenth Century**, ed. Leo Schrade. Monaco: Éditions de L'Oiseau-Lyre, 1956-
PortM   82.   **Portugaliae Musica**. Lisbon: Fundaçao Caloriste Gulbenkian, 1959.
PMMM   83.   **Publication of Medieval Musical Manuscripts**. Brooklyn: Institute of Mediaeval Music, 1957-
PäM   84.   **Publikationen älterer Musik**, ed. Theodor Kroyer. Leipzig: Breitkopf & Härtel, 1926-1940.
PAM   85.   **Publikationen älterer praktichser und theoretischer Musikwerke**, ed. Robert Eitner. Berlin: Gesellschaft für Musikforschung, 1873-1905.
LP   86.   **Le Pupitre**, ed. François Lesure. Paris: Heugel, 1967-
RRMR   87.   **Recent Researches in the Music of the Renaissance**. New Haven, CT: A-R Editions, 1964-
SCMA   88.   **Smith College Music Archives**, ed. Alfred Einstein. Northampton, MA: Smith College, 1935-
        89.   **Study Scores of Musical Style**, ed. Edward R. Lerner. New York: McGraw-Hill, 1968.
SMMA   90.   **Summa Musicae Medii Aevi**, ed. Friedrich Gennrich. Darmstadt, 1957.
        91.   **Thomas Morley Editions of Italian Canzonets and Madrigals, 1597-1598**, ed. Catherine A. Murphy. Tallahassee, FL: The Florida State University, 1964. (**Florida State University Studies**, No. 42)
TEM   92.   **Treasury of Early Music**, ed. Carl Parrish. New York: W. W. Norton, 1957.
TECM   93.   **The Treasury of English Church Music**, ed. Gerald H. Knight and William L. Reed. London: Blandford Press, 1965.
LMA   94.   **Treize livres de motets parus chez Pierre Attaingnent**, ed. Albert Smijers. Paris: L'Oiseau-Lyre, 1934-
TCM   95.   **Tudor Church Music**, ed. Percy C. Buck, Edmund H. Fellowes, Alexander Ramsbotham, Richard Runciman Terry, Sylvia Townsend Warner. London: Oxford University Press, 1923-1948.
VOTS   96.   **Van Ockeghem tot Sweelinck**, ed. Albert Smijers. Amsterdam: Nederlandse Musiekgeschiedenis, 1949.
WE   97.   **The Wellesley Edition**, ed. Jan LaRue. Wellesley, MA: Wellesley College, 1950-

INDEX